THE SEA POWER
OF THE STATE

THE SEA POWER
OF THE STATE

by

S. G. GORSHKOV

Admiral of the Fleet of the Soviet Union
Commander-in-Chief of the Soviet Navy

ROBERT E. KRIEGER PUBLISHING COMPANY
MALABAR, FLORIDA
1983

Original English Edition 1979
Russian Edition Copyright © Voenizdat 1976
Translation Copyright © 1979 Pergamon Press Ltd.
Special Reprint Edition for Naval War College, 1983

Printed and Published by
ROBERT E. KRIEGER PUBLISHING COMPANY, INC.
KRIEGER DRIVE
MALABAR, FLORIDA 32950

All Rights Reserved.
Translated from Morskaya moshch gosudarstva 2nd revised edition
published by Voennoe Izdatel'stvo Ministerstva Oborony SSR,
Moscow, 1976.

Printed in the United States of America

Library of Congress Cataloging in Publication Data

Gorshkov, Sergei Georgievich, 1910-
    The sea power of the state.

    Translation of: Morskaia moshch gosudarstva.
2nd rev. ed., 1979.
    Reprint. Originally published: Annapolis, Md. :
Naval Institute Press, cl979.
    Includes index.
    1. Sea-power. 2. Navies—History. 3. Naval art
and science—History. I. Title.
V25.G6713 1983   359'.009   82-21294
ISBN 0-89874-589-6

Contents

Foreword to the English edition

On agreeing to publish this book in English the author proceeded in the knowledge that this is the language of nations that for centuries have contributed to the development of naval science. Our knowledge and mastery of the World Ocean, the progress of shipbuilding and navigation, and the discovery of new lands and sea routes to them, all bear witness to this. These nations have left their mark too, on the founding and development of military-naval art. Their rich historical experience is conclusive evidence of the important role played by the seas and oceans in the progress of civilization.

We Soviet sailors remember how, during the worst and most bloody war in world history, unleashed by fascist Germany and militarist Japan, the Soviet Union, the United States and Great Britain—or the 'Big Three' as it then was—formed the basis of the alliance against Nazi Germany. In this great battle which raged over all oceans and many seas, the seamen of the allied countries, from both civil and military fleets, co-operated directly with each other in decisions concerning their common objectives in the struggle against the enemy.

The military alliance of our countries and of our armed forces and fleets, further strengthened by our common suffering in war, proved to be a key factor in our great victory, which saved mankind from the threat of fascist subjugation.

Whilst themselves conducting difficult military operations against the powerful enemy, Soviet seamen followed with unwavering attention and concern the valiant struggle waged by their American and British allies in distant seas and oceans. There were occasions, especially in the north, when we fought together with our allies—in a united battle front, thus further strengthening the military solidarity and alliance between our countries and fleets. We learned to understand each other regardless of the language in which we spoke.

It would only be fair to recall here how the Soviet Union took the brunt of military action and played a decisive role in bringing down the fascist coalition—this has been universally recognized and repeatedly acknowledged by leaders in the West. However, although we consistently fulfilled our duty to the alliance in the post-war years, we became the object of a protracted 'cold war', which more than once threatened to turn into another world conflict using the latest weapons of mass destruction.

It is quite natural that the USSR, while guided by a desire for world peace, in order not to be taken unaware was obliged to safeguard its own security—and thus the Soviet fleet was born. The vital need for such measures is discussed in this book on the basis of the irrefutable facts of recent world events. Furthermore, the author gives a Soviet explanation for the sea power of the state, emphasizing its economic importance—as well as its military aspects—in the circumstances of today. Convinced that this economic factor will remain firm and constant, the author believes that the seas and oceans must above all serve to raise standards of living and to consolidate amicable relations between nations.

The military aspect of sea power is of but transitory importance, which will continue to decrease as world peace becomes more secure.

This belongs, however, to the realm of the future. Thanks to the constant efforts on the part of the socialist countries and all other peace-loving forces there has been a noticeable thaw, a *détente* in international relations. In the West, anti-Soviet propaganda is still rife, while the military budget continues to soar. New types of weapons are being invented and new military and military-naval bases established, constituting firm evidence of armed strength.

L. I. Brezhnev, General Secretary of the Central Committee of the CPSU, gave a clear and convincing reply to this show of force when he appeared on French television on 5 October 1976: "The Soviet Union has never threatened anyone and is not doing so now. It is ready to agree to mutual restriction on armed forces at any time.

"We are obliged—I repeat, obliged—to protect our defence systems, because we are faced with an unrestrained arms race".

The author knows from personal experience, as do the Soviet people, what war means and he fervently hopes that wisdom and good sense will prevail so that the immeasurable resources of the World Ocean may be put to serve the cause of peace and prosperity.

The world community, and indeed the reader of this book, could play an important part in the realization of these worthy aims.

Moscow   **SERGEI GORSHKOV**
31 March 1978

Introduction

Marxism sees the geographical environment as one of the many important factors influencing the development of human society, and the most important element of that environment is the World Ocean. It occupies almost three-quarters of the surface of our planet and possesses enormous biological, energy and mineral resources.

Man's use of the World Ocean over many centuries led to the creation of merchant and fishing fleets, which led in turn to the expansion of trade and the construction of numerous bases and ports. With the development of the science of the oceans, the research fleet is steadily growing. The littoral position of many countries has prompted the appearance in them of specific branches of industry favourably influencing the economic development of these countries. The seas and oceans have for long been a specific area of rivalry and armed conflict, entailing the creation of special arms systems and the birth of forces subsumed under the term "navy".

It is reasonable to consider that the totality of the means of harnessing the World Ocean and the means of defending the interests of the state when rationally combined constitute the sea power of the state, which determines the capacity of a particular country to use the military-economic possiblities of the ocean for its own purposes.

It is legitimate to consider the sea power of the state as a system characterised not only by the presence of links between its components (military, merchant, fishing, scientific research fleet, etc.) but also by the inseparable union with the environment—the ocean in the mutual relations with which the system expresses its wholeness.

The importance of the individual components making up sea power is not constant but determined by specific historical conditions, although the dominant importance of the navy always remains.

Because of this, study of the military aspects of sea power is very important, having regard to the significance attached to navies by the most powerful imperialist states.

At present, in the epoch of sweeping scientific discoveries and their use for military requirements, the technical possibilities of conducting combat operations in the oceanic sphere have considerably grown.

Both in the preparation by international monopoly-capital of a world war and local wars which in the last quarter of the century have become an integral part of the policy of the imperialist states, an important role is assigned to navies, which have moved into the forefront of modern diverse combat agents. For example, the leaders of the Pentagon consider the naval forces of the USA as a most essential part of the strategic nuclear forces, capable of inflicting in a short time tremendous damage on land installations situated far from the coast, and this decisively colours the situation in all theatres of military operations. By concentrating nuclear arms in the sphere of operations of the fleet they hope to shield their own territory from nuclear strikes.

Guided by such views of the role of naval forces in a world war, the camp of imperialism employs oceanic strategy as a basic concept of its military doctrine. This strategy starts from the premise that practically all land objectives are within reach of attack from the ocean and the oceanic nuclear systems themselves are most mobile and not very vulnerable because of their ability to use deep water for defence and the huge expanses of the oceans for concealment. Therefore, even now, extensive areas of the World Ocean have already been turned by the imperialists into launching points for highly mobile, covertly acting, carriers of long-range strategic missiles launched from under water and always ready for combat.

It is generally known that missiles of the nuclear system of the US navy are aimed at Russia from different directions. Moreover, on the sea borders of the Soviet state numerous naval and military air bases have been set up by the USA and aggressive anti-Soviet blocs—NATO, CENTO and others—and the member countries of these blocs are in a position to deploy their aircraft-carrier forces and shore-based aviation at distances from which major targets are well within reach in the territory of the Soviet Union and the countries of the socialist community.

All this creates a constant threat to the security of our country and, should the imperialists unleash a war, predetermines the conditions, radically differing from those obtaining in the period of the Great Patriotic War. The last war was a continental war. The struggle in the sea and oceanic theatres was a struggle in secondary directions and its influence on the course and outcome of the war, though substantial, was not decisive. Now we are threatened by a coalition of maritime powers which, together with land armies, aviation and missile forces, dispose of powerful modern naval forces.

Therefore, despite the policy of *détente* in international affairs pursued by the CPSU and by the Soviet state, and the steadfast implementation of the peace programme adopted at the 24th CPSU Congress, and developed at the 25th, we are forced to devote necessary attention towards improvement of Soviet state defence. The establishment of the country's systems of defence from oceanic attack plays an important part in these defensive measures.

The role of combat in oceanic directions in the general efforts of the armed forces has greatly increased and in certain conditions these directions may become paramount. At present, a fleet with its strikes from the sea is capable of changing the course and outcome of an armed struggle even in continental theatres of military operations.

Equipping the fleets with nuclear missile weapons has introduced much that is new into tactics and operational art and has made it necessary to alter the design of ships and create new forms of technology and arms.

Together with one of the most important and all-embracing tasks of the fleet—destruction of the enemy's ships—a qualitatively new task has appeared: the curbing of the enemy's military-economic potential by directly acting on his vitally important centres from the sea. Military operations at sea as on dry land are governed by general permanently operating laws. They cannot be conducted divorced from the goals of that policy, the continuation of which was war. Lenin pointed out that ". . . politics is reason, while war is only a tool and not vice-versa. Consequently, it only remains to subordinate the military point of view to the political".[1] Therefore, in modern conditions, too, it is not without interest to follow in the historical sense the dialectical link between the development of the naval forces and the goals of the policy of the states which they are intended to serve.

The sole agent waging armed struggle has always been the army and the fleet which even in peace time continue to serve as an instrument or tool of the policy of states. Many examples from history indicate that both under feudalism and capitalism foreign policy problems have always been solved on the basis of the military might of the "negotiating" parties and that the potential military power of a particular state, created in line with its economic possibilities and with reference to its political orientation, has often enabled it to conduct an advantageous policy to the detriment of other states not possessing the corresponding military power.

The development of the armed forces is most intimately bound up with the history of socio-economic formations and the means of material production particular to them. Their flourishing or decline is determined by the process of emergence or breakdown of the particular formation. In periods of change of one socio-economic formation for another, more progressive form, progress in the military sphere has also been considerably speeded up.

A revolutionizing influence on the development of the armed forces and the art of deploying them has always been exerted by technical discoveries. This expresses the regularity of the impact of the economic development of society and the growth of its productive forces on the military sphere. Lenin wrote on this: "Military tactics depends on the level of military technology . . . ."[2]

Without embarking on a detailed examination of changes in the structure of the armed forces of states on the historical plane, we would merely note that all maritime countries without exception have usually had or tried to have both an army and fleet, or as Peter the Great figuratively put it: "Any potentate with a land army has one hand but he who also has a fleet has two hands."[3]

The importance of the army and navy with a given development of technology and economic possibilities has always been determined by the prevailing politico-strategic situation, the relative position of the states or the character of coalitions. At some stages of history the main role was played by land forces and at others by navies. The place and role of each branch of the armed forces of a country might change both in peace and wartime depending on technical transformation, the enemy, geographical conditions, etc.

The experience of history also testifies that each branch of the armed forces makes its own definite and always weighty contribution to victory. There have virtually been no pure land and no pure sea wars, one principle remaining

[1] *Lenin Collection,* XII 2nd ed., 1931, p. 437 (Russian edition).
[2] V. I. Lenin, *Complete Collected Works,* 13, p. 374 (Russian edition).
[3] *Marine Regulations,* St.P., 1720, p. 2 (Russian edition).

unchanged: the results of a victory in a campaign or in a war as a whole can be consolidated only by the land forces capable by their actual presence of asserting its reality.

The conditions for achieving victory are created only with properly organized, equipped and prepared branches of all the armed forces. Each of them has its own modes of operations, sphere of deployment and conditions for interaction. The able (or, on the contrary, unskilled) use of these modes often determines the success (or failure) of the operation, the campaign and even the war as a whole. Therefore, the basic tenet of Soviet military science is the principle of interaction of all branches of the armed forces. Only their concerted efforts can bring victory. As far back as 1921, M. V. Frunze wrote about this in his work devoted to the formation of the Red Army. The idea of the decisive importance of the joint operations of the army and navy in all links of armed combat is clearly expressed in his work *A Unitary Military Doctrine and the Red Army*.[4]

The problems of the harmonious combination of rationally balanced branches of the armed forces and their concerted efforts are also now particularly acute for us. It is known that the forces of aggression and militarism, though hard pressed, are far from being rendered harmless. In the post-war years they have started over thirty wars and armed conflicts of different magnitudes and are threatening to unleash a new world war. Under these circumstances, our powers of defence assume the utmost importance for ensuring the peaceful development of the Soviet country and the countries of the socialist community. L. I. Brezhnev, making his formal report from the Central Committee of the Communist Party of the Soviet Union to the 25th Congress of the Party, said: "And no one should doubt that our Party will do everything necessary to ensure that the glorious armed forces of the Soviet Union shall in the future, too, have available all the resources necessary for implementation of their responsible task of standing guard over the peaceful labour of the Soviet people and of being a bulwark for universal peace."[5]

Therefore, it is very important to consider the problems of deploying the various branches of the armed forces in historical, existing and future terms in order to substantiate the tendencies and patterns of change in their role and place in war and peacetime.

On the basis of this, the author outlines some ideas on the role and place of fleets in different historical epochs and at different stages of development of military technology and military art.

Starting from the specific features of the navy as a military factor which has also been used in peacetime for demonstrating the economic and military power of the state beyond its confines, and the fact that, of all branches of the armed forces, the navy is best capable of operationally ensuring the state interests of the country beyond its borders, we feel it necessary to look at the problems associated with its specific nature.

The present work shows the fleets in wars of the past and their role in the

[4] M. V. Frunze, *Selected Works,* Moscow, Voenizdat, 1951, pp. 137-160 (in Russian).
[5] L. I. Brezhnev, Review Report from the Central Committee of the CPSU to the 25th Congress of the Communist Party of the Soviet Union, Moscow, Politizdat, 1976, p. 100.

emergence and development of states. However, it is not the author's intention to present an all-embracing picture of the development of the naval forces and the means of their operations. This is done only to the extent necessary to show the growth of the significance of the fleets and confirm the development of the patterns which took shape in the past. On the basis of analysis of the present distribution of the forces in the world arena and evaluation of the ratio of forces in the conditions of a threat by the imperialists of unleashing a global nuclear war, the author attempts to show the need for the presence of a powerful navy as part of the armed forces of our state which would be in a position to counter threat to our country from the imperialist states from the seas and oceans.

Special attention in the work is paid to the post-war development of navies and the new concepts of their utilization and closer definition of their role and tasks in present conditions and in the immediate future.

The book shows that in the development of the fleets of many countries in the post-war period a special place is taken by the comprehensive perfecting of submarine forces. In the now highly-varied type of forces of the fleet, of prime importance are submarine nuclear missile systems of strategic purpose. At the same time, growing importance is being assumed by multi-purpose atomic submarines as universal forces of the fleet intended to solve a wide range of problems in fighting at sea.

It is natural that the growth of the importance of the submarine forces makes necessary the intensive development of submarine-hunting forces of the fleets and therefore the tendencies of their development will be considered.

The work also shows the place of surface craft as part of modern fleets, starting from the premise that scientific-technical achievements have exerted a fundamental influence on the views of their role and combat resilience. Together with the perfecting of individual earlier classes of ships, for example, aircraft carriers and landing craft, qualitatively new ones have appeared—submarine-hunting, including helicopter-carrying missile ships, and also ships with dynamic principles of support—hydrofoil and air cushion.

Considerable attention is also paid to such an important element of fighting power of any modern fleet as naval aviation. The tendency for aviation capability to be widely adopted in surface craft of different classes is shown in connection with the production of aircraft with shortened or vertical take-off and landing.

Nor does the book ignore the ever-growing interest in oceanic problems which is being clearly shown in our time in various social groupings in the world. Oceanic problems are regarded from different points of view: economic, political and military—with their dialectical links and mutual dependence.

The author wishes to express his sincere gratitude for valuable advice and assistance to Admiral V. N. Alekseyev, Admiral V. S. Sysoyev, Rear-Admiral K. A. Stalbo, Rear-Admiral V. N. Usenko, First Rank Captain N. P. V'yunenko, Professor V. G. Bakayev and also all those who helped in the preparation of the book.

After publication of the Russian-language edition, the author received a number of comments and requests from readers. Having gratefully accepted these, the author has made some corrections in the original text in preparing the book for publication abroad. A number of changes which have taken place latterly in international affairs have also made necessary some other corrections.

CHAPTER 1

The Oceans and the Sea Power of the State

SINCE ancient times the ocean has attracted man with its secrecy and minatory force, holding out the promise not only of the means of existence but of a route to unexplored lands. It has promised him incalculable wealth, but has concealed great dangers. Therefore one of the most illustrious pages of the history of mankind is associated with the conquest of the ocean and the penetration of its secrets.

The importance of the ocean cannot be overestimated in the development of productive forces and accumulation of wealth by states. As a rule, civilizations emerged and developed precisely on the shores of the seas and oceans. Countries whose population was associated with seafaring became economically strong earlier than others. At a definite stage of the history of mankind the acute need was felt to make use of the vastness of the waters of the seas and their riches. The wider the possibilities for using this wealth, the greater the prominence assumed by the conditions governing the emergence and formation of such a category as the sea power of the state which to a certain extent characterizes the economic and military power of a country and hence its role on the world stage.

Different Views on the Sea Power of the State

The essence of the sea power of the state, in our view, is how far it is possible to make the most effective use of the World Ocean or, as is sometimes said, the hydrosphere of the earth, in the interests of the state as a whole.

In the definition of the sea power of the state we include as the main components possibilities for the state to study (explore) the ocean and harness its wealth, the status of the merchant and fishing fleets and their ability to meet the needs of the state and also the presence of a navy matching the interests of this state, since antagonistic social systems exist in the world. Of course, the character of the use of the ocean and the degree of development of these components are ultimately determined by the level of economic and social development reached by the state and by the policies it pursues.

For the Soviet Union, the main goal of whose policy is the building of communism and a steady rise in the welfare of its builders, sea power emerges as one of the important factors for strengthening its economy, accelerating scien-

1

tific and technical development and consolidating the economic, political, cultural and scientific links of the Soviet people with the peoples and countries friendly to it.

The material expression of that aspect of the sea power of the state which is linked with the economy of the country is offered by the merchant, fishing, and research fleets, the science of the ocean ensuring study and exploitation of its riches, the various branches of industry extracting and processing the gifts of the ocean and also staffs of scientists, designers, engineers and technicians and the renowned army of seafarers with its diverse, complex and prestigious branches. At the same time sea power, naturally together with other components, also includes the ability of our armed forces to protect the country from threat of attack from the oceans. This aspect of sea power assumes greater importance the greater the military threat to our security.

The material expression of this aspect of sea power, characterizing the real capacity of our country to ward off aggression from the oceans, is the constantly developing and increasingly sophisticated Soviet navy called upon, in unison with our valiant armed forces, to guarantee the building of communism by decisively thwarting any attempts by aggressors to encroach on the great gains of the workers.

This in no way means that the sea power of the country depends only on the real fighting strength of the navy. It must be regarded primarily as the capacity of the state to place all the resources and possibilities offered by the ocean at the service of man and make full use of them to develop the economy, the health of which finally determines all facets of the life of our country including its defence capability. In this context the concept of sea power to a certain degree is identified with the concept of the economic power of the state. Accordingly sea power may be regarded as a constituent part of economic power. Just as the latter determines military power, sea power, mediated by the economy of the state and exerting an influence on it, carries within it an economic and military principle.

The circumstances which force us to include in the concept of the sea power of the state prerequisites of a military character are due to factors at international level, notably the existence of imperialism, extending its rapacious ventures also to the hydrosphere. Therefore, as long as imperialism exists the inclusion of the military component in the concept of sea power of the state is an imperative necessity. In these conditions the navy must be regarded as one of the most important components of sea power, serving as a reliable guarantee of the security of our country and an important means of ensuring its interests at sea.

The imperialist states use their sea power primarily as an instrument of aggressive policy for subjugating and holding down countries and peoples, as a means of exacerbating the international situation and unleashing wars and military conflicts in different parts of the world. The military theoreticians and ideologists of imperialism, for example in the USA, view sea power not only as a most crucial means of threatening socialism but also as a force capable of holding in check their allies in aggressive military blocs and ensuring in these blocs their dominant position and the overriding influence of the American monopolies.

Thus, a fundamental difference in the understanding of sea power by the Soviet Union and the imperialist powers stems from their class essence. It also determines the goals, tasks and means of applying the various components of sea power, notably the navies to which in the imperialist states is assigned the role of one of the main tools for gaining world dominance. This also explains the fact that the concept of sea power of the imperialist states is being increasingly overshadowed by its military aspects to which are subordinated all its other aspects which they serve.

In essence the concept of sea power of the state is identified by them with such a category as naval power or naval forces. Moreover, an attempt is often made to replace military power by this concept, thereby emphasizing their intentions to continue to concentrate in the sphere of operations of their fleets the main strategic, in particular, nuclear missile, potential of the armed forces. Western strategists often give to sea power an unjustifiably hypertrophied significance. Its status and its relation to the power of other countries are used to explain many events in the world and even the development of the history of whole peoples and countries, as has been done by US naval theoreticians. Their current followers, seeking from the standpoint of "sea power", "sea force", "naval power" to explain those most highly complicated events and processes which occur on the world scene, inevitably arrive at the contrived conclusion that it is necessary to step up still further the naval arms race.

In the expansion of sea power the imperialists see ways of further plundering nations, filling the so-called power vacuum in certain areas of the world due to the breakdown of the whole colonial system and the appearance in its remnants of an ever larger number of independent states embarking on the path of independent development. These states are regarded by the ideologists of sea power of imperialism as fair game for their aggressive pursuits which can be "ensnared" as they cynically assert, primarily with the aid of the naval forces. Such "ideological" justifications are widely backed up by force of arms, as witness the more than thirty wars and conflicts unleashed by the imperialist circles of different countries since the end of the Second World War and involving navies. They have invariably fulfilled the role of the "big stick" with which the national liberation movements have been ruthlessly suppressed in countries selected by the imperialists as victims of their aggression.

The need to expand sea power by the imperialist states is also justified by the large number of commitments of these countries to the "defence of democracy and anti-communist regimes" in different parts of the world. Using the old methods of colonial policy—terror and blackmail, intervention, economic and political dictation—the imperialist powers now more and more often resort to new forms of colonial expansion, masking them by so-called aid and assistance. How the famous "aid" and "assistance" have been carried out is sufficiently well known to the reader by the examples of Korea and Vietnam, Greece, Panama, and many other countries.

Among the arguments used to justify expansion of the military components of sea power are the tremendous scale of American big business involved in the economies of overseas countries and the rapid growth of American sea trade, the annual volume of which exceeds 400 million tons. Here the navy is given the role of guarantor of the economic expansion of the American monopolies, the role of an accomplice in robbing the peoples of many countries dependent on the USA in economic, political and military fields.

Manifestly standing on their head all the processes of world social development, the new-styled advocates of sea force agree in recognizing sea power as the dominant factor in the creation of a new type of "regionalism", i.e. economic groupings of countries a decisive role in the economy of which is alleged to be played by the use of giant ships in sea trade. "Arguments" are advanced for justifying the need to protect the cargoes on these ships by the force of arms of the fleets. There is no lack of such "justifications" of the essence and content of sea power and merely to list them would tire the reader.

We have mentioned only some of the most widespread concepts of sea power directly linked with political and economic issues and used mainly for propagandist purposes intended to hide the essence of the aggressive plans of imperialism. The ideologists of imperialism resort to deliberately vague phraseology to mask the unsavoury aspects of their aggressive policy, namely those which they consider it better to hide from foreign eyes than reveal to public gaze.

But there also exist frankly militaristic concepts which with cynical bluntness expose that which others conceal. They express the view of the heads of the military industrial complex whose whole *raison d'etre* lies in the whipping up of war hysteria and of extracting ever new grants for stepping up the arms race, representing the main item of their income and profits. Sea power, as they claim, is no longer confined to the huge expanses of the oceans and is now breaking into the continental masses, supplementing and even replacing military power, the level of which is determined above all by the ability to hit with nuclear strikes ground targets deep in the territory of the enemy at any point of the globe. In this connection sea power is increasingly acting as a stimulator of repeated "decisive" revisions of existing strategies for waging war.

A new reorientation of the armed forces of the USA is now taking place in a situation in which the basic tasks in war must be inevitably solved by delivering powerful strikes from the sea with the three main elements of the naval forces: ballistic missiles from atomic submarines, aircraft-carrier aviation and the marines. The destructive force of nuclear strikes is seen as a new, additional measure of sea power used in operations of the fleet against the shore. This is promoted by the wide use of submarines with atomic power, lessening the traditional dependence of the fleets on the disposition of strategic positions in oceanic and sea theatres and on the "geography" of their bases with the possibility of extending the sphere of aggressive moves to new areas of the World Ocean.

But not only this draws the gaze of the ideologists of the military-industrial complex to naval power. "It would be tragic if US soil were the only delivery base that we had, for then the total enemy effort could be directed against our homeland. Fortunately, naval power provides an excellent alternative. It gives us a means of using the oceans as the delivery base, while retaining the enemy base as the point of weapon impact," wrote one such, Admiral K. Ricketts. "These precious attributes of naval weapon systems provide advantages that accrue only to those who recognize and exploit the unique characteristics of the sea."[1] Here, as we see, sea power is displayed as a means capable of shifting the threat of retaliation further into the ocean away from those who are preparing nuclear aggression against mankind.

Among the factors promoting the growth of sea power are the other achievements of scientific and technical progress, in particular artificial earth satellites, already used by imperialist forces for the purposes of intelligence, communications and navigation. Like many other achievements of science and technology marshalled in the service of imperialism they are regarded only from the angle of their use for military purposes, especially for expanding the strike force of the fleets.

This brief perusal of the concepts of sea power current abroad indicates their narrow, utilitarian direction and their subordinate position in preparing for war. Sea power, according to these concepts, is determined by new measurements of the destructive force of naval weaponry, the ever lower costs of distant troop transports, the extension of the impact of naval arms to land masses, wide international commitments, by the aggressive alliances of maritime states, and also by control over the seas in specific regions where the forces enjoying superiority may be brought into action at any moment.

Recently all countries of the world have shown a growing interest in the use of the infinite wealth of the World Ocean for economic purposes. The highly varied resources of the oceans used in the interests of humanity would make it possible to solve many major problems in the field of power, food, recovery of useful minerals and in the development of the transport, economic, cultural and scientific links of countries in different areas of the world. However, activity in this field is often regarded by the leading maritime powers of the imperialist camp from the angle of military preparations.

"If all the aspects of sea power are related to the proper interests of the USA" declared the US Secretary of the Navy P. Ignatus, "then it should be noted that to ensure the maintenance of military operations with the aim of preserving the flexibility of independent operation it is necessary to have a large and modern merchant fleet sailing under the American flag. Without a strong merchant fleet a number of independent variants of military decisions may be overlooked. With superiority in the technical achievements of use of the oceans, the USA must open up new regions for extending American influence on an international scale. This primacy in the exploration of the oceans may prove very important for the future development of US sea power, closely associated with its national economy. Similarly, superiority in questions of oceanography helps the USA to maintain its lead in the scientific world and also to reap the fruits of the practical advantages from the corresponding results which very often cannot be predicted in advance. Prestige in the international world is important not only for foreign purchasers of American products but also for the international relations of the USA, resting on its sea power." (Retranslated from Russian).[2]

Similar examples showing the aggressive essence of the sea power of the

[1] Ricketts, K. "Naval power—present and future", *United States Naval Institute Proceedings,* 1963, No. 1, p. 39.
[2] *United States Naval Institute Proceedings,* 1970, No. 4, pp. 26-31.

imperialist states and its reactionary content could also be given in relation to other aspects of their foreign policy, basically orientated to the infamous "position of strength". However, even the examples presented above are sufficient to understand the true intention of the sea power of the imperialist states used by them in peacetime first and foremost as a principal attribute of "gun diplomacy" and in wartime as a most important means of major strategy, the principal content of which is to an increasing degree taken up by oceanic strategy.

As indicated above, we regard sea power as an involved complex of different components relating to the economy of the country and the policy of the Communist Party, its defence capability, the knowledge and training of personnel and the practical realization of all those possibilities opened up by the use of the seas and oceans in the building of communism.

The Ocean and its Significance

The ocean with which is connected the origin of all life on our planet is of the greatest importance for the life of mankind. Present-day flora and fauna developed from organisms that used to live in the waters of the ocean, which continues to remain an active focus of life.

The influence of the oceanic environment on the economy of states is tremendous and multifacetted. The seas and oceans hold the largest stores of varied industrial raw materials and energy. Across the seas and oceans run the most important and most economic lines of communication between countries. The amount of living matter synthesized in the ocean many times exceeds all that which the land creates. The ocean may thus be seen as one of the main sources for solving the food problem of the growing world population. The annual world fish catch from an area accounting for about 10 per cent of the surface of the ocean is 60 million tons but by 1985 it may be up to 100-120 million tons. A possible future source of protein is plant and animal plankton, the stores of which in the ocean are enormous. The first steps in this direction have already been taken.

The chemical and mineral resources of the World Ocean are practically inexhaustible. It has been estimated that if one could sediment all the salt of the ocean, its floor would be covered by a layer of salt 57 metres thick. In the sea part of the planet are concentrated some 90,000 million tons of iodine, 5000 million tons of uranium, up to 3000 million tons of manganese, vanadium and nickel, 10 million tons of gold, 270,000 million tons of heavy water, thousands of millions of tons of magnesium, potassium, bromine and calcium and millions of tons of silver, thorium and other rare elements. One cubic metre of sea water on average contains 30 kilograms of sodium chloride, 1.3 kilograms of magnesium and 66 grams of bromine, 99 per cent of the stores of which on our planet is in the ocean.

Only a few substances dissolved in sea water are as yet amenable to man for industrial exploitation. The problem has been economically and technically solved for obtaining from sea water cooking salt, magnesium, bromine, potassium, iodine and some other substances. Thus, with world production of cooking salt at 22 million tons a year, one-third is obtained by evaporation of sea water. The annual world recovery of magnesium from sea water is 300,000 tons and bromine 100,000 tons. Ways have been found of obtaining from sea water uranium, gold and other valuable elements. The scope and scale of the work on the extraction from water of rare and scattered elements are such that in the not too distant future they may bring major changes in world economics.

On the surface of the ocean floor very rich accumulations of iron-manganese concretions[3] are found, containing as many as 30 chemical elements, the principal ones being manganese (25 per cent), iron (14 per cent) and also cobalt, nickel, copper, titanium and vanadium. In content of valuable metals these formations are incomparably richer than the ores found in the bowels of the earth.

Although the treatment of deep-water ores is a new development, even now projects to raise them from the bottom at comparatively cheap cost are being proposed. Thus, the extraction of iron-manganese concretions has already begun in some countries.

The depths of the sea bed comprise enormous energy resources. Rich oil and gas deposits have been found in the Persian and Mexican Gulfs, in the western part of the Caribbean Sea, in the North Sea, on the Pacific Coast of the USA, on the coast of West Africa, in the East and South China Seas and in other areas. The geological oil reserves discovered at depths down to 300 metres are tentatively put at 420,000 million tons. Moreover it is assumed that the main oil and gas deposits are not under dry land but in the sea, since two-thirds of the oil-gas-bearing territories known on dry land are located on the sea coast. And although mankind can make full use of all this wealth only in the future, even now the importance of harnessing it is rapidly growing. Prospecting for oil and gas is taking place at nearly every point of the continental shelf. About one-quarter of the world production of oil is now lifted from the floor of the seas and oceans. It is expected that in the next ten years the annual volume of the marine production of oil will reach one-third of total world production.

The ocean floor is also rich in other useful minerals. Coal seams have been found on the western coast of the USA and on the shores of Chile and Australia. In Newfoundland, iron and copper ores are extracted and iron ore reserves in this region are put at over 3000 million tons. In the Mexican Gulf on "iron islands" sulphur is being extracted from the bottom. The maritime extraction of tin, thorium and titanium ores and also diamonds, pearls, sand, gravel and coquina is also being pursued.

Interest in the ocean is heightened by the possibilities opening up of using the thermal, mechanical and chemical energy of the waters of the ocean.

According to the estimates of scientists, the energy of the sea tides exceeds more than two thousand times the annual energy store of all world rivers. The harnessing of even a small part of this energy will make a telling contribution to the energy resources of mankind. Engineering thought is now concentrated on wide experimentation on the use of the tidal variations of the sea level and the difference in the water temperature of the upper (25-30°C) and deep (5-10°C)

[3] Sedimentary rock deposits.

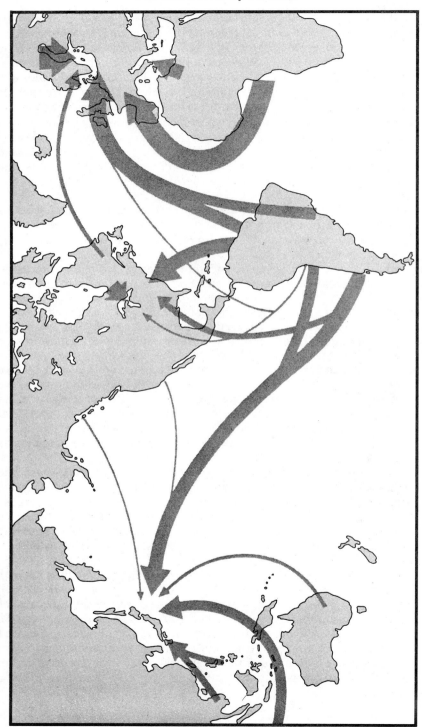

Fig. 1.   Diagram of International Seaborne Iron Ore Cargoes

layers of the ocean. In 1959 France was the first country in the world to bring into service a 9000 KW plant based on an experimental tidal station with a rated power of 320 MW. In the USSR the Kislogubsk tidal power-station recently came into service and projects of tidal stations in Lumbovsk Bay and Mezensk Gulf are in hand. Small tidal power-stations are operating in China. Some countries are already building hydrothermal power-stations. When all the technical difficulties have been overcome and the stations begin to work, a new, practically inexhaustible source of energy generated by the ocean will be opened up.

The transport significance of the ocean is very considerable. Across the oceans and seas run the main trade routes of the world linking continents, countries and peoples. If the lines of the navigation routes of ships in the course of a year are plotted on a map, then the World Ocean will be found to be covered by a veritable web of routes, though of differing thicknesses. This lack of uniformity primarily depends on the level of development of the economies of the countries situated on the shores of the oceans and seas, on their resources and the foreign trade requirements directly linked with them, the natural conditions of navigation, the economic desirability of carrying cargoes by water and also on the political situations which build up in the relations between individual countries in different parts of the world. Particularly instructive and constant are the causes connected with the natural or historically-shaped distribution of natural resources and productive forces.

Thus, a well-defined pattern is offered by the cargo flows of sea transport of oil from the countries of the Near and Middle East to the West—Europe and the USA, and to the East—to Japan and the countries of South-East Asia, the carriage of grain from the USA, Canada and Australia to the countries of the European continent and also machinery and manufactured goods from the industrially developed countries of Europe and America to the less developed countries of the African and Asian continents.

The economies of the developed capitalist countries largely depend on sea transport, especially on the importation of different kinds of raw materials and provisions. This is confirmed by the fact that about 90 per cent of the total volume of foreign-trade marine shipments consists of raw materials and foodstuffs. In the last few years the volume of oil and oil product shipments has grown apace (about 10 per cent a year). The volume of shipments for individual types of cargo is roughly distributed percentagewise as follows: oil and oil products 55, iron ore 10, grain and coal 5 each, fertilizers 3, timber, sugar, bauxites 1.5-2 each and with about 25 for piece and other types of cargo (Figs. 1-4). The predominance of raw materials and foodstuffs among the cargoes carried determines not only the character of international sea shipments but the whole system of international economic links—the volume, commodity structure and direction of the international cargo turnover.

The role and the place of oceanic transport in the economy of many states in the past also determined the importance of the oceans, which for long has remained practically unchanged.

The Atlantic Ocean is of prime importance for shipping and international trade. In the Atlantic basin are situated the most industrially developed regions

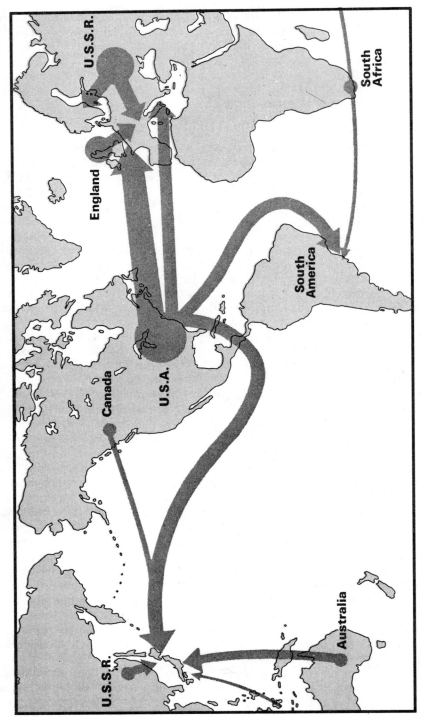

Fig. 2. Diagram of International Seaborne Coal Cargo Flows

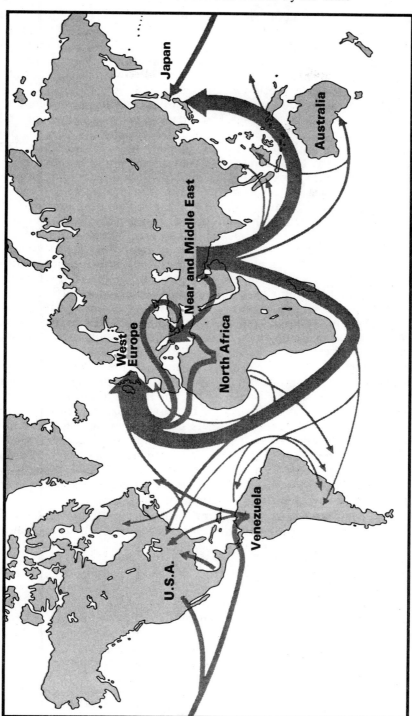

Fig. 3.   Diagram of International Oil Cargo Flows

in which some 800 million people live. The area of this ocean exceeds 93 million sq km or almost 26 per cent of the total area of the World Ocean. The distance, for example, from Copenhagen to New York is over 7000 km and to the Panama Canal 10,000 km. On the coast of the Atlantic Ocean are three-quarters of the sea ports of the world which handle over 70 per cent of the cargoes carried across the World Ocean.

In the Atlantic Ocean the communications in its northern part stand out in importance and intensity of shipping. Here, daily (on average) one finds 4000 merchant vessels, a good number of which are on passage between ports. Across the North Atlantic run over 100 regular lines of the USSR, USA, England, France, Italy, Netherlands, West Germany and other countries.

The main transoceanic cargo flows in the North Atlantic pass in directions linking the ports of Western Europe to the ports of North America (over 21 per cent of cargo turnover); the ports of North America with the ports of South-West Europe, North Africa and the Middle East through the Straits of Gibraltar (about 12 per cent of cargo turnover); and the ports of Western Europe with the ports of Central and South America and the countries of the Pacific through the Panama Canal (over 10 per cent of cargo turnover). After the closure of the Suez Canal in 1967 as a result of Israeli aggression, greater importance was attached to the routes running from the ports of Europe and North and South America around Africa. The importance of these communications will also obviously grow in the future despite the re-opening of the Canal, since recently an increasing role is beginning to be played in world shipping by large-tonnage ships—so-called supertankers and others with large draught.

The role of Atlantic communications is enhanced by the exceptional military significance of this theatre. In fact here are spread out the armed forces of the main aggressive bloc of imperialism—NATO, and from here the most powerful nuclear missile strikes may be delivered by submarines and aircraft-carrier planes of the imperialist fleets on targets of the countries of the socialist community. In the Atlantic (including the Mediterranean) are concentrated the principal forces of the fleets of the main imperialist powers. Here, there are constantly present 70-80 per cent of the fighting ships of the USA and Great Britain, including five of the six squadrons of the ballistic missile submarines and four of the six aircraft-strike formations of the USA.

Across the Atlantic pass the basic communications of NATO which link the group of European countries belonging to this bloc to its main arsenal, the United States of America. The military significance of these communications is enormous. For example, in the Second World War over 2200 large convoys including more than 75,000 ships sailed to Europe across the Atlantic. In the same period coastal communications handled some 7700 convoys including over 170,000 ships.[4]

Among the seas of the Atlantic basin of the greatest importance is the Mediterranean, on the shores of which are 18 European, Asian and African states with different political outlooks. In them live over 300 million people. Some of these states belong to the aggressive blocs of NATO and CENTO,

[4] V. A. Belli *et al.*, *Blockade and Counter-Blockade* (in Russian), p. 398 , Moscow, Nauka, 1967.

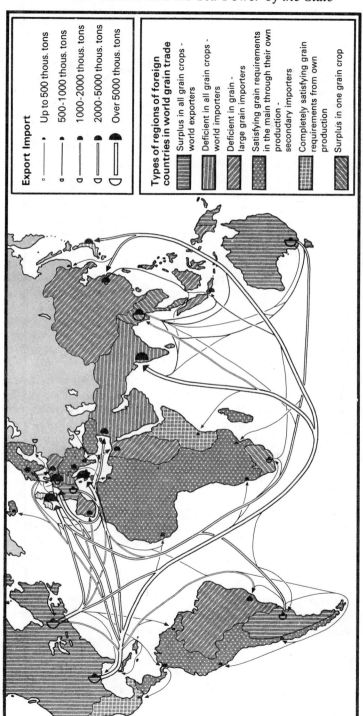

Fig. 4. Diagram of International Seaborne Grain Cargo Flows

others to the group of so-called non-aligned countries or those waging a tough struggle for their independence.

The economy of many Mediterranean states is connected with the extraction of so-called strategic fossils such as oil, and chrome. The fight for predominant influence in the sphere of extraction of these fossils forms an important part of the policies of many capitalist countries. Through the Mediterranean run the most important communications along which fuel is supplied to the countries of Europe and the USA. In the Second World War ships with a tonnage of over 154 million registered tons passed through the Mediterranean from the countries of Africa and Southern Europe to England and back. In 1940 alone the ships of the Axis powers carried to North Africa alone over 5 million tons of cargo.[5]

Thus, across the Atlantic Ocean pass the main transport arteries of the western countries on the continuous functioning of which closely depends their economy. Therefore, the military ideologists of NATO consider the Atlantic Ocean with its seas the main oceanic theatre of military operations and concentrate here the main forces of their fleet.

The Pacific is the largest ocean in the world and is of great importance for shipping and international trade. In the countries of the basin of this ocean live over 1000 million people. The area of the Pacific is almost 180 million sq km or half the entire area of the World Ocean or one-third of the surface of the earth. The states situated on its opposite shores are separated by enormous distances. Thus, from Vladivostok to San Francisco is over 8400 km, from Petropavlovsk-Kamchatka to the Panama Canal 14,800 km, and from San Francisco to Manila 11,500 km.

The Pacific takes about 20 per cent of world shipping, the busiest routes being the American-Asian, American-Australian and Asian-Australian.

Recently much importance has been assumed by the communications through which oil is supplied from the ports of the Persian Gulf to Japan. The most lively is the movement of ships on the American-Asian route joining the ports of North America and the Panama Canal to the ports of Japan, the Chinese People's Republic, the Philippines and the Straits of Singapore. The economic importance of the Pacific theatre is largely determined by the dependence of the countries lying there on oceanic communications ensuring the requirements of the economy and the armed forces.

The Pacific coast of the USA is the location of many centres of the atomic, missile and aviation industries, shipbuilding, production of synthetic rubber, aluminium, etc. It now constitutes a large base of American imperialism providing with military technology not only the armed forces of the USA but also the other capitalist states of the American continent, Asia and also Australia.

The imperialist states in the Pacific theatre are united under the aegis of the USA into military blocs. A number of bilateral agreements have been concluded between the USA and Japan, South Korea, Thailand, the Taiwan regime and governments of other countries. The USA has installed military bases in foreign countries and maintains advisers and large contingents of land, air and naval forces. The waters of the Pacific are continuously patrolled by American

[5] V. A. Belli *et al.*, *Blockade and Counter-Blockade* (in Russian), pp. 669-670, Moscow, Nauka, 1967.

ballistic missile submarines. In the Far East the main strike force of the USA is the Seventh Naval Fleet.

For the United States of great importance in the Pacific are military shipments meeting the requirements of the armed forces. Sea shipments predominate despite the considerable developments of air transport. Thus, in three years of military operations in Korea over one million persons and 370,000 tons of cargo were delivered by air from the USA to Korea and Japan and back. In this same time sea transport and the fighting ships of the USA and their allies carried about 5 million persons and 74 million tons of various items of cargo. Thus, for every ton of cargo supplied to Asia by air, above 200 tons of cargo was delivered by sea, and of each six members of the occupying forces five arrived by sea. In connection with the war in Vietnam in 1967 the USA carried across the ocean into South-East Asia 2.5 million tons of cargo.[6]

The Indian Ocean is playing an increasing role in the economies of the developing countries of South Asia and East Africa. In the countries of its basin live some 1000 million persons. This is the third biggest ocean, with an area of almost 75 million sq km (over 20 per cent of the World Ocean). The greatest distances between the southern tips of Africa and Australia (Agulhas and South Capes) are 10,750 km, along the equator 6300 km and along the meridian 60°E longitude about 10,600 km. The Indian Ocean takes about a tenth of world shipping. The economic importance of the Indian Ocean lies essentially in the fact that along it run world trade routes linking Europe and America with South Asia, East Africa, Australia and the oil-bearing regions of the Near and Middle East. Across the Indian Ocean run the routes from the Black Sea and Baltic ports of the USSR to the ports of the Far East and also to India, Pakistan, Bangladesh, Indonesia, Burma and other countries.

The situation in many countries of the Indian Ocean basin is determined, on the one hand, by the endeavour of imperialism to maintain in new forms its former dominance and, on the other, by the stubborn struggle of the peoples of these states for complete political and economic independence and struggle against foreign bases on their territories and neo-colonialism in all its manifestations.

The Arctic Ocean is the smallest of all, occupying an area of only a little more than 13 million sq km with a large part of this stretch of water, roughly 8 million sq km, being accounted for by the Barents, Kara, East Siberian and Chukov Seas, the Kaptev Sea and others.

It takes only a one-hundredth part of world shipping. Over the Arctic Ocean into the arctic seas embracing the northern coasts of the Soviet Union, Norway, USA, Canada and Greenland pass the shortest air routes between Eurasia and the American continent.

The importance of this ocean is determined by the great economic significance of the territories of the USSR lying next to its coast. The Northern sea route running along the Soviet coast is of enormous importance for our country's economy despite the extreme complexity of navigation of ships along it. The navigation period in the Arctic lasts from the end of June to September and is about 90-120 days.

[6] See *History of Naval Art* (in Russian), pp. 551 and 558, Moscow, Voenizdat, 1969.

The link by sea with the islands and the northern coast of Canada is also possible only for three to four months of the year and this in heavy ice.

Study of the oceanic environment

Despite the fact that the seas and oceans played a crucial role in the history of the development of mankind and that man in the search for new spheres of application of his capacities at first turned to the ocean and only then to the near-earth air space and then to the cosmos, much still remains unknown in efforts to harness the hydrosphere. In it there are a lot of blank spaces which the peoples during their history have never yet reached. Therefore, even now the sea is perhaps the least studied area of the planet.

To harness the World Ocean and use its resources it is necessary to have a detailed and comprehensive knowledge of the hydrosphere of the earth, understand the processes occurring in it, its influence on dry land and atmosphere and the shaping of the weather, and have reliable information on the resources present in the hydrosphere and possible means of exploiting them. Knowledge is also required ensuring the safety of navigation in the oceans and seas and flights over them. Man is studying ever more deeply and probingly the ocean, harnessing it and unravelling its secrets. The World Ocean is the property of all mankind and only through the friendly efforts of all peoples and countries is it possible in full measure and with full return to make it serve man.

It is known that the processes occurring on the surface and deep in the water masses have a major influence on the whole nature of the earth and yet, much that is observed is still not clear and remains unexplained. The main difficulty in discovering the secrets of the the deep lies in the specificity of the oceanic environment itself and the relative inaccessibility of its study by modern technical means.

Scientific enquiry into the oceans began in fact some 200 years ago. However, only in the middle of the twentieth century did the complex science of the World Ocean take shape.

The main aim of oceanographic research today is to accumulate general scientific knowledge on the World Ocean and draw up a reliable picture of the distribution of the flows, waves, temperature, salinity, underwater relief, magnetic and other geophysical fields. The results of research are being taken as the basis for developing reliable methods of forecasting processes occurring deep in the waters of the oceans and seas and in near-surface atmospheric layers. All this is being used for preparing recommendations on ship design and for measures ensuring the safety of navigation of ships and aircraft flights.

An important independent line of research is the prospecting for the organic and mineral raw material resources of the oceans, developing measures for their rational exploitation and preparing recommendations on the preservation and protection of the oceanic expanses from pollution.

The developed capitalist countries (primarily the USA, England, France, Japan, West Germany and Canada) attach very great significance to the problems of exploring and harnessing the World Ocean and are taking a series of measures aimed at extending work in this area. The most important are the development of perspective plans for exploring and harnessing the ocean with a sharp increase in budgetary allocations for this work and also the setting up of special organs co-ordinating the activity of different organizations, scientific centres, private companies, firms and institutions of learning.

Since 1966 in the USA, the National Board for Marine Resources and Technical Development, co-ordinating work in this field, has worked with the President under the chairmanship of the Vice-President.

Close attention is also being paid to the problems of co-ordinating oceanographic research in other capitalist countries: in particular in Japan the Inter-Departmental Committee on Marine Science and Technology has been formed, in France the National Centre for Oceanographic Research and in West Germany the Technical Committee, etc.

Increased interest in oceanographic research is also indicated by the steady growth of budgetary expenditure for these purposes in a number of the major capitalist states. However, as Table 1 shows, the bulk of these allocations is for military purposes.

Thus, of the total sum allocated within the national oceanographic programme of the USA in the 1972-73 fiscal year (667 million dollars) the most important items of expenditure were those directly or indirectly connected with military preparations (over 409 million dollars).

A report of the Marine Science Commission of the US Congress entitled *Our Nation and the Sea* was published in January 1969 in the USA (US Government, *Congressional Record,* Washington, 1969, January 15, 351-4). It contained recommendations for a considerable expansion of the activity of the Federal Government in exploration of the World Ocean, the harnessing of its resources and gradual increase of about 7-10 per cent per annum in allocations for these purposes over the next 10 years (1971-1980).

TABLE 1

Volume and Distribution by US Agencies of Allocations for Oceanic Research (in millions of dollars)

	1970-71	1971-72	1972-73
Department of Defense	224.9	238.0	252.0
Department of Commerce	140.9	161.0	195.0
Department of the Interior	30.3	35.0	41.0
National Science Foundation	48.9	67.0	69.0
Department of Transportation	27.3	56.0	53.0
Department of Health, Education and Welfare	6.7	6.0	5.0
State Department	8.3	9.0	10.0
NASA	2.1	4.0	6.0
Environmental Protection Agency	17.0	18.0	26.0
Other agencies	11.0	11.0	10.0
Total	517.4	605.0	667.0

As recommended by Congress, this Report presented information on the rough cost of implementing the extended exploration programme for the World Ocean and the harnessing of its resources between 1971 and 1980. According to this information the fulfilment of the whole programme within ten years would cost some 10,000 million dollars. It was planned to increase the allocations for these purposes gradually and by 1980 bring them up to 2000 million dollars per annum.

The growth of budgetary provisions for the purpose of exploring and harnessing the ocean in some other capitalist countries is indicated by Table 2.

TABLE 2
Growth of Budgetary Provisions
for Exploring and Harnessing the
Ocean (in millions of dollars)

Countries	1970	1971	1972
France	13.7	17.6	21.5
West Germany	38.8	47.5	53.5
Japan	13.9	20.0	26.7

The leading countries of the world are exploring the World Ocean using surface oceanographic vessels, exploratory submarines and deep-water craft, specially equipped aircraft and helicopters, artificial earth satellites, fixed platforms and systems set up on the sea bottom and also anchored and floating buoy stations. The future may see the use for this purpose of independently-operating devices moving freely over the ocean bottom. At the present stage the main means of conducting various oceanographic explorations in extensive regions of the World Ocean remain surface oceanographic vessels.

A technique has now been devised for exploring the oceans and seas which represents a combination of such methods as synchronous oceanographic and meteorological surveys, determination of the parameters on standard hydrological sections, surveys of the bottom relief and determination of the elements of the magnetic and gravitational fields of the earth.

In the last few years a method of oceanographic proving-grounds which can be used to establish patterns of space-time variation in large stretches of the ocean at long time intervals has become firmly established.

In the future the best method of exploration will evidently be that based on the development of a global system of independently operating anchored or drifting oceanographic stations, backed by study from ships and artificial earth satellites which, in addition, will receive data from oceanographic stations and transmit it to land units collecting and processing this information.

A special place in oceanic exploration belongs to oceanographic expeditions which have been conducted for over 150 years. The first such work in the open ocean was carried out at the beginning of the nineteenth century by the Russian seafarers I. F. Kruzenstern and Yu. F. Lisyansky, travelling round the world on the ships *Nadezhda* and *Neva*.

In 1820, the Russian expedition of F. F. Bellinshauzen and M. P. Lazarev on the ships *Vostok* and *Mirny* discovered a new continent—Antarctica.

Extensive oceanographic explorations were made by the Russian seafarers F. P. Wrangel in the Arctic Ocean (1820-24) and the Pacific (1825-27) and by F. P. Litke in the Pacific (1826-29).

In 1872-76, the English round-the-world expedition on the ship *Challenger* studied the relief of the ocean floor and also the physical and chemical properties of surface and deep oceanic waters.

The end of the nineteenth and beginning of the twentieth centuries is characterized by considerable widening of the geography of exploration. The greatest interest among the explorers in various countries was aroused by the bleak, poorly accessible, polar regions of the World Ocean. Thus, in 1878-9 the ship *Vega*, under the command of the well-known Swedish polar explorer A. E. Nordenskiöld, made the first through journey along the Northern sea route, looking for sea animals.

A special place in study of the Arctic belongs to the well-known Norwegian polar explorers F. Nansen (1893-96) and R. Amundsen (1918-24).

Russian land explorers long ago explored the Arctic. In the eighteenth century this activity assumed national proportions. Then the major expeditions under the direction of Bering, Chirikov, the brothers Laptev and other outstanding seafarers put on the map nearly all the northern coast of Asia. In 1898, the most powerful icebreaker in the world, the *Yermak*, was built according to the ideas of the outstanding Russian naval commander and scientist S. O. Makarov, giving a considerable boost to study of and, especially, mastery of the Arctic.

The beginning of the twentieth century saw a number of Arctic expeditions, the most important of which in scientific terms were those carried out in 1911-15 under the direction of B. A. Vil'kitsky on the icebreakers *Taimyr* and *Vaigach*.

With the victory of the Great October Socialist Revolution the young socialist state embarked on a systematic planned study of the Arctic basin. In March 1921 the Floating Marine Scientific Institute (PLAVMORNII) was set up by decree of the Soviet authorities.

In 1932-33 wide international explorations of the Arctic under the aegis of the Second International Polar Year were carried out. In this period the Soviet Union equipped 15 oceanographic expeditions with the aim of making a detailed study of the geophysics of the Arctic regions and the conditions for navigation over the course of the Northern sea route. In 1937, the first explorations of the Arctic from the scientific research drift stations *North Pole* were begun. Since 1954, two such stations have been in permanent operation in the Arctic Ocean. They are the scene of oceanographic, meteorological, aerological, actinometric, magnetic, ionospheric, glacial, astronomic and hydrographic investigations which are of great practical importance for the operational servicing of shipping over the Northern sea route.

In addition, since 1948 the Arctic has been explored by unmanned automatic radio-meteorological stations. Today in the ice of the Arctic Ocean as many as twenty to thirty such stations are set up each year. They communicate by radio to shore posts information on wind direction and speed, air temperature and atmospheric pressure and also ice drift.

Despite the fact that the exploration of the southern near-polar regions were begun almost simultaneously with those of the waters of the Arctic, up to the second half of the 'fifties they were of a sporadic character, and only since then have comprehensive international explorations of Antarctica been started, both by regular expeditions from different countries and by the scientific bases and observatories set up there.

The first Soviet observatories in Antarctica were set up in the period of implementation of the programmes of the International Geophysical Year and the Year of International Geophysical Cooperation (1957-59). Joint study of Antarctica is now being undertaken by twelve countries, the work of which is coordinated by the International Scientific Committee for Antarctic Exploration.

The temperate and low latitudes of the World Ocean up to the 'thirties of this century were studied from time to time, covering small stretches of water. The most important of them were the explorations in the Pacific and Atlantic carried out by S. O. Makarov on the corvette *Vityaz* in 1886-89, resulting in a detailed description of the water regimen of the Pacific, the comprehensive explorations carried out by the German expedition on the ship *Meteor* in 1925-38 which covered practically the whole water stretch of the Atlantic Ocean and the oceanographic and geophysical explorations of US scientists in the Pacific on the ship *Cornet* in 1928-29. It is hard to overestimate the importance of these first extensive explorations.

Interest in oceanographic explorations grew particularly after the Second World War. Table 3 is instructive in this respect.

TABLE 3
Number of Oceanographic Explorations carried out on Individual Basins*

Periods	Atlantic Ocean and its seas		Pacific Ocean and its seas		Indian Ocean and its seas		Arctic Ocean and its seas		World Ocean	
	No.	%	No.	%	No.	%	No.	%	No.	%
1849-1956	1485	10	1193	8	81	0.5	905	6	3664	24.5
1957-1960	1218	8	699	5	64	0.5	405	3	2386	16.5
1961-1964	1831	12	947	6	180	1	435	3	3393	22
1965-1972	2589	17	2065	14	263	2	640	4	5557	37
Total	7123	47	4904	33	588	4	2385	16	15,000	100

* According to the oceanographic records of the World Oceanographic Research Centre

The exploration of the oceans has been most concentrated in the period between 1957 and 1972. In these fifteen years 75.5 per cent of all expeditions organized since 1849 were carried out.

As the diagram presented in Fig. 5 indicates, our motherland has made a basic contribution to this.

The growing demands of the national economy have led to the need for wider study of the World Ocean. The solution of regional problems is now gradually taking second place, giving way to global explorations of three interacting media: the ocean, the atmosphere and the lithosphere. In this connection a tendency can be discerned towards concerting the resources and means of different states for study and harnessing of the ocean.

Thus, in 1957-59 the above-mentioned international explorations were undertaken under the programme of the International Geophysical Year and the Year of International Geophysical Cooperation involving over 70 expeditionary ships from 17 countries. In the period of these explorations extensive and highly valuable material was obtained on the seas and oceans, in particular the physics of the sea, the history of the earth, phenomena influencing the weather and climates and life in the World Ocean. In the period between 1959 and 1965 the Indian Ocean international expedition was organized, its main tasks being study of the physical processes in the atmosphere and ocean, establishing the zones of the oceanological fronts, determination of the thermal balance and the water exchange of the ocean, study of the geological structure of the bottom and identification of new resource areas.

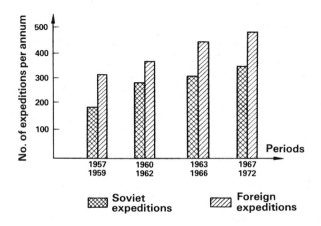

Fig. 5.   Average Number of Expeditions per year over the World Ocean at various Periods

Of great importance in the development of international co-operation in the field of oceanographic research was the setting up in 1961 at UNESCO of the Intergovernmental Oceanographic Commission (IOC), under the guidance of which international expeditions were run concerned with study of the tropical part of the Atlantic Ocean (1963-64), the exploration of Curaçao (from 1969), joint explorations of the Mediterranean (since 1969) and the Caribbean and adjacent regions (since 1970).

The programmes of these expeditions include exploration of the geophysical and dynamic fields of the ocean and also work on the problem of the interaction of the ocean and atmosphere.

For the purpose of preparing for international work on the programme of exploration of global atmospheric processes planned for 1974, the USSR in 1972 carried out explorations as part of the National Tropical Experiment in the Atlantic Ocean. In the course of this experiment for the first time in the history of study of the ocean and atmosphere a wide range of aerometeorological and oceanographic observations were made simultaneously from scientific research craft.

An even greater union of the efforts of countries is planned in the explorations of the World Ocean. These explorations will provide most valuable material necessary to mankind for the wide utilization of the enormous riches of the hydrosphere.

The most studied ocean is the Atlantic.

Table 4 shows that the greatest contribution to the exploration of the Atlantic Ocean has been made by the Soviet Union, USA and England. Undoubtedly the Soviet Union does not intend to surrender its position of a leading oceanographic power in the world. The successful resolution of the problem of studying the World Ocean in our country is connected above all with changes in the quality and increase in the number of ships and of technical means for exploration.

TABLE 4

Contribution of Different States to the Exploration of the Atlantic Ocean in
the Period between 1849 and 1972

State	Number of expeditions in the Atlantic	Percentage of total number of expeditions
Russia and the USSR	2137	30
USA	1567	22
England	997	14
France	498	7
Canada	427	6
Denmark	285	4
Argentina	214	3
Norway	214	3
Spain	71	1
Iceland	71	1
Other states	641	9
Total	7122	100

The main and most economic means of conducting exploratory and other operations to master the World Ocean are surface craft constructed to specially formulated designs and fitted out with appropriate equipment and machinery.

Our country at present has some 150 exploratory vessels with a displacement of over 500 tons (Table 5).

Most of the Soviet scientific research vessels in their design, tactical and technical characteristics and equipment are right up to date.

The development and improvement of Soviet research vessels is being continued with the aim of devising oceanic resources of varying function with maximum integration of apparatus, securing exploration in all spheres with the greatest possible number of parameters, which naturally also predetermines increase in the displacement of such vessels.

To carry out theoretical and applied research in all areas of the oceans and the seas, our research and expeditionary vessels are fitted with modern storm,

TABLE 5
Basic Tactical and Technical Characteristics of Some Types of Exploratory Vessels of the Soviet Union

Type of ship	Function of ship	Displacement, tons	Economic speed, knots	Travelling range, miles	Crew	Scientific staff	Number of laboratories
Akademik Kurchatov	Comprehensive oceanographic explorations	6700	16	20,000	86	81	28
Nikolai Zubov	Comprehensive oceanographic explorations	3000	14	11,000	68	40	14
Passat	Weather-ship	3700	13	15,000	60	52	5
Arktika	Hydrographic investigations	1500	14	8000	41	14	3
Aelita	Fishery investigations	900	11	7000	28	4	3

navigational and exploratory equipment. Ship computers make it possible, during exploration, to analyse and process all the information on the relief and composition of the sea bottom, the physical fields of the earth in the ocean and hydrological and meteorological processes in the aquatic environment and in the atmosphere above it. With the aid of modern equipment it is possible to measure depths down to 11,000 metres for all inclines of the sea bed and to study the hydrophysical fields at all oceanic levels with a high degree of accuracy. In practical exploration wide use is made of automatic deep-water buoy stations strung out from exploratory vessels. Individual vessels make extensive surveys of the upper layers of the atmosphere above the ocean, using meteorological rockets.

A whole number of explorations in the ocean can be made only with the aid of exploratory submarines and deep-water craft. In addition, experience in the use of deep-water craft has shown that they possess a number of important advantages over probes, trawls, buoys and other resources used for exploration from surface vessels. Deep-water craft allow scientists to carry out multi-plane and sustained investigations of phenomena in their natural setting and of marine life in natural conditions.

In their tactical and technical characteristics deep-water craft are highly varied. Depending on the purpose and tasks facing the craft, they may have a displacement from two or three to several hundred tons, independent operation potential from 10-15 hours to several days, and an operating range from 30-40 to several thousands of miles at a speed of two or three to 25 knots.

While the Soviet Union occupies a leading place in world exploratory oceanographic science in the production of surface exploratory vessels, in some aspects of the production of deep-water craft we somewhat lag behind the leading Western countries where wider use is made of bathyscaphes, bathyspheres and other deep-water devices. This places before Soviet scientific and industrial organizations the task of overcoming the lag in the exploration of the deep-water oceanic world.

Soviet scientists have made considerable advances in solving existing problems in the field of oceanography. The explorations of Soviet expeditions in the oceans in the last few years have been marked by a number of fundamental discoveries.

Thus, the expeditions on the exploratory vessels *M. Lomonosov* (1959) and *Akademik Kurchatov* (1969) discovered and explored the strong counter currents in the equatorial and north-western Atlantic Ocean at depths of 100-500 metres called the Lomonosov current and the Antilles-Guyana counter current. Our scientists have discovered and studied the Lomonosov, Mendeleev and Hakkel ranges in the Arctic Ocean and also a number of depressions in the Pacific.

Soviet oceanography has made a considerable contribution in the field of experimental and theoretical investigations aimed at studying the physical system "ocean-atmosphere", the space-time variability of hydrophysical fields and working out methods of hydrometeorological and ice forecasting in the ocean.

Step by step, Soviet oceanologists are acquiring the necessary scientific data furthering the progress of science and raising the efficacy of the national economy of our motherland. A considerable share in all major international expeditions is, as a rule, taken by the Soviet Union. We must not in the future lessen the share of our participation in world efforts to study the oceanic environment but continue to develop the fleet of exploratory vessels and develop the industry producing modern instruments for oceanographic research, improve the coordination of the activity of all departments engaged in this important field of understanding of our planet and perfect the training of professional specialists—oceanologists, hydrographers and others that this science needs.

Here it is pertinent to stress that we need to see instruments perfected for oceanographic explorations. The requirements for ever more diverse information on the water environment and the thickness of the bed of the oceans and seas, the need for monitoring ongoing changes occurring in this medium and also the timely and continuous processing of the whole mass of ongoing information require the large-scale introduction of modern electronic measuring and computer systems. The scientific and industrial organizations of our country must greatly increase their efforts in the organization of oceanographic research so as not to lose the leading place which the Soviet Union rightfully holds in world oceanographic science.

Problems of combating the pollution of the oceans

The swift development of industry and agriculture and also the intensive use of the riches of the sea have caused wide-scale pollution and created a threat to the life of animal organisms both of inland fresh waters and in the seas and oceans.

It is quite natural that as mankind becomes more aware of the tremendous importance of the ocean as a source of vital resources and the need for its comprehensive study grows, problems of preserving and developing these resources also arise and hence also problems of combating pollution of the oceanic environment directly and very dangerously threatening its riches.

Of late, the fight against pollution of the ocean has ceased to be a purely scientific problem and is at the centre of attention both of the governments of many countries and international organizations. At the Conference held in October 1973 in London an International Convention for the Prevention of Pollution from Ships was adopted, intended to replace the 1954 International Convention on the Prevention of Pollution of the Sea by Oil. The new Convention stiffens the demands for measures to prevent such pollution.

In the Soviet Union the protection of the waters from pollution is regarded as a general task of the state. The law "On the Protection of Nature in the RSFSR" was adopted by the third session of the Supreme Soviet of the RSFSR of the fifth convocation as far back as 1960. In December 1972 a resolution of the Central Committee of the CPSU and the USSR Council of Ministers "On strengthening protection of nature and improved use of natural resources" was adopted.

From the January 1973 issue of *Courier,* the UNESCO journal, we have as the ten main pollutants of our planet:

(1) Radiation—arises from atomic weapons testing and the operation of nuclear-powered ships and vessels, in the production of nuclear fuels and arms manufacture. Exceeding the permissible doses may lead to malignant neoplasms and genetic mutations.

(2) Oil—pollution occurs on transporting oil by sea, in sea disasters and in extracting and purifying it, with dire ecological consequences: pollutes the coast, causes death of plankton organisms, fish, sea birds and mammals.

(3) DDT and other pesticides—very toxic for crustaceans even in very low concentrations. Gaining access to water stretches, they kill fish and poison organisms serving as food for the fish and also human foodstuffs.

(4) Mercury—contained in the combustion products of fossil fuels, paint production wastes and is released on enrichment of ores. Mercury, one of the most dangerous pollutants of foodstuffs, especially those of marine origin, is able to accumulate in the body, exerting a harmful influence on the nervous system.

(5) Phosphates—contained in sewage. The main sources are chemical detergents, fertilizers washed from the soil and waste products of farms engaged in intensive animal husbandry. The main pollutant of the waters of rivers and lakes.

(6) Lead—contained in exhaust gases. Other sources undertaking processing lead ores, the chemical industry and pesticides. It is a toxic element with cumulative properties, acts on the enzyme systems and metabolism of living cells and accumulates in sea deposits and in fresh water.

(7) Carbon dioxide—forms on combustion of various carbon-containing compounds (power, industry, heating). Increase in the content of this gas in the atmosphere may cause a dangerous rise in the temperature over the earth's surface, which is fraught with dire geochemical and ecological consequences.

(8) Carbon monoxide—a very toxic gas which may disturb the thermal balance of the upper atmosphere. The main sources are internal-combustion engines, the metallurgical industry and oil distillation plants.

(9) Sulphur dioxide—contained in exhaust gases, the fumes of power and industrial plants and ovens. Pollution of the air with it exacerbates respiratory diseases, inflicts harm on plants and corrodes limestone constructions and some synthetic fabrics and materials.

(10) Nitrogen oxides—they produce smog, promoting heavy proliferation of aquatic vegetation, which leads to depletion of the oxygen reserves in water, death of fish and deterioration of the quality of the water. The main sources are internal-combustion engines, jet engines, blast furnaces, industrial chemical plants, forest fires and immoderate use of chemical fertilizers.

The greatest danger to the resources of the World Ocean and mankind as a whole is posed by the pollution of the waters by radioactive substances and oil products. The natural radioactivity of the ocean, in the main, is produced by potassium-40, and the artificial chiefly by strontium-90 and caesium-137.

All marine organisms possess a selective capacity to accumulate radioactive substances and concentrate them in large amounts. Algae and phytoplankton concentrate radioactive isotopes to tens of thousands of times their content in the water. Radioactive isotopes are also actively taken up by animals living in the water. Thus, fish which make distant migrations are contaminated with radioactive substances and act as carriers. For marine organisms the most dangerous are cerium, caesium and yttrium, and for man strontium-90.

The main sources of radioactive pollution of the environment are nuclear explosions which are accompanied by the formation of radioactive substances. Much of the long-lived radioactive products of explosions under the influence of climatic and meteorological factors enters the waters of the World Ocean.

Despite the 1963 Moscow Treaty banning nuclear explosions in the aquatic environment, the atmosphere and outer space, France and China, not signatories to this international document, continue to test nuclear weapons. Between 1960 and 1973 France carried out 51 explosions, and China 15 between 1964 and 1973. All these explosions substantially added to the total number of radionuclides deposited in the biogenesis zone.

The development of atomic power has brought with it the acute problem of burying radioactive wastes since the amount grows from year to year. The practice of burying radioactive wastes in open areas of the seas and oceans has been widely adopted. In 1969 alone, off the shores of Spain, Euroatom buried some 11,000 tons of radioactive waste in the Atlantic Ocean.

Despite the regulatory measures, the dumping of radioactive wastes is leading to pollution of the flora and fauna of the seas and oceans. Having regard to the system officially endorsed in the USA for the dumping of radioactive wastes of atomic submarines, it may be expected that large quantities of radioactive isotopes will be introduced not only in coastal waters but also in open stretches of the World Ocean.

Pollution of sea waters and shores with oil products has become a world disaster. Oil films on the surface of the oceans and seas greatly worsen the aeration of sea waters leading to the formation of stagnant hydrogen sulphide zones, secondary pollution of the bottom and destruction of the benthos. It is generally known that oil pollution destroys beaches and leads to fires.

At present 25 per cent of world merchant fleet tonnage is made up of tankers and about 50 per cent of motor vessels. On pumping out ballast waters and washing tanks about half a million tons of oil products are annually dumped into the seas and oceans, from where the tides deposit them on the beaches. No small role in the pollution of sea water is played by the oil-processing and petroleum industries.

Reference was made above to the ever-increasing amount of oil extracted in the ocean. If it is assumed that less than 5 per cent of the oil in marine industrial activity will be subject to leakage, even then tens of millions of tons of it will enter the open ocean. This makes clear just how acute has become the battle against pollution of the waters of the World Ocean by oil and oil products.

Several international conferences, including those in 1954 and 1962, have been concerned with the danger of oil pollution of the oceans and seas.

Other sources of pollution of the seas and oceans are the effluents of industrial and municipal enterprises situated on the sea coasts and also on the banks of rivers flowing into the seas and oceans. The volume of the effluent discharged daily into the rivers and seas has assumed mammoth proportions. At the same time little attention is paid to the construction of purifying plants of various kinds. Many countries have failed to show the necessary firmness with industrial establishments polluting the water environment with production wastes.

An especially great danger to the resources of the World Ocean is presented by the dumping of the waste products of the chemical industry. Sewage contaminating coastal waters with toxic substances has a destructive effect on marine flora and fauna. The dumping into the sea of unpurified sewage brings with it the pollution not only of the water but also, the beaches by pathogenic bacteria which may carry diseases.

In the light of all this it may be stated that the World Ocean, despite its cosmic dimensions, is in danger. The efforts of all mankind are necessary to forestall this danger.

Here it is pertinent to recall the words of the great Karl Marx: "Even the whole of society, the nation and even all simultaneously existing societies taken together are not the owners of the earth. They are only its occupiers using it and as *boni patres familias* must leave it improved to the next generations".[7]

Merchant and Fishing Fleets— Constituent Parts of the Sea Power of the State

An important component of the sea might of the state is marine transport which since ancient times has held one of the leading places among other forms of transport. Nowadays in the total transport cargo flow it accounts for 75-80 per cent of international shipments. This is the most economic form of transport due to the high carrying capacity of ships, relatively small capital investments in fitting out sea routes and the lowest gross expenditure of power per speed of displacement of cargo. For these reasons the cost of sea shipments is 40-45 per cent lower than for rail and over 20 times less than by road.[8]

[7] K. Marx and F. Engels, *Works,* 2nd ed., Vol. 25, Part II, p. 337 (in Russian)
[8] See *Vodny transport,* 1971, 28 Jan. (in Russian).

As world production grows, so does the need to move its products both within state territory and between different countries. The endeavour by each state to use its own means is perfectly natural. Hence the need to possess the necessary merchant fleet, ensuring the economic and political independence of foreign trade and helping not only to save on the expenditure of foreign currency on ship freight but also in certain conditions derive considerable currency earnings for one's budget. For many so-called maritime countries with a developed merchant fleet the currency earnings from sea shipments are an important source covering the deficit of the currency balance. As V. G. Bakayev, who for a long time headed the Soviet merchant fleet, writes in his work *The USSR on the World Sea Routes,* " . . . such a major capitalist country as England, systematically having an adverse balance of trade, largely covers the deficit from income earned by turning over about half its fleet to the transport of cargoes of foreign charterers.

"The same crucial role in the balance of payments is played by the earnings from the shipping of Norway, Denmark, Greece, Sweden and some other countries. For example, the annual net income of the Norwegian merchant fleet exceeds 700 million dollars. In the balance of payments of Sweden, income from shipping amounts to 17-19 per cent. . . ."[9]

The volume of marine shipments in the world is continuously expanding. While at the beginning of the 'fifties the sea-going ships of the world carried between countries and continents some 600 million tons of cargo a year, in 1970 it had already reached 2400 million tons.

If it is also remembered that the sea-going fleet is practically the only form of transport capable of mass shipment of cargo between continents while the income from shipping plays a considerable role in the balance of payments of many states, its tremendous economic and political importance becomes obvious.

The merchant fleet, in addition, is considered by many countries not only as an important means of economics but also an important reserve of the navy in the event of war. For example, the American naval command regards the merchant fleet in wartime as a constituent part of the armed forces. In this connection the construction of the US merchant marine and its development is governed not only by economic factors but also the need to solve purely military tasks which will inevitably be set for the merchant fleet in wartime. This is to support at a necessary level the military-economic potential of the country by ensuring the uninterrupted transport of strategic raw materials and finished products and the provision of all forms of supply to military bases situated on the territories of other countries and also the sea and oceanic transport of troops and military cargoes.

The English journalist David Fairhall in his book *Russia Looks to the Sea* quite frankly writes that with the construction of new merchant ships ". . . the American Government pays for specific 'defence features' which makes ships readily convertible to a wartime role of naval auxiliary.

"In the post-war years it was paying out an annual average of nearly 80 million US dollars in subsidies. By 1960 more than half the 500 or so US flag

[9] V. G. Bakayev, *The USSR on the World Sea Routes* (in Russian), pp. 7 and 8, Moscow, Znanie, 1969.

vessels in foreign trade were subsidised . . .", and then goes on to say, "If a merchant vessel is built with government aid the Secretary of the Navy can and does request the inclusion of national defence features to ensure, under the 1936 Act, that it shall be 'capable of serving as a naval auxiliary'. American commentators on Soviet sea power", writes this English journalist, "are fond of pointing out ways in which new Russian merchant ships could be adapted for military use in wartime . . . without reminding readers of the explicit nature of their own Government's provisions in this respect".

He then discloses the content of these measures: "Other examples of defence features are heavy lift gear, roll-on and roll-off facilities to load military vehicles, extra evaporator capacity to provide extra water for troops, and duplicated controls which would be less vulnerable to damage. If the Federal Maritime Board judges that such equipment is not commercially necessary it is paid for by the Government. For example, a freighter costing about 13 million US dollars might include 90,000 dollars worth of defence features."*

The press reported, for example, that the liner *United States*, with 2000 passenger berths, could be rapidly adapted for transporting a 14,000-strong division.

American military specialists affirm that in planning the transport of landing troops it is necessary to proceed from the calculation that for each soldier in a modern mechanized army with a complete combat cover, four tons of displacement of ships plus two tons for their monthly supply are necessary.

As is known, merchant ships are widely used for material and technical supply of fighting ships at sea. In this connection in the naval and merchant fleets of many countries of the world much attention has recently been paid to means and treatment of the organization of cargo transfer at sea and also the re-fuelling of ships and vessels underway. The press has reported that tankers designed in the USA (with an atomic power plant) with a displacement of 31,400 tons must be able to ensure the transfer at sea to another vessel of 2380 cub.m. of fuel an hour at a speed of travel of 15 knots.

Thus, the mercantile marine fleets of the capitalist countries are being developed with reference to the requirements of war as an important means of supplying the navies and also for the transport of large contingents of troops, their arms and supplies.

In the light of this the merchant fleet must be regarded as a universal component of the sea power of a country which has a most important role in war and peacetime.

In this connection the development and use of merchant fleets of various countries in peacetime are constantly in the sphere of that economic and political struggle in the international arena which continues to remain an unchanged accompaniment of antagonistic social systems. Even now the struggle in this field, which may be characterized as a struggle for influence on world sea communications, is constantly intensifying with the development of world production, interstate trade and economic links. The problems of national and international sea shipping are becoming all-embracing and ever more acute.

* David Fairhall, *Russia looks to the Sea*, pp. 89, 90-1, London, 1971.

All this has led to a rapid expansion of the civil fleet.[10] While in 1950 in the civil fleet of the world there were 30,852 vessels, on 1 July 1973, 59,606 vessels were registered. The total gross tonnage of the fleet in 20 years has gone up almost three times and has reached 289,927 thousand registered tons.

At present, according to Lloyd's, 110 states have a civil fleet. The total full tonnage of the vessels of the fleet of capitalist states on 1 July 1973 was 264.2 million registered tons as compared with a figure of 224 million on 1 July 1971, i.e. an increase in two years of almost 18 per cent.

Table 6 indicates the concentration of tonnage in a small number of countries. Thus. six capitalist maritime powers (Liberia, a large part of whose fleet belongs to American and Greek owners, Japan, England, Norway, Greece and the USA) account for 55 per cent of gross tonnage.

TABLE 6
Number of Ships of the World Civil Fleet and their
Gross Tonnage by Country in 1974

Country	No. of ships	Gross tonnage, registered
Liberia	2332	55,321,641
Japan	9974	38,707,659
England	3603	31,566,298
Norway	2689	24,852,917
Greece	2651	21,759,449
USA	4086	14,429,076
Panama	1962	11,003,227
Italy	1710	9,322,015
France·	1341	8,834,519
West Germany	2088	7,980,453
Sweden	785	6,226,659
Holland	1358	5,500,932
Spain	2520	4,949,146
Denmark	1349	4,460,219
India	451	3,484,751
Cyprus	722	3,394,880
Singapore	511	2,878,327
Canada	1231	2,459,998
Brazil	471	2,428,972
Somalia	276	1,916,273
Total	61,194	311,322,626

Table 6 does not present the data for a number of countries. These data are taken into account in the totals.

The development of the world merchant fleet after the Second World War and especially in the last ten to fifteen years has been along the lines of increase in the speed of ships, their size, carrying capacity and specialization. The size and gross tonnage of merchant ships are continuously growing. Thus, while in 1968 there were 12 giant ships, notably tankers, with a gross tonnage upwards of 100,000 registered tons, in 1973 there were 293. It should also be noted that while the group of ships with a gross tonnage of up to 4000 registered tons intended in the main for service in limited areas is over 65 per cent of the total

[10] Here and hereafter the statistical data on the world fleet are taken from Lloyd's reference books in which by the term "civil fleet" is meant simultaneously the transport (merchant) and fishing fleets.

stock of the merchant fleet, the total gross tonnage of these ships amounts to only 13 per cent of the total tonnage of the world merchant fleet.

Together with increase in the average size of ships there is also a rapid rejuvenation of the fleet leading to considerable qualitative improvement. The process of rejuvenation is well illustrated in Table 7.

TABLE 7
Change in the Distribution of Gross Tonnage of the World Merchant Marine by Age of Ships

Age of vessels	1951 1000 reg. tons	%	1957 1000 reg. tons	%	1963 1000 reg. tons	%	1971 1000 reg. tons	%	1973 1000 reg. tons	%
Less than 5 years	12,427	15.3	23,080	22.1	60.806	31.3	91,750	37.1	111,628	38.2
5-9 years	40,667	49.4	16,130	15.4	44,035	22.7	55,074	22.3	70,280	24.3
10-14 years	6141	7.5	36,668	35.1	33,949	17.7	43,292	17.5	43,997	15.3
15-19 years	2569	3.2	10,380	10.0	17,952	9.2	24,653	10.0	32,600	11.2
20-24 years	5446	6.7	3124	3.0	19,096	9.8	11,120	4.5	13,660	4.7
Over 25 years	14,500	17.9	15,075	14.4	18,314	9.3	21,313	8.6	17,762	6.3
Total	81,750	100	104,457	100	194,152	100	247,202	100	289,927	100

Thus, in 1973 ships less than 10 years old had over 62 per cent of the total tonnage. Today, ships whose time of service does not exceed four years form the majority and have the largest gross tonnage.

Among the most important qualitative changes in the vessels of the merchant fleet is also the increase in the speed of travel (see Table 8). While during the Second World War the speed of most merchant ships did not exceed 8-10 knots, now it is up to 14-16 knots and many container-carriers now travel at up to 22-24 knots.

TABLE 8
Speed of Ships of Different Types
in Knots

Ships	Pre-war years	50's	60's
Universal	10-11	12-15	18-20
Container	13-15	14-20	20-26
Tankers	10-11	14-15	15-17
Fishing vessels	8-10	12-14	15-17

On average, in the last 30-35 years the speed of a "mean statistical" ship of the world fleet has increased by 60-70 per cent but in ships of different types the tendency for the speed to rise varies. The speed of tankers is increasing relatively slowly. In the pre-war years the seaborne transport of oil and oil products was at an average speed of 11 knots. This has risen for modern tankers to 16 knots while only individual fast bulk ships, the number of which is small, have a speed of about 19 knots.

The tendency for the speed to rise is most clearly observed in line shipping.

Until recently the speed of these ships did not exceed 16-18 knots. However, already in 1970 the world merchant fleet included some 230 dry-cargo ships with a speed above 20 knots. Cargo liners are now being commissioned with a speed of 20-24 knots and container ships 22-27 knots. The average speed of container ships now being built exceeds by 35 per cent the corresponding figure for conventional ships under construction and intended for transporting general cargoes. An American container company has ordered eight container carriers which will have a speed of 33 knots.

Diesels have come into the widest use in sea transport. Ship diesel power is steadily growing. Only 15 years ago, on output of 10,000 h.p. was the limit for a single unit. Now it already exceeds 40,000 h.p. and in this time the gross consumption of fuel has fallen by about 20 per cent, while diesel efficiency has reached 42 per cent. In the near future all ship installations with a power of up to 25,000 h.p. will apparently be diesel-powered.

A comparatively new type of main engine in the merchant fleet is the gas-turbine aggregate. The few gas-turbine ships at present are essentially experimental. However, this type of engine has encouraging prospects of being widely adopted in the merchant fleet by virtue of large savings and the possibility of obtaining compact high-power units.

The growth of the size of ships and their speeds requires the creation of ever more powerful ship power units. Atomic power units with an output range from 60,000 to 150,000 h.p. will apparently be used. At present, atomic ships are already in service in the USSR, USA and West Germany. The leading place among the capitalist countries producing atomic power plants is taken by the USA. However, work on the building of atomic ships has still not moved from the experimental stage.

As we see in the field of merchant shipbuilding, an increasingly conspicuous influence is being exerted by scientific and technical progress, the utilization of which lies within the power of the developed countries with a strong shipbuilding base and high individual potential. As a result of this influence and the ever-growing requirements of many countries for mass sea shipments, sea transport vessels of new types have been built which are of great interest from the military-economic point of view.

These are first and foremost ships completely or partially fitted to carry cargo in containers. Container ships or cellular container carriers exist in which all the cargo room consists of modules for carrying and stowing containers, semi-container carriers in which some of the holds or only one hold are of cellular construction (if necessary they may also be used both as container carriers and conventional universal ships) and, finally, combined ships—container trailers and barge-carriers.

In 1970, container shipments in the USA reached 14.3 million tons, England 9.7 million tons, Japan 4.8 million tons, Holland 3.2 million tons, Belgium 2.9 million tons and West Germany 2.1 million tons.

On 1 July 1973 there were in world service 394 modern container carriers with a total gross tonnage of 5,899,000 registered tons, the largest number of container carriers being owned by the USA—104, England 92, Japan 37 and West Germany 48 vessels.

About 60 per cent of container carriers are used in two main transport directions: Europe-North America and USA-Far East and South-East Asia. The rest operate in the directions of Europe-Australia, North America-Mediterranean, USA-Australia and on some other runs.

It should be noted that the bulk of military cargoes may also be carried in containers, which is confirmed by the experience of supplying US troops in Vietnam.

Ships with horizontal loading and unloading facilities (roll-on roll-off type) have been greatly developed. By the beginning of 1971 in the world fleet there were over 130 such ships, 80 per cent of them having been built in four years with a deadweight of 14,000-23,000 tons and speed of travel 20-25 knots. These ships are usually fitted with stern gates. In addition, foregates and side ports are provided in some cases to speed up loading operations. The special features of these ships are the presence fore and aft (for large-tonnage ships) steering devices, suspended car decks, an absence of cargo-lifting gear characteristic of conventional transport ships and the wide use of automation.

Ships with horizontal loading and unloading are particularly effective as military transports since they are capable of carrying military technical supplies and containers. The speed of handling operations on them is higher than on container carriers since they may, simultaneously with the unloading of driven vehicles, remove containers from the deck. A serious defect of container trailer carriers consisting in the need for mooring only to aft is removed on container trailers of the *Parall* type. The ramp on them is located at an angle to the centre line of the ships, so making it possible to moor to the usual quay sideways on. In this connection the role of such ships in military transport has grown even further.

Much ground has also been gained by such specialized ships as barge-carriers which may also be widely used for military purposes.

Barge-carriers first appeared in the USA at the end of the 'sixties with the construction of ships of the LASH type intended for transporting shallow barges with a mass of 500 to 1000 tons. On 1 July 1973, there were in service 20 barge-carriers of different types with a total gross tonnage of 565,000 registered tons, 16 belonging to the USA, two to Norway and one each to Holland and West Germany.

Each barge-carrier is a universal dry-cargo ship. It can carry not only barges but also containers, wheeled vehicles, helicopters, packaged cargoes on trays and also bulk cargo.

The modern US barge-carrier of the CB type is capable of carrying a motorized rifle brigade (this used to need five C-3 type transports). The troops may be landed on a poorly-equipped shore.

To receive barge-carriers in a number of world ports (in the USA, Los Angeles, San Francisco, Houston, Galveston, and in Europe, Rotterdam, Bremerhaven, Barcelona) special docks and shore installations for unloading them are being constructed.

Specialists consider that the use of barge-carriers makes it possible to achieve five- to ten-fold the productivity in loading operations as compared with the conventional cargo ship, to cut the idle time of ships and the number of aids used for shipments and also reduce capital investment in the construction of port installations and, as a whole, expenditure on loading and unloading.

Very interesting changes are taking place in the tanker fleet. Tankers play a very important role in providing countries with raw materials and energy resources and also in providing the armed forces with fuel. The mean annual growth rate of the world tanker fleet between 1965 and 1971 was 10.4 per cent. In 1970, international shipments of liquid fuel rose to 1370 million tons.

The gross tonnage of the ships of the world tanker fleet in 1973 was 115,365 thousand registered tons, i.e. 39.8 per cent of the gross tonnage of the total merchant fleet. The largest number of tankers is registered in Liberia (29.4 million tons), Japan (14.2 million tons), Great Britain (14.1 million tons) and Norway (11.2 million tons).

Over 60 per cent of the carrying capacity of the world tanker fleet is made up of tankers with a deadweight from 50,000 to 372,000 tons. A well-defined tendency in the development of the tanker fleet is the growth of the role of large-bulk oil vessels with a deadweight increase from 100,000 to 300,000 tons.

The maximum size of tankers in the last 20 years has increased 17 times. This is connected with the fact that the operation of large-tonnage vessels has proved more economical. For example, the cost of transporting oil on a tanker with a carrying capacity of 100,000 tons over a distance of 10,000 miles is only 31 per cent of that for carriage over the same distance on a 10,000 tonner. Therefore it is not by chance that there has been a sharp increase in the number of orders for tankers with a carrying capacity of 250,000 to 300,000 tons, although their relative place among tankers in service is still insignificant—only 1.3 per cent.

There are important reasons which hold back the building of large tankers. One of the main ones is the lack of preparedness of ports to receive them because of shallow depths and the danger of heavy pollution of an area of water in the event of damage or destruction of such a supertanker.

Possessing a large mass and high inertia, even with a speed of 14-16 knots and with steering gear, they are not easily manoeuvrable. To cut down the speed of their movement Japan has even devised special parachutes reducing the length of run of the ship after the main engine has stopped.

Great importance in the merchant fleet has been assumed by liquefied-gas carriers intended for carrying liquefied petroleum and natural gases. On 1 July 1973, there were in service 374 gas carriers with a gross tonnage of 2,276,000 registered tons.

The biggest vessels of this class have a capacity of up to 71,000 cub.m. Their average capacity is, however, about 6500 cub.m. Ships with a capacity of 95,000 cub.m. are now being built for petroleum gas and 125,000 cub.m. for natural gas. The main routes for transport of liquefied gases are Algeria to France, England, USA, Italy and Spain, Libya to Italy and Spain and Alaska to Japan and the USA.

Let us take a brief look at the basic data characterizing the merchant fleets of some capitalist maritime powers.

The merchant fleet of Japan in gross tonnage comes second in the world, ships with a service life of under 10 years accounting for 86 per cent of the total tonnage of its merchant fleet. The rapid growth of the Japanese merchant fleet in the last few years has been achieved as a result of state support for shipbuilding and shipping companies.

Since 1956 the shipbuilding industry of Japan has come to occupy first place in the world in gross tonnage of merchant vessels under construction. Making full use of its productive forces, Japan, according to rough calculations, could build in one year merchant vessels with a tonnage of over 9,000,000 registered tons.

As Japanese specialists claim, should there be a sharp increase in the requirements of the country for warships such an industrial shipbuilding base will be able to ensure the building of ships of all classes with a total displacement of up to 300,000 tons a year with simultaneous construction of merchant ships with a total gross tonnage of 4-4.5 million tons.

Despite the fact that Great Britain continues to remain one of the leading maritime powers, her share of merchant shipping is steadily decreasing. The gross tonnage of the ships of the merchant fleet in the period between 1968 and 1972 rose by over 5 million registered tons, but her share in the world merchant fleet fell from 11.6 to 10.6 per cent. The merchant fleet of Great Britain in gross tonnage now comes third in the world after those of Liberia and Japan. The age of the ships of the merchant fleet of Great Britain corresponds to the average world level i.e. 60 per cent is made up of ships not more than 10 years old.

The recent period has seen a considerable increase in the growth of the tanker fleet of Great Britain, accounting for 40 per cent of the gross tonnage of the British merchant fleet. The tanker fleet numbers 600 vessels, including 50 supertankers, the largest British tanker *Universe Ireland* having a deadweight of 326,000 tons.

Great Britain has a developed shipbuilding industry with an annual output capacity of merchant ships of up to 3 million tons and is also capable of building warships of all classes in large numbers.

The Norwegian merchant fleet takes fourth place in the world. It is of primary importance to the country's economy: 90 per cent of the tonnage of her vessels is used in shipments between ports of other states, 8 per cent between the ports of Norway and other states and 2 per cent between her own ports.

Some 80 per cent of the gross tonnage of Norway's fleet is accounted for by ships less than 10 years old. In the main the fleet is represented by large-tonnage ships and there is no doubt that the tonnage will continue to grow, particularly since Norway is a country with a highly-developed shipbuilding industry.

The shipbuilding industry of Norway includes some 150 undertakings building ships with a total tonnage of up to 500,000 registered tons a year.

On 1 July 1971, the merchant fleet of Greece had 2241 ships with a total gross tonnage of 15,329,000 registered tons (5.8 per cent of world tonnage) including 304 tankers (5,205,000 registered tons). In addition, Greek shipowners own some 1250 ships (18 million registered tons) registered under flags of other countries.

As judged by the position on 1 July 1973, the Greek merchant fleet came fifth among the merchant fleets of the world, increasing in two years by 4,166,000 registered tons.

The shipbuilding industry of Greece is poorly developed, the main source for replenishment of its fleet being foreign yards.

The United States of America has a merchant fleet which takes seventh place in the world. Under the Merchant Marine Act adopted by the US Congress in 1936, the USA must not become dependent on foreign shipowners and yards and must dispose of a merchant fleet consisting of ships constructed in the USA belonging to the citizens of the USA and manned by citizens of the USA. Such ships must carry out all coastal shipments and a considerable part of foreign trade cargo shipments. In wartime they may be used by the armed forces as auxiliaries.

During the Second World War, the USA built up a very large merchant fleet. In 1945 its gross tonnage was about 59 per cent of the tonnage of the merchant fleets of all capitalist countries, but this fleet was poorly balanced and had low operational qualities. Therefore, in 1946 the partial sale of ships, mothballing and delivery for scrap were begun.

The new law on the marine merchant fleet and the shipbuilding programme adopted in 1970 were aimed at regenerating the former sea power of the USA in the world freight market. On 1 July 1973, the US merchant fleet had ships with a gross tonnage of 14,312,000 registered tons of which 5,000,000 was accounted for by the reserve. It should be noted that the bulk of the merchant fleets of Liberia and Panama belongs to American shipowners. They use the "convenience" flags of these countries for extracting superprofits by paying minimum taxes and hiring low-paid crews whose pay is outside the control of the US trade unions.

Some 60 per cent of the gross tonnage of the US merchant fleet is represented by ships with a service life of more than 20 years. The US Government has adopted a ten-year programme of fleet renewal envisaging the construction of 300 ships. The new ships will be designed with reference to their use for military purposes on the basis of the experience of waging war in Vietnam where the ships of the merchant fleet ensured a large volume of military shipments. Provision is made in the first place for the building of tankers, barge-carriers and universal ships.

The USA has a developed shipbuilding industry, the productive possibilities of which enable it, if brought together, to undertake the annual building of fighting ships of all classes with a total standard displacement of some 1,700,000 tons and merchant vessels with a total carrying capacity of about 16,000,000 tons.

The West German merchant fleet takes eleventh place in the world. Most of the ships (80 per cent) are under 10 years old, an insignificant percentage are ships which have been in service for over 25 years. Federal Germany quite rapidly restored her shipbuilding industry in the post-war period. The country now has over 50 shipbuilding yards. Shipbuilding undertakings employ some 80,000 workers. Container ships and large-tonnage tankers are being constructed and an atomic cargo ship has been built. The shipbuilding industry of West Germany is marked by a concentration of yards—88 per cent of the productive forces are concentrated in Hamburg, Bremen-Bremerhaven, Kiel and Emden alone.

The largest container ships are being built by the yards of Howaldstwerke-Deutsche Werft AG. High-speed (up to 33 knots) container ships are being built at the AG Weser and Rheinstahl-Nordseewerke yards.

Analysis of the data published in the foreign press reveals the following tendencies in the development of the world transport fleet in the near future.

The dry-cargo fleet will continue to be rapidly replenished with large fast container ships without their own loading facilities for work on lines with stable cargo flows, and also with smaller and slower container carriers with loading cranes for delivering containers to unequipped ports. Third-generation container carriers with a carrying capacity of up to 40,000 tons taking 2000 or more 20-foot long containers will come into wider use. Further increase in container carriers will be limited not so much by the technical possibilities as by the business outlook and the size of canals and locks.

For work on short lines linking areas with a developed network of motorways, trailer ships will be built with horizontal means of loading and discharging (so-called roll-on roll-off ships).

To ensure non-transfer shipments between sea and river ports barge-carriers will be built. They apparently will be widely used for purely marine shipments as a means of shortening idle time. A "boundary" variant of such ships may turn out to be modular ships with an entirely detachable, interchangeable cargo part.

The building of universal dry-cargo ships will fall off, but will increase for specialized ships adapted for shipping strictly defined types of cargo. The number of merchant ships built and adapted for sailing in icy conditions and of icebreakers will increase.

The building of fast passenger ships and also relatively low-speed ships for long cruises is increasing.

It may be supposed that the new transport vessels will possess the following characteristic features.

The speed of the ships of a number of categories will substantially rise. The first to rise and probably in the near future exceed 30 knots will be large container and trailer ships, barge-carriers and other vessels with a reduced time of loading operations. It is planned to achieve the rise in speed in the main by using more powerful equipment.

The use of the hydrofoil principle which ensures a speed of 40-50 knots will be limited to passenger ships with a displacement of not more than 1000 tons since further increase in the displacement of such ships is economically disadvantageous and technically complicated.

More promising for the building of large, fast merchant vessels is the principle of movement on an air cushion, the efficiency of which rises with increase in the size of the ship. The displacement of ships on an air cushion will be determined by the possibilities of producing high-output power systems.

The size of ships for transporting mass cargoes will increase and the tonnage of ships for transport of bulk cargoes will exceed 250,000 registered tons.

In connection with the rise in the speed and size of ships and hence of their power, gas-turbine and steam-turbine equipment will come into wider use and, later, economical atomic power plants. On ships with a lower power of the main engines light diesels and diesel-reducing systems will be widely employed.

The comprehensive automation of ship technical systems will gain more ground, so helping to reduce crew size sharply and improve the economic use of equipment.

The continuous increase in the volume of oil and oil product shipments (in 1976 it will possibly exceed 2400 million tons) will mean a bigger world tanker fleet. One of the most important tendencies in the development of the bulk-oil fleet is an increase in tankers. The carrying capacity of the biggest tankers already reaches 500,000 registered tons (the problem of building a tanker with deadweight of 1 million tons is under study).

From the forecasts of the Japan Steel and Tube Company the average carrying capacity of commissioned tankers will be 190,000 tons, and a third of the tankers in service will have a carrying capacity of over 100,000 tons in 1981.

Further growth of the tonnage of tankers is held back by the depth and conditions of passage of canals and straits. The number of ports capable of receiving large-tonnage tankers is increasing from year to year.

A most important adjunct to the merchant fleet has always been the ports, constituting the terminals of sea communications. There are now some 420 large sea ports in the capitalist countries, the cargo turnover of each of which exceeds a million tons. Naturally their development has been affected by such major events as the appearance of giant ships for different purposes including ships capable of carrying mass cargo shipments in containers under the "door to door" system. The requirements for the operation of the latest ships, the main characteristics of which are shown in Table 9, determine the dimensions of the approach fairways to the ports and the fairways in straits, the size of the quays and their depths and other characteristics of ports and harbours.

In the main, to handle large-tonnage tankers road quays of varied design and oil-transhipment bases are now being built and deepening work undertaken at existing quays. One of the first oil-transhipment bases was the Bantry Bay base, built in the south of Ireland, which can handle giant tankers with a draught of up to 25 metres. The Bantry Bay transhipment base constitutes a road quay 30 metres deep. This wharf is connected to the shore by a boom along which run two pipes for crude oil. The store installations consist of 12 tanks with a capacity of 95,400 cub. metres for crude oil, two ballast tanks, bunkering capacities and auxiliary equipment.

TABLE 9
Main Characteristics of Ships of the Latest Types

Type of ship	Total carrying capacity, thousand tons	Length, m	Breadth, m	Draught, m
Tanker	500	380	67	26.5
Tanker	200	340	50	15.5
Ore carrier	150	305	48	16.5
Ore carrier	80	260	35	14.5
Dry cargo	30	210	26	11.5
Dry cargo	20	175	23	10.5

Giant tankers deliver oil from the ports of the Persian Gulf here, then tankers with a capacity up to 100,000 tons take the oil to the ports of the European continent.

The oil-processing plants on the European continent receive crude oil from pipelines from six main ports: Rotterdam (Netherlands), Brest and le Havre (France), Trieste and Genoa (Italy) and Wilhelmshaven (GFR).

The ports of Rotterdam, Brest and le Havre can take large-tonnage tankers with a capacity of up to 250,000 tons, Genoa up to 220,000 tons, Wilhelmshaven up to 210,000 tons (for an incomplete load) and Trieste up to 200,000 tons. Japan has ports capable of receiving large-tonnage tankers with a capacity of 200,000-300,000 tons (Yokohama, Tiba and a number of others).

However, only some twenty ports in the world can receive ships with a draught of 15 metres and more. Even the USA does not have any; it plans to raise by 1985 the import of oil and natural gas to half that consumed in the country. Into the USA each day come 2 million tons of oil and oil products and their transhipment requires 2600 tankers with a capacity of 47,000 or 500 tankers with capacity of 250,000 tons. To receive and process the cargoes of supertankers it is planned to build three deep-water ports—one in the east, another on the west coast of the USA and a third in the Gulf of Mexico.

In connection with the development of container shipments the traditional functions of a port as an accumulation and distribution centre and a terminal point for different forms of transport are receding into the background. At the same time the role of the port as a transfer node in a unified transport system is growing. The port must pay far more attention than before to shortening the idle time of container ships working to a tight schedule, not only by reducing the time of cargo handling but also by cutting down the number of auxiliary operations. The cargoes must also be in port for a minimum time. Therefore, great importance is attached to improvement of the water approaches, pilotage service and port fleet, rail and car access routes, parking places, etc.

In all the large ports of the highly developed capitalist states special container areas and quays have been or are being created. In the last few years, among the European ports, Rotterdam has become the largest container transfer centre. In 1971 in this port some 320,000 containers were transhipped. Rotterdam is also the port with the largest cargo turnover in the world; in 1971 it was 231,700,000 tons, comprising imports of 169,800,000 tons and exports of 61,900,000 tons.

In the very near future the character of port installations will also be affected by the appearance of ships on air cushion and hydrofoil, the significance of which for cargo shipment and passenger transport over small distances will probably grow.

Thus, the development of the main world ports is in the direction of major deepening operations, the construction of new deep-water quay installations, the equipping of special container areas and quays capable of rapidly handling container carriers and specialization in the ports.

The Soviet merchant marine fleet, like the fleet of any state, is a constituent part of the sea power of the USSR. The transformation of our country in the years of Soviet power into a highly developed industrial power, the steady growth of the economic might of the USSR and the continuous expansion of its foreign trade links have been responsible for the swift development of the marine transport of the USSR.

The sea transport of the Soviet Union has been converted into an advanced, technically well equipped and highly profitable branch of the national economy which fully meets the economic requirements of the country.

The USSR marine fleet now comes second in cargo turnover among other forms of transport of the country. The role of seaborne shipments is particularly great in the life of the Far East and the North where the merchant fleet is practically the only form of transport ensuring the conveyance of the most varied cargoes to numerous points of the coast.

For the Soviet Union of particularly great importance is sea transport, necessary for ensuring external trade. The work of the fleet in this link accounts for some 90 per cent of the total volume of its cargo turnover.

The building of the Soviet merchant fleet is being successfully developed within the framework of socialist economic integration embracing many spheres of its activity. Its importance has become even more telling in connection with the transport requirements of the countries fighting for their freedom and independence and also of the developing countries striving to gain economic independence but, as a rule, not having their own merchant fleet.

In foreign trade the Soviet Union is free of the capitalist freight market. It can maintain and develop trade relations with any maritime country with its own merchant fleet.

The successful fulfilment by sea transport of the plans of post-war development permits complete satisfaction for the requirements of the national economy and helps to guarantee that the external economic links of the country will not be shaken by unforeseen circumstances similar to the Cuba blockade or the closure of the Suez Canal.

The Soviet merchant marine fleet is assuming ever greater weight in world shipping by expanding shipments for foreign freight charterers. It thereby discharges the task important for the state of the export of transport services and year by year makes a considerable contribution to the state's foreign currency balances.

In the history of the development of our merchant marine fleet, as of the national economy as a whole, a very important stage was the Great Patriotic War of 1941-45. In the course of the war, the merchant fleet, hand in hand with the navy, did work of tremendous importance by meeting the needs of the fronts and economy of the country with transport of products of importance to the national economy and for military supplies. In many cases sea communications were the main and sometimes the only lines of conveyance of military cargoes. Soviet merchant ships sailing in nearly all seas and oceans ensured the transport links with the Allied countries, often exposing themselves to enemy air and submarine strikes. In the course of the heroic combat work in the period of the Great Patriotic War the Soviet merchant fleet numbering 800 ships with a total carrying capacity of over 2 million tons by 1941 lost 363 ships with a total capacity of some 700,000 tons.

The great and sustained work of the Soviet people in restoring the national economy made it possible by 1950 to bring the level of cargo shipments by the merchant marine up to the 1940 level and by 1965 the carrying capacity of the Soviet merchant fleet exceeded 8,500,000 tons.

In the following years the merchant marine of the USSR continued to develop at a fast pace. While in 12 years (from 1946 to 1958) the cargo turnover of the Soviet merchant marine increased from 15,900 to 57,400 million ton miles, i.e. 3.6 times, later it took only seven years to achieve the same growth.

In 1973 the gross tonnage of our fleet (including ships of the transport, fishing and research fleets) reached 17.4 million registered tons. The Soviet Union, from the twelfth place it occupied in the tonnage of the world merchant marine before 1960, has moved into sixth place. This completely secured the foreign trade requirements of the Soviet Union, the turnover of which increased from 2900 million in 1950 to 31,300 million roubles in 1973. In 1973 the Soviet merchant fleet had 1602 ships with a total carrying capacity of some 14 million tons. Yearly its stock is being replenished by a large number of new ships of the most varied types and categories. In 1973 the fleet received over 80 ships with a total carrying capacity of over 700,000 tons and in 1974 its stock increased further by almost 90 ships with a capacity of some 900,000 tons.

As a result the Soviet merchant marine in its age composition is younger than the world fleet as a whole. Thus, ships in service for less than 10 years represent for the USSR 64.4 per cent of total gross tonnage as against 62.7 per cent for the world fleet.

The merchant marine of the USSR has ships for different purposes, from coastal navigation ships to the largest ships such as the tanker *Krym* with a carrying capacity of 150,000 tons,which makes it possible to undertake shipments in any area of the World Ocean. It includes dry-cargo vessels and tankers, ships for carrying timber materials, coal and ore, icebreakers and icebreaker-transport ships, container carriers, ships for mixed navigation in seas and rivers and ships of other types. The carrying capacity of the Soviet tanker fleet by 1973 had reached almost 5 million tons.

The Soviet Union also has a large fleet of passenger ships sailing on 17 international and many coastal lines.

Our merchant marine fleet consists not only of ships. In the Soviet Union there are over 70 ports with an annual cargo turnover of not less than 1 million tons each. Most of them have deep-water and mechanized quays, good warehouse facilities and well-laid-out territory with access routes.

On the Far Eastern coast and on the Black Sea new large ports are being built, well exceeding in technical equipment and throughput the largest existing ports of our country. The level of the complex mechanization of the loading-unloading operations is growing from year to year. All this has made possible a sharp rise in the throughput capacity of the "sea gates" of the USSR. The Soviet merchant marine is served by over 30 ship-repair yards ensuring together with the crews of the ships the good technical state of the fleet.

The entire productive activity of the Soviet merchant marine is directed by 17 sea steamship companies organizationally forming part of three associations: Sevzapflot, Yuzhflot and Dal'flot. To them are subordinate registered ships, ports, repair yards, damage-recovery and other organizations directly linked with the work of the fleet, its victualling and servicing. In the fleet much work is done to perfect control at all levels, starting from the ships and ending with the whole, for which automated planning and control systems are being devised and introduced.

The Party and the Government envisage the further development of the merchant marine of the USSR. It is planned to increase the cargo turnover, replenish the fleet with new, highly economical universal and specialized ships, increase the throughput of the sea ports and expand the output of the ship-repair establishments.

Thus, in the future too it is planned to develop all the components of the merchant marine, forming a single whole of this branch of the country's national economy and its sea power.

The fishing fleet (in its widest sense) is a constituent part of the civil fleet and an important component of the sea power of the state. The role of this fleet has sharply grown as a result of progress in the mastery by mankind of the World Ocean and increase in the scale of use of various marine products of animal and plant origin for food and industrial purposes. Its most important task consists in ensuring the solution of the acute food problem facing mankind.

According to official data of the FAO the food situation of the population of the world is unfavourable, mainly due to lack of animal proteins in the food intake from which lack some 2,000 million people suffer, i.e. half the entire world population. Such an abnormal situation, with a rise in the population of the planet, is sharpened by capitalist relations in the majority of countries. Mankind is therefore looking more and more often towards the potential biological resources of the World Ocean.

People have engaged in the catching of fish and marine animals from time immemorial, although the development of fishing fleets on an industrial basis began in the second half of the nineteenth century in connection with a sharp increase in protein requirements and technological improvements in sea navigation.

At first this process was slow. Thus, in the period from 1850 to 1900 the mean annual growth of the world catch came to what is now a modest figure—about 40,000 tons. In the period between the two world wars growth was considerable—1.3 million tons, and in the post-war period this has risen on average to 2.3 million tons.

Of the greatest importance in sea and ocean fisheries is fish (89 per cent), followed by molluscs (5 per cent), crustaceans (2.3 per cent), marine animals (1.8 per cent) and aquatic vegetation.[11]

In the period between 1948 and 1967 the world fish catch and recovery of other sea products almost trebled—from 22 to 62 million tons. However, after 1967, despite considerable improvement in the technical equipment of the fishing fleets, the growth rate of the catch fell appreciably. One of the reasons for this is the depletion of fish stock, resulting from heedless intensification of catching in important, earlier well-exploited, traditional fishing grounds. Therefore, a question on the agenda is the need to regulate the catching norms of certain fish species and marine animals and to devise an overall

[11] *The Fishing Fleet of the Capitalist Countries* (in Russian), pp. 10-11, Moscow, Sudostroyeniye, 1971.

scientifically-based system of conducting sea-fishing.

The recovery of marine biological resources now yields about three-quarters of all the earnings of mankind from the World Ocean. Throughout the world over 7 million people are now engaged in industrial fishing. The world catch of fish and other sea products reaches a level of 70 million tons a year, comparatively close to that optimally attainable—determined with reference to the real yearly natural reproduction of the biological mass of sea products and the conditions of their spread in the oceans.

Many hundreds of thousands of rowing, sailing and motor boats are engaged in the world in fishing and marine animal catching. However, the basis of the modern fishing fleet is afforded by power-driven large ships intended for catching fish and marine animals in remote areas of the seas and oceans, processing the products, storing and carrying them to shore bases.

Lloyd's World Register divides modern fishing craft according to their function into two main groups: trawlers and other fish-(animal) catching vessels with a gross tonnage from 100 to 4000 registered tons and over, and fish factories and carriers (in our terminology, transport refrigerators and processing floating bases) with a gross tonnage from 100 to 10,000 registered tons and more.

Modern fishing vessels possess considerable seaworthiness, a long operating range and independence of action. They are, as a rule, equipped with the latest navigational, sonar and radio—electronic devices and fishing and technological gear.

A decisive role in the development of the world fishing fleet in the post-war period was played by the research undertaken in different countries, in the first place in the Soviet Union, in the sphere of fish biology, forecasting the areas and routes of their movements, working out on this basis new ways of prospecting fish wealth and the necessary technical means for detecting it and also new and more refined methods of catching, processing, storing and delivering the products to the consumer.

The growth of the recovery of sea products, using the fishing fleet, plays an essential role in the production of foodstuffs and raw materials for the functioning of many branches of industry. Almost 80 countries of the world are now engaged in industrial fishing. In size of fish catch the Soviet Union comes third after Peru and Japan.

In 1974, the world large-tonnage fishing fleet had 17,955 ships (100 registered tons and more) with a total gross tonnage of some 10.7 million tons[12] including 17,262 fishing ships (trawlers, seiners, animal catching vessels, etc.) with a total tonnage of 7.33 million tons and 693 fish factories and carriers with a total gross tonnage of about 3.45 million tons.

Among the capitalist states Japan has the greatest number and total tonnage of ships in the fishing fleet, while Peru has the largest catch.

The fishing fleet of Japan in 1974 had 3198 ships with a total tonnage of some 1,260,000 registered tons. Some three million people are engaged in fishing in that country. The annual catch is over 8,600,000 tons of fish and other marine products. Fish is one of the staple products and an important export item.

[12] *Lloyd's Register of Shipping,* p. 12, London, 1974.

The Republic of Peru, whose fishing fleet in number of vessels and total tonnage comes only eleventh in the world (604 vessels—about 125,000 registered tons), has, thanks to its immediate proximity (30-50 miles) to the richest Pacific fishing grounds, the biggest fish catch in the world—over 9 million tons a year.

The major fishing countries are the United States (1577 large-tonnage vessels with a total tonnage of about 358,000 registered tons), Norway (606 ships with a total tonnage of 204,000 registered tons) and the Republic of South Africa (143 vessels with a total tonnage of 75,000 registered tons). Each of these countries yearly catches from 2 to 3 million tons of fish and other sea products. Among the other fishing capitalist countries an important place is taken by England, Canada, Spain, Denmark, Chile and others with an annual catch of over 1 million tons.

It is significant that Peru and Japan have about one third of the world fish catch and the leading 15 fishing countries about four-fifths[13] (these countries include Peru, Japan, the USSR, the Chinese People's Republic, Norway, USA, the United Arab Republic, India, Spain, Canada, Denmark, Chile, Indonesia, Thailand and England).

The bulk of the products of world sea fishing before 1957 was drawn from the Atlantic Ocean, especially its northern part. Then the centre of gravity shifted to the Pacific which by 1970 accounted for about 55 per cent of the world catch, more than half of which came from the northern part. At the same time 41 per cent of the world catch was obtained in the Atlantic, more than two-thirds coming from the northern part.

The Indian Ocean accounted for some 5 per cent of the world catch of sea products.

The experience of two world wars showed that fishing vessels were widely used as part of the navy for solving auxiliary and combat tasks chiefly in the sphere of defence and protection of ports and areas housing naval bases.

Our country has a large fishing fleet which forms the basis of its fish industry. The foundation of the Soviet fishing fleet was laid on 9 December 1918 when, by the decision of the Supreme Economic Council, the Fish Catching and Fish Industry Board was set up in Russia (Glavryba).

In the following years the state put large resources into the expansion of the technical base of sea fisheries and primarily into the acquisition and building of ships.

The war seriously held back the development of Soviet fishing and its fleet. It suffered the heaviest losses in the Azov-Black Sea and the Baltic and Northern basins. The shore establishments of the fish industry, ports and building yards were put out of action and some 5000 ships were lost. Our fish catch dropped sharply.

After the end of the war work was undertaken with new vigour to build and develop the Soviet fishing fleet. And now in the remotest areas of the World Ocean one can meet fishing vessels flying our flag.

Our fishing fleet in the ninth Five-Year Plan moved into a phase of radical technical re-equipment, greatly extending the sphere of the industry.

[13] See S. D. Osokin, *The World Ocean*, Moscow, Prosveshchenie, 1972.

At present, 87 per cent of the total fish catch in the USSR comes from oceanic fishing grounds. The intensity of fishing has trebled despite the fact that many capitalist states have extended their territorial water zones and established special fishing zones up to 200 miles wide, so that up to 40 per cent of the area of the fishery shelf with a possible fish catch of 10 million tons a year has been closed to the fleets of other countries.

The contraction of the fishing bases together with increase in the radius of action of the fleet in the World Ocean has also stimulated development of the catch at greater depths. While before the Second World War trawling was carried out at depths up to 200-400 metres, this has now gone up to 1000 metres. The Soviet Union is ahead of other countries of the world in mastery of deep-water catching grounds. Research into deep-water trawling is also being conducted in West Germany, Spain, France and England. In these countries ships of various types are capable of trawling to depths of 600-1000 metres.

The Soviet fishing fleet in number of vessels of different functions now occupies first place among the major fishing fleets of the world. It has catching, processing and transport ships and also the necessary means of supply.

The ships of the Soviet fishing fleet are distinguished by their universality, i.e. have different catching implements. Thanks to this they are not tied to the seasons for catching of particular fish species and are capable of completely processing the catch. They are economically very efficient.

The further development of the fishing fleet is dictated by the fact that the fishing grounds will continue to move further away from shore bases. The character of work of fishing vessels will change with a corresponding change in the structure of the fishing fleet. The stock of catching vessels will be augmented by supertrawlers intended for automatic work in distant areas with harsh meteorological conditions. There will be an increase in the number of medium-sized universal catching vessels intended for work as part of expeditions and also independently in nearby fishing grounds where the use of large catching vessels is inefficient. The number of specialized catching vessels and supply ships will increase.

Bearing in mind the development of shipbuilding techniques, it may be supposed that new fishing vessels in the near future will have power equipment with a much greater output, not only enabling them to raise productivity sharply by using trawls of increased size and catching at increased trawling speeds and at great depths, but also increasing the mobility of the fleet as a whole.

New power possibilities open the way to the further refinement of the technology of processing the catch, and will permit a considerable improvement in the working and living conditions of crews while increasing the safety of navigation.

The further development of the fishing fleet will make a significant contribution to the provision of the Soviet people with foodstuffs. At the same time the extension of the areas of operations of the fishing fleet will add to our knowledge of the World Ocean as a result of wide oceanographic, meteorological and other explorations of the oceanic sphere carried out alongside fishery work.

Thousands of seamen of the merchant and fishing fleets, spending many months at sea, demonstrate to the whole world the attachment of our people to seafaring, the love of this hard but fine vocation which our ancestors practised many centuries ago, and are exploding the myth of the "land" peculiarity of the Russian nation and of all the Soviet peoples.

The sea power of the Soviet Union primarily rests on the remarkable contingent of professional seafarers who have devoted their lives to the alluring and very tough vocation of the sea.

International Problems of the Law of the Ocean

The World Ocean is immense, but however grandiose its expanses, the interest of all countries of the world in the utilization of the hydrosphere and its resources is so great that to ensure the freedom of sea navigation, fishing and scientific exploration it was found necessary to introduce international regulations which are a constituent part of the peaceful co-operation of all countries.

These regulations found reflection in international maritime law fixing the legal regime of the expanses of the World Ocean and the activity of the state in the sphere of sea navigation and the use of the hydrosphere in peace and wartime.

Being an integral part of international law, international maritime law is guided by all its principles such as the principle of peaceful co-existence, the principle of respecting state sovereignty, the principle of the peaceful settlement of international disputes, etc. At the same time, as a branch of international law directly associated with the use of the oceans and seas, it has its own distinctive principles, for example, the principle of freedom of the open sea, the principle of immunity of warships and others.

International maritime law establishes the legal foundations of the operations of independent states and rules of mutual relations between them and their organs in the seas and oceans. A distinctive feature of modern international maritime law is the formulation of its norms on the basis of mutual agreements and negotiations between independent sovereign states, including states with different socio-economic systems.

Modern international maritime law covers a wide range of problems. They include, for example, the legal regime of the open sea, territorial and inland waters, the adjacent zones, straits and canals, demilitarized and neutralized sea zones and territories, the floor of oceans and seas and the continental shelf, freedom to conduct scientific explorations in the open sea, fishing and the conduct of marine industrial activity, control of pollution of the ocean, the legal position of warships and naval navigation and other no less important problems.

International maritime law also includes norms and rules worked out as a result of many centuries of efforts by maritime states aimed at the safety of sea navigation and giving aid to victims of disasters at sea. In this area on the basis of wide international co-operation a number of international laws have been adopted and are in force.

As long as imperialism exists, the danger of the outbreak of new wars remains. In this connection the international rules of waging war retain their significance including the rules of waging war at sea. The relations between warring states at sea, between warring and neutral states, the legal definition of belligerent individuals and ships, problems connected with the arming of merchant ships, the legal validation of the legality of a sea blockade and the determination of its zone and other problems form part of international maritime law.

Thus, international maritime law is an important instrument ensuring the rights and the obligations of sovereign states whose interests touch in different spheres of utilization by mankind of the oceans and seas. It influences the practical activity of the navies which require international legal safeguarding of their daily activities, i.e. creation of the most favourable conditions for solving the problems posed on the basis of strict observance of the norms and principles of international maritime law.

The growth of the operational and strategic potential of modern navies, the wide use of them by states for achieving their political ends and the tremendous success of military shipbuilding have promoted the creation of conditions in which considerable forces of the fleets are permanently at sea far from their main bases. One of the specific features of the activity of navies in the second half of the twentieth century as compared with the recent past is the sharp rise in the sailing schedules of formations and individual warships in different parts of the World Ocean. This plus the colossal growth of the merchant and fishing fleets is promoting increase in the number of contacts at sea between warships of different states, between warships and merchant vessels and also between local authorities and warships on calls at the ports of foreign states. Such contacts in peacetime are particular to the highest degree only to one branch of the armed forces of any state—the Navy.

Underway, a warship may be in the waters of the open sea, territorial or inland waters, pass through straits and other parts of the World Ocean the legal regimes of which have their own peculiarities and exercise a definite influence on navigation. On the other hand, the legal position of the warship itself also regulates its operations in areas where it may come into contact with foreign warships, civilian vessels and authorities.

The legal position of a warship in the open sea, territorial waters or ports of foreign states is now determined by its immunity based on the principle of sovereignty of the state resting on the generally recognized principle of equality of states in international relations. Any warship is regarded as a specific organ of the state and operates with the full authorization of its authorities and at the same time is a representative of the armed forces. Therefore, the activity of any warship at sea may involve tasks of a military-diplomatic nature. The commander of a warship outside his own inland and territorial waters and executing the tasks assigned must observe and strictly fulfil all the international agreements concluded by the state of his flag and also take into account special aspects of the national legislation of foreign coastal states. Therefore international maritime law is studied in all institutions training marine officers. Knowledge of its basic tenets and apt application to his activity is not only a direct service obligation of each Soviet naval officer but also serves as a yardstick of his erudition and understanding of behaviour at sea.

The World Ocean has been used by mankind from time immemorial. As the first class society in history—the slave-owning system—grew stronger, sea navigation developed, then serving as one of the important means of developing the slave trade and commodity exchange. This period saw the origin of certain unwritten sea customs the observance of which was considered obligatory, and which after a certain time were fixed in written documents of a contractual nature and assumed the significance of international norms. Thus, in the third to second centuries B.C. there appeared the Code of Rhodes recognized by the Greeks and Romans. The norms of this code were later called the Rhodes Maritime Law. The seventh century saw the appearance of the sea code of Byzantine law—the "Basilica", regulating the trade of the countries of the Levant. Later, other compendia of maritime rules and customs came into their own, all directed at protecting the commercial interests of the most powerful slave-owning states of that time and based on the concept "might is right". However, even then ideas of the freedom of the open sea were expressed. For example, under classical Roman law it was considered that the air, running water and the sea, by virtue of natural law were intended for the common use of all peoples.

With the transition to the feudal mode of production, the large slave-owning states broke down into a multiplicity of small independent principalities. The feudal lords considered themselves not only the unrestricted masters of their own lands but the owners of the rivers cutting through their property and also of the seas and oceans.

The drive of sovereign lords towards self-enrichment led to numerous inter-necine wars providing the only means of territorial acquisition. This in no small measure was promoted by the higher level of development of productive forces and techniques as compared with the slave-owning system. The possibility emerged of breaking away from the shores with the aid of a fairly sophisticated sailing fleet and of embarking on the search for new lands and the acquisition of their riches.

The epoch of the great geographical discoveries gave a fillip to the development of sea navigation and with it to piracy, the slave trade and campaigns of conquest. In this period "might is right" assumed even greater importance, which was also reflected in maritime law.

The seizure by the maritime powers of newly-discovered lands at the same time led to the appropriation of certain sea spaces. Thus, in 1494 and 1529 Spain and Portugal agreed to divide up their spheres of influence in the World Ocean: Spain announced exclusive rights to sail in the Western Atlantic, the Gulf of Mexico and the Pacific Ocean, while Portugal claimed the Eastern Atlantic and Indian Ocean. These maritime powers appropriated to themselves the right to pursue and seize as booty all foreign ships appearing in the waters under their control, levy custom duties and also to try the crews of these ships by Spanish or Portuguese law.

In the Middle Ages other states also laid claim to ownership of the seas: Denmark to the northern seas situated between Norway, Iceland and Greenland, Genoa to the Ligurian Sea and the Gulf of Lyon, England to all the seas and oceans bathing its possessions; and Venice declared itself owner of the Adriatic.[14]

Challenging such pretensions to the open sea, the developing bourgeoisie and its ideologists demanded freedom of sea navigation and freedom of economic links. Thus in 1609 the Dutch jurist Hugo Grotius in his book *Mare liberum* presented a convincing case for the protection of the freedom of the open sea, directed against the dominance of England at sea.

Thus, in the period of the emergence of capitalist relations an active struggle began against the reactionary principle of the feudal law of ownership of the seas and a struggle for their recognition as free. This important progressive step in the field of international maritime law opened the way to the appearance of other positive norms. With the further economic and social development of society the role of the principle of freedom of the open sea steadily grew and in the modern epoch has assumed special importance.

The need for equal freedom of navigation over the seas and oceans was primarily due to the economic requirements of states since the development of productive forces led to the formation of a world market and hence a world freight market. International trade could not exist without transport and it could only be sea transport.[15]

The cause of freedom of the seas was also taken up by the main revolutionary class—the proletariat—forming their own awareness of law, and by their ideologists. ". . . The sea as a general common highway of all nations", wrote Karl Marx in 1861, "cannot be under the sovereignty of . . . any . . . power".[16]

A definite role in the development of maritime law was played by the International Congresses meeting in Vienna (1815) and Paris (1856). These Congresses, for all their reactionary nature, adopted, in particular, such progressive resolutions as that on the freedom of shipping on certain international rivers, condemnation of the slave trade, the abolition of privateering and limitation of the law of seizure.

Although the principle of the freedom of the open sea was generally recognized and established from the second half of the eighteenth century, the feudal and bourgeois states fighting for dominance in the seas and for capture of foreign lands constantly violated it.

In the nineteenth and twentieth centuries the USA, England, Germany, France and other capitalist states sought to continue the policy of dominance at sea which grossly violated the bases of the principle of the open sea. Thus, for example, the United States, after the end of the Second World War, under the guise of "protecting" freedom of sea navigation tried to restore the old policy of dictating to others in the open sea, in particular, by introducing the practice of the illegal shadowing by its war planes of cargo vessels, clearly intended to intimidate.

In the period of capitalism, as in all preceding socio-economic formations based on private ownership and exploitation of man by man, international law

[14] See S. V. Molodtsov, *International Legal Regime of the Open Sea and Continental Shelf,* p. 11 (in Russian), Akad. Nauk SSSR, Moscow, 1960

[15] See O. Khlestov, *International Legal Problems of the World Ocean,* p. 48 (in Russian), Mezhdunar. zhizn, 1973, No. 2.

[16] K. Marx and F. Engels, *Works,* 2nd ed., Vol. 15, p. 439 (in Russian).

was used principally in the interests of the ruling classes and the sphere of its operation was confined only to the so-called civilized states. The uncivilized, i.e. colonial, nations did not enjoy the protection of international law.

Thus, at different stages of the development of society international law, as a whole, and maritime law, in particular, did not remain unchanged and each period of history has its own international law.

Modern international law characteristic of the epoch of transition from capitalism to socialism was already shaped after the Great October Socialist Revolution under the potent impact of new principles in international relations not known in any earlier epoch. This law is intended to regulate relations between states of different socio-economic systems on the basis of the principles of the sovereign equality of all states, their mutual respect and peaceful co-existence. It has progressive norms, created in our time with the most active and direct participation of the Soviet Union and other socialist states, with retention of the positive norms and principles of past epochs.

The existing principles of international maritime law are codified in numerous conventions and contracts, in particular, in the 1958 Geneva Convention, representing the first compendium of norms and principles of international maritime law backed by many years of practice.

However, current international maritime law is not a compendium of frozen canons. Its individual precepts are continuing to develop and improve. This process is primarily determined by such political factors as the immeasurably greater influence on the development of international relations of the collaboration of the socialist states, the rise in political activity in the international arena of developing countries including those which have recently freed themselves from colonial dependence, and also the further deepening of the general crisis of capitalism. In addition, the development of modern international law is greatly influenced by the possibilities, extended as a result of scientific-technical progress, in reclaiming the enormous natural wealth of the World Ocean.

In modern conditions the legal regulation of the activity of states in the World Ocean is complicated by a number of circumstances. The most important of them are:

the fundamental differences in the political and economic interests of states with different socio-economic systems determining their different approaches to the solution of international legal problems;

the encouragement by the imperialist powers of the greedy drive by monopoly capital to seize for the purpose of prospecting and industrial development huge areas of the sea floor beyond the continental shelf, which will inflict harm on other states of the world;

certain contemptuous tendencies of the ruling classes of some states, accompanied by a desire for the purpose of deriving material gain without expenditure of resources on the development of their own economy, to dictate to other states the conditions of use of the World Ocean.

The circumstances listed, together with others, have contributed to the appearance of tendencies towards a revision of the basic principles and practically all the tenets of modern international maritime law codified by the system of the 1958 Geneva Convention and other international legal acts.

One such principle is that of the freedom of the open sea. The imperialist states in words constantly champion its observance although it is precisely they who, carrying out a policy of "overthrowing communism", of aggression and strangling national liberation struggles, are seeking to use the freedom of the open sea for their own military-political and economic purposes.

Thus, to counter the activity of the Soviet navy in the World Ocean, their ships have everywhere created obstacles to the sailing of our ships in the open sea, have drawn closer to them over short distances and manoeuvred in their direct proximity with sham use of weapons, etc. Their planes have not only constantly accompanied Soviet ships in the open ocean but have shadowed them from impermissibly low, dangerous heights and distances. However, this practice has not produced the desired results since brute force has been counterposed by the distinguished skill of Soviet commanders, their boldness and resilience, high military discipline, the sea lore of the crews of Soviet ships and also by firm knowledge and strict fulfilment of the norms of international maritime law.

As a result of a number of meetings of military delegations of the two countries, an agreement was prepared and signed in May 1972 between the government of the Union of Soviet Socialist Republics and the government of the United States of America on the prevention of incidents in the open sea and in the air space above it. Defining the mutual obligations of the parties, the agreement confirmed the principles recognized by international law and, in particular, the 1958 Geneva Convention on the open sea.

Despite the fact that the agreement is bilateral, it may be open to other interested countries to subscribe to it. The practical implementation of this agreement appreciably improved the situation in the open sea. However, the attacks of the imperialist powers on the principles of international maritime law continued. These attacks were assisted to a certain extent by the unreal draft treaty on sea space put forward by Malta in August 1971, proposing a radical change of all the modern principles of international maritime law including the principle of freedom of the open sea.

In particular, the draft envisaged the division of the entire World Ocean into sea spaces of two legal categories: national—width of 200 nautical miles with a regime practically not differing from that of territorial waters, and an international—the so-called general legacy of mankind. While in the national sea space it was proposed that the full power of authority be handed over to the coastal state, the international sea space must, as the authors saw it, be controlled on behalf of the international community by a special international organization possessing wide, full supranational powers.

The appearance of the Malta draft was promoted by the endeavour of some developing maritime countries to seek new sources of supplies for their economic development. One such source in their view may become the World Ocean and its bed, especially those parts of it which are most promising from the point of view of economic utilization. Therefore, they are also seeking to bring them under their own jurisdiction in order then to use them as a source of profit not requiring any expenditure.

As a reason for revising international maritime law references are also made to the imperfection of the 1958 Geneva Convention which it is argued were worked out only by the maritime powers from the position of "might is right" and without regard to the interests of the developing countries and the absence in this Convention of precise norms defining the limits of territorial waters and continental shelf. It is common knowledge, however, that the 1958 Conventions were worked out and adopted with the participation of the developing countries. Forty-nine of the 86 participants at the 1958 Law of the Sea Conference were from the developing countries (20 Latin American and 19 Asian). As regards the absence of indicators for the exact delimitation of territorial waters and of the continental shelf, a resolution of such questions undoubtedly does not require revision of the existing law on maritime spaces.

Seeking to buttress the claims to the huge expanses of the open sea, a certain group of states have put forward a variant whereby the absence of a formally-fixed norm entitled each state to define the widths of its territorial waters as it sees fit, irrespective of the point of view and the interests of other states.

In contrast, other states quite rightly maintain that unilateral and unlimited extension of territorial waters is not allowed under modern international law. The solution of this problem cannot depend only on the will of the coastal state since it is always of an international character despite the fact that the extension of territorial waters in all cases is a unilateral action.

Thus, one of the most important causes of the attempts made by some countries to impose on the world community a radical revision of existing international maritime law and, in particular, revision of the principle of the freedom of the open sea essentially lies in the clash between economic and political interests of different groups of countries.

The vast majority of states, basing themselves on the norms of international maritime law and generally recognized practice, quite justifiably consider that to ensure those interests for which territorial waters are established, it is necessary to introduce a limit the same for all and not exceeding 12 nautical miles. However, among these states there is a certain group which, agreeing with the establishment of such a standard norm, believes it necessary in addition to territorial waters to establish a wider zone of economic interests, extending the jurisdiction of coastal states to its resources.

With the problem of the width of territorial waters is intimately connected the problem of the freedom of passage through international straits and flight in the air space above them. All the straits of importance for shipping may be divided into several categories. One of them includes the straits lying away from the international sea routes. Such straits are of great importance in the main only for the states adjacent to them and, therefore, the regulation of shipping in such straits always was and must remain a prerogative of the national authorities.

Coming into quite a different category are the straits linking individual seas and oceans and intensively used for international shipping (for example, the English Channel, Gibraltar, Singapore, Kithira and many others). By virtue of historically-established norms of ordinary maritime law in such straits there has always existed and must exist freedom of passage for ships and flight of aircraft on the basis of the equality of all flags, since all the states of the world are interested in the normal functioning of international sea routes.

However, some countries whose shores are washed by the international straits, on the pretext of protecting their sovereignty and ensuring security, act against this freedom by seeking to bring under their control all international shipping and in some cases damage the legitimate vitally important interests of individual states.

The Soviet Union is anxious to see that in the straits used for international shipping freedom of passage for ships and the flight of aircraft of all countries is ensured, with observance of the guarantees of the security of coastal states. Unless such freedom is ensured it is inconceivable and practically impossible to implement the generally recognized principle of freedom of the open sea promoting the normal development of mutual relations between states.

Another set of problems on international maritime law is closely bound up with the widening of possibilities for the virtually nascent industrial harnessing of the resources of the sea bed outside territorial waters. Although the general principles of the legal regulation of such activity on the continental shelf were fixed in the 1958 Geneva Convention on the continental shelf, the problem of its external boundary has remained open since in the Convention this boundary relates to a site where the depth of the covering waters permits the exploitation of natural wealth.

The lack of a solution to the problem of the external limits of the continental shelf and the reality of industrial exploitation of its wealth at considerable depths gave rise to an endeavour to divide the whole World Ocean into two parts: one coming under the national jurisdiction of coastal states and the other forming a so-called international region. The idea is to exploit the resources of this region under the control of a specially-created international organ vested with wide, full powers in the sphere of the activity of states prospecting and working its living and mineral resources, levying licence or leasing fees for the use of parts of the sea bed and the distribution of the returns between the participants of the agreement, having regard to the special interests of the developing countries.

The trend towards the division of the sea bed is closely connected with that towards the establishment of 200-mile economic zones or zones of patrimonial sea, since in the 200-mile zone bordering the continents dwells the bulk of the biological species of commercial importance. In addition, this zone practically overlaps nearly all the geological continental shelf where so far profitable working of useful minerals has alone been possible.

Most of the developing and some developed capitalist states, on the problem of the regime of the economic zone or patrimonial sea, start from the premise that coastal states must enjoy in them exclusive rights to animate and inanimate resources. In addition, they must exercise in them control over the conduct of scientific explorations by other states and the pollution of sea water. One of the reasons for putting forward and supporting this concept is the wish of some states to substitute it for the not widely popular idea of 200-mile territorial waters.

As regards marine scientific research, mankind has always been interested in the detailed study of seas and oceans, which play an enormous part not only in man's economic activity, but also in influencing the very conditions of mankind's existence on our planet.

The multitude of unresolved problems in this sphere, the need for enormous capital investment and the interest of most countries in the results all create the pre-requisites for a considerable extension of international collaboration in study of the World Ocean.

Such activity should be encouraged in every way possible by members of the international community, as called for in the many resolutions of various UN agencies and of other international organizations. Nevertheless, some states distort the meaning of such resolutions, and cite the formal absence of convention regulations which would secure freedom for scientific research in the open sea. They strive as much as possible to limit such research and bring it under their control by using the already existing international machinery.

We consider impermissible any limitations on scientific research in an area as enormous as the open sea. The Soviet Union and other fraternal socialist countries strongly support the securing, on the basis of conventions, of freedom for scientific research in the open sea as a normal part of international maritime law, as well as the retention of other, already codified, freedoms of the open sea.

The problem of preventing the pollution of man's environment, including the World Ocean, by harmful substances in modern conditions in connection with the further development of industry, shipping, the extraction of oil and gas from the sea-bed, and widening of scientific exploration of the sea-bed, also has great topical importance. Its solution is possible on the basis of a rational combination of international agreements and national legislation. However, of great importance here is the maximum preservation of the generally recognized freedom of shipping in the open sea which cannot be subordinated to foreign control.

In the Soviet Union this problem is receiving much attention, as witness in particular the legislative and administrative acts adopted by us in the past few years alone, including the 24 February 1974 Decree of the Presidium of the USSR Supreme Soviet entitled *Increasing responsibility for pollution of the sea by substances harmful to human health or to live marine resources,* and also the participation of the Soviet Union in many international agreements concerning the prevention of the pollution of the sea with oil and other noxious substances.

The current level of scientific and technical progress and the further development of the many-sided activity of states in the World Ocean have made it necessary to erect in its waters and on its bed various artificial installations of industrial and scientific importance. The scale of such activity is indicated, for example, by the fact that in different regions of the continental shelf many hundreds of drilling installations have been set up merely to extract oil. The erection of artificial installations is now a reality not only on the continental shelf and its over-lying waters but also far beyond them.

However, the problem of the legal norms regulating the activity of states connected with the building and running of artificial installations and ensuring the safety both of shipping and the installations themselves and also the protection of the environment from pollution has not been solved by modern international law. So far there are only norms regulating in broad terms the creation of artificial installations on the continental shelf, intended for industrial prospecting and working of the the natural wealth of the sea-floor and its depths. As for the disposition and legal position of artificial installations carrying out other tasks or set up outside the continental shelf, there are still no international legal acts regulating this form of activity. In the next few decades such a situation may create obstacles both to the construction of such installations and to shipping and other lawful activity carried out on the basis of the principle of the freedom of the open sea, as fixed by international agreements.

The Soviet Union stands for the rational resolution of this problem, having regard to the interests of the whole international community, including states with no outlet to the sea, and is calling for the quickest closing of this gap in modern international law.

The problem of the status of artificial installations on the sea-bed outside the 12-mile territorial waters limit is closely connected with the problem of banning the use of the sea-floor outside these limits for military purposes, forming part of the problem of stopping the arms race with a subsequent cut in arms and then disarmament. In this field definite progress has already been achieved. The efforts of the Soviet Union and other peace-loving countries have led to the signing and coming into force of the international treaty banning placement on the bed of the seas and oceans and in their depths beyond the 12-mile zones of coastal states of nuclear weapons and other types of weapons of mass destruction. Efforts are being made to bring about the complete demilitarization of the sea-bed outside these limits.

Some states legitimately tie the question of the demilitarization of the sea-bed to the question of banning atomic submarines outside territorial waters proper, i.e. in practically the entire World Ocean, ignoring the principle of ensuring the equal security of states with different socio-economic systems. This question cannot be solved in isolation from such questions, for example, as the banning of the setting-up of military bases on foreign territories, the banning of flights of aircraft with nuclear weapons on board outside national territory, and the like.

The Soviet Union has always stood and continues to stand for a policy of stopping the arms race and narrowing the sphere of military activity of states not in a one-sided way, but on the basis of the principle of ensuring the equal security of interested states.

The paths of further development of international legal regulations on the use of the World Ocean and its bed are of no little importance to the Soviet Union—a great maritime power. The countries of the whole world are now faced with the choice: either radical break-up and complete revision of the present norms of modern maritime law; or further development and improvement of these norms on the basis of existing international conventions and agreements which in contractual form lay down the principles and norms of maritime law evolved over the centuries and justifying themselves in practice.

In view of the situation facing the Soviet Union and, objectively, all the states of the world, it is extremely important to defend the principle of freedom of the open sea as an essential condition for the further progressive development of international maritime law. It is also important to defend the freedom to conduct scientific exploration since otherwise the efforts of many states in the further exploration of the World Ocean will be confronted with insurmountable obstacles. Attempts to bring under the control of coastal states or of an international organization the conduct of scientific exploration in the World Ocean may do irreparable harm to the future activity of mankind in this still little-explored sphere.

Of great importance is the outcome of the struggle for establishing a single 12-mile limit for the width of territorial waters with maintenance of the freedom of shipping through international straits. A positive solution to this problem in the international sphere, with definite guarantees ensuring the security of coastal states and protection from pollution of the surrounding environment, will help to remove serious interference in international shipping in the straits and will help to establish mutually advantageous business relations between states.

Of no little importance in the working out of an international regime of the sea bed and eliminating the threat of spread to this area of the arms race is the proposal of the USSR to place a complete ban on the use of the bed of the seas and oceans and their depths for military purposes. A positive solution to this problem will have a favourable influence on international security and will further concert efforts to prospect and work the resources of the World Ocean.

Between 20 June and 29 August 1974, in the capital of Venezuela, Caracas, was held the second session of the Third UN Law of the Sea Conference at which 138 states were represented. The agenda included over 100 items, covering practically all international legal problems earlier discussed by the UN Committee on the Sea Bed. Among the most important were problems such as fixing a 12-mile limit for the width of territorial waters, setting up 200-mile economic zones and determining their regimes, freedom of passage through the straits used for international shipping, the regime of the open sea, freedom of scientific exploration not connected with the prospecting and working of oceanic resources, the outer limits of the continental shelf, the regime of the sea bed outside the continental shelf, prevention of the pollution of the marine environment, and so on.

All these questions were the subject of lively discussions. To bring closer together the policies of different states and hasten the solution of the fundamental problems the Soviet delegation, starting from the premise that all questions of maritime law are interrelated and must be solved "as a package", declared their readiness to go for the establishment of 200-mile economic zones, providing positive solutions are found to the other main problems of maritime law (establishment of a 12-mile width of territorial waters, freedom of passage through the international straits, freedom of navigation, freedom of scientific exploration, determination of the outer limits of the continental shelf, determination of the regime of the sea bed, prevention of pollution of the marine environment and permission for the fishermen of other states to fish part catches in the economic zone if the coastal state does not catch its full annual permitted quota). This proposal of the Soviet Union received the support of a large number of delegates from other states.

The second session of the Third UN Law of the Sea Conference was able to take only the first step towards working out a new convention: the order of adoption of the decisions at the conference was regulated, the essence of the problems was more closely defined and the attitudes of the states toward them were brought closer together and practical bases worked out for adopting certain decisions on a number of important problems of maritime law at the next stages of the work.

The third session of this conference, held between 17 March and 9 May 1975 in Geneva, also did not adopt any decisions on the essence of the problems considered since it failed to overcome serious disagreements on basic issues of maritime law. However, the Geneva session prepared an unofficial draft of a single text of a new Convention, which was accepted as the basis for further discussion at subsequent conference sessions.

The current development of the productive forces of society is in considerable measure associated with the harnessing of the wealth of the ocean and using its energy potentials. This problem is now engaging the attention of all mankind. From being a national problem, as it remained for many years, it has become international, has passed outside the orbit of the policy of individual countries and assumed an international character. Its solution now demands the united efforts of many states, which also finds reflection in the conclusion of a number of international agreements and the acceptance by many countries of definite obligations. They include the mutual obligations of the countries of Comecon and also an agreement between the governments of the USSR and the USA on co-operation in the field of exploration of the World Ocean, signed in Washington on 19 June 1973.

Our motherland, possessing powerful transport, fishing and exploratory fleets is establishing close international contacts associated with the use of the riches of the ocean and its exploration. These contacts and also the enhanced authority of the Soviet Union have enabled it to become a regular participant in all the main agreements and conventions determining the existing international mutual relations of states regulated by the norms of international maritime law.

The peace-loving policy of the Soviet Communist Party and the Soviet Government, deep respect for national peculiarities, traditions and interests of other states and the unswerving pursuit of Leninist principles of internationalism govern the contribution of the Soviet Union to the solution of the problems of international maritime law, which serves the interests of the mutual regulation of the relations of sovereign states in the use of the oceans. The contribution of the Soviet Union to the general practice of international maritime law is rationally combined with the struggle for the observance of the interests of the Soviet Union and the countries of the socialist community.

From an examination of the basic aspects of the sea power of the Soviet state follows the obvious conclusion that, possessing sea power and tirelessly expanding it, our country is acquiring ever new possibilities for the further development of the economy and of science, improving the welfare of the Soviet people and strengthening defence capacity. The constantly growing sea power of our country ensures the ever wider use of the immense resources of the World Ocean in various branches of the national economy. It opens up new prospects for the further development of science, the rapid and effective deployment of the theoretical results of oceanographic research for the economic development of the country and helps to maintain the leading positions of our country in the world science of the oceans. The use of the resources of the World Ocean in association with the further development of science in this field is opening up new directions in the economic and political integration of the socialist countries, expanding the sphere of their international co-operation and raising the prestige of the Soviet state in the international arena.

The growing sea might of our country ensures the successful conduct of its foreign policy, helps constantly to widen trading, merchant scientific and cultural links with other countries and to strengthen the constructive co-operation of states with different social systems and it places in the hands of our people a most important means for fulfilment of its historic mission—the constant expansion of economic aid to all countries which have begun independent development.

Illuminating only in broad terms those aspects of the sea power of the country which are associated with politics, economics, international law and science, and considering that sea power is an important factor in strengthening the defence capabilities of our country which makes it possible for its armed forces to repel aggression directed from the oceans—which in the post-war years has become more dangerous for the Soviet Union and the countries of the socialist community than in the past—we intend in the following chapters to deal in greater detail with the military side and show the need of our country for a strong and properly organized navy.

CHAPTER 2

Pages in the History of the Navies

As stated, among the components of the sea power of the state, fundamental is the navy with all its diverse and ramified organization—this is made up of ships, aviation and other forces, organs of command, control and communication, material back-up supply systems and bases, research organs with their ships and test centres.

Each stage creates the complex organism of its navy according to its own views and experience, beginning with the tasks set for the fleet by the political leadership and economic potential of the country.

A fleet cannot be built by blindly copying its composition and organization from some blueprint, be this the blueprint of the fleet of the mightiest state. However, there is much in common, which allows one to compare the power of fleets and evaluate their fighting or operational potential and degree of technical perfection.

This common identity springs primarily from the unity of the environment where the fleet is called upon to operate, i.e. the oceans, and also from the unity of shipbuilding principles and other sciences, on the basis of which the seaworthiness, strength, fighting and other qualities of a ship are appraised, and from that common factor which determines the considerable possibilities of using the oceans as developed lines of intercontinental communication and trade.

In solving the problems of trade, reliable lines of communication, links between peoples, fishing and marine industries, people far back in antiquity learnt to know individual coastal regions of the seas and oceans. The maritime position of many countries promoted the development in them of specific branches of industry, which naturally left its imprint on the development of the armed forces of states engaged in varying degrees in the building of navies and using them in wars.

Navies have always played a major role in strengthening the independence of states whose territories are washed by the seas and oceans and in their economic and cultural development. The strength of the fleets was one of the factors helping states to move into the category of great powers. Moreover, history shows that states not possessing naval forces were unable for a long time to occupy the position of a great power.

And it could not be otherwise, for the sphere of operations of the fleets is the seas and oceans. The continents are in essence giant islands whose total area barely reaches 150 million sq.km. They are surrounded, tied together and held in many respects (in particular, climatic) in permanent dependence by the World Ocean, the surface of which is equal to 350 million sq.km.

As shown above, the seas and oceans serve as an inexhaustible source of diverse food resources, industrial raw materials and energy. Across the seas and oceans runs the most important and most economically advantageous lines of communication between countries comprising the trading and other links between peoples. All this determines the special role of the seas and oceans in the economic growth of state.

The general growth of the economy of maritime countries and the growth rate were promoted by the creation in them of many branches of industry and economy dependent on the sea, resulting in the higher industrial development of these countries. Therefore, it is not by chance that the countries whose population was associated with seafaring became strong economically and militarily before others. These included, in different periods of history, Spain, England, Holland, France, Portugal, Turkey and the USA. All modern great powers are maritime countries.

Thus, both military necessity and the development of the economy, bound up with the sea, and political struggle have always and on an ever-growing scale encouraged states to create, possess and support navies suited to their times.

As man came to know and harness the ocean, the scale of use of the marine environment for military purposes grew—defence of one's country and the seizure of foreign possessions. At present, in the epoch of spectacular scientific discoveries and their utilization for military needs, the possibilities for waging combat operations in the oceans have grown incredibly. In this connection the oceanic theatres instead of their former significance—to be only the encounter areas of the sea forces of warring sides in a struggle for oceanic communications or in landing operations—have been transformed into extensive areas for releasing sea ballistic missiles launched from submarines and the operations of planes taking off from the deck of aircraft-carriers.

To understand better the possibilities of the present-day fleet and to gain an idea of its lines of development in the future, it is very useful to look at the processes of its development in the past and the role played by navies in the system of the armed forces of states in strengthening their independent position.

From the oceans in the past there used to be mostly the threat of invasion, the possibility of which was determined by the relative strength of the fleets and land armies. Since the creation of systems of sea strategic weapons, they now hold also the threat of delivery of devastating strikes on regions located on the territory of an opponent.

In this connection combat operations in oceanic theatres now form an important part of the armed struggle as a whole. Finally, the oceans have also lost their former significance as defence barriers which, during two world wars, reliably shielded the countries of the Western hemisphere from the devastating inferno and havoc wrought on the countries of Europe.

The role and significance of oceanic theatres in modern conditions have correspondingly changed. The enormously expanded strike possibilities of the naval forces and the endeavour of the leading military figures of the imperialist states to achieve with their aid a predominant position in the solution of strategic tasks provide the main criterion determining the role and importance of the oceanic theatres from a military point of view.

It should also be noted that the expanses of the oceans and adjacent seas are not only the most extensive strategic zones of deployment of major sea forces and disposition of launching sites of submarine missile-carriers, but are also stretches where in different directions and in regions highly advantageous for the Western powers lie numerous island territories convenient for setting up support points, forward lines, naval and air bases. This has enabled the imperialist member states of aggressive blocs to surround the Soviet Union and the countries of the socialist community with strong groupings of land, sea and air forces, and launching sites for missiles located on land and at sea. The combat deployment of all these forces is connected with the use of powerful fleets intended for the direct waging of combat operations or for comprehensive supply to other groupings. Thanks to the wide front and great depth of oceanic zone emplacements, the imperialists are capable, at minimum cost, of staggering their fleet forces and manoeuvring them in various directions, creating, in a relatively short time, strong groupings in selected areas of the World Ocean, from which they can deliver nuclear strikes against the territory of the USSR.

America, separated from Europe by the vast expanses of the Atlantic Ocean, has for centuries been safe and not experienced the horrors of war. It grew used to its safety and impunity, finding itself protected by its powerful fleet. Today the position has changed and oceanic areas are now the least secure in the US defence system. Today, if the US imperialists were to launch a war against the countries of the socialist community, the territory of the USA, unlike in past wars, might become a theatre of combat operations and the oceanic expanses might be turned into an arena of bitter struggle between the fleets to make full use of sea power for solving important strategic tasks.

Fleets of the Western Countries in the Sixteenth to Nineteenth Centuries

Each socio-economic formation has created navies corresponding to its economic and technical potential. For example, in a slave-owning society the basis of the fleets consisted of flat-bottomed, rower-powered, rarely seagoing, ships. At that time the compass did not yet exist and sailing was only inshore. For fighting at sea, cold weapons were used—bows, spears, stone-throwing catapults, and therefore the tactics of sea fighting added up to ramming and, as a rule, to hand-to-hand boarding combat.

In the epoch of feudalism the ships of the fleet were fitted with sails, acquired a keel and were more stable, but remained small. In this period, artillery came into use on ships. This brought considerable changes in the tactics of sea fighting although ramming and boarding still persisted for a long time.

The advent of capitalism on the world scene led to a radical change in the material-technical basis of armed struggle—the formation of a steam fleet, powerful artillery arms and heavy armour. The rivalry between artillery and armour for a long time determined the new trend in the development of naval shipbuilding and naval art—it was necessary to work out ways of employing the navies adequate to the new means of waging battle at sea. Considerable changes in the development of the fleets resulted from the advent of submarines and of aviation capable of operating at sea. Finally, the recent period has seen even more profound and revolutionary changes in the development of the fleets, associated with the construction of atomic-powered ships with nuclear missile weapons.

These steps in the development of the fleets were not only stages in technical improvement of ships. Simultaneously with development of the material-technical basis of the fleets their basic designation changed, their role in the politics of states in peacetime grew, the place of the fleets in the system of armed forces changed and the role of combat operations at sea grew.

In slave-owning society and under feudalism, together with land forces the fleets took part in numerous wars and even then served as the most important and often sole means of transport and invasion of hostile territories by armies. They were used to protect their own sea-trade routes and disrupt the sea trade of the enemy.

In the sixteenth to seventeenth centuries comes one of the turning points in the history of mankind—the epoch of the great geographical discoveries, the period of primary accumulation of capital and the emergence of capitalism.

"The era of the colonial enterprises which now opened up for all the maritime nations was also the stage of the formation of large navies for defending the recently-founded colonies and the trade with them. From this time begins a period richer in sea engagements and more fruitful for the development of sea arms than any preceding one."[1]

In this stage many countries of Western Europe converted their fleets into one of the instruments of primary accumulation of capital, seizure of colonies, enslavement of the peoples of whole continents and their plunder. The fleets became the instrument for bitter battles between rivals in colonial robbery for domination in the colonies and in the sea lanes.

Since the main territories of the possible colonial possessions of the European states lay beyond the seas and oceans, a most important role in the battle for colonies, and the partition of the world associated with this, was played by the navies, which were the instruments of this division.

"The opening up of gold and silver mines in America, the uprooting, enslavement and burial alive of the native population in the mines, the first steps to the conquest and plunder of the East Indies, the transformation of Africa into a hunting ground against black-skinned people—such was the dawn of the capitalist era of production."[2]

This "dawn" arose in bitter struggle for the seizure of colonies and oceanic trade routes with their key positions such as Gibraltar, Singapore, Malta, and many others. The chief force in this struggle were the navies of the European powers.

[1] K. Marx and F. Engels, *Works,* 2nd ed., Vol. 14, p. 382 (in Russian).
[2] K. Marx, *Capital,* Vol. 1, 1951, p. 754 (in Russian).

The first in the search for new lands and their colonization were Spain and Portugal. The sea expeditions of Columbus, Vespucci, Magellan, Vasco da Gama and other seafarers not only discovered the American continent, charted the sea route round Africa to India and China and explored many islands in the Pacific Ocean, but also opened the way to the colonization of these regions and countries. The operations of the fleets in discovering and colonizing new lands were successful and held out such alluring and exciting prospects as to allow the first two major predators—Spain and Portugal—to conclude a treaty dividing the world between themselves in order not to lose the wealth seized and not allow "third states" to join in the colonial plunder. Such a line of division was established in 1494 in the Atlantic Ocean and in 1529 in the Pacific Ocean.

Following the Spaniards and Portuguese, the search for new lands was joined by the English, French and Dutch. Russia had no outlet to the oceans at that time, did not possess a fleet and, therefore, could not take part in the partition of the world.

Spain in the sixteenth century firmly occupying the place of a great power and owning enormous colonies was not able, however, to make use of the wealth plundered from the colonies to develop industry and build a fleet. The Spanish fleet did not progress and shipbuilding did not develop. After the defeat of the "invincible Armada" by the more modern English fleet, Spain ceased to hold her former place among the great world powers and gradually, unable to defend her overseas possessions, lost them and passed into the category of a third-rate state, largely the result of the loss of her sea power.

In the middle of the seventeenth century Holland, with the most powerful fleet in the world, was able to develop to the full a colonial system and reach the pinnacle of her might. Soon her main rival became rapidly-developing England, possessing economic superiority over Holland. The struggle between these countries reachd its climax in the wars known in history as the Anglo-Dutch wars. The arena of the main engagements in them was the North Sea. After several sea battles won by the English, Holland was forced to concede defeat. She then became a second-rate colonial power. Her fate was sealed by the victory of the industrial capital of England over the commercial capital of Holland, the military expression of which was the superiority of the English fleet (or, in the final analysis, the sea power of England).

Karl Marx had this to to say "... Mercantile dominance is already now connected with the greater or lesser preponderance of the conditions of existence of large industry. It is worth, for example, comparing England and Holland. The history of the decline of Holland as a dominant mercantile nation is the history of the subordination of mercantile to industrial capital."[3]

England often used her navy for the direct enrichment of the country. Suffice it to recall that many English ships and vessels in royal service operated like pirates: pillaged the merchant ships of other countries, seized them and brought them into English ports, disrupting the economy of her rivals. Thus the fleet, from being a consumer, became the source of enrichment of the state.

The hub of the policy of England was always the endeavour to occupy the position of "ruler of the seas" personifying a world political power. To achieve

[3]K. Marx, *Capital*, Vol. 3, p. 345 (in Russian).

this goal, she opted for the path of downgrading by all possible measures her rivals at sea to the status of powers not capable of withstanding the strength of her fleet.

At the beginning of the eighteenth century France began capitalist develop-ment. By enslaving overseas countries with the aid of her fleet she was also transformed into a huge colonial empire, owning Canada, large territories in the Mississippi valley, a number of West Indian islands, part of India and extensive areas in Africa.

By this time the struggle in the international arena for economic hegemony, colonial possessions and dominance in world trade had shifted to the sphere of rivalry between England and France. The culmination of this struggle was the Seven Years' War of 1756-63 involving nearly all the states of Europe including Russia. "... England and France fought in the Seven Years' War for colonies, i.e. waged an imperialist war. . . ."[4]

The main events in this war unfolded at sea so that in the clash of the main opponents the most important role was played by their navies. The political goals of this war were reached in the engagements of the English and French fleets, as a result of which France, losing all hope of achieving domination or even a predominant position at sea, was forced to surrender to England her possessions in North America and India.

From the middle of the eighteenth century England firmly held the rank of the first world sea power, resting on the strongest fleet in the world. She held her dominant position in the capitalist world for almost two centuries.

The operations of the English colonizers aimed at impeding in all ways the development of industry in the colonies, their endeavour to keep them only as suppliers of raw materials and consumers of the goods of British industry, brought about a war for independence in the most developed colonies in North America. On the side of the Americans operated the fleets of the old rivals of England—France, Holland and Spain. A positive role for the Americans was also played by the policy of Russia, declaring so-called armed neutrality sup-ported by the strength of the Russian fleet and not allowing England to block-ade America. The English had to wage war in conditions in which their fleet was greatly inferior to the combined fleet of their opponents. The unfavourable ratio of forces at sea and the impossibility of sending troop reinforcements unimpeded from the metropolitan country forced England, after several engagements lost by her on land, to recognize the independence of the United States of North America.

This war once again confirmed the growth of the influence of the naval forces on the course and outcome of armed conflict. In it the combat operations of the fleet shifted from the European seas to distant oceanic areas sharply raising the significance of oceanic communications.

The new conditions of the combat operations of the fleets set higher demands on the seaworthiness of ships and their fighting resilience. This increased the size of ships, changed their designs, intensified their arming and ushered in the use of armouring. The considerable growth of the possibilities of rapidly-developing capitalist industry promoted the swift development of the fleet and

[4] V. I. Lenin, *Complete Collected Works,* Vol. 30, p. 7 (in Russian).

its arming.

The role of the navies in the political struggle grew, particularly in the wars of the French bourgeois revolution at the turn of the eighteenth and beginning of the nineteenth centuries.

The main organizer of these wars was the English bourgoisie, seeking to gain a complete hold on the colonial possessions still left to France. England transferred the burden of the struggle on the continent to her European allies, confining her own participation in the wars essentially to sea operations. At the same time the counter-revolutionary big bourgeoisie coming to power in France after the Thermidorian upheaval brought to the fore the task of breaking the colonial power of England. For this the Bonaparte expedition to Egypt was undertaken with the further purpose of seizing India. The French troops, unknown to the English fleet, performed a "marche-manoeuvre" at sea and began successful combat operations in Egypt.

It should be noted that the sea expedition of Bonaparte was exposed to great danger had it encountered the English fleet under the command of Nelson. At that time the chain of errors of Nelson and chance factors saved the French expedition. It was only two and a half months later that the English fleet caught up with the French ships anchored in Aboukir Bay and scattered them.

The defeat of the French fleet first affected the fighting capacity of that part of the army which was in Egypt. Napoleon was forced to abandon the expedition to India and confined himself to operations in the main on Egyptian territory.

Thus, although France possessed strong land armies, the weakness of her fleet became one of the main causes of the failure of the plans of the major political action of the French Government—the shattering of the colonial power of England by conquering Egypt and India.

Napoleon, continuing the struggle, decided to make a large-scale landing directly in the British Isles for which 2600 various transport vessels were prepared. A mortal threat hung over England. Yet again the weakness of the French fleet played a role fatal for France. The preparation for the invasion dragged on. At the same time the advance of the Russian forces under the command of Kutuzov forced Napoleon to abandon completely his plans to land in England.

On 21 October 1805 in the Atlantic Ocean off the shores of Spain took place the famous Battle of Trafalgar in which the English fleet under Nelson's command inflicted a heavy defeat on the Franco-Spanish fleet. The importance of this battle, like the role of the English fleet in the struggle with Napoleonic France, has been enormously exaggerated by Anglo-American ideologists. For example, *Fyffe's History of Modern Europe* claims that "Trafalgar was not only the greatest naval victory, it was the greatest and most momentous victory won either by land or by sea during the whole of the Revolutionary War. No victory, and no series of victories by Napoleon produced the same effect upon Europe. . . ."[5]

One cannot agree with this. As is known, the fight against Napoleon went on for many more years and in it the main role was played by Russia in crushing the

[5] Quoted in A. T. Mahan, *The Influence of Sea Power on the French Revolution and Empire*, Vol. 2, p. 152, Moscow-Leningrad, Voenmorizdat, 1940.

French army in the 1812 Patriotic War. The victory of Russia had a decisive influence on the political situation in Europe. As for the Battle of Trafalgar, in its political consequences it was, of course, not an ordinary combat clash of fleets. After a number of defeats for the French fleet, its final crushing at Trafalgar showed the total inability of France to wage war at sea against the more sophisticated English fleet consisting of better-quality ships manned by better-trained crews and employing tactics new for that time. England and her colonies became practically invulnerable to strikes from the sea. This untied the hands of the English bourgeoisie to organize and finance new alliances for continuing the struggle against Napoleonic France. France was compelled, finally, to abandon plans to fight at sea and to seek other means of war against her main foe, unconnected with the sea.

The Russian Fleet in the
Seventeenth to Nineteenth Centuries

Because of the political and historical conditions of its genesis, the development of the fleet of Russia—the largest continental state in the world—was quite distinctive. The Russian fleet moved into the sea expanses when the fleets of the strong sea powers of the West already held sway there. For the record, it should be noted that expansionist schemes characteristic of the major states of that epoch were by no means alien to the policy of the Russian State under the Czars.

History patently confirmed that without a strong fleet Russia could not take its place among the great powers. This was well understood by Peter the Great who is rightly considered the founder of Russia's regular fleet. Indeed with the aid of this fleet the tough centuries-old fight of the Russian people for the return of the outlets to the Baltic taken from them was brilliantly accomplished. However, the lessons of this struggle with foreign invaders were not always properly understood by the Russian autocracy, often underestimating the possibilities residing in the power of the fleet; and so Russia in many cases suffered harm. This was also promoted by the constant centuries-old propagation by states hostile to Russia, headed by England, of the idea that it was useless for a large continental power to have interests at sea. To lend conviction to such propaganda, the aspersion was widely used that the Russians were not a maritime but a land nation, that the sea was alien to them and that they were incapable of navigation.

This psychological and at times physical influence was heightened after the fleet of Peter the Great drew equal in its power with the English fleet, which the English bourgeoisie saw as a challenge to its self-proclaimed right to be "ruler of the seas".

Indeed, starting from the third century our ancestors waged wars in the Black, Mediterranean and Caspian Seas. History shows that already at that time the Old Slav tribes undertook ambitious sea voyages, suggesting that sea navigation by the ancestors of the Slavs of the northern Black Sea region, the Dnieper and other regions of eastern Europe was already developed in earlier times. The fact that in 269 A.D. these tribes brought a large fleet and crushed Athens, Corinth and Sparta and reached Crete and Cyprus, makes it perfectly obvious that, for the Old Slav tribes populating the southern regions of our country, sea navigation and knowledge of sea routes on the Black, Marmora, Aegean and Mediterranean Seas were already far from new.

The sea navigation of the Old Slavs was of a distinctive character and emerged as a consequence of the needs of economic development. Our rivers, with a relatively calm flow, since ancient times were not only the most important lines of communication and outlets to the seas, but also the starting points for sailing the seas. This distinctiveness of Slav sea navigation was expressed in the peculiarities of shipbuilding and the tactical methods employed in combat operations at sea.

The fighting expeditions of the Slavs and their penetration into slave-owning Byzantium had an important influence on changing the political map of the Balkan peninsula and the nearby regions of Europe of that time. The Slav conquests hastened the destruction of the slave-owning system of Byzantium, weakened by internal struggle, and contributed to its establishment of feudalism.

As well as the sea-fighting campaigns of the Slavs in the third century already mentioned, history retains data on the invasion by the Slavs of the Balkan peninsula, repeated assaults on Constantinople, their struggles in Thrace and Hellas, and the expeditions of the Eastern Slavs to Italy and the island of Crete undertaken in the sixth to seventh centuries. The seafarers of the Kiev and Novgorod states had superb mastery of sea matters. This is well borne out by the numerous sea campaigns of the ninth to twelfth centuries of which the better known to us are the campaigns of the Kievan Prince Oleg, in particular the campaign in 907 A.D. leading to the capitulation of Constantinople and the conclusion of the first written trade treaty (911 A.D.) ensuring the unhindered navigation of Russian vessels through the Black and Mediterranean Seas.

On the growth of the Kievan state in the ninth to eleventh centuries, Karl Marx in *Secret Diplomacy of the Eighteenth Century* wrote: "The old maps of Russia when laid out before us show that this country at one time possessed in Europe even larger dimensions than . . . now. Its continuous growth between the ninth and eleventh centuries is noted with alarm. We have already referred to Oleg hurling against Byzantium 88,000 men and dictating . . . the peace conditions affronting the dignity of the Eastern Roman Empire. We have also referred to Igor who made Byzantium his own tributary and to Svyatos-lav . . . and finally Vladimir who conquered the Crimea . . . ."

The campaigns of the Russians for the seas have been quite well illustrated in Russian historical and imaginative literature. Many foreign scholars have also written about Russian seamen of that period. For example, the English researcher F. Jane wrote of the Russian fleet that it could claim greater antiquity than the English fleet. Centuries before British ships were built, the Russians were already fiercely fighting in sea battles and at least a thousand years ago were considered the best seamen of the time. In the eleventh century the Russians were already engaged in sea crafts and trade in the White Sea, penetrated into the Pechora region, travelled to Novaya Zemlya and into the

Kara Sea. From the twelfth century the maritime activity of the Russians also spread into the Baltic Sea. In the thirteenth century Novgorod, in a long and bitter struggle with the Swedes and with the Teutonic Knights, the highlights of which were the victories of Alexander Nevsky over the Swedes at Neva in 1240 and over the German "psalm knights" on Lake Chud in 1242, occupied an important position in trade on the Baltic Sea, as a result of which it joined the Hanseatic League of maritime mercantile towns.

The incursion of the Tartars destroyed Russian sea power in the southern seas and cut off Russia from the Black and Caspian Seas. In Russian hands remained only the White Sea coast and a small part of the shore of the Gulf of Finland at the mouths of the Neva and Narva where the Novgorodians withstood their enemies, stubbornly endeavouring to keep them back from the Baltic Sea.

The Tartar yoke and the subsequent Polish and Swedish interventions for long held back the development of Russia. This difficult period for our country, lasting some five centuries, also affected the development of the fleet. Russia at that time completely lost her sea trade. The Western countries, not subject to such severe tribulations, sheltered from the incursion of the Tartar hordes by the Slavs, rapidly developed and created powerful fleets which were widely used for conquering colonies and developing sea trade.

As a result of the centuries-long but unsuccessful struggle for an outlet to the Baltic Sea Russia, under the Stolbovo peace treaty (1616), was completely cut off from her former Baltic shores. The Swedish king Gustavus Adolphus called this peace one of the "greatest favours of the gods" and declared that it would be hard for the Russian people to jump over the hurdles erected.

However, the drive of the Russians to the sea, arrested in the southern and Baltic Seas, was directed northwards where they explored the whole seashore from Pechora to the Sea of Okhotsk and obtained the first information on Sakhalin and the Shantar Islands. In the south the Don and Zaporozhie Cossacks, despite counter-action from strong adversaries, came to the sea from the Dnieper and the Don and carried out bold raids on the Black Sea coast.

It must be recognized that the prolonged propaganda hostile to Russia found support among the influential satraps of Russian Czarism who, in every way possible, impeded the building of a fleet and achieved expenditure cuts, preventing it from being kept in a necessary state of readiness.

The narrowness of the thinking of highly-placed Czarist servitors did not fail to leave its mark. Their reactionary ideas of setting off the fleet against the army and their failure to understand that the power of a country's armed forces depends on a harmonious development of both components of a single organism did serious damage to the country's defence capacity over a considerable period. An example confirming this is afforded by the actions of War Minister Kuropatkin. Before the Russo-Japanese War he wrote in his diary: "Yesterday, together with Witte . . . we easily convinced the sovereign of the need to stop spending on the fleet and the Far East".[6] This points, if not to treason, at any rate to the crudest misapprehension of the interests of the state.

Hostile propaganda tirelessly affirmed that Russia was not a maritime but

[6] A. I. Sorokin, *The Russo-Japanese War, 1904-05*, p. 19 (in Russian), Moscow, Voenizdat, 1956.

only a continental country and needed a fleet only for resolving the modest task of coastal defence.

Russia, possessing a sixth of the land of the world, was undoubtedly the biggest continental power of the world. But at the same time she had always been a great sea power. The sea borders of Russia were almost twice as long as the coastal line of the United States and almost fifteen times the coastline of France. The land which borders the sea in Russia, USA and France is much the same: about two-thirds of their state borders are represented by the coasts of the seas and oceans. The sea borders of Germany (before the Second World War) amounted to only one-third of all her borders. But despite this, no one reproached Germany for seeking to have a powerful fleet even though a continental country.

The enemies of Russia no less widely used techniques of falsification of its military history, claiming that all her victories had been achieved by land armies, that she must set off the army against the fleet and that the Russian army could be powerful only by getting rid of the fleet. Thus, Kuropatkin in 1900 declared to the Czar: "The lessons of history have taught us to travel along that path over which our ancestors trod and to see the main strengths of Russia as being her land army . . .".[7]

In fact the fleet did not take part in only two of the 33 wars which Russia waged in the 200 years preceding the First World War (1849 Hungarian campaign and the 1877-79 Akhaltekinsk expeditions).[8]

In this connection one cannot fail to note that in the Russo-Japanese war, according to Lenin, the chief problem was predominance at sea. In the article *The Fall of Port Arthur,* Lenin wrote: "The military blow is irreparable. The problem of predominance at sea is solved—the chief and fundamental question of the present war . . . . The Japanese have so far more rapidly and more heavily reinforced their military forces after each major engagement than the Russians. And now achieving complete dominance at sea and completely destroying one of the Russian armies, they are able to send twice as many reinforcements as the Russians".[9]

Even now bourgeois propaganda, headed by the ideologists of the USA and directed against the need for the Soviet state to have a powerful navy is still continuing on a wide scale.

Comparatively recently, on 4 August 1970, Richard Nixon, then US President, stated: "What the Soviet Union needs is different from what we need. They're a land power . . . We're, primarily, of course, a sea power and our needs, therefore, are different."[10] It does not need saying that Nixon's statement, which is a modern variant of the old attempts of English politicians and leaders of the British Admiralty to show that Russia has no need of a strong navy, has no bearing on the actual state of affairs and contradicts the whole course of development of our fleet in the past and the interests of our state today.

[7] War Reports of General-Adjutant Kuropatkin, Vol. 4, Warsaw, Printed District H.Q. printing house, 1906, p. 68 (in Russian).
[8] See K. F. Shatsillo, *Russian Imperialism and the Development of the Fleet,* p. 12 (in Russian), Nauka, 1968.
[9] V. I. Lenin, *Complete Collected Works,* Vol. 9, pp. 153-54 (in Russian).
[10] *Washington Post,* 5 August 1970.

For a variety of reasons Russia's fleet developed far from uniformly. Individual surges of the sea power of Russia gave way to long periods of decline and weakness and each time a reduction in the naval strength of Russia produced new difficulties on her historic path and had serious consequences which usually could not be corrected despite considerable efforts. This was the case in the 1853-56 Crimean War, the outcome of which was decided in advance by the superiority of the Anglo-French fleet. The under-estimation by the Czarist government of the role of the fleet had the result that under the terms of the 1856 peace treaty Russia was forbidden to have a fleet in the Black Sea.[11]

The lessons of that war were not heeded by the autocracy in the 1877-78 war with Turkey, when the appearance in the Straits of the English fleet forced the Russian army, already standing at the walls of Constantinople, to withdraw without achieving the main goal of the war—the gaining of free access to the Mediterranean.

This was also true in the 1904-05 Russo-Japanese War. The inactivity of the Russian fleet at the start of it as a result of incompetence and sheer treachery of the military command, and then the crushing of the fleet, could not fail, as Lenin noted, to have a decisive influence on the harsh outcome of this war for Russia.

In periods of decline the fleet lost its active features, became only a defence force lacking the qualities of a most important instrument of the policy of the state. The Russian fleet, especially after the industrial revolution in the leading capitalist countries when the general weakness of Russia was clearly manifest, became relatively ever weaker. This testifies to the loss by Czarist Russia of her status as a great world power conducting her own independent policy, her conversion to a supplier of cannon fodder for the imperialist predators in their struggle for their interests, a struggle alien to the Russian people.

Considerable difficulties for Russia also stemmed from her geographical position making it necessary in each of the separate sea theatres to have a fleet which would be capable of resolving the tasks facing it.

However, despite all difficulties, the fleet wrote into the history of our homeland many remarkable heroic pages and played an important role in the history of the development of Russia.

The history of the regular Russian fleet is usually taken to begin with Peter the Great. Karl Marx, characterizing that epoch, said that one could not imagine a great nation so cut off from the sea as Russia before Peter. "No great nation has existed nor was capable of existing in such an intracontinental position as was at first the state of Peter the Great; no nation would ever agree to see its shores and mouths of its rivers wrenched from it. Russia could not leave the mouth of the Neva, the only route for disposing of the products of the Russian North, in the hands of the Swedes."[12]

Russia could not reconcile herself to being cut off from the sea and continuously fought for outlets to the coast.

The struggle of Russia for outlets to the sea urgently demanded the creation of a navy without which this goal could not be reached. The building of the fleet under Peter the Great was a logical extension of the development of the Russian

---

[11] In 1871 Russia succeeded in lifting this humiliating ban.
[12] K. Marx, *Secret Diplomacy of the Eighteenth Century* (in Russian).

state and in fact meant the regeneration in new conditions of the qualities of a seafaring people particular to the Russian people.

To solve this problem in a backward country and in the short time allotted by history, the Russian people had to overcome exceptional difficulties.

It was decided to begin the breakthrough to the sea by taking Azov, which would shelter Russia from the Turko-Tartar threat. The then existing international situation and system of military-political alliances (Russia, Poland, Austria and Venice against Turkey) confirmed the soundness of the choice of this approach.

However, the first Azov campaign (1695) showed that the army alone, without the assistance of the fleet, was not in a position to take Azov, which was receiving constant assistance by sea. Sustained work on building a fleet already made it possible in the spring of 1696 to muster ships for a siege and to capture Azov by joint efforts of army and fleet. This successful experience of a coherent interaction of land and sea forces in taking a sea fortress differs advantageously from similar but unsuccessful operations by the English in their bid to capture Quebec (1691) and Saint-Pierre (1693).

True, the seizure of Azov in no wise solved the problem of restoring outlets to the seas for free sea trade. It was still necessary to solve the problem of taking possession of the shores of the Kerch Strait, under the control of Turkey. In addition, a tough and stubborn fight lay ahead with one of the strongest powers of that time—Sweden—which had already dominated northern Europe for some 150 years and with especial stubbornness counteracted the attempts of the Russians to move out to the Baltic coasts and sail in the Baltic Sea. Russia needed to reconstruct her economy on a new basis, create a modern army and at the same time build a fleet more rapidly, without which successful operations in the Baltic Sea zone were impossible.

The appearance of a Russian fleet in the Baltic immediately made itself felt during combat operations of emergence at the mouth of the Neva and possession of Kotlin Island, and also in defence of the new capital being built on the banks of the Neva—St Petersburg. In 1708, when the Swedes undertook a combined assault by large land and sea forces on Petersburg, the Russian fleet was already an impressive force. It had twelve battleships under sail and several hundred small vessels, powered by oarsmen. This assault failed ignominiously under the blows of the Russian army and fleet.

On 27 June 1709 took place the successful Battle of Poltava—a most important moment in history—marking the end of Sweden as a great power. But the goals of the war were nevertheless not reached, and twelve long years of stubborn battle still lay ahead.

To clear the Gulf of Finland of the hostile fleet it was necessary to conquer Vyborg. This removed the direct threat to Petersburg and opened the way for the fleet to the Finnish skerries. An attempt to solve the task by the land armies alone did not lead to the fall of the fortress. Vyborg was taken later by the closely interacting land and sea forces, followed by Riga, Pernau, Arensburg and the Moonsund (Suur väin) Islands and Reval. In all these battles an increasing role was played by the fleet. Gradually, it became the most important factor in the continued stubborn fight. The joint operations of the galley ships and the troops disembarking from them resulted in the occupation in the summer of 1713 of Helsingfors and Åbo, which brought within direct striking distance the coasts of Sweden and her capital. Despite this the Swedes in no way considered themselves defeated and were confident that their battleships would be able to destroy the Russian fleet and not allow a "march-manoeuvre" of its landing parties through the Gulf of Bothnia.

England and France and, later, other states fearing the growing strength of Russia and the total collapse of Sweden, hatched endless intrigues against Russia and pressurized her. However, Peter the Great firmly insisted on the complete securing for Russia of the shores of the Baltic Sea occupied by him. He drew this confidence from the young Russian fleet, achieving a resounding victory over the Swedish fleet at Hargo in 1714 and becoming a formidable force ensuring the independence of Russian policy in the Baltic Sea sphere.

The matter was not confined merely to intrigues and diplomatic pressure by foreign states. In the summer of 1719 England decided to set in motion her own armed forces. Her fleet entered the Baltic Sea. Heartened by this move of the English the Swedes led their ships out to sea. In the engagement at the Island of Osel the Russian battle forces under the command of N. A. Senyavin completely vanquished the Swedish squadron, capturing some of her ships. Then the Russian galleys under the cover of the battle fleet landed large groups in the Stockholm region.

At the end of 1719, Britain concluded a military alliance with Sweden directed against Russia, which inspired the Swedes to continue the war. Yet the Russian Baltic Fleet continued to grow. According to a general estimation, in the world by that time there were only two powerful fleets—the English and Russian. The fleets of other sea powers were much weaker.

In 1720 heavy English naval forces again moved into the Baltic. However, the Russian fleet continued active landing operations on the shores of Sweden and won a victory over the battle forces of the enemy in the engagement at the Island of Gotland. In 1721, despite the presence in the Baltic of the English, the Russian armed forces compelled the Swedes to lay down their arms and on 30 August 1721 signed a peace treaty under which Sweden permanently gave up the coastal regions of the Baltic Sea occupied by the Russian forces. The treaty was vivid proof of the importance of the fleet and the support by it of land troops in achieving the goals of the war.

The fleet, despite the intervention of England and other powers, did not allow the results of the Poltava victory to be undermined and brought Russia into the ranks of the most powerful sea powers of the world.

On the medal struck in honour of the victory over Sweden is inscribed: "To the Fleet goes the honour of ending the war, since to have done so by land alone would have been impossible". This is one of the striking examples of the influence of the fleet on the achievement by Russia of major successes in the international arena.

While waging battle for the return of the outlets to the Baltic Sea, the Russian state expanded to the east as far as the Pacific Ocean.

In the seventeenth century the Russians prospected the enormous territory of Siberia and the Far East remarkably fast. The results of these explorations are geographical discoveries of world significance.

In 1632, Yakutsk was founded—the starting point of the break-through to the Pacific Ocean. From here the expeditions of I. Moskvitin, M. Stadukhin, S. Dezhnev, E. Khabarov and others explored the territory of the Far East and its coast. In 1649 Okhotsk was established—the first Russian port on the Pacific Ocean. By the beginning of the eighteenth century. V. Atlasov had explored Kamchatka where the port of Petropavlovsk-Kamchatka was founded in 1740.

From the middle of the eighteenth century Russian manufacturers, headed by G. Shelekhov, setting up the Russo-American Company began to conquer North West America and the Aleutian Islands.

By 1800 Alaska, the Aleutian Islands, Sakhalin and also many islands in the Pacific Ocean had already been secured for Russia. Russia came out on to the coast of the Pacific Ocean but her position here lacked stability because of the weakness of the Russian fleet in this area, and also in connection with the aggressiveness of other states, seeking to seize Russian possessions in the northern areas of the Pacific.

After the death of Peter the Great in 1725 the Russian fleet gradually began to show signs of decline and break-up. The ships became out of date and were not replaced in good time by new ones, their upkeep steadily worsened and shipbuilding contracted.

The new 1741-43 Swedish-Russian war, thought temporarily enlivening the activity of the fleet, highlighted its serious shortcomings, resulting from loss of attention by Russian ruling circles to its construction and development. However, in this war, too, the Russian fleet played a most important part in defence of the shores of the Baltic Sea and of Petersburg. Yet, after the war, the process of decline of the Russian fleet continued and Russia gradually lost the status of a great sea power. At the same time she was faced by the ever more urgent task of restoring the outlets to the southern seas. This was bound to regenerate the fleet and enhance its role in the armed forces system, as indeed happened later.

In 1769 the building of a fleet was renewed at the old Petrovsk yards. Already in the 1768-74 Russo-Turkish War much aid to the forces engaging the Turks on the western coast of the Black Sea was provided by a Danube flotilla, which crushed the powerful sea forces of the Turks. The Azov-Black Sea fleet, commanded by A. N. Senyavin, opened up for the Russians the way from Azov to the Black Sea, which settled a problem the solution of which had already begun in 1696 with the capture of Azov. The young Black Sea fleet won a series of famous victories over the more numerous groupings of the Turkish fleet, and thwarted the landing of the enemy in the Crimea, thereby promoting the establishment of Russia on the shores of the Black Sea.

During the many years of struggle for outlets to the sea Russia was able to create a strong naval fleet and shipbuilding industry with great potential. The talent of Russian officers and admirals showed itself in advanced naval art and shipbuilding science. The famous traditions of the Russian sea school, giving the world and our homeland such illustrious fleet commanders as Spiridov, Ushakov, Senyavin, Lazarev, Nakhimov and Makarov and such remarkable shipbuilders as Sklyaev, Vereshchagin, Kurochkin, Yershov, Titov, Bubnov and Krylov, are preserved and augmented by Soviet naval seamen.

Russia in the Mediterranean

The Mediterranean Sea is called the cradle of the might of the great fleets. This sea has also been the arena for famous feats by Russian seamen.

The latest historical research shows that even in ancient times the peoples of the Black Sea region, the Balkan peninsula, the Aegean archipelago and Asia Minor over many centuries communicated with each other over the sea routes. Navigation, at that time ensuring the requirements of trade, favourably influenced the economic development of the peoples of these areas. The tribes populating the extensive steppes and forested steppes of eastern Europe and all the Black Sea coast, thanks to the marine channels of communication were drawn into trading, cultural, political and military relations with the most developed ancient states of the Mediterranean. These links played a very important role in the development of the economy of the peoples living near the Black Sea and the development among them of handicrafts and also exerted a positive effect on the development of their socio-political life.

The Russian state had a beneficial effect on the development of commercial shipping in the Mediterranean basin and in the Baltic Sea. The military successes of Russia in the struggle with her enemies ensured the reliability of the famous waterway built up by the ninth century "from the Varangians to the Greeks" and this furthered the development of the trade of many countries of Europe, Asia and Africa.

From the eleventh century Novgorod merchants went on trading missions to the Mediterranean countries not only along the rivers but by sea around Europe to Constantinople. The Russian state took a number of measures to ensure the safety of the sea-trading routes even to the point of joint struggle with Byzantium against pirates in the Aegean Sea.

From the second half of the eleventh century and up to the Tartar-Mongolian incursion, Russian trade in the Mediterranean promoted the development in Russia of feudal relations. As the Russian state came to be divided up, the sea voyages were now undertaken by individual principalities. Caravans of Russian merchant ships went to overseas countries until the Mongolian-Tartar invasion cut off Russia from the southern seas.

However, the Tartar-Mongolian conquerors could not take from the Russian people their innate pull to the sea. The seafarers of Russia, usually on ships of foreign merchants, continued to sail in the Mediterranean for trading and diplomatic purposes and also often for the purpose of pilgrimage. In those hard times Russian freemen in the lowlands of the Dnieper and Don upheld the country's tradition of sea-going. The bold sea campaigns of the Don and Zaporozhie Cossacks augmented the past fame of Slav sea navigation in the southern seas. The sea campaigns of the Cossacks became particularly active in the sixteenth century when to their aid came the unified centralized Russian state, not only supporting the fight of the Cossacks but also often organizing it.

The struggle with Turkey and its dependent the Crimean Khanate was long and hard. The Osman empire, in population and area and also in military-economic resources, was one of the most powerful states of that time. The Turkish army and fleet were considered one of the strongest in the world. Therefore, the fighting successes of the weakly-armed Cossacks in this struggle were of no little importance in the defence of the southern regions of the Russian state and were an inspiring example for the peoples of the Mediterranean, rising in the fight against the Turkish oppressors. Being pertinacious and skilful warriors, the Don and Zaporozhie Cossaks in the sixteenth to seventeenth centuries turned the water expanses and the shores of the Black and Azov Seas into an arena of fierce clashes with the Turkish army and fleet. One of the episodes of this struggle worth mentioning was the capture by the Cossacks of the Turkish fortress of Azov (1637) and holding it for five years. In 1641 the Turks sent against the fortress captured by the Cossaks a 200,000-strong force and about 300 ships. After a siege lasting three and a half months the Turks, without breaking the resistance of the Cossaks and sustaining heavy losses, were forced to raise it and evacuate the surviving troops. It was only a year later (1642) that the Cossacks voluntarily quit the fortress after first destroying its fortifications. They arrived at this decision by agreement with the Russian government seeking to avoid a major war with Turkey.

The victory of the Russian regular army and fleet won with the taking of Azov by Peter the Great in 1696 was a brilliant outcome of the two-century struggle of the Russians for the right to free navigation in the southern seas. Not only did Russia again emerge on the shores of the Sea of Azov as a result of this victory: the treaty with Turkey provided for the unhindered sailing of Russians into the Mediterranean.

An illustrious page in history was written by the first Archipelagean expedition of the Russian Baltic fleet in the Mediterranean (1770-74) under the command of Admiral G. A. Spiridov, undertaken to conduct major military-political actions against Turkey and also in support of the uprising of the Balkan peoples enslaved by the Turks. The Balkan squadron, consisting of 10 battleships and a number of other ships, overcoming enormous difficulties, was concentrated in the Mediterranean. It was set tasks considered completely insoluble. But the squadron brilliantly executed them. In a decisive engagement at Cesme (24-26 June 1770)[13] it destroyed the Turkish fleet on which Admiral G. A. Spiridov commanding the squadron reported: "All honour to the all-Russian fleet! . . . The enemy war . . . fleet was attacked, smashed, crushed, burnt, blown into the sky, sunk and reduced to ashes . . . and we ourselves became dominant over all the Archipelago".[14]

For several years the Russian squadron conducted military operations far from its own shores. It destroyed the Turkish fleet in engagements at Chios and Cesme, blockaded the Dardanelles, interrupted the sea communications of the Turks and made numerous landings, thereby diverting the enemy from the main northern Black Sea route. The squadron captured 20 islands of the Archipelago and a number of coastal towns including some on the coast of Syria. The Turks were under constant threat of a blow from the Russian fleet against Constantinople from the south.

[13] In the Cesme engagement the Turks lost all their ships—15 battleships, six frigates, 50 other vessels and 10,000 crewmen.

[14] *Combat Chronicle of the Russian Fleet*, p. 97 (in Russian), Moscow, Voenizdat, 1948.

The activity in the Mediterranean Sea of the Russian squadron which for several years maintained its fighting capacity with its own forces, and the brilliant victories won by it over the larger fleet of the enemy, were a remarkable example of the lengthy operations of a major sea unit totally cut off from its home bases. This detachment of the Russian fleet enhanced the authority of Russia in the international arena and attracted warm sympathy for the Russians from all the peoples of the Mediterranean.

The successful operations of the Russian army and fleet compelled the Turks to conclude a peace treaty, under which Russia acquired lands between the Bug and Dnieper, finally secured for herself the Azov Sea and an outlet from it to the Black Sea and also received the right of unhindered commercial navigation in the Black Sea with passage into the Mediterranean. The Crimea was recognized as a state independent of Turkey.

Using the power of her fleet, Russia, without a war, in 1783 finally took over the Crimea where the main base of the Black Sea Fleet was set up—Sevastopol. However, the struggle in the southern seas did not end there.

The rapid political emergence of Russia became for states hostile to her a reason to support Turkey in its attempts to make the Russians give up their acquisitions on the coast of the Black Sea by military force. Another country to be drawn into the war against Russia was Sweden, whose rulers still cherished hopes of winning back the lands around the Baltic.

In August 1787 Turkey began military operations, drawing the Russian forces to the southern borders of the state. Taking advantage of the fact that, apart from the Baltic Fleet, there were almost no armed forces in the Petersburg area, Sweden in the summer of 1788 declared war on Russia, brought her fleet into the eastern part of the Gulf of Finland and placed the capital of Russia in a critical position. The main burden of the war with Sweden fell on the Baltic Fleet, which successfully defended our shores, and, after a number of victories, crushed and drove off the Swedish fleet and exerted a decisive influence on the outcome of the battles on the territory of Finland. Obviously, with no Russian fleet here the land forces alone, because of their insufficient numbers, could not have dealt with the Swedes so quickly.

The foreign powers supporting Turkey and Sweden in this war passed from diplomatic pressure to threats. England moved her fleet into the Black and Baltic Seas, Prussia concentrated troops at the Russian border. But the military operations in the South went Russia's way. A strong detachment of the Turkish fleet arriving in Ochakov to support her army was crushed by the Liman flotilla, so enabling the Russian troops to capture Ochakov. The Turkish battle fleet suffered a defeat at the hands of the Black Sea fleet at Kerch and then was finally crushed at Cape Kaliakria. Thanks to the able operations of the Black Sea fleet under the command of the outstanding Admiral of the Fleet F. F. Ushakov, the Turkish fleet was expelled from the Black Sea and its army, deprived of support from the sea, at the end of 1791 ceased resistance. In 1792 a peace treaty was concluded at Jassy, under which the coasts of the Black Sea from the Dnester to Novorossisk went to Russia.

At the end of the eighteenth and beginning of the nineteenth centuries the international situation was extremely complex. Following the bourgeois revolution France waged a fierce struggle against England, which had for long been a capitalist country and had seized the main colonial regions of the world. A political struggle was going on between France and Russia seeking to make use of the legacy of the German empire by that time in decline. In this period the only question was whether the small German states would form a Rhine alliance with France or Russia. Such a complex situation led to repeated sharp turns in the policy of the major countries of Europe and to change in the direction of their principal war efforts.

In 1798-1800 Russia, in alliance with England, Austria and Turkey, conducted military operations against France. Units of the Russian army under the command of the outstanding army leader A. V. Suvorov displayed wonders of heroism in distant Switzerland and northern Italy. The Russian squadron in the Mediterranean under the command of Ushakov freed from French ownership the Ionian Islands, from where it took an active part in driving out the French from Italy. One of the most brilliant exploits of the fleet was the taking after a three-month siege of the strong Corfu fortress. Known to history are the impassioned words of Suvorov who, learning of this, declared: "Our great Peter lives! What he said on the defeat in 1714 of the Swedish fleet . . .—Nature made Russia unique, it has no rival—this we now see. Hurrah! To the Russian fleet . . . I now ask myself: Why was I not at Corfu even as a midshipman?"[15]

For comparison we would recall that at the same time the English Fleet under the command of Admiral Nelson was in the second year of laying siege to the weaker La Valetta fortress on the island of Malta and could not take it.

The political implications of the victories of the Russian fleet in the Mediterranean Sea were very considerable. Napoleon attached great importance to the Ionian Islands. In his view, they represented the most important starting point for the development of military operations against Egypt, the Balkans, Constantinople and the south of Russia. Therefore, the expulsion of the French by Ushakov's squadron from the Ionian Archipelago radically altered the position in the Mediterranean Sea. The Russian fleet showed itself to be a most potent instrument of foreign policy. Its operations brought into the orbit of Russia's influence Italy, Sardinia and even Tunis. The fleet, working together with the army, took a decisive part in the liberation of Naples and Rome.

The flourishing of naval art in Russia in the second half of the eighteenth century coincided with the tempestuous development of the whole of Russian military art. The Russian army, thanks to Suvorov, greatly added to their famous fighting traditions. But the credit for such service in the fleet goes to Ushakov.

Only in the Soviet period was Admiral Ushakov worthily appraised and his name borne aloft. Western European and American historians even now taking their cue from the American Mahan continue to downgrade Ushakov, considering that he was only a dutiful pupil of Nelson and thanks to this successful. However, mere comparison[16] of the dates of major engagements carried out

[15] *History of the Russian Army and Fleet*, p. 57 (in Russian), Moscow, Obrazovanic, 1913.
[16] The main victories of Admiral Ushakov were won on the Island of Phidonis in 1788, at the Strait of Kerch and at Tendra in 1790, at Cape Kaliakria in 1791 and the taking of Corfu in 1799. The victories of Admiral Nelson refer to later dates: at St. Vincent in 1797, in Aboukir Bay in 1789 and at Trafalgar in 1805.

under the direction of the two celebrated admirals shows that Ushakov scored the principal sea victories well before Nelson was able to display his talents as a commander of the fleet.

After the departure of the main forces of Ushakov's squadron some of the forces of the fleet and marines were left in the Mediterranean to ensure the security of the Ionian Islands. And only after several years did Russia, in order to counter new attempts by the French to make grabs in the Balkans, and also in order to protect the Ionian Islands as bases of the Russian fleet in the Mediterranean, again begin to concentrate here the forces of the fleet under the command of Admiral D. N. Senyavin (Second Archipelagean Expedition) who had to cope with a very complex and fast-changing military-political situation.

At the end of 1806, Turkey, urged on by Napoleon, declared war on Russia; this completely changed the tasks of the Russian Mediterranean squadron whose main goal had become the capture of Constantinople by a strike from the south. This task had to be solved jointly with the allied English fleet. However, the true intentions of England were not to allow the capture by the Russians of the Black Sea straits and to consolidate their dominion in the Mediterranean Sea. Under the influence of the provocative operations of the English, D. N. Senyavin was forced to confine himself to a blockade of the Dardanelles. Yet in the course of the military operations in the battle of the Dardanelles and in the Athos engagement he smashed the Turkish fleet.

While the Russian Fleet was achieving brilliant victories in the Aegean Sea, on the Niemen, peace negotiations were in progress between Napoleon and Czar Alexander I. One week after the Athos engagement the Treaty of Tilsit was signed (25 June 1807) which sharply changed the foreign policy of the Czarist government, concluding an alliance with Napoleon. As a result, Russia, before the invasion of the French, gained a respite bought at an extremely high price. The territorial gains of Napoleon in Western Europe were recognized, Russia undertook to take part in the continental blockade of England and to begin war with her, to cede to France and Turkey all the strategic positions in the Mediterranean Sea gained by the Russian fleet, to pull out of the Mediterranean all Russian ships and place the squadron at the complete disposal of France.

This sharp turn in the foreign policy of Russia proved extremely harsh for the Russian Mediterranean squadron. Only in August 1809 did some of the crew of the squadron return home.

It was only 20 years later, in 1827, that the Russian squadron went back to the Mediterranean and again with the beneficial mission of providing aid, this time to the Greek people. The Russian squadron of Admiral Gaiden together with the English and French squadrons had to force the Turkish occupation forces in Greece to cease the extermination of the Greek population fighting for national independence. The joint operations of the allied fleets ended in the famous Navarin engagement (October 1827) in which the more numerous Turkish fleet was completely crushed.

After the Navarino engagement a Russian squadron remained in the Mediterranean under the command of Admiral Rikord, which in the 1828–29 Russo-Turkish war successfully solved the task of a tight blockade of the Dardanelles and the Turkish coast. Later, although the Russian fleet did not engage in military operations in the Mediterranean, its ships and whole squadrons regularly visited this area.

Thus, the Mediterranean Sea from ancient times has been of immense economic and strategic importance to Russia. Through it operated the trade and cultural ties with the Mediterranean and other countries of the world. Here over a long period lay the most important line of defence of Russia from attack by enemies from the south.

Even greater defence significance for our motherland has been assumed by the Mediterranean Sea in modern conditions: now the possibilities of the imperialist aggressors for attacking the Soviet Union directly from this area have enormously grown in connection with the fact that here is permanently stationed the US Sixth Fleet with its aircraft carriers and atomic submarine missile carriers.

The Russian fleet in the period of the industrial revolution

By the end of the Napoleonic wars the Russian fleet had entered a difficult period. This was one of the gloomiest epochs in its history, the result of the failure of the Czarist rulers to understand the importance of the fleet in the fate of Russia. Ungifted leaders were put in charge of the fleet, such as Admiral Chichagov who considered the fleet as a burdensome luxury unnecessary for the state. His successors—the reactionary French emigré, the Marquis de Traverse and the German von Müller—continued the destruction of the fleet. The Decembrist Shteingel thus characterized the then existing state of the fleet: "... the finest creation of Peter the Great has been utterly destroyed by the Marquis de Traverse".[17]

The ships virtually did not put to sea. The sailors were used for ancillary duties. Russian admirals were replaced by foreigners. There was wholesale embezzlement. The well-known Russian Admiral V. M. Golovnin wrote: "... if rotten, scantily and poorly-armed ships and senile, infirm fleet commanders without knowledge of the sea and its spirit, inexperienced captains and officers and ploughmen, called sailors, and pressed into ship crews. can make up a fleet, then we have one."[18]

Against the background of the general decline of Russia's sea power the positive phenomena in the activity of the fleet were even more distinctly set off, such as the round-the-world expeditions undertaken on the initiative of leading naval officers, including the entire pleiad of Decembrist seamen. The crews of the expeditionary ships preserved the best traditions of the Russian fleet. From this environment emerged the celebrated fleet commanders M. P. Lazarev, P. S. Nakhimov, V. A. Kornilov and others.

No small role in the preservation of fleet traditions was played by the activity of seafarers and industrialists in the Aleutians, the Kurile Islands and the

[17] From letters and notes of the Decembrists, A. K. Borazdin (Ed), p. 61 (in Russian), St. Petersburg, 1906.
[18] Quoted from an article by G. Ye. Pavlov 'The Decembrist Nikolai Bestuzhev and his Experience of the History of the Russian Fleet', in N. A. Bestuzhev, *Experience of the History of the Russian Fleet*, p. 9 (in Russian), Leningrad, Sudpromgiz, 1961.

western coasts of North America. Naval ships under the general guidance of the industrialists Shelekov, Baranov and others, perseveringly took control of the coast of North America and of islands from Alaska to St. Elias Cape. However, the further fate of these lands was decided in advance; the Czarist government did not attach due significance to the newly acquired regions which it was impossible to hold without creating strong naval forces in the northern part of the Pacific Ocean.

The time drew nearer for payment for the failure of Czarism to grasp the importance of the fleet in the country's development, and of its under-estimation as an instrument of policy and as an armed force. The 1853-56 Crimean War was approaching. England and France continued the policy of pushing Russia out of the Mediterranean and sought to take into their own hands the economy and finances of Turkey, which itself cherished the hope of regaining its domination of the northern shores of the Black Sea.

An important role in this war was to be played by the fleets since the main adversaries (the Anglo-French and the Russians) were separated by large distances which could be covered only with the aid of the fleet.

The war took place in the period of the industrial revolution which began in the capitalist countries of Western Europe, where heavy industry very rapidly developed bringing a technical revolution in military matters. For navies this was the period of the transition from the sailing to the steamship with metal-armoured hull, screw propeller and powerful armament.

The English and French with general superiority over the Russian fleet in battleships and frigates, possessing more than twice as many, had more than ten times as many steamships. Moreover, all the Russian steamships were paddle-ships. The technical backwardness of the Russian fleet meant that it had to adopt a defensive and not an active combat posture which was in conflict with the essence of a most mobile branch of power intended to seek out and destroy the enemy at sea.

The chief theatre of the war became the Black Sea and the central event of the whole war was the eleven-month-long heroic defence of Sevastopol. The war began with the Sinope battle in which the Turkish fleet was destroyed. This event is inscribed in gold letters in the book of fame of the Russian fleet. However, with the entry of the Anglo-French fleet into the Black Sea, the technically backward and weak Russian Black Sea fleet was not destined to continue the struggle at sea. The Russian command decided to use the weapons and crew of the fleet for the direct defence of Sevastopol on land.

The enemy with superior sea forces embarked on a geographical expansion of the war. Combined Anglo-French squadrons sailed into the Gulf of Finland where they met the stubborn resistance of the weaker Russian sea forces, yet able to ward off the attack on St. Petersburg.

In the White Sea the Anglo-French engaged in "hit-and-run attacks" on Russian and Lopar villages and in the destruction of the meagre property of poor fishermen"[19] and, of course, did not achieve any important goal. In August 1854, an Anglo-French squadron approached Petropavlovsk-Kamchatka which was defended only by two ships and a small garrison. How-

[19] K. Marx and F. Engels, *Works,* 2nd ed., Vol. 11, p. 522 (in Russian).

ever, in an unequal fight the Russians displayed high resolution and were victorious, forcing the allied squadron to beat an inglorious retreat.

Despite the heroism shown by the Russians in this war, backward Czarist Russia sustained a heavy defeat. The Crimean War, costing the warring countries "an incalculable sum and over a million human lives",[20] ended with the conclusion of a peace treaty in Paris on 30 March 1856. Russia had to cede the mouth of the Danube and part of southern Bessarabia, and give up its protectorate over the Danube principalities. The harshest condition of the treaty was the ban on Russia having a naval fleet in the Black Sea. This circumstance once again emphasized the special importance attached to the fleet in international relations. Russia was pushed even further back from achieving the cherished goal of her policy—unimpeded access to the Mediterranean Sea.

The Crimean War was an exceptionally important turning-point followed by major shifts in the socio-economic life of Russia. The country entered on the path of developing capitalism and healing the wounds inflicted by the war.

In 1871, Russia secured the lifting of the humiliating ban on having a fleet in the Black Sea. However, while obtaining this right, Czarism did not change its attitude to the fleet, did not understand the need for it and did not take resolute measures to restore the sea power of Russia. Yet, as a result of the 1870-71 Franco-Prussian War, favourable conditions were created for solving contentious questions with Turkey by military means. Using the situation created, Russia in 1877 declared war on Turkey.

By the start of that war the Black Sea Fleet was in a very sorry state. Apart from two weak and clumsy battleships, so-called Popov ships, it included only a few small obsolete ships. Necessity demanded the arming and use in military operations of the comparatively fast steamers of the commercial fleet and also steam cutters and sloops. On these ships Russian seamen under the direction of young and vigorous commanders waged successful combat operations and were able to paralyse the activity of the Turkish battleships.

The Russian army was put through severe trials, but as a result of a series of heroic victories it drew near to Constantinople. Just a little more effort and the prolonged struggle for an outlet to the Mediterranean would have been successfully completed. However, when the Russian troops were at the walls of Constantinople an English squadron appeared in the Straits. Its impact proved really magical. The independence of the policy of Russian Czarism wavered in the face of threats from England and Austria, personified in this squadron. Russia in substance not having a fleet to protect the Black Sea coast and surrounding regions was forced to yield. She again had to pay for the fact that Czarist leaders, under-estimating the importance of the fleet in international relations and wars, obstinately refused to strengthen the sea power of Russia.

The peace treaty was submitted for examination to an international congress in Berlin (1878). The ruling adopted by the congress again pushed Russia away from outlets to the Mediterranean and had a very adverse effect on the position of the Slav peoples of the Balkan peninsula. The territory of Bulgaria was more than halved and that of Montenegro considerably reduced. As against this,

[20] *Ibid.,* Vol. 22, p. 39.

non-belligerent Austro-Hungary received the right to Bosnia and Herzegovina and England to Cyprus.

And although as a result of the war the strategic position of Russia somewhat improved, the advantages accruing to her under this peace treaty in no way matched the efforts she had made. And this merely because she did not have a strong fleet.

The Berlin congress became the starting-point for a new alignment of forces in Europe. It laid the foundation for the division of the major powers into two hostile groupings: Russia and France against Germany and Austro-Hungary. England and the US acted as arbiters. The question of the right gained by Russia to unhindered outlets to the Mediterranean became much more complicated, was put off for an indefinite period and could now find a solution only in the arena of world war.

For over a hundred years the most important axial line of the policy of Russia in the south was the constant endeavour to achieve a free outlet to the Mediterranean. This promised not only major commercial-economic advantages but the strengthening of its influence on the Balkan and Asia Minor peninsulas. And while the Black Sea Straits were in the hands of a long-since weakened Turkey, such a task could be considered within the reach of Russia only if other powers kept out of the struggle. Therefore, whenever the main European states were deflected in other directions, Russia again returned to the principal goal of her policy in the south, seeking to achieve freedom of trade and shipping in the Mediterranean.

The wars waged here extended over some thirty years and took millions of human lives, but Russia was able to secure herself only on the northern and eastern parts of the Black Sea shores. She could not move closer to her goal despite the victory of the Russian forces.

In the struggle for outlets to the southern seas Russian Czarism often turned out to be bankrupt in the final periods of a war, when there was particular need for a naval force on which an independent policy could rest to make the enemy and the states supporting him agree to peace conditions advantageous to Russia. One of the strongest land powers in the world, Russia possessed to the south a fleet only strong enough to take on the Turkish Fleet. But as soon as other powers came into a war, chiefly threatening with sea power, Russia was forced to give way and sometimes sustained defeats, lost the independence of her policy and came under the dictation of the Western European powers.

In this connection it must be stressed that Peter the Great could not have so consistently pursued the policy of securing for Russia the shores of the Baltic Sea, without submitting to the demands and threats of other powers backed by demonstrations of sea force, if by then a powerful navy, occupying second place in the world, had not been in existence.

Thus, for over a century of the fight for outlets to the southern seas, the relative weakness of the Russian fleet was one of the most important causes of the failure to achieve this goal.

Our brief persual of the role of the fleet in the history of Russia, in her emergence and economic development, leads to the main conclusion: at all stages of the life of the country her armed forces needed a powerful navy, matching the interests of a world power.

The Fleets in the Wars of the End of the Nineteenth and Beginning of the Twentieth Centuries

At the end of the nineteenth and the beginning of the twentieth centuries capitalism passed into the imperialist stage. "Imperialism, as a higher stage of the capitalism of America and Europe and then Asia was fully in being by 1898-1914. The Spanish-American (1898), Anglo-Boer (1899-1902), Russo-Japanese (1904-5) Wars and the economic crisis in Europe in 1900 are the main historical landmarks of the new epoch of world history".[21]

By that time the main capitalist countries, chiefly with the aid of their fleets, had divided nearly all the territory of the globe. The countries first on the path of capitalist development and possessing strong fleets were able to capture the lion's share of these territories. Thus, for example, England, beginning colonial seizures as far back as 1583 (Newfoundland), over three hundred years ably using in peacetime and in war the might of her fleet by various ways and means, managed by the end of the nineteenth century to take possession of colonies over ninety times the size of the metropolitan country.

The centre of the struggle to divide and redivide the world shifted to the Pacific Ocean, on whose shores lay a still undivided and weak China. Here were sent squadrons of the fleets for executing the expansionist ambitions of the main imperialist powers. The first to begin the plunder of the Chinese people were the English and French imperialists followed by younger predators—USA, Germany and Japan. Russian Czarism, which was military-feudal imperialism with all its characteristic qualities (barbarity, despotism, coercion, unlimited exploitation of the multi-national population of the country and a policy of grab in relation to neighbouring countries), also joined in the war.

Irreconcilable contradiction between the colonizers engendered a series of conflicts and wars in the Far East in which the navies continued to be the main means of achieving the political ends of the imperialist states.

Sino-Japanese War

The industrial development of Japan after the 1863 bourgeois revolution soon enabled her to create a navy, by using which Japanese imperialism concentrated its aggressive pursuits on the seizure of the territories of China which was an economically backward state with a very weak fleet.

In 1894 Japan, supported by the USA and England, and without declaring war, attacked China and since the enemies were separated by sea, this largely determined the most important role of the navies in the war.

Japan, able with the aid of the fleet to prevent China from concentrating seaborne troops in Korea, invaded southern Manchuria. Then the army, landed again by the fleet on the coast of the Yellow Sea in the region of Bitseivo and Talien Wan, with the co-operation of the fleet captured the Liaotung peninsula with the main Chinese naval base of Port Arthur.

[21] V. I. Lenin, *Complete Collected Works* (in Russian), Vol. 30, p. 164.

Japan moved from the islands to the Asian mainland and the major countries of the world saw this as a potential threat to their expansion. The peace treaty between Japan and China concluded in April 1895 was opposed by Russia, Germany and France possessing imposing sea forces capable of threatening the Japanese island state. Japan had to give up the Liaotung peninsula and Port Arthur.

The problems of the new Far East node of the contradictions of imperialism came to the fore in world politics. The Sino-Japanese war demonstrated the particularly important role of the fleets in achieving the political aims of states in the conditions of more complicated struggle for the redivision of the world.

Spanish-American War

By the end of the nineteenth century the policy of the USA had assumed all the features peculiar to an imperialist power. America sought for itself its first major victim. The nearest and most convenient object of its aggressive pursuits proved to be the Spanish colonies situated in the Caribbean Sea and also the islands of the Philippines and Guam. These islands were to ensure the further expansion of the USA in Asia. At the first convenient occasion in 1898 the Americans launched a war. The main role in the war was assigned to the fleet whose forces were expected to deliver decisive blows primarily at the Spanish fleet depriving the enemy of the possibility of receiving reinforcements by sea from Spain. Therefore, in preparing for war they created a navy surpassing the fleet of backward royal Spain. The theatres of the war were the Caribbean and the western Pacific.

Exploiting their superiority at sea the Americans landed on Cuba. When the West Indies squadron of Spain attempted to break out of Santiago into the ocean, the technically more sophisticated American ships smashed it. The Spanish garrison of Santiago, deprived of the support of the fleet, soon capitulated. The struggle in the Caribbean Sea was virtually over.

The victory in the Philippines region also cost the Americans little. The weak Asian squadron of the Spaniards was destroyed in Manila Bay. The US marines without a fight moved into the capital of the Philippines (Manila), not allowing the true victors there—the Filipino insurgents whose operations beforehand had freed the islands of the archipelago of Spanish troops.

Under the peace treaty Cuba, Puerto Rico, Guam and the Philippines became American colonies. The USA occupied a dominant place in the Caribbean, secured itself in the Western hemisphere and gained advantageous positions in the Pacific Ocean, at the approaches to China.

The victory of the USA over backward Spain was the direct result of the superiority of the Americans at sea. The fleets in this war played a most important and decisive role. After the Spanish-American War came a long period in the USA of unrestrained naval arms build-up. The fleet and the marines moved into first place in the US arms system.

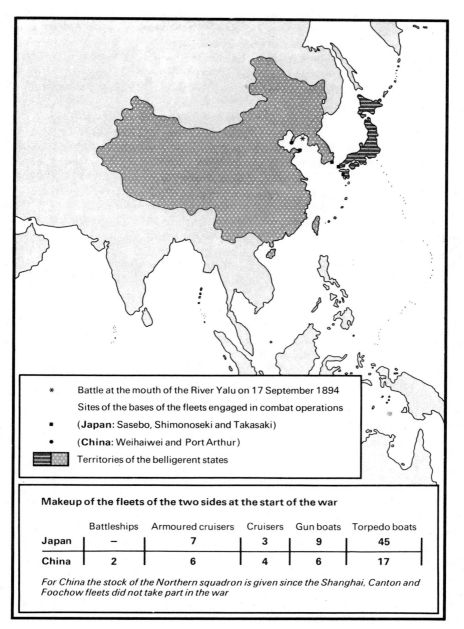

* Battle at the mouth of the River Yalu on 17 September 1894

Sites of the bases of the fleets engaged in combat operations

■ (**Japan**: Sasebo, Shimonoseki and Takasaki)

• (**China**: Weihaiwei and Port Arthur)

Territories of the belligerent states

Makeup of the fleets of the two sides at the start of the war

	Battleships	Armoured cruisers	Cruisers	Gun boats	Torpedo boats
Japan	–	7	3	9	45
China	2	6	4	6	17

For China the stock of the Northern squadron is given since the Shanghai, Canton and Foochow fleets did not take part in the war

Fig. 6. Sino-Japanese War of 1894-95

Role of the fleets in the Russo-Japanese War

The contradictions in the Far East were fraught with new wars. A war between Japan and Russia ripened. The attack by Russia together with France and Germany on the terms of the Sino-Japanese peace treaty paved the way for an open political struggle between Russia and Japan. The capture in 1897 by the Russian fleet and troops of the Kwantung region and the setting up of the base of the Russian Pacific squadron in Port Arthur further exacerbated the situation.

In connection with the so-called Boxer Uprising in 1900, troops were sent into China by all the main imperialist competitors: England, Japan, USA, Germany, France and Russia. From then on, the contradictions between these imperialist states became even sharper.

After the occupation by Russia of Manchuria, the main issue of the Far East policy of England, Japan and the USA became the ousting of Russia from the regions she held and the inclusion of them in their own possessions. Japan, egged on by England and the USA, openly worked for a war against Russia and stepped up preparations for it. In 1902, Japan and England signed a treaty directed against Russia. In it the allies specially undertook to keep a fleet stronger than the Russians in Far Eastern waters. This clearly pointed to the intention of the enemies of Russia to assign to the fleet a prime role in the impending armed clash.

The USA sought to whip up a war between Japan and Russia in the hope that they would weaken each other, primarily their fleets, so allowing the Americans to seize key positions in the Pacific Ocean and China. The US President warned the governments of France and Germany that America would take Japan's side if they gave any assistance to Russia. Thus, Russia was alone against a strong island power the basis of whose strategic force was a navy, a power supported by an alliance and the support of at least two of the largest maritime states in the world—England and the USA—whose principles of using the fleets for solving military-political tasks were well known. These circumstances were to determine the direction of the preparations of the conflicting parties for a possible war. The different approach to the preparation of the armed forces of the two sides was a clear expression of the far-sightedness of the political leaders of Japan and the absence of this quality in the statesmen of Czarist Russia.

The Japanese Government paid close attention to the building of a powerful fleet, allocating to it the bulk of the state budget and the war indemnities received from China following the Sino-Japanese war. The USA and England widely subsidized Japan and, in fact, were its arsenal. British shipyards built nearly all the Japanese armour-plated ships, possessing the best tactical specification and arms of the times. Japan under the guidance of German instructors also created a large army for invading the mainland. Naval and army officers had experience of war in China and were very familiar with the peculiarities of that theatre of war.

A different picture was presented by the preparations of Czarist Russia for the approaching war. The ruling circles of Russia, while realizing that their Far-Eastern ambitions could be realized only by war, failed to take the necessary vigorous and precautionary measures. The influence of this inactivity on the preparedness for war was further heightened by the fact that the strategic situation in the Far East was not in Russia's favour—the Siberian and Chinese Eastern railways still did not have enough capacity to ensure the uninterrupted and rapid concentration and supply of Russian troops in the theatre and the armed forces of Russia present in the Far-Eastern theatre were not ready for war, particularly not the Pacific fleet, greatly inferior to the Japanese fleet as Table 10 shows.

The short-sighted Russian Command and the Czar failed to grasp the seriousness of the situation in the Far East and the role of the fleet in the coming war. Therefore, timely measures to strengthen the Pacific Fleet by drawing on the sea forces of the Baltic and Black Seas were not taken. Moreover, the Russian Pacific Fleet was scattered in different seas. In the Yellow Sea, which was the main sea theatre, the fleet had only eight armour-plated ships.

The construction of the fleet's bases in the Pacific Ocean was far from complete and therefore Port Arthur constituted neither a sufficiently reliable fortress nor an equipped naval base capable of withstanding the blows of the enemy and of being a secure ship base.

TABLE 10
Composition of the Forces of the
Russian and Japanese Fleets in the
Far East at the Beginning of the
Russo/Japanese War*

Classes of ships	Russia	Japan
Squadron battleships	7	6
Armoured cruisers	4	8
Cruisers	7	12
Destroyers and torpedo boats	37	47

* See: *History of Naval Art,* p. 82 (in Russian), Moscow, Voenizdat, 1969.

Thus, by the beginning of 1904, fundamentally isolated, not ready for war and disposing of a weak navy in the Far East, Russia stood face to face with the whole might of international monopoly capital which had put Japan forward as its shock-troop representative.

The most important strategic goal in the war, according to Japanese plans, was the gaining of dominance at sea which was supposed to be attained by a sudden attack on Russia's Pacific Fleet and the destruction of the Port Arthur squadron and the Russian shore-based ships in Korea and China. Then the successive landing of armies was planned on the Liaotung peninsula and capture of Port Arthur by crushing the main grouping of the Russian forces in southern Manchuria, followed by the seizure of the whole of Manchuria and the Ussurisk and Amur regions.

Taking advantage of the favourable international situation and the general military unpreparedness of Czarist Russia, Japan on 9 February 1904 unleashed a war enjoying superiority in quality and numbers at sea over the

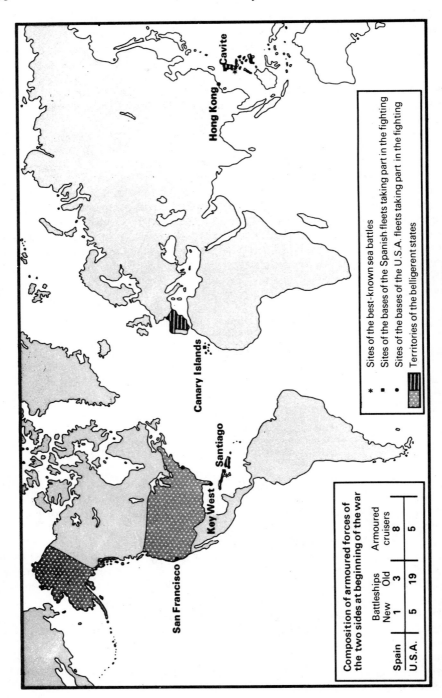

Composition of armoured forces of the two sides at beginning of the war			
	Battleships		Armoured cruisers
	New	Old	
Spain	1	3	8
U.S.A.	5	19	5

Sites of the best-known sea battles

Sites of the bases of the Spanish fleets taking part in the fighting

Sites of the bases of the U.S.A. fleets taking part in the fighting

Territories of the belligerent states

Cavite

Hong Kong

Canary Islands

San Francisco

Key West

Santiago

Fig. 7.   Spanish–American War of 1898

Russian fleet. Moreover, the bases of the Japanese fleet ensured its dominance in the lines of transport of troops to the continent. The Japanese army also outnumbered the Russian land forces and this ratio could not be changed in a short time in Russia's favour because of poor transport facilities.

The war began with a sudden attack by the Japanese fleet on the Russian sea forces in Port Arthur and Chemulpo, which, though greatly weakening the Russian squadron, still did not lead to domination by the enemy at sea.

Was this attack really sudden? Was there not enough information on the preparations of the Japanese for war?

The repeated warnings of the Russian naval agent in Japan on the operations of its fleet gave every reason to expect a strike. Early in January he reported that Japan was calling up reservists, chartering steamships capable of shipping two divisions of troops, had stopped long-distance steamship journeys and that the Japanese fleet was moving into Korea. On 18 January the agent reported the laying of defensive minefields, that the scale of the preparations indicated the wide plans of Japan and on 24 January telegraphed on the general mobilization in Japan. But the Czarist government turned a blind eye to all these warnings and the war hit the Russian ships out of the blue.

When the war had started the Czar appointed as Fleet Commander in the Pacific Ocean Vice-Admiral S. O. Makarov who knew the enemy and the theatre of military operations well and was a recognized authority in sea tactics. However, the Czarist governor in the Far East and the Fleet Commander had opposed views on the role of the fleet in war and also the use of its forces in the conditions pertaining. Makarov's proposals on the active operations of the fleet and the raising of its battle readiness encountered obstacles. The ships for a good part of the time were at their bases and did not conduct reconnoitering operations nor active struggle against sea shipments of the Japanese. After the death (14 April 1904) of the Fleet Commander on the flagship *Petropavlovsk,* blown up on mines, the active operations of the Port Arthur squadron ceased.

The Russian army, though greatly reinforced, under the blows of the Japanese retreated to the north and effective measures were necessary to weaken the thrust of the Japanese. The real force for this could only be a fleet capable of interrupting or limiting the flow of seaborne reinforcements for the Japanese army and of threatening its islands. This was understood too late.

On 24 August 1904 the belated decision was taken to despatch from the Baltic Sea a second Pacific squadron. Its timely linking with the Port Arthur squadron could have radically altered the situation in the whole theatre of operations in favour of Russia, but the time for this was allowed to go by.

Indeed, if such measures had been taken earlier, the balance of forces in the Far East would have been different (Table 11).

The Japanese command, using the favourable conditions created at sea, concentrated the main efforts on Port Arthur. It sought to break the resistance of its defenders and destroy the squadron based there even before the arrival of reinforcements from Europe. The siege grouping of the Japanese was strengthened and a fierce assault on the fortifications of Port Arthur was mounted.

Refraining from using the still quite powerful forces of the fleet directly intended for battle at sea, where through its operations it could have given the greatest aid both to besieged Port Arthur and all the Russian forces in Man-churia, the incompetent Russian war chiefs decided to disarm the ships and use their arms and crews directly in the land defence of the fortress without realizing that the existing conditions radically differed from the position at Sevastopol in 1854-55, where such a decision was fully justified. The Port Arthur garrison fought heroically for eight months. Although the possibilities of defending the fortress were not fully exhausted, on 2 January 1905 it was handed over to the Japanese undefeated. And although the fall of Port Arthur is considered a turning point in the course of the war, largely pre-determining its outcome, in fact the break came with the arrest of the active operations of the Russian fleet, i.e. after the first stage of the struggle for domination at sea had ended in the defeat of the Russians.

TABLE 11
Composition of Forces of the Fleets in the Event of the Timely Arrival of the
Second Pacific Squadron in the Far East

Classes of ships	Russia			Japan
	Port Arthur and Vladivostok squadrons	Second Pacific Squadron	Total	
Squadron battleships	7	8	15	8
Armoured cruisers	4	1	5	8
Coastal defence armour-plated ships	–	3	3	–
Total of armour-plated ships	11	12	23	16
Cruisers	7	8	15	15
Destroyers and torpedo boats	37	9	46	63

Note. The increase in the number of ships as compared with the pre-war period was achieved by Japan essentially by using the shipbuilding industry of England and Anglo-American credits.

It was not until 15 October 1904 that the second Pacific squadron under the command of Rozhestvensky began to move from the Baltic to the Far East. The history of the Russian fleet and indeed of other fleets still did not know of such a distant and long movement of a huge fleet consisting of a variety of ships, some of which were not fully seaworthy, with no experience of combined long-distance oceanic travel. Over the entire route the squadron did not have a single base of its own for resting the crew, for repair and supply. Most of the shores along which it passed belonged to hostile England. As it moved away from its Western bases the Russian squadron was faced with the increased danger of sudden encounters with the enemy's fleet, which made the passage extremely complicated. However, the heroism and high sea qualities of the Russian seamen made it possible to overcome all difficulties.

As the squadron was standing off the shores of Madagascar, Petersburg learned of the fall of Port Arthur and the destruction of its squadron. But the Czar and his entourage saw in the second Pacific squadron the last hope of victory in the war and did not alter the tasks assigned to it.

Completing a matchless, almost eight-month passage without losing a ship, the Russian squadron on 14 May 1905 entered the Korean Straits. Waiting for it here was the Japanese fleet, more sophisticated and long ready for battle and relying on a whole system of nearby bases. The outcome of the Tsushima engagement was decided in advance. Despite the heroism of the men valiantly fighting in the Tsushima battle, the second Pacific squadron suffered a heavy defeat because the enemy surpassed it primarily in weapons and fighting technique. Most of the Russian ships were destroyed in the battle and some were interned in foreign ports.

The question of domination at sea was finally solved in favour of the Japanese. Lenin wrote: "The Russian navy was finally destroyed. The war was irredeemably lost . . . . We are faced not only with a military defeat but also the complete military bankruptcy of the autocracy".[22]

The Russo-Japanese war ended with this crushing of the Czarist fleet. The government became convinced that it was pointless to continue the war, and, faced with an incipient revolution, seeing it as a harbinger of the complete collapse of the autocracy, brought the war to an end. Japan had also completely exhausted its forces and had to appeal to the American President to mediate.

State, economic, political and military backwardness, the complete misunderstanding by Czarism of the importance of sea power for Russia, which were the basic causes of the weakness of the fleet, led Czarism to military defeat. The true victors in this war turned out to be the imperialists of the USA, England and Germany for their rivals in the Far East and the Pacific were greatly weakened and burdened with debts.

Under the Portsmouth Peace Treaty, Japan received the right to lease the Kwantung region with Port Arthur and approaches, to it went the southern part of the Manchurian railway, the southern part of Sakhalin and the preferential rights of Japan in Korea were recognized.

As a result of the severe lessons of the war, influential Russian society began to understand better the importance of the fleet in modern warfare and encouraged the Czarist government to set about the quickest rebuilding of the fleet. The building of the fleet attracted the greatest Russian shipbuilders: A. N. Krylov, V. V. Konstantinov, N. I. Kuteinikov, I. G. Bubnov and others. But as shown by subsequent events, the Czarist rulers remained true to type and did not change their attitude to the fleet. Its construction continued to remain essentially based on its prestige value to the state, ignoring the need for Russia to possess sea power. Therefore, the construction of the fleet was of a chance character not pursuing specifically defined tasks but only fitting its forces to the forces of foreign fleets; hence the slavish imitation of foreigners in the types of ships often imperfect and obsolete. There was a complete failure to allow for the conditions in which the ships must operate and also the special requirements peculiar solely to Russia for the building of the fleet, stemming from her geographical position. The most important of these was the potential need for inter-theatre manoeuvre by the forces because of the separation of the sea theatres. It was necessary to take into account the absence of possessions and sea routes between the separate theatres equipped with base sites, which was

[22]V. I. Lenin, *Complete Collected Works,* Vol. 10, p. 252 (in Russian).

largely the result of the neglect by Czarism of securing for Russia a whole number of the islands and overseas territories discovered by Russian seafarers. We would recall, in passing, that the main cause of the loss of these territories was the ingrained misunderstanding of the importance for Russia of sea power. Russia was forced to create in each sea separate fleets which, as a rule, were weaker than the fleets of potential enemies in any given theatre. Obviously, the solution of the problem of the inter-theatre manoeuvre by the naval forces called for the building of ships with a long operating range and also an exceptional strategic farsightedness of the leadership to ensure the timely concentration of forces in the necessary theatre. There can be no doubt that, had Rozhestvensky's squadron been transferred to the Far East before the start of military operations or even before the fall of Port Arthur, the war would either have been put off or its course considerably changed.

The history of the wars which Russia waged convincingly shows that, whenever the Czarist rulers did not pay sufficient attention to the development of the fleet and keeping it up to date, Russia either suffered defeats in wars or her policy in peacetime did not achieve what it was intended to achieve.

The Fleets in the First World War

The unevenness of the economic and political development of the imperialist states embittered the struggle for the redivision of the world and brought to the fore a new and even graver war.

Political preparations for the forthcoming war had already long been in hand. The imperialist countries were split into two hostile groupings: the Central European alliance headed by Germany, and the Triple Entente headed by England. The approaching war could only be a world, imperialist war. In parallel went the process of accelerated preparations of the armed forces. Special attention was paid to the careful analysis of the experience of the Russo-Japanese war which had seen the largest sea engagements involving the most sophisticated ways of fighting at sea. That war showed that the importance of the fleets in military operations had markedly increased. This fundamental conclusion was accepted by nearly all the principal imperialist states, at once embarking on the construction of ships with reference to the experience of the Russo-Japanese war.

Another conclusion was the recognition of the dominant role of heavy armour-plated armed ships in fighting at sea. The efforts of all the maritime powers in preparing for the First World War were accordingly directed at creating surface fleets and also at working out ways of making the guns a match for armour-plated squadrons. These views were reflected in the building of powerful battleships—dreadnoughts.

The next most important weapon of the fleet was recognized as being the torpedo, first used in the Russo-Japanese war from surface ships, which led to sophistication and large-scale construction of destroyers and light cruisers with torpedo launchers and armaments.

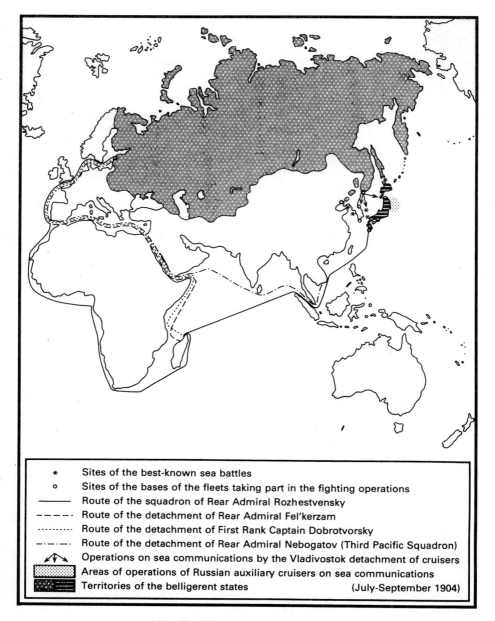

*	Sites of the best-known sea battles
○	Sites of the bases of the fleets taking part in the fighting operations
——	Route of the squadron of Rear Admiral Rozhestvensky
— — — ·	Route of the detachment of Rear Admiral Fel'kerzam
· · · · · · · ·	Route of the detachment of First Rank Captain Dobrotvorsky
— · — · — ·	Route of the detachment of Rear Admiral Nebogatov (Third Pacific Squadron)
↙↑↘	Operations on sea communications by the Vladivostok detachment of cruisers
▓▓▓	Areas of operations of Russian auxiliary cruisers on sea communications
▓▓▓	Territories of the belligerent states (July-September 1904)

Fig. 8.   1904-05 Russo-Japanese War

All the other problems of building fleets, in particular the creation of submarine forces, under the influence of the past war were relegated to the background, although the achievements of science and engineering of that time already enabled industry to build quite sophisticated submarines.

A considerable and highly negative influence on the one-sided trend in the development of the fleets was also exerted by the Mahan theory of "dominance at sea" taken as irrefutable, in line with which only the engagement of the major battle forces or the blocking by the fleet of the enemy in his home base could lead to victory at sea. Submarines were thought incapable of ensuring dominance at sea.

The preparations of Russia for the First World War proceeded against a complex political setting. The results of the Russo-Japanese war showed the shakiness of Russian Czarism and its inability to solve successfully the main affairs of state. Revolutionary demonstrations and armed uprisings, begun on the heroic *Potemkin,* did not cease until the start of the new war and shook the foundations of the autocracy.   After the Russo-Japanese war the Russian fleet was thoroughly debilitated and incapable of fighting the German fleet in open waters. Despite the objective and urgent need to reconstruct the fleet, the Czarist government dallied. Therefore, for a long time it was not clear what kind of a fleet Russia needed and what tasks it would have to discharge in a forthcoming war.

It was not until 1911 that a law was finally adopted serving as the basis for defining the specific composition of the effective forces of the Baltic fleet.[23] As for the Black Sea fleet and Siberian flotilla, the idea was to define more clearly their composition later, depending on the changes in the strategic military situation in these theatres.

The Baltic fleet, to which special importance was attached in ensuring the right strategic flank of the front of the armed struggle and the defence of the capital from the strikes of the strong German fleet, was given the task of not allowing the enemy to land in the eastern part of the Gulf of Finland. It must be granted that the Baltic fleet brilliantly discharged this task, taking as the basis of the plan of military operations the idea of defensive combat at the Nargen minefields off Porkkala-Uude. The Black Sea fleet was supposed to ensure dominance in the Black Sea and be ready to begin battle for the possession of the outlets to the Mediterranean. It was also expected to be ready to destroy the enemy's fleet at the artillery point and minefield off Sevastopol.

The approach of world war became ever more obvious, yet the shipbuilding programmes, begun late, were poorly fulfilled. Thus, the first battleships laid down in 1909 for the Baltic fleet, in 1911 for the Black Sea and at the end of 1912 the battle cruisers for the Baltic fleet had not been finished by the start of the war. The destroyer-building programme was more successful. Thus, the Baltic and Black Sea fleets entered the war having ships with obsolete equipment.

---

[23] This document envisaged that by 1924 the effective forces in the Baltic Sea would include: 16 battleships, eight armoured cruisers, 18 cruisers, 72 destroyers and 24 submarines.

At the same time the Russian fleet rapidly and successfully perfected nearly all types of weapons and means of combat which possessed better combat properties than foreign models. Positive results were also achieved in the combat preparations of the fleets.

State of navies by the start of the First World War

As a result of the one-sided consideration of the experience of the Russo-Japanese War, by the start of the world war enormous battle fleets had been created in the main countries.

The strongest was the British fleet which apparently could ensure the security of its huge colonial empire and sea links with all the countries of the world.

The German fleet relying on a rapidly-growing industrial base developed at a tempestuous pace, furthering the technical sophistication of its ships. As Table 12 shows, by the start of the war the fleets of the Entente included 99 battleships as against 53 for the Alliance of Central Powers, almost double. The general balance of forces became even worse for the German grouping after the entry

TABLE 12
Composition of the Forces of the Navies by the Start of
the First World War

Classes of ships	Entente				Central Powers		
Battleships—dreadnoughts and battle cruisers	29	4	–	33	19	3	22
Battleships—pre-dreadnoughts	40	17	9	66	22	9	31
Cruisers	82	24	12	118	44	10	54
Destroyers	225	81	62	368	144	16	160
Submarines	76	38	15	129	28	6	34

into the war on the side of the Entente of the USA and Italy, as is confirmed by Table 13.

In addition, the British fleet possessed a widespread system of bases, both at home and in the colonies. The very geographical position of England in relation to the bases of the German fleet created favourable conditions for a sea blockade of Germany and gave considerable advantages to the British fleet in operations against the surface ships of the enemy.

The plan of the British Admiralty was aimed at strangling Germany's economy by disrupting her sea shipments, and at establishing dominance at sea by blockading the German shores. The bases of the homeland were envisaged as always having superior battle forces, capable in favourable conditions of inflicting in a general engagement a decisive defeat on the German fleet should it take to sea.

The French fleet by agreement with the English and, later, with the Italian fleet, were deployed in the Mediterranean where they could use the developed system of bases in its western part.

The Sea Power of the State

TABLE 13
Composition of the Forces of the Navies after the Entry of the USA and Italy
into the First World War

Classes of ships	England	France	Russia	Italy	USA	Total	Germany	Austria-Hungary	Turkey	Total
Battleships— dreadnoughts and battle cruisers	42	7	5	5	15	74	24	4	1	29
Battleships— pre-dreadnought (squadron battleships)	31	14	9	6	25	85	21	9	1	31
Cruisers (including armoured)	88	22	12	18	26	166	26	12	2	40
Destroyers	339	83	76	34	75	607	195	17	9	221
Submarines	131	40	34	36	54	295	138	13	–	151

The Austro-Hungarian fleet from the start of the war was bottled up in the Adriatic.

Germany's fleet relied on bases advantageous for its defence against strikes from the sea but had no bases providing direct outlets to the ocean. Its system of bases permitted rapid concentration of forces only in the North or Baltic Seas.

The German Command reckoned on weakening the British fleet by destroying it piecemeal during the blockade by the English of Germany's shores. Thus, the idea was to match the forces of the fleets and then in a general engagement to inflict a decisive defeat on the English. This would have allowed Germany to operate freely in the seas and later by sea blockade to strangle England, reaching the ultimate goals of the war—to redivide the world in Germany's favour and create a most powerful colonial empire. Large-scale operations of cruisers against the sea shipments of the English were envisaged. Participation of the fleet in military operations in land theatres was not planned. The Baltic theatre for the German fleet was thought of in the initial period of the war as secondary.

It is not without interest to note the following: in planning intensely offensive ground operations in the spirit of a lightning war the Germans had little regard for losses, but planned with special care the operations of the fleet for fear of losing large ships.

In 1914 the sides reached the point of war. Only a reason for unleashing it was needed and naturally this was found.

The main culprit in unleashing the First World War, generated by the contradictions of the imperialist states, was German imperialism distinguished by the greatest aggressiveness. It openly opted for such a coercive redivision of the world which would forever ensure Germany a leading place on the planet.

The point must be made that the other imperialist countries too were guilty of unleashing the war and also entered it with predatory aims. The Entente and the Central Alliance confronted each other.

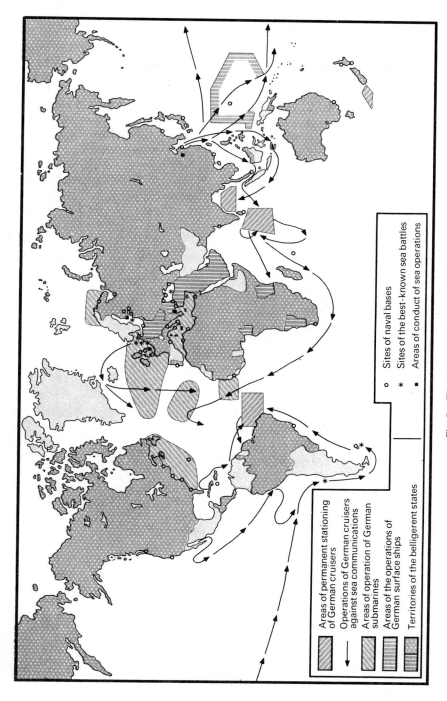

Fig. 9. The 1914-18 First World War

Areas of permanent stationing of German cruisers

Operations of German cruisers against sea communications

Areas of operation of German submarines

Areas of the operations of German surface ships

Territories of the belligerent states

o Sites of naval bases

* Sites of the best-known sea battles

■ Areas of conduct of sea operations

This was "war between two groups of rapacious great powers for dividing up the colonies, enslaving other nations and for gains and privileges on the world market".[24]

As is known, the German plan for the lightning destruction of the French army and the capture of Paris failed. Both sides in the western theatre went over to protracted positional warfare. German strategy on the western front entered an impasse.

Nor were the desired results produced by the operations of the cruiser squadrons and individual cruisers, widely deployed by Germany against the sea communications of the Entente but not proving very effective. US neutrality, kindly disposed to the Entente, and the entry into the war on its side of Japan, out to seize the German colonies to provide itself with favourable positions for widening expansion in China and the subsequent struggle for dominance in the Pacific Ocean, also helped to eliminate the threat to oceanic movements. Already by the end of 1914 the main cruiser forces of the Germans, though causing some tension in oceanic communications, were destroyed, and the support points in the colonies of Germany at which the cruisers were based were captured.

Nor were any appreciable results given by the operations of the German fleet to weaken the British naval forces. Despite this, Germany still hoped by a victory over the British fleet in a decisive sea engagement to change in its favour the outcome of the battle at sea and thereby fundamentally influence the outcome of the whole world war. The British fleet was also getting ready for such an engagement. The possibility of measuring up against each other was finally offered by the well-known Jutland engagement in May 1916.

The Battle of Jutland

This battle (30 May-1 June 1916) was the greatest sea engagement of the whole war involving the main battle forces of the British and German fleets.

In evaluating the engagement many authors have seen only a certain indecisiveness displayed by the fleet commanders, especially the British; have noted the absence of a willingness to take a risk for fear of losing large ships; have called the engagement a "cat and mouse" game; and have written that the admirals present in the line of fire were on the whole distinguished by less resolution than generals, who usually during battle deploy their forces from the rear. For these reasons many consider that the Jutland engagement produced no results.

However, such a view in our judgement is quite incorrect. The appraisal of any engagement, as is known, may be made not by comparing the extent of the losses sustained in it by the opposing sides but by how far the goals set for the engaging forces are accomplished.

Let us look from this angle at the results of the Jutland engagement of the fleets.

Germany sought in this engagement to bring about a sharp turn in the course of the war in her favour, to crush the British Grand Fleet and provide herself

[24] V. I. Lenin, *Complete Collected Works*, Vol. 27, p. 1 (in Russian).

with freedom of operations in order then, by an unrestricted sea blockade, to strangle England. A victory would have meant the lifting of the sea blockade on the Central Powers, the severe effects of which on the economy they were already painfully experiencing. But the German High Sea Fleet proved incapable of solving these tasks.

England strove to maintain the existing position at sea and to intensify blockade operations against Germany. These aims were in essence achieved by her in the engagement.

Thus, the Jutland engagement determined the absence of any change in the further general course of a drawn-out war, returning it to a struggle of potentials which held out no success for Germany.

The Jutland engagement meant the loss of the hopes of the German Command for breaking the sea blockade of Germany, further depletion of her military might and loss of the war. The battle showed that it was mistaken to transfer to the new conditions the experience of the Russo-Japanese war on the use of major uniform battle forces of the fleet as the principal and sole ones for achieving victory in battle at sea. The engagement became a watershed, after which came the period of recognition of the need for interaction in a sea battle of the diverse forces and equipment of the fleets.

The depletion of military-economic resources and growth of the revolutionary movement in the countries of the warring coalitions, especially the German grouping, forced their governments to seek ways of hastening the end of the war. The economies of England and France, drawing across the seas on the resources of nearly the whole world, were such as to allow these countries to wage a long war with expectation of success. Germany, because of the blockade from the sea, experienced an acute shortage of industrial raw materials, food and human resources and, therefore, a long war promised defeat. Austro-Hungary was held only with the aid of German bayonets and pursued a line for a separate withdrawal from the war. In Russia there was a growth of the revolutionary movement which Czarism was no longer able to contain.

In January 1917 Lenin wrote: "In 29 months of the war the resources of both imperialist coalitions have been sufficiently determined, all or nearly all the possible allies . . . drawn into a slaughterhouse, the forces of the armies and fleets have been tested and re-tested, measured and re-measured".[25] "There has begun . . . the turn from an imperialist war to an imperialist peace".[26]

In these conditions Germany, losing hopes of an early end to the war by the efforts of the land forces and not achieving her aims in the Jutland engagement of the battle fleets, feverishly sought other ways of achieving victory in a short time. And a way out appeared to have been found: to disrupt by unrestricted operations of submarines the sea shipments of England, forcing her capitulation before the American forces arrived in Europe.

The leaders of Germany, including the land command, saw in unrestricted submarine warfare the sole and last possibility of salvation and probably of achieving victory or at least an honourable peace.

---

[25] V. I. Lenin, *Complete Collected Works,* Vol. 30, p. 340 (in Russian).
[26] *Ibid.,* p. 241.

Germany had embarked on the submarine blockade of England already at the start of the war, but then waged it very irresolutely, fearing to exacerbate relations with the neutral states, primarily the USA.

However, on the insistence of Hindenburg and Ludendorff, in February 1917 the unrestricted operations of submarine forces began. At first 26 or 27 submarines permanently operated against the English communications. In later months their number grew. The losses of the merchant fleet of the adversary mounted, only about 10 per cent of the losses being made good. The unrestricted submarine blockade forced England almost to her knees. The situation was so bad that the necessary reserves were sought from among the forces at the front and England herself was on the brink of economic disaster.

To combat the German submarines already operating without any restrictions of international law, the Entente mustered its enormous anti-submarine naval forces which included a large number of ships, planes and airships. The system of convoys was increasingly introduced. Other measures were also taken to fight submarines especially on the approaches to and in the bases themselves. As well as sowing more minefields off the shores of Germany, a huge minefield was laid between the Shetland Isles and Norway which was to cut off the access of submarines to the ocean from the North Sea. However, despite great efforts and expenditure, this minefield did not live up to the hopes placed on it. The general level of losses of merchant ships continued high.

And yet in the last period of the war the effectiveness of the submarine blockade waned as the German Command, relying on submarines to solve the main task, did not resort to other branches of the forces of the fleet to ensure success. The German fleets and aviation in substance did not wage battle even against the anti-submarine forces of the enemy. The submarine forces were left to their own devices. To the thousands of ships and other means of anti-submarine defence newly brought into the fight, Germany replied only with single new submarines. Imperialist Germany, whose war machine, as a whole, was approaching a catastrophic end by delaying the wide use of the submarine forces and by not backing their operations with its entire sea might, ultimately proved incapable of fulfilling the task of effectively blockading England by submarine. Yet the allies, receiving heavy reinforcements and aid from the USA, continued to expand their efforts in the fight against the underwater foe. In 1918 for these purposes they had already enlisted some 9000 ships of different classes, 2500 planes, a large number of airships and balloons and also over 700,000 men. The decline in the effectiveness of the submarine blockade was also influenced by the ever-growing replacement of cargo vessels which, however, did not exceed the losses until 1918.

But despite the fact that the main goals were not reached with the aid of the submarine forces, submarines had a considerable influence on the general course of the war. They largely paralysed the sea shipments of the adversary and allowed Germany to carry on with the war.

In 1915-18 German submarines completed over 2500 combat operations including 1700 (68 per cent) in 1917-18. In the war they destroyed merchant shipping with a tonnage of over 11 million registered tons, which surpassed by

22 times the results of the operations of the German cruisers on the sea communications in 1914-15. In the course of the fighting operations the Germans lost 178 submarines, including 132 (74 per cent) in 1917-18.[27]

Submarines achieved no little success also in the fight against surface fighting ships, sinking in the war 156 ships, including 10 battleships, 20 cruisers, 31 destroyers, etc. And although surface ships were not robbed of the possibility of solving the tasks facing them, their activity was seriously impeded. Mine-laying submarines extended the danger of mines to areas of theatres which had earlier been considered safe in this respect. But despite the considerable successes of German submarines Germany was unable to defeat England. A decisive influence on the outcome of the war was exerted by the general economic and military superiority of the countries of the Entente, allowing them in the end to break the resistance of the Germans on land and at sea.

A very adverse effect on Germany's position was also exerted by the military-strategic miscalculations of her leaders, the result of which was first and foremost the belated start of mass production of submarines. A certain role was also played by the miscalculations on the German side in evaluating the possibilities of her adversaries for restoring the heavy losses of merchant ships and also developing an effective system of combating the submarine menace. These circumstances made it impossible to reveal fully the great potential possibilities of submarines in waging armed struggle at sea.

The Russian fleet had a considerable influence on the general course of the fight against Germany and its allies. On the situation in the Baltic Sea considerably depended the success of the maritime operations of the groupings of the forces in the strategic maritime direction which, in turn, could not but influence the position on the whole Russo-German front. In addition, of great importance for Germany were the sea shipments of iron ore from Sweden which were threatened by the operations of the Russian fleet.

At the start of the war the Baltic fleet set up a defence system including a central minefield position which, together with the fortifications of Reval and Sveaborg, became the main node of defence in the Baltic. In the course of the war it was strengthened by advanced fortified positions on the Moonsund Islands and Åbo-Land. To the rear of this system was the fortified Kronstadt region. The defence of the Gulf of Finland made sure that the capital would be safe from sea strikes. Its power was so obvious that the Germans not once risked an attempt to overcome it. The position covering entry to the Bay of Riga, set up in a short time, twice came under attack from large forces of the German fleet, proving itself an effective barrier.

The Baltic fleet ensured the stability of the right flank of the land front. This was particularly vividly expressed with the shift of the flank of the front to the coast of the Bay of Riga and also in the Moonsund operation in the autumn of 1917.

The Moonsund operation involving the whole main stock of the German fleet had the far-reaching aims of combating revolution and uniting the Central Powers with England, the USA and France. Lenin, assessing these events,

[27] See *History of Naval Art* (in Russian), p. 117.

wrote: "Does not the complete inactivity of the British fleet and also the English submarines in the capture of Ösel by the Germans demonstrate . . . that between the Russian and British imperialists, between Kerensky and the Anglo-French capitalists, a deal has been made to hand over Peter' to the Germans and so strangle the Russian revolution? I think it does".[28]

But the Baltic fleet foiled this plan and the Germans could take only the Moonsund Islands, which as they themselves admitted were not all that necessary. This "victory" later played a negligible role.

The operations of the Baltic fleet on the sea communications of the enemy, assuming special importance in the conditions of the blockade of the German shores, held an important place in the general plan of upsetting Germany's economy. And this task the Baltic fleet discharged successfully. One of the brightest pages of its history was provided by the blockade operations in the southern part of the sea, where in the autumn of 1914 and during 1915 minefields were secretly and widely sown, paralysing the movement of the fighting ships and transports of the enemy, forcing him to curtail sea shipments (especially the essential Swedish ores) and for a long time to refrain from active operations in the Baltic.

A considerable influence on the course of the military operations of the Caucasian and later also the Rumanian fronts was exerted by the activity of the Black Sea fleet. At first the Turkish fleet was inferior in strength to the Russian. However, after being joined by the German battle cruisers *Goeben* and *Breslau,* outstripping in speed the old Russian ships, the enemy's fleet was able to activate his operations. On 29-30 October 1914 he staged a raiding operation on Odessa, Sevastopol, Feodosiya, the Kerch Strait and Novorossiisk. This raid, because of the confusion of the Black Sea fleet command, went unpunished for the enemy and was the beginning of the participation of Turkey in the war and of combat operations in the Black Sea.

Later, strengthened by new battleships, the Russian fleet was able to block the surface ships of the Germano-Turkish fleet, sharply curtail sea shipments of the enemy, go over to systematic operations around his coasts and give direct aid to the sea flanks of the land fronts with artillery support, landing parties and transport of troops and supplies.

The Black Sea fleet, by upsetting the enemy's sea communications, by mass mine-laying and operations against bases and ports, made him pass to shipments exclusively on small vessels, which had an adverse effect on his troop reinforcements and considerably reduced supply to the main regions of Turkey of coal, oil and other provisions.

The experience gathered by the Baltic and Black Sea fleets in the First World War turned out to be a valuable contribution to the development of the naval art of our country.

The fate of the First World War was decided on the land fronts. Here were concentrated the bulk of the forces, weapons and military technique and here the sides sustained the heaviest losses. Much of the economic resources of the

[28] V. I. Lenin, *Completed Collected Works,* Vol. 34, p. 347 (in Russian).

coalitions went on ensuring the waging of combat operations on land. But the positional character of the war and the practically insignificant movements of the troops deep into the territory of the opposing sides never created a critical situation liable to lead to the capture or exit from the war of one of the countries of this or that coalition. The opposing fronts wore each other down in the line of fire, and war production expanding in the rear caused ever greater privations and suffering to the working people.

In fact, the German army in the first days of the war invaded the territory of France and conducted all subsequent operations on French soil. However, this in no way brought France nearer to defeat.

The eastern front played a most important role in crippling German plans, since at the start of the war the offensive of the Russian troops in Galicia and East Prussia drew off considerable forces of Germans from the western front, and therefore the Russians to a certain extent were the creators of the "miracle of the Marne". The activity of the Russian army in 1915 enabled the allies to strengthen the positional front in the west. The Brusilov offensive in 1916 saved Italy from defeat and helped to bring Rumania in on the side of the Entente.

However, these successes of Russia at the start of the war and later successes of Germany on the eastern front did not produce an acute crisis in the situation in the land theatres.

The operations in the oceanic and sea theatres did not in the history of the First World War take such a place as they had done in the wars earlier considered by us. But the decisive character of the operations of the fleets in individual strategic directions produced at particular stages of the war the most acute crisis situations with a profound influence on its course. For example, the German submarine blockade of 1917 brought England to the brink of catastrophe. The dependence of the English economy on imported raw materials and also the fact that without the carriage of foodstuffs the British population was threatened by starvation made the country particularly sensitive to a sea blockade. In this direction, too, German submarines delivered a blow of staggering magnitude (in the war they sank 65 per cent of the merchant navy of the British Empire, the most powerful of pre-war years). Britain had never been exposed to such great danger in her entire history.

The expansion of the anti-submarine forces of Britain and the coming into the war of the United States of America with its strong fleet ultimately led to failure by the Germans to win the battle for dominance on the oceanic seaways.

The struggle in the oceanic and sea theatres had a profound influence on the course of the operations and campaigns in the land theatres. This influence was of a strategic character. Here it is firstly necessary to note the long, continuous blockading operations of the British fleet conducted with the aim of undermining Germany's economy, isolating it from its colonies and foreign markets and not allowing German sea forces beyond the North Sea.

Germany, despite the very fast growth of industry and its advanced character in the pre-war years, was cut off in the course of the war from all its colonies, conquered markets and overseas raw materials. For Germany the most important condition for achieving victory was to keep the war short, a goal its economy could reach. A long war for it was tantamount to defeat. In contrast, the transformation of the war into a long one gave Germany's adversaries a gain in time necessary for strangling the German economy and largely guaranteed the achievement of final victory.

A major role in turning such a Blitzkrieg desirable for the German government into a long war was played by the navies of the Entente. They were able to isolate Germany and thereby introduce a new factor in armed struggle—its duration.

The endeavour of the allies to cripple Germany's economy was expressed in a whole system of techniques of economic warfare, but the principal one was the planned execution of blockade by the fleet. The sea blockade extended the war not only to the military strength of the Germans but also to the source of this strength. In the end it deprived the German army of superiority in technical provisions and ensured that superiority would lie with the other side. The blockade also had an exceptional influence on the political condition and morale of the population of Germany.

The blockade turned such an important economic factor as the German merchant navy into a useless group of vessels bottled up in their ports. True, Germany could still trade through bordering neutrals which, of course, was not a bad source of sustenance for the German economy, but it could not prevent all the dire consequences of a systematic sea blockade. This only put off the denouement.

Another asset of the navies was that they ensured the transport of large contingents of land troops across the seas and oceans, which had a direct influence on the success of the operations of the Entente armies. In addition, some countries neutral at the beginning of the war, under the influence of the might of the Entente fleet, turned against Germany.

It is also necessary to note the almost complete absence in the course of the First World War of such a form of joint operations of the fleet and army as landing operations. In fact, only one attempt was made to stage a large landing operation, in the Dardanelles. However, the operations of the allies in this venture did not come off and this unsuccessful experience long remained a factor holding back the development of the theory and practice of such landings.

In the course of the First World War an important place in the general efforts of the fleets was taken by the struggle of the fleets for dominance at sea. It was regarded as one of the measures ensuring the achievement of strategic and operative goals in the oceanic and sea theatres of military operations. These goals, as stated, formed the basis of the German and English plans for waging war at sea and were vigorously pursued by the opposing sides. The main means of achieving dominance at sea were considered by both sides to be sea blockade and general engagement of the battle forces of the fleets.

The results of the First World War sharply affected the state of the naval forces. The Royal Navy lost pre-eminence at sea and Britain was forced to give up the "two-power standard"[29] to which it had firmly clung before the war. Now England found it hard to maintain her fleet at the level of the strongest, the American fleet.

[29] The British Navy according to this principle was supposed to match in its power the next two strongest fleets in the world.

Germany was deprived of the right to have a navy. Its main forces, including all its submarines, were handed over to the countries of the Entente for division. Germany was categorically forbidden to build submarines. In addition, the victors received all cargo ships above 1600 tons and half of the smaller ships left to Germany. The equipment of all the shipbuilding yards was made over to England as compensation for the German ships taken to Scapa Flow and scuttled there by the German Command contrary to the treaty. Such a heavy toll precisely on the German Navy also testified to the particularly great significance of the fleet in wartime.

However, the restrictions set by the victors on the building of the fleet and armed forces of Germany proved short-lived. The striving of the leading imperialist circles to crush at any price the Soviet system in our state took precedence over the true national interests of the Western countries. The Anglo-French and American imperialists saw as the main aim of their policy in that period setting Germany, Italy and Japan against the Soviet Union. To this end they gave generous aid to Germany to restore its military-industrial potential, and with the coming to power of Hitler at first relaxed and then in effect lifted all the restrictions on the development of German arms.[30]

Nor was it possible to stop or at least regulate the naval arms race between the victorious countries; at first on the initiative of the Japanese militarists and then of the German fascists in the 'thirties', the naval arms race developed with a vigour never seen before.

The Fleets in the Second World War

After the First World War and the splitting of the world into two socio-political systems, the policy of the imperialist powers was largely determined by their constant desire to destroy the Soviet Union. In the first half of the 'thirties two foci of a new world war emerged. The first focus sprang up in 1931-32 as a result of the invasion of Manchuria by the forces of militarist Japan. This conflict contained the danger of a major war by Japan against China, the Soviet Union and also the USA and Britain. The second war focus appeared in 1933-35 in connection with the Fascist putsch in Germany and the active preparations beginning for a war against the USSR and the Western countries. German Fascism, with the support of world reaction, in 1936 unleashed a civil war in Spain, seized Austria and after the Munich Pact occupied Czechoslovakia in 1939.

The USA, Britain and France were quite confident that the armed power of Germany, restored by them, would be directed against the Soviet Union and ensure the destruction of Communism; and that Germany itself, weakened in such a war, would for a long time be incapable of standing up to other imperialist powers. Encouraged by the liberal subsidies of international monopoly capital, the military-industrial and political chiefs of Hitler's Germany rapidly got ready for war, mobilized industry, directed the development of the whole economy on war lines and ensured the corresponding ideological processing of the German people.

[30] A decisive step in this direction was the 1935 Anglo-German agreement under which Germany was allowed to rebuild its navy to within one-third the size of the British.

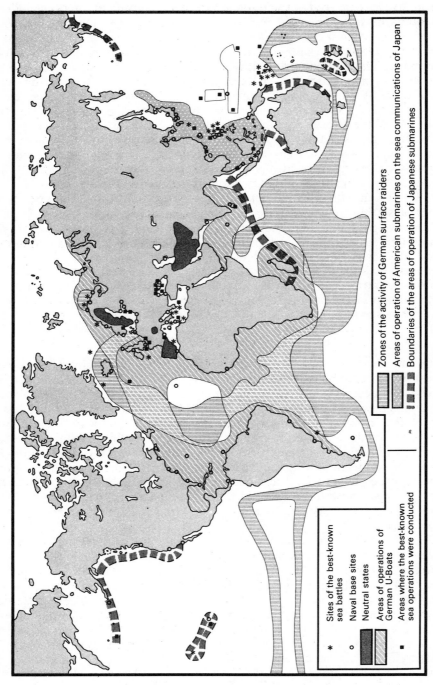

Fig. 10.   1939-45 Second World War

The restrictions of the Treaty of Versailles opposing the arming of Germany were soon cast aside and the country openly went over to the creation of powerful armed forces necessary for a predatory war.

In 1935 the Anglo-German sea agreement was concluded. It, in fact, repealed the restrictive articles of the Versailles Treaty on naval arms and untied the hands of Hitler's Germany to build up a powerful navy. Already by the end of 1939 Germany possessed an army and air force surpassing any of the armies of the capitalist world, and capable in Hitler's view of establishing dominance in Europe. However, this dominance was not the final goal of the pursuits of Fascist Germany. It was merely the basic pre-requisite for creating a pan-Hitlerite colonial empire. Therefore the attainment of the main political goal—the gaining of world dominance—was divided into two main stages. The first covered the establishment of dominance in Europe and the destruction of the Soviet Union, without which the gaining of world dominance was considered impossible; and the second the seizure of overseas colonial possessions.

This policy demanded that the Fascist leaders pay special attention to the creation first and foremost of ground and air forces. But since the attainment of world dominance was connected with the seizure of colonies, Fascist Germany also planned to build powerful naval forces capable of ensuring it the position of the strongest power. The Z plan sought to cover 9-10 years, and (worked out in 1934) envisaged the creation in the first place of battleships, aircraft carriers, cruisers and a large number of submarines.

The breakdown of the 1936 London Conference on the problems of further regulation of the building of fleets acted as a signal for an unrestricted arms race by the imperialist powers. The very attempt to regulate naval arms by various international agreements, as repeatedly noted in history, especially after the First World War, testifies to the special importance which the major imperialist countries attached to the naval forces. The German Navy by the beginning of the war was weaker than those of England and France. But Germany had allies in aggression—Fascist Italy in Europe and Japan in the Pacific possessing large fleets (Table 14).

TABLE 14

Balance of the Forces of the Navies of the Coalitions at the Start of the Second World War

Classes of ships	England	France	Total	Germany	Italy	Total	Ratio
Battleships	15	7	22	2	4	6	3.7:1
Aircraft carriers	6	2	8	–	–	–	–
Heavy, light and anti-aircraft cruisers	66	19	85	11	22	33	2.6:1
Destroyers and torpedo boats	119	70	189	42	128	170	1.1:1
Submarines	69	77	146	57	115	172	0.8:1

The dogmas of Mahan and Colomb left an indelible mark on the plans to use the fleets of the Western countries in war. Thus, in the plans to use the German fleet the main role in the struggle at sea was assigned to the battle forces. The Hitlerites reckoned that a cruiser war would interrupt the sea communications of Britain with her allies and colonies and making the war a total war would undermine the economic potential and morale of Britain.

The role of aircraft and submarines was under-estimated by the Germans. It was perfectly obvious that such tasks and means of operations did not match the real possibilities of the German fleet, well inferior in fighting power to its opponents.

England and France saw in their fleets a means of gaining dominance at sea through a general engagement and also a means of effecting an economic blockade and delivering strikes from the sea on vulnerable coastal targets of the enemy. Aircraft and submarines were assigned by the allies, like the Germans, a secondary role for which they had to pay dear in the course of the war.

Thus, the starting point of the British plan of military operations at sea was that the conditions of the situation in a future war would not greatly differ from those of the First World War, and the plan envisaged the fleet exercising a long sea blockade of Germany and the protection of her own sea communications. The French fleet and some of the forces of the British fleet relying on a developed system of bases were planned to be used to ensure dominance in the Mediterranean.

The Second World War ". . . broke out within the capitalist world as a result of the sharp accentuation of the antagonisms between the capitalist countries by reason of the operation of the law of unevenness of their development under imperialism. The responsibility for its outbreak lies with imperialism as a social system, the ruling classes and the governments of the largest capitalist powers. . . .

"The Second World War generated by the mutual struggle of the capitalist powers began as an imperialist war on both sides. . . . But it could not arrest, and still less remove, the objective processes of the gradual mounting of the just struggle of the peoples against Fascist oppression. . . . The invasion of the European countries by the Hitlerites was answered by stiffened resistance giving it a clearly marked anti-Fascist, national-liberation character. . . . The Great Patriotic War, to which the peoples of the USSR rose headed by the Leninist party, became the most important constituent part of the Second World War, the acme of a just war—a war in defence of the socialist homeland."[31]

In the first period of the war (1939-41)—from its start to the attack by Fascist Germany and its satellites on the USSR—the navies played an important role and exerted a fundamental influence on the course of the war.

After the destruction by Germany of Poland, England and France, still hoping to turn Fascist aggression against the Soviet Union, for a long time in essence waged no military operations on the land front. The long period of the phoney war ensued. Taking advantage of this, the Hitlerites were able calmly to concentrate troops against the Western powers with the aim of crushing them and establishing dominance in Western Europe as a necessary condition for the attack on the USSR.

[31] *History of the Second World War* (in Russian), Vol. 1, Moscow, Voenizdat, 1973, viii, xi-xiii.

The sole theatre where active fighting was waged in this period was the sea theatre. The struggle here had not ceased right from the start of the war. Its main task was to disrupt the oceanic and sea shipments of the enemy. The German fleet for this purpose used large surface ships and submarines. Although their operations did not lead to the desired convulsion of the British economy, it forced the Royal Navy to thin out its ships to many areas of the World Ocean to protect its links with the different countries of the world.

As a result, in the area of the coastal waters of northern Europe, the Hitlerites were presented with a favourable situation and in April 1940, using nearly all the available forces of the fleet supported by superior air power, they suddenly staged sea and air landings in Norway and in a short time captured it. At the same time they occupied Denmark. This operation had a considerable influence on the further course of the war. It improved the strategic position of the northern flank of the battle front of the Germans, extended the possibilities of combat activity of their fleet, especially submarines, and provided Germany's economy with supplies of Scandinavian iron ore over protected coastal sea routes.

On 10 May 1940 the phoney war ended. The Hitlerite troops concentrated on the western front, invaded Belgium and Holland, then France, cut to pieces the Anglo-French armies and approached the English Channel, pushing to the sea in the Dunkirk district nine British and eighteen French divisions. Over 850 different boats and craft were needed by the allies to evacuate to England 338,000 men, leaving to the enemy all their heavy equipment.

The Munich policy of the ruling Anglo-French circles culminated in the ignominious capitulation of France with the threat of invasion of the British Isles by German troops. The aerodromes of the Fascist air force moved up to England's doorstep and Germany's submarine bases were moved to the oceanic coast, beyond the lines of blockade, almost touching the main routes of British sea transport.

The plan of Hitlerite Germany to gain dominance in Western Europe, chiefly by the forces of the land troops and aviation, appeared to be close to a successful completion. But there remained defiant England and it was impossible to make her surrender in the absence of adequate naval forces. And again the Germans sought, as in the First World War, to find a way out of this stalemate in their submarine fleet. In November 1940 at a conference with Hitler an extended submarine building programme was adopted in order, with the aid of these craft, to strangle England by submarine blockade. But the Hitlerites were unable to put into full operation the programme drawn up of combating England in the war already being waged. Not possessing the necessary complement of submarines, and having a weakened fleet of surface ships as a result of the destruction of the raiders operating on English communications and of the latest battleship *Bismarck* on her first outing into the Atlantic, the German Command was forced to give up the plan of vanquishing England and to revise the agenda for gaining sea dominance.

A new period of the world war was approaching—the attack on the Soviet Union—which Hitler saw as the main obstacle in the way of achieving his crazy aims. Fascist Germany now concentrated its entire activity on preparing for this attack. All the military operations of the western front were relegated to the background. The plans to capture England, Switzerland and Sweden, liquidate the small Western European states, conquer India, the Middle East and Africa—all this was left in abeyance pending the successful fulfilment of the Barbarossa plan. Devastation of the USA and the capture of the American continent were also made conditional on the solution of the task of destroying the Soviet Union.

The perfidious attack of Fascist Germany on the USSR, involving by far the greater part of the armed forces of Germany and its satellites, determined the start of a new period in the course of the world war, sharply changing the whole situation.

The war in the European theatre assumed an explicitly continental character and the operations of the fleets in the Atlantic theatre including the Mediterranean, Baltic and Black Seas were increasingly aimed at meeting the requirements of the land forces emphasizing the land nature of the greatest battle in history.

A somewhat different position was later created in the Pacific theatre of military operations where the fleets played a more independent role. This gave the military operations a sea character and brought to the fore the practice of waging combined land-sea operations.

The main theatre where the fate of the whole Second World War was decided remained the European theatre, with the indisputably most important Soviet-German front. That is why the role of the fleets in the war and their influence on its general course cannot be considered in isolation from this main theatre of military operations.

At the same time the military operations in the Pacific which, though they could not decisively influence the outcome of the Second World War, are very instructive from a historical point of view as an example of the importance of the fleets in wars between states separated by the oceans. Such separation of the adversaries by stretches of water and the attendant important role of the fleets had also often been a feature of past wars (Sino-Japanese, Spanish-American, Russo-Japanese) and have become a generally recognized principle.

The attack of Nazi Germany on the Soviet Union and the concentration of all its efforts in the east immediately and decisively affected the course of the military operations in the other theatres, primarily the Atlantic. Air raids on England and against her shipping ceased almost completely. Again, as in the First World War, German submarines operating against British shipping were left to fend for themselves. Large surface ships and a large part of the submarines of the German fleet were switched to bases in northern Norway to give the maximum assistance to the eastern front, where a struggle was being fiercely waged on the communications linking our country with the allies. England was in a position to take measures to protect her sea communications and upset the enemy's shipments without special interference. The Battle for the Atlantic passed into the relatively calm channel of the already customary fight against German submarines not supported by other forces.

However, despite such conditions and the swift development of the anti-submarine forces of the Anglo-Americans, these proved capable only of considerably reducing the successes of the German submarines but not of removing the submarine threat before the end of the war.

The further course of the war showed that a decisive role in the destruction of Nazi Germany and its allies was played by the Soviet Union and her armed forces. The events on this, the main front exerted a decisive influence on the character of the struggle also in other theatres of military operations, including the oceanic.

Winston Churchill, then British Prime Minister, said, in a report to the War Cabinet on 20 January 1943: ". . . all our military operations taken together are on a very small scale compared . . . with the gigantic effort of Russia."[32] He also uttered the famous words: ". . . the Russian resistance broke the power of the German armies."[33]

The Japanese military historian Hattori, assessing the importance of the capitulation of the German Fascist troops at Stalingrad, wrote: "From that moment the initiative on the Soviet-German front completely passed from the German troops. This radically altered the plans of the three countries. . . ."[34] (Germany, Japan and Italy—S.G.).

In 1944 US Secretary of the Interior Ickes said this about the dependence of the situation in other war theatres on the operations at the Soviet-German front: "The greatest gift which the Russians gave the United Nations was time, without which England could not have even healed the wounds sustained at Dunkirk and the United States could not have developed war production and created armies and fleets. . . ."[35] (Retranslated from Russian.)

General Charles de Gaulle declared on 2 December 1944: "The French know what Soviet Russia has done for them and know that it was precisely Soviet Russia which played the main role in their liberation".[36]

Stettinius, a major political figure in the USA, wrote in 1949 when the war was over: "The American people should not forget that they were not far from catastrophe. If the Soviet Union had been unable to hold her front the Germans would have been in a position to capture Great Britain. They might also have seized Africa and in this case they could have set up a jumping-off ground in Latin America".[37] (Retranslated from Russian.)

The success of all the major large landing operations of the allies in Africa and Europe was also ensured by the operations of the Soviet armed forces, not allowing the Nazis to manoeuvre with their forces to repel the invasion forces or destroy them.

Many prominent Soviet military figures have also stressed the direct impact of the events on the Soviet-German front on the course of the war on other fronts. Thus, Marshal of the Soviet Union A. A. Grechko in his book *The Battle for the Caucasus* wrote; "Victory at Stalingrad, Kursk, on the Don and in the

[32] Winston Churchill, *The Second World War, London, 1949-54, Vol. IV*, p. 613.
[33] *Ibid.l* Vol. III, p. 152.
[34] R. Hattori, *Japan in the 1941-45 War* (in Russian), pp. 293, 294, Voenizdat, Moscow.
[35] *Krasny flot.*, 27 June 1944.
[36] *Soviet-French Relations during the 1941-45 Great Patriotic War*, p. 340 (in Russian), Moscow, Gozpolitizdat, 1959.
[37] Quoted in L. M. Yeremeyev, *Through the Eyes of Friends and Enemies. The Role of the Soviet Union in Smashing Fascist Germany* (in Russian), p. 150, Moscow, Nauka, 1966.

Caucasus greatly strengthened the positions of our allies in the Middle East and the Mediterranean basin and facilitated victory in North Africa over the army of General Rommel".[38]

Also incontrovertible is the influence of the general strategic position created on the main Soviet-German front on the course of the military operations in the Pacific. The choice by the Japanese of the southern variant for the start of their aggression, the subsequent refusal to continue the offensive and going over to strategic defence were the consequence of the failure of the Blitzkrieg and the series of defeats inflicted on Hitler's Germany by the Soviet armed forces.

Despite the predominantly continental character of this war, the fleets of the warring countries discharged a number of major tasks having no small influence on the course of the struggle as a whole. Thus, the successes of the Allies in the Mediterranean, at first in North Africa and then in Italy, were to a certain extent determined by the operations of the fleets ensuring the disembarking of large invasion forces in North Africa, on the island of Sicily and in the Appenine peninsula. At the same time the fleets of the Allies interrupted supplies to Rommel's troops, brought across the Mediterranean, which predetermined his defeat. These partial successes on a secondary battle front played their own positive role in the course of the war, although they drew off relatively small forces of the Hitlerites.

By their victories our valiant armed forces finally gained for themselves the initiative and in 1943 went over to a series of inter-related major offensive operations. Hitler's plans to stabilize the position on the Soviet-German front and to switch troops to meet the long-awaited invasion by the Allies of Western Europe were frustrated. England and the USA could no longer put off the opening of a second front. But by that time there no longer remained any doubt that the Soviet Union was in a position to smash Fascist Germany and finish off the war without the direct participation of the Allies.

The landing of Allied troops in Normandy in June 1944 was the greatest landing operation in the history of war. Its preparations went on for thirty months unopposed by the enemy. The operation involved huge forces of the fleet, land armies and aircraft. Some 4500 landing ships and vessels were used to carry the invasion force by sea. The landing on the coast was undertaken with the aid of 4000 different landing devices. It was secured by over 2000 fighting ships and some 14,000 planes.

With the opening of the Second Front in the summer of 1944 the USA and England made their own greatest but belated contribution to the cause of victory over Fascist Germany. However, the deliberately deferred opening of the Second Front did not become a turning point in the course of the war as is often depicted by Western historians. ". . . by next spring the way things are going in Russia now, maybe a Second Front won't be necessary", declared US President F. Roosevelt in 1943.[39] As can be seen, the importance of the Second Front was then no longer decisive and it could not help the Soviet troops, but on the contrary it was they who created favourable conditions for the invasion of

[38] A. A. Grechko, *The Battle for the Caucasus* (in Russian), p. 456, 2nd ed., revised, Voenizdat, Moscow 1973.
[39] E. Roosevelt, *As He Saw It,* p. 156, Duell, Sloan and Pearce, New York, 1946.

Western Europe by the Allies, allowing them to build up massive forces and outstrip the Nazis with a navy twelve times and an air force 22 times as big as theirs.

As stated, in the Pacific, unlike the other theatres, the operations of the navies had a more fundamental influence on the course of the armed struggle. Here the main adversaries—the USA and Japan—were separated by oceanic expanses which in itself already pre-determined the special and even decisive role of the fleets. The main form of combat activity in this theatre was provided by the marine landing operations of both sides and the blockade operations of the American fleet. All the other fighting operations of the armed forces of the contestants were aimed either at securing the disembarking of marine invasion forces and shielding them or at countering sea landings, and were constituent parts of the landing or anti-landing operations.

The sea forces of the adversaries in the Pacific theatre before the start of the war were almost equal (Table 15) excluding aircraft carriers, in which the Japanese had a three-fold lead.

The war in this theatre began on 7 December 1941 with a sudden attack by the Japanese fleet on the main base of the American Pacific fleet in Pearl Harbour. The strike by Japanese carrier planes sank and damaged the one cruiser and eight battleships at the American base, and destroyed over 300 planes.

Having smashed in three days an English squadron in the Gulf of Siam and in February 1942 in the Java Sea the hastily assembled Anglo-Dutch-American squadron, the Japanese secured dominance at sea. This allowed them in the first stage of the war to undertake offensive operations unhindered. In two months the Japanese seized the Philippines, the Malayan peninsula with the biggest English base at Singapore, the Dutch East Indies, Burma and a number of Pacific islands. Into their hands fell huge resources, but time and transport facilities were needed to enlist them for war.

TABLE 15
Balance of Naval Forces in the Pacific before the Start of
the Second World War*

Classes of ships	USA	Great Britain	Holland	Total	Japan	Ratio
Battleships	9	2	–	11	10	1:0.9
Aircraft carriers	3	–	–	3	10	1:3.3
Seaplane transports	–	–	–	–	6	–
Cruisers	24	9	3	36	36	1:1
Destroyers	80	13	7	100	113	1:1.1
Submarines	56	–	13	69	63	1:0.9

* See S. Roskill, *The Fleet in War*, p. 510 (in Russian), Voenizdat, Moscow, 1967.

Occupying vast spaces, the Japanese, under the influence of the radical turn in the course of the whole war brought about as a result of the battle at Stalingrad and deepened by the subsequent victories of the Soviet Army, went over to strategic defence as early as 1943.

Western historians try to demonstrate that the turn-round in the course of the war in the Pacific came long before Stalingrad, namely in the engagement off Midway Island successful for the Americans (3-6 June 1942) in which four Japanese carriers and only one American carrier were sunk. However, the balance of naval forces set up after the engagement off Midway Island contradicts these claims.

Even then Japan's fleet retained superiority in forces, possessing (including those newly brought into commission) eight aircraft carriers as against four American. In battleships and cruisers the balance was also in favour of the Japanese. Even the character of the combat operations of both sides, following the Midway Island battle, indicates that no turn in the course of the war occurred. The Japanese continued to stage landings and conduct an offensive on New Guinea and the Solomon Islands and created a more serious position for the forces of the Allies by destroying two further American carriers (*Wasp* and *Hornet*). Churchill wrote that in the "autumn of 1942 the Americans . . . appealed . . . for one or more British carriers, . . . that an intense crisis had arisen in the Solomons."[40] In fact the Americans at that time were left with only two damaged carriers, the *Saratoga* and *Enterprise*. There was a real threat of invasion of Australia by the Japanese. What sort of turn in the course of the war was this?

Also untenable is the attempt by Western historians to present as a turning-point in the course of the war in the Pacific theatre the landing of one division of US marines (1942) at Guadalcanal, which fought there lengthy battles with variable success. These attempts are refuted by President Roosevelt who, in his Report to Congress and to the Nation on the State of the Union and the State of the War on 7 January 1943, declared that the successes at the Midway and Guadalcanal Islands ". . . were essentially defensive. They were part of the delaying strategy that characterized this phase of the war."[41]

If at this difficult moment for the Allies (31 December 1942) the Japanese Imperial Staff decided to drop their offensive strategy and go over to defence, the most important cause of this transition to a new stage of the war was the victory of Soviet troops at Stalingrad over the main forces of the Fascist coalition, when for the first time the faith of Japanese militarists in the strength of the German army was badly shaken. "The victory of the Soviet Army at Stalingrad was a heavy blow not only for Germany but also for Japan and Italy."[42] Japan knew perfectly well that "if Germany ever weakened, Japan would rapidly be faced with world coalition".[43]

Another reason why the Japanese went over to defensive operations was that the scale of the expansion and predatory appetite of Japan were incommensurate with the ability of its naval forces to secure the prolonged protection of the

[40] Winston Churchill, *The Second World War*, Vol. V, p. 18.
[41] *The War Messages of Franklin D. Roosevelt*. The President's War Addresses to the People of the United States, to the Congress of the United States and to Other Nations, Supplement, November 7 1942 to July 30 1943, p. 29.
[42] *History of the War in the Pacific*, Vol. IV, p. 16 (in Russian), Inost. Lit., 1958.
[43] *Nuremburg Trials, Collection of Proceedings*, Vol I, p. 402 (in Russian), Moscow, Gosyurizdat, 1952.

territories seized and harness their economic resources. And the economy of Japan itself, depending on the import of raw materials from other areas of the world, limited its possibilities not only of expanding the forces of the fleet in the course of war but also in making good the losses sustained from the blows of the Americans.

The United States of America was in a different position. Its industry was not exposed to the action of the enemy, was provided with raw material resources and worked with ever greater momentum. Thanks to this, the Americans in a short time achieved superiority over Japan at sea.

Thus, the course of events in the war in the Pacific theatre once again confirmed that in these conditions the political ends which were to be achieved by military means were directly dependent on the potential of the fleet to ensure their attainment.

On 1 February 1943 the evacuation of the Japanese troops from the island of Guadalcanal began. In the spring of 1943 a new shorter defence line was established. In the summer of 1943 the Japanese shortened still further the defence belt, taking it to the Caroline and Marianas Islands, and drew off the main fleet forces to rear bases.

By the autumn of 1943 the economic advantages of the USA were already making themselves felt in the Pacific. Superiority at sea irrevocably passed to the Americans, who went over to the offensive.

In connection with the switch by the Japanese to defence, of the greatest importance was the sea transport of troops between the homeland and the oceanic defence lines, and also the delivery of strategic materials from the captured areas of the southern seas to Japan. However, this transport was the most vulnerable link in the Japanese defence system. And when the initiative passed to the Americans and they began offensive operations, the Japanese were unable either to manoeuvre their forces on the defence line in the ocean or protect the carriage of strategic materials to Japan from the countries of the southern seas.

The struggle for sea communications in the Pacific assumed a distinctive and largely one-sided character. Japanese submarines operated against large fighting surface ships of the enemy and were not used on his lines of communication. Therefore, American sea shipments were virtually left untouched by the Japanese fleet.

The USA from the start of the war mostly employed submarines against Japanese sea shipments. And it was not until 1944 that aircraft and surface ships were drawn into the conflict. Because of the weakness of the protection of Japanese communications, the operations of the American fleet to disrupt them proceeded in simple conditions.

As a result of the struggle for communications and the strikes of American aircraft on industrial targets in the Japanese islands, by 1945 the economic potential of Japan had been undermined. It could no longer make good the losses in fighting ships and aircraft, whereas the USA continued to step up the building of ships and planes, the bulk of which was deployed for operations against Japan in the Pacific.

All this allowed the Americans to build up a decisive lead in forces and to dominate in the areas of conduct of operations. Moreover, influenced by the protracted war and the defeats of the Nazis on the Soviet-German front, the Japanese did not risk the main force of their navy in the defence of the captured islands, leaving it to small garrisons unsupported from either sea or air.

Offensive operations of the American fleet began at the end of 1943, at first not directed against the main forces of the Japanese fleet, but against the peripheral garrisons on the islands captured by the Japanese.

TABLE 16
Growth of the Forces of the US Fleet

Classes of ships	1941*	1944**
Aircraft carriers (heavy, light, escort)	7	125
Battleships	16	23
Cruisers, light, heavy and anti-aircraft	36	67
Destroyers and escort ships	180	879
Submarine hunters	–	Up to 900
Submarines	112	351
Landing and disembarking ships and devices	–	Over 75,000

* See L. M. Yeremeyev and A. P. Shergin, *Submarines of Foreign Fleets in the Second World War*, p. 375 (in Russian), Voenizdat, 1962.
** *Reference Book of the Ship Complement of World Naval Fleets*, p. 295 (in Russian), Voenmorizdat, Moscow-Leningrad, 1945.

The fight to break through the Japanese outer defence line highlighted a further important quality of the fleet—the ability to undertake a wide man-oeuvre with considerable forces. The Americans, thanks to the superior forces of the fleet, were able to choose at their own discretion the directions of the strikes. The result was the Japanese were often late in coming to the aid of their island garrisons. The US fleet, breaking through the outer defence line of Japan in the autumn of 1944, went over to operations against the inner defence line running through the islands of the Philippines. Here in the waters of the archipelago took place the biggest sea engagement of the Second World War, in which Japan used the main forces of its fleet. As a result of this battle the Japanese fleet sustained heavy losses fatal to it. It lost four carriers, three battleships, ten cruisers, eleven destroyers and two submarines.[44] This engagement had a considerable influence on the further course of military operations in the Pacific theatre, pre-determining the subsequent successes of the Americans.

The last major landing operation of the Americans in the Pacific Ocean was that of their troops on the Island of Okinawa. The fight for this island, despite the six-fold superiority of the American forces over the enemy's garrison and their complete dominance at sea and in the air, went on for three months, which does not suggest great skill in this operation.

The raids of American aircraft on the towns and ports of Japan increased, but its land army on the Pacific islands sustained insignificant losses, since the

[44] *Sea Atlas* (in Russian), Vol. III, Part 2, Supreme Naval Command publishing house, 1963, sheet 48.

garrisons were small in number. The Kwantung army in Manchuria, representing the most powerful and best fighting grouping of the land troops of Japan, remained untouched. Such an important military-economic base of Japanese imperialism as industry in Manchuria and Korea not only did not suffer from military operations but even continued to develop. All this enabled Japan, despite the sharp weakening of the Japanese fleet and loss of the territories earlier seized by it in the southern seas, to continue the war. It banked, not without reason, on the possibility of anti-Soviet deals with its capitalist enemy.

In 1945 Japan possessed large armed forces reckoning armies of many millions and also 8400 planes and 600 warships, including four carriers, six battleships, seven cruisers, 44 submarines, etc.[45]

Victory over it demanded a sustained struggle with the enlistment of large land forces, which the Allies did not have. Therefore, the Americans worked out plans for a long war with Japan, envisaging the disembarkation of an invasion force on the island of Kyushu at the end of 1945 but not until 1946 in the Tokyo region and possibly even later. That is why the entry of the USSR into the war against Japan was so necessary for the Allies. Without it, it was not possible to break the determination of the Japanese militarists to continue the war, as convincingly testified by the telegram of the Commander-in-Chief of the Japanese forces in China, General Okamura, 12 August 1945 to Tokyo: "We realize that the entry into the war of the Soviet Union has made the position even worse. However, having in the territory of Japan proper an army of up to seven million men and an expeditionary army on the mainland of up to a million men whose fighting spirit continues to remain high, we are ready for the decisive crushing of the enemy. Now the land army has become the main support of the Empire. . . . The fate of Imperial Japan is being decided in Manchuria."[46]

It is known that in fulfilling their obligations as allies the Soviet Army and Navy with a powerful blow smashed the Kwantung army and the Japanese support points on Sakhalin and the Kurile islands, after which Japan was forced to surrender unconditionally.

The main tasks solved by the fleets in the course of the Second World War

The Second World War as a whole, as stated above, was continental since its main goals were reached on the land fronts. However, some strategic tasks in the European theatres could not be solved without the participation of large forces of the fleets. For example, the struggle for communications was conducted almost exclusively by the forces of the fleets. Although the operations at sea were, as a whole, of a subordinate character in relation to the strategic tasks solved on land, they had a considerable influence on the course of the war.

The main forms of military operations of the fleets in the Second World War must be seen as being the struggle for sea communications aimed at undermining the military-economic potential of the enemies and the protection of their

[45] N. I. Smirnov, *The Sailors of the Pacific Fleet in the War against Imperialist Japan* (in Russian), Morskoi sbornik, 1970, No. 8, p. 7.
[46] R. Hattori, *Japan in the 1941-45 War*, (in Russian), p. 573.

own sea shipments and marine landing operations on a scale hitherto unknown.

The importance of the battle for sea communications in the general scope of military operations at sea was not the same for all theatres. In the Atlantic Ocean its scale and intensity exceeded similar operations in all other theatres. Thus, the struggle for sea communications was the basis of all the activity of the German fleet. The special attention to it may be confirmed by the fact that the heads of the Allied states at the Casablanca Conference (1943) recognized the need to deploy the main resources of the united nations primarily in the fight against the threat stemming from German submarines.

The scale and intensity of the struggle for communications gradually grew in the course of the war, which was also characteristic of the First World War. Unquestionably the greatest mistake of the German Fascist leaders was to develop the struggle for the Atlantic communications on a wide scale only several years after the start of the war, when it had become clear that their plans on land had failed. A no smaller error was that of waging the struggle virtually only with submarines, without backing them up with other kinds of forces, especially aircraft. Because of these errors the Allies were able to build up in massive numbers the forces and resources for protection from the strikes of the submarines and to make good the loss of cargo vessels. Therefore, although the influence of the struggle for communications on the general course of the war was considerable, it could not become decisive. This struggle gradually waned and lost all value. The only new thing about it was that it encompassed all the sea and oceanic theatres except Antarctica. It was waged most persistently around communications converging on England and Japan.

An important feature of the war on sea communications was the use of different kinds of forces and also the elaboration and introduction of new types of weapons and technical means such as radar, sonar devices, new types of submarines and anti-submarine ships, homing torpedoes, under-water diesel plants, etc. The development of armaments naturally brought changes in the methods of using the forces, led to submarines hunting in packs, obliteration of the boundaries between night- and daytime operations, the organization of special operations in signal traffic, sharp increase in the strikes on ports and bases as part of the struggle for communications, and to much else.

It is worth noting that despite the extreme threat to submarines from the anti-submarine forces not a single operation or other specially organized combat operations aimed at crushing and destroying the forces of the "anti-submarine war" took place. This undoubtedly was a major shortcoming in the system of struggle for communications.

The various branches of the forces of the fleets performed differing roles in the struggle for sea communications. Thus, of all the cargo ships sunk, submarines accounted for 65 per cent, aircraft about 20 per cent and surface ships 6 per cent, with 8 per cent of the ships being destroyed by mines.

Submarines confirmed their possibilities, already identified in the First World War, despite the much greater counter-action of the forces of anti-submarine defence. As well as destroying cargo vessels they were also able to inflict serious blows on warships and operate successfully against enemy submarines.

Although aviation did not make full use of its potential, it brought radical changes into the struggle at sea as a whole. It must be emphasized that the aviation forming part of the fleets operated, as a rule, more effectively than that which was temporarily made available to the fleet for fighting the sea foe. But while aircraft took only a second place in sinking the enemy's cargo ships, in the protection of their own sea communications they rank first—they accounted for over 40 per cent of all the submarines of the Axis countries sunk.

The role of surface ships in the fight against sea shipments was limited. The number of large surface ships solving this task was insignificant because of the serious threat they faced from submarines and aircraft. At the same time surface ships occupied a most important place in the protection of their communications, destroying over 35 per cent of the submarines of the Hitlerite coalition. It must also be recognized that as aircraft became technically more sophisticated and their numbers grew, the surface ships themselves became their carriers, consolidating their position as part of the fleets.

In evaluating the general results of the struggle for sea communications in the course of the Second World War, let us see whether submarines justified their use as a basic means of combating the enemy's shipping.

During the Second World War the Germans sunk 5150 merchant ships, 54 per cent of this number (68 per cent of the tonnage) accounted for by submarines. The most effective operations of submarines were in 1939-42: in that time they sank 2177 cargo vessels. From 1943 the effectiveness of the operations of submarines began to fall sharply and in the second half of the war they managed to sink only 651 ships.

The results of the operations of Japanese and Italian submarines against shipping introduce no special corrections to the information presented. The submarines of the Japanese fleet in the war sank, according to American figures, 147 merchant ships, and according to French figures 170 ships, with a total tonnage of 776,000 registered tons. The submarines of the Italian fleet (according to German figures) sank 105 ships with a total tonnage of about a million registered tons.[47]

What were the real causes of the change in the effectiveness of the strikes of the submarines? The main cause undoubtedly lay in the turn in the course of the war as a whole brought about on the Soviet-German front and directly influencing the course of events in all other theatres.

The influence of the general turn in the course of the war on the struggle for communications in the Atlantic was expressed in the fact that Nazi Germany was forced to concentrate its main efforts on the eastern front and weaken its forces in the Atlantic, taking from this theatre primarily aircraft and a considerable part of the ship complement. The allocations earmarked for the German fleet for this reason fell from 12.1 per cent of the total allocations for the armed forces in 1942 to 5.6 per cent in 1944. The number of operating submarines of the Axis countries also diminished.

Exploiting the weakening of the Germans in the western theatre due to the turn in the course of the war, the Allies made sea landings in North Africa, in Sicily and on the Appenine peninsula and compelled Italy to capitulate. This

[47] L. M. Yeremeyev and A. P. Shergin, *The Submarines of Foreign Fleets in the Second World War* (in Russian), pp. 66-69 and 334.

enabled them to transfer considerable sea forces from the Mediterranean to the Atlantic. An important role was also played by the anti-submarine forces of the Allies, the creation of which, in connection with the concentration of the main efforts of the enemy on the eastern front, presented no special difficulty. Against the German submarines operated 5500 specially constructed anti-submarine ships and 20,000 small craft. To every one German submarine there were 25 ships of the Allies and 100 planes, and for each German submarine at sea were 100 English and Americans.

However, although the anti-submarine forces pressed the submarines hard, they could not discredit and dethrone them as happened, for example, to battleships. In fact, submarines proved capable even in 1945 of continuing the battle. Of all the armed forces of Germany only the submarine fleet, right up to the end of the war, represented a most serious threat and the "anti-submarine war" ended only after the territory of Germany had been occupied by Allied armies.

A negative influence on the effectiveness of the operations of submarines was also exerted by the delay in their technical improvement and the diminished level of the training of German submarine crews, which also made it easier for anti-submarine forces to move ahead in competition with submarines. The intensified building of new Series 21 submarines begun by the Germans and the switch to the mass production of U-boats with more advanced Walter power units, though belated, clearly showed that even pre-atomic submarines had sufficient possibilities for successfully overcoming the advantages enjoyed by the anti-submarine forces.

In the "Battle for the Atlantic" a most important role was played by the building, developed in the USA and England, of cargo ships. In the war years they built merchant ships with a total tonnage of 42.5 million tons. i.e. almost double the losses suffered.

Thus, for the second time in history Germany in the course of a war fundamentally changed its pre-war views on the use of the navy and went over to the wide use of submarines for the struggle for sea communications but with a certain delay. And yet in the period of the Second World War Germany, building over 1100 submarines, took a heavy toll of the merchant fleets of her adversaries, destroying as much as 60 per cent of the pre-war stock. But it could not do more. The main reason for this, as we see it, is that the submarines did not have the support of other forces, notably aircraft, which could have been an irreplaceable means of reconnaisance, to fulfil the tasks of destroying anti-submarine forces and also to act against the economy of the opponent, particularly his shipbuilding industry, and to inflict blows on cargo ships in the ocean.

Such support was particularly necessary for the submarines of that time, still not fully underwater, and forced to surface periodically for charging accumulator batteries, which was also the main cause of their detection and defeat. Thus, the experience of the Second World War gives a graphic idea of the role which the ensuring of the operations of submarines directly in the ocean ought to play. In going over to their mass use, the German Command, however, left them to their own devices. Throughout the war not a single attempt was made to counter the anti-submarine forces of the Allies in an organized way from operating with total impunity. Herein evidently also lies the reason why 70 per cent of the German submarines were lost in transit to the areas of combat operations.

The battle of the US Navy against the marine shipments of Japan went quite a different way. By the start of the war, Japan had a merchant fleet with a total tonnage of 6.4 million registered tons and seized the merchant shipping of other countries with a total tonnage of 830,000 registered tons. Its potential for restoring losses was comparatively weak and the number and quality of the forces for protecting convoys were plainly inadequate.

Strange as it may seem for an island power, the Japanese fleet was not at all ready to protect sea shipments.

To combat Japanese shipments the Americans were able to make wide use of submarines, surface ships and aircraft and also mine-laying in Japanese waters, mostly from aircraft. Such conditions of the struggle for communications and the balance of the naval forces of the two sides enabled the Americans to sink in the war 2143 Japanese cargo vessels with a total tonnage of some 8 million registered tons,[48] seize control over the sea communications linking Japan to the territories in the southern seas and also to lay mines in the Japanese ports and at their approaches.

However, the Americans left alone the sea communications linking Japan to such economically important regions as Manchuria and Korea and to the Japanese armed forces stationed there. In fact, the strongest grouping of the Japanese land forces and the powerful economic base on the Asian mainland, and the communications with them, were not touched at all by the military operations of the Americans and allowed Japan to continue the war.

The sea blockade of Japan by the Americans was thus partially successful. For this reason the results of the struggle of the American fleet to disrupt the sea shipments of the enemy for all its impressiveness was not enough to make Japan surrender.

Thus, the fight for oceanic communications, for which huge forces of the fleets in the Atlantic and Pacific Oceans were mustered, in no small measure weakened the economy of the warring sides. This, in turn, had a considerable influence on the general course of the war, though not leading to decisive results.

The abundance of landing operations was quite unexpected for most fleets of the world, which at the start of the war were totally unprepared for this type of operation.

Basing themselves on the experience of the unsuccessful Dardanelles operation in the First World War, all the maritime powers failed to devote attention to landing operations. The potential of anti-landing defence was exaggerated and the increased offensive potential of land forces on a coast overlooked.

In the course of the Second World War the warring sides (leaving aside the Soviet fleet) staged over 500 landings, not counting minor diversionary reconnaisance raids. The Soviet fleet in the years of the Great Patriotic War mounted over 100 landings, varying in scale.

[48] M. F. Stepanov, *Replenishment of the Naval and Merchant Fleets in the Second World War* (in Russian), Morskoi sbornik. 1959, No. 11, p. 84.

Landing operations, as a rule, involved a large number of diverse forces and equipment in the concentration of which, on a battle unit at the front, no single form of operations could rival. Landing operations are characterized by a particularly high saturation of combat clashes of varying degree, heavy combat losses and considerable expenditure of material-technical resources. They were often accompanied or preceded by a major engagement to destroy the enemy's forces at sea. A frequent distinguishing feature of the landing operations of foreign fleets was that they, as a rule, were conducted in a comparatively favourable setting in the course of a successful strategic offensive in a given theatre.

Considerable changes in the methods of disembarking invasion forces in the course of the war occurred under the influence of the ever-growing use of aircraft. Dominance in the air in the area of an operation was an essential pre-requisite for its success even if the enemy predominated in naval strength. By the end of the war, airborne landings had become an obligatory constituent part of naval landing operations.

The success of landing operations in the Second World War was determined by a considerable increase in the offensive possibilities of the forces of the fleets, their increased capacity to break through the defence of the enemy and attain the aims of the operation, and also by the mass use of landing craft and disembarking devices. In the course of the war there were only two miscarriages in disembarking operational invasion forces (Midway, Port Moresby) and not a single unsuccessful operation on a strategic scale. This was explained by the general military-political conditions favourable for the invaders and also by the concentration of the strength of the invasion force outstripping the defence. In the whole war not a single successful anti-landing operation was undertaken with delivery of powerful and successive blows on the enemy, from the points of assembly to the area of disembarking of the invasion force on a coast. The reasons for this were usually either the belatedness of the intelligence on the preparations by the enemy of the landing or the lack of means for strikes at all stages of the operation.

All in all, landing operations in the course of the Second World War took one of the leading places in the armed struggle at sea. In individual theatres, in particular in the Pacific, where the land forces of the warring sides did not meet face-to-face, landing operations and the accompanying combat clashes of the fleets formed the main content of the armed conflict.

While in the First World War such an important type of operation of naval forces as the destruction at sea of the strike groupings of the forces of the enemy's fleet was conducted separately from other combat operations of the fleet, being as it were self-sufficient, in the Second World War such operations were nearly always constituent parts either of the struggle for oceanic communications or landing operations. The importance of artillery weapons as a decisive means of achieving victory in battle sharply diminished so that the battleships—the main carriers of large-calibre armaments—lost their pre-eminent place in the navies. Sea battles were often waged with use of aircraft at distances far exceeding the range of artillery fire.

In the course of the Second World War the scale of combat operations against naval forces in the bases and also the destruction of important military and economic targets on the shores of the enemy increased. While in the First World War only five surface ships and submarines were destroyed in their bases (or about 1 per cent of all ships lost), in the Second World War up to 158 ships were destroyed (8 per cent of all ships lost). It should be noted that aircraft accounted for some 80 per cent of ships destroyed and damaged during raids on the bases.

The Second World War made it necessary to re-evaluate the role of individual types of forces forming part of the navies and also the importance of the fleets themselves in the system of the armed forces of the country.

In the course of the war the fleets became less homogeneous. They began to include different kinds of forces in a ratio optimal for battle at sea. Techniques were also developed and refined for combined action on the enemy with varying forces and a variety of weapons for more thoroughly prepared and varied combat orders.

The experience of combat operations at sea in the First and Second World Wars confirmed the need to move over to the building of balanced fleets. The powerful Japanese fleet of the period of the Second World War not, however, having the necessary forces to do battle with American submarines and protect its shipments, is an example of an unbalanced fleet.

As for the importance of the different types of forces for the fleets, the most important event in the course of the war turned out to be the ending of the use of battle fleets which had held sway for centuries. The experience of the war made all states abandon the building of new battleships and with the end of the war they took them out of service. Primacy among surface ships passed to aircraft carriers.

Submarines became the most important means of battle at sea. And if individual states in the pre-war period under-estimated their possibilities, in the course of the war they changed their views on the use of submarine forces. Thus, Hitlerite Germany, having at the start of the war only 57 submarines, during it built 1131 (not including midgets). It should be noted that despite the swift development of the forces and resources of anti-submarine defence of the enemies, the number of German submarines steadily grew and on 1 January 1945 was 493 units.

Earlier the view was repeatedly expressed that submarines are a weapon of the weakest fleet and that strong fleets have no need of them. However, this view was flatly rebutted by the experience of the war when, for example, it became clear that the submarines of the strongest American fleet performed a most important role not only in the fight against Japanese shipping but also against surface ships and submarines. This led to the very rapid construction of submarines in the war years in the USA, the number of which almost trebled.

The building of submarines also proceeded apace in other countries. In the main imperialist states during the war 1630 submarines were built—almost four times as many as there were in the fleets at the start of the war. And despite the huge losses (1195) of submarine units, their number by the end of the war was more than twice that before it.[49]

[49] M. E. Stepanov, *The Replenishment of the Naval and Merchant Fleets in the Second World War* (in Russian), Morskoi sbornik, 1959, No. 11, p. 83.

Naval aviation, both carrier and land-based, swiftly developed in the war years. Its specialization became necessary, resulting in the appearance of strike (torpedo-carrying and bombing), anti-submarine, pursuit and reconnaissance aircraft. In the course of the war, aviation firmly took its place among the main and leading branches of the fleet.

In parallel went the building on an enormous scale of anti-submarine and anti-aircraft ships and craft. In the war some 6000 were built and by mid-1945 their share in the fleets had risen several times as compared with pre-war.

Other surface ships were also given a further boost. Surface ships of new classes appeared, built in massive numbers, such as special escort and landing craft. They completely justified their use and now form part of navies. The sea-landing operations widely used in the Second World War demanded the creation, in addition to landing craft, of special landing-disembarking devices. Thus, the US naval forces by the end of the war had over 200 specially constructed large landing craft and several thousand units for disembarking equipment.

Thus, the navies made a fundamental contribution to the armed struggle and played an important role in the Second World War which was of a clearly marked continental character. The activity of the fleets was largely directed to helping the land fronts and meeting their requirements, which logically stemmed from the character of the armed conflict.

Of special importance was the fact that, taking on itself the blow of the main part of the armed forces of Germany and its satellites and then holding up and destroying them, the Soviet Union gave the Allied states the opportunity to develop their military-economic potential, mobilize their armed forces and undertake the wide and massive building of the fleets without interference.

The Creation of the Soviet Fleet

The history of the Soviet Navy was made by the Great October Socialist Revolution. The Navy invariably took a most active part in the struggle to gain power, in the armed protection of the young Soviet Republic from the war thrust of international reaction and internal counter-revolution. The famous revolutionary and fighting traditions of the seamen of the Russian fleet, their devotion to the cause of Lenin and high organizational capacity brought them into the first ranks of the fighters against the enemies of October.

One of the important conditions ensuring the victory of the revolution was that the Party succeeded in creating an armed bulwark of revolution uniting the workers' Red Guard with the masses of revolutionary sailors and soldiers. The close link of naval seamen with the workers hardened in revolutionary battles and the constant leadership of the Central Committee of the Party were determined by the vigorous development of the revolutionary movement in the first place in the Baltic fleet and the active participation of naval seamen in the fight for the victory of October. Relying on the seamen of the Baltic fleet, the Bolsheviks were able to intensify work to win over the soldiers of the regular army and the seamen of other fleets and flotillas.

By the autumn of 1917 the Russian fleet in all theatres had over 1100 fighting ships and auxiliary vessels and numbered some 180,000 men. The bulk of its forces was in the Baltic and was based at Helsingfors, Reval, Kronstadt and Petrograd. This was the real and powerful force of the proletarian revolution which, according to Lenin's idea, together with the workers' detachments and troop units on the side of the revolution, was by a combined attack to take over all the key positions. In line with this, the Baltic fleet was assigned a decisive place in the plan of the armed uprising. Lenin wrote that the uprising "... *may* and must be solved by Petersburg, Moscow, Helsingfors, Kronstadt, Vyborg and Reval. . . . The fleet, Kronstadt, Vyborg, Reval may and must go to Petersburg, smash the Kornilov regiments, raise both capitals, set in motion mass agitation for power, immediately handing over the land to the peasants and immediately offering peace, bring down the Kerensky government and create this power."[50]

Under the Lenin plan the Baltic fleet was to ensure the protection of Petrograd from a possible sea strike of the German fleet and take a direct part in the fighting in the capital and at its approaches.

After the historic decision of the Central Committee for an armed uprising the Baltic fleet prepared itself to discharge the tasks devolving on it: bring fighting ships into the Neva and bring under fire the Winter Palace and other important points, ensure combat interaction with the detachments of the Red Guard and soldiers of the garrison, seize the railway lines leading to Petrograd and deploy large forces of seamen for joint combat operations with the Petersburg proletariat.

Fulfilling the will of the Party and Lenin, the Baltic seamen sent large forces to Petrograd. The battleship *Zarya svobody* entered the sea canal to use its whole fire power in aid of the revolution. A detachment of its seamen occupied the station at Ligovo. Seamen of the No. 1 fleet crew seized the Petrograd-Oranienbaum railway line. The cruiser *Aurora* and the minelayers *Amur* and *Khoper* took up station on the Neva to bombard the Winter Palace. Torpedo boats moored at the quay on Vasilevsky Island. A combined sea detachment from Kronstadt numbering over 10,000 men and about 4,500 seamen from Helsingfors arrived in Petrograd to take part in the seizure of the post office, telephone and telegraph stations, bridges, railway stations, power stations, the buildings of the chief army HQ and the Winter Palace. The seamen also took over control of the railways linking Finland with Petrograd and did not allow the forces of counter-revolution to sever the bridges in the city, so creating favourable conditions for the victory of the revolution.

At 9.40 p.m. on 7 November the historic shots from the *Aurora* rang out. The assault on the Winter Palace began, ending at 1.50 a.m. on 8 November. The bourgeois government, under a convoy of sailors, was moved to the Petropavlovsk fortress. The armed uprising had won. The workers and peasants of Russia led by the party of communists took state power into their own hands.

Lenin personally despatched detachments of sailors to the key regions of the struggle for power. Baltic seamen were sent to Moscow to support detachments of the Red Guard and took part in the crushing of the counter-revolution.

[50] V. I. Lenin, *Complete Collected Works*, Vol. 34, p. 390 (in Russian).

Seamen formed the main force eradicating the chief focus of counter-revolution at the front—the staff of the High Command in Mogilev.

A great contribution to the struggle to establish Soviet power was made by the seamen of the Black Sea fleet and the Arctic, Caspian, Amur, Siberian, Saimin, Amu-Dar'ya and Chud flotillas.

Lenin held in high regard the services of the naval seamen as steadfast fighters for the liberation of the working people. In a speech to the First All-Russian Congress of the Navy on 22 November (5 December) 1917 he said: "In the fleet we see a brilliant model of the creative possibilities of the working masses, in this respect the fleet has shown itself as an advanced detachment".[51]

An indication of the recognition of the services of naval seamen to the revolution was the following event important to the fleet. In December 1917 in the elections to the Constituent Assembly Lenin was put forward as a candidate for Deputy in five electoral districts, including the Baltic fleet district. In this connection he wrote to the Commission on the Elections to the Constituent Assembly that he wished to go forward as a candidate from the Baltic fleet. Thus, Lenin became the deputy for the Baltic.

Naval seamen in the Civil War

Power was gained but the next task was to keep and protect it from numerous enemies. The interventionists and White Guards tried to strangle the young Soviet state. Plots and mutinies took shape and fronts of the Civil War were formed. The fight against counter-revolution and the interventionists widened.

Naval seamen at the call of the Party stepped into the first ranks of the defenders of Soviet power. They took an active part in smashing all the main foci of counter-revolution in the country, fought the White Finns, the troops of Kerensky and Krasnov, the bands of Kaledin at Rostov-on-Don, the troops of the Central Council in the Ukraine, the White Poles in Byelorussia and detachments of the Otaman Dutov at Orenburg.

The victory of the revolution in Russia met with the fierce resistance of all the forces of the old world. Against the young Soviet Republic stood Germany, England, France, Japan, USA and their satellites, seeking to destroy the first state of workers and peasants in the world. And thus military intervention began in 1918. Acting as stranglers of the freedom of the peoples, the governments of these countries took it upon themselves to support Kolchak, Denikin, Yudenich, Wrangel and Pilsudski.

On 18 February 1918 German troops went over to the offensive all along the line of the front. The ships of the Kaiser's fleet entered the Gulf of Finland to strike at the heart of the revolution—Petrograd. The German armies quickly moved ahead and soon reached Reval (Tallinn), Pskov and Narva. A frightful threat hung over the Soviet land. With the growth of the external and internal threat the Red Guard and the temporarily formed detachments were no longer in a position to solve successfully the tasks of protecting the revolution and defending the country. The Party took measures to set up the Workers-Peasant

[51] V. I. Lenin, *Complete Collected Works,* Vol. 35, p. 114 (in Russian).

Red Army and the Red Fleet which were formed in the course of a bitter struggle.

On 28 January 1918, Lenin signed a decree on the organization of the Worker-Peasant Red Army and on 11 February the creation of the Worker-Peasant Red Fleet. The first People's Commissar on Naval Affairs was the bolshevik seaman P. E. Dybenko from the Baltic. These decrees made by Lenin laid down the foundation for building the Soviet armed forces represented by an army and fleet of a new socialist type.

The backbone and cementing force of the units created were Petrograd workers, the revolutionary-minded soldiers and naval seamen who had heroically battled against superior forces of the enemy.

The morale-fighting qualities of the naval seamen displayed in battles for the emergence and the protection of the young Soviet Republic were highly esteemed by the military command. Thus, already in January 1918 a directive of the People's Commissariat on Military Affairs stated: "In connection with the formation of detachments of the socialist army and their impending rapid despatch to the front it is necessary to detail a platoon of comrade seamen to each echelon formed of volunteers (complement 1000 men) in order to weld them".[52] As a result, in the units of the young Red Army operating in the Petrograd direction, the main one at that time, to each thousand Red Army men there were some 40 seamen.

The position of the Baltic and Black Sea fleets had then become extremely difficult. The People's Commissar for Foreign Affairs G. V. Chicherin said at that time that the question of the fleet was at the centre of the entire action of German diplomacy. The Baltic fleet, based at Helsingfors and Reval, under the Brest-Litovsk peace terms, had to be immediately withdrawn to Russian bases or be disarmed. The Germans reckoned on seizing our ships which could not break through the ice of the Gulf of Finland. However, the ships of the Baltic fleet on the direct instructions of Lenin successfully completed an heroic "ice voyage" arriving in Kronstadt and Petrograd. The fleet was saved from possible seizure of its ships by German troops. This gave stability to the defence of the capital and consolidated the position of the Soviet Republic.

In the summer of 1918 the imperialists. setting themselves the task of breaking through from the sea to Petrograd, concentrated considerable forces of the Royal Navy in the Gulf of Finland. To stop the English interventionist fleet from reaching Petrograd, the ships of the Baltic fleet on 14 August laid a dense minefield of almost 1500 sea mines blocking the way of the enemy to Petrograd from the sea. The shore artillery of Kronstadt set up an unbreakable defence firing line protecting the citadel of the revolution. The failure of the interventionists and White Guards to capture Petrograd was a great service rendered by the fleet.

In the years of the Civil War the Baltic fleet was a base and smithy for resources in the creation of the whole Soviet fleet. From its units came ships, aircraft and arms and Baltic seamen became the main nucleus in forming numerous flotillas and detachments.

In the south of the country the Germans occupied the whole of the Ukraine

[52] *Central State Archives of Navy,* folio r 5, op. 1, section 149, 1. 26.

and therefore the Black Sea fleet had to move from Sevastopol to Novorossiisk. Since Novorossiisk was also threatened by occupation, the ships, to avoid seizure by the Germans, on the order of Lenin, were scuttled in Tsemessa Bay.

The 1918 November revolution in Germany removed from our motherland the bondage terms of the Brest treaty. However, the respite provided by the treaty soon ended. Open foreign armed intervention began. In the spring of 1918 the first fronts appeared. The Soviet Republic was ringed by enemies.

In March 1918 the troops of the interventionists landed in Murmansk, in April in Vladivostok and then in the Black Sea ports. It should be noted that they were disembarked from the sea and operated where the Soviet Republic had no naval fleet. In the Baltic Sea, where quite a strong fleet was maintained, the interventionists hesitated to make a landing.

The outstanding commanders of the Civil War, the main events of which took place on land, realistically evaluated the importance of the fleet for the interventionists and saw it as a force capable of fundamentally influencing the course of the armed struggle. As Commander-in-Chief of the Armed Forces of the Soviet Republic S. S. Kamenev wrote on this: "In his fighting qualities the enemy, with a larger number of trained command staff and better technical means, was stronger than the Red Army.

"Another no less characteristic feature of the general situation was the supply to the enemy's rear lines from the seas. Across the seas the enemy had a constant link with the Entente. Hence the constant support by the Entente of the ever-weakening forces and means of the enemy. Without this support the enemy would probably have been forced to withdraw after the first battles unsuccessful for him."[53]

In other words, the fleets of the imperialist states in the years of the Civil War and foreign intervention served as the main instrument of their policy used to destroy by force of arms the great gains of October.

At the same time the limitation of the possibilities of the Soviet Red Fleet, inferior in number of ships and arms to the fleets of the hostile coalition, made much more complicated for us the conditions of armed struggle on all fronts of the Civil War. Red Army troops were forced to fight against the armies of the interventionists after they had seized bridgeheads and set up on them support points and supply bases. To attack the enemy while crossing the sea or not allow reinforcements of his troops sent by sea could not be done by the young Soviet armed forces, not having the fleet necessary for this.

The Communist Party and the Soviet Government took all possible measures to safeguard the sea lines of the young Soviet state. Lenin in July 1918 wrote to the People's Commissariat on Naval Affairs: "I strongly urge that all measures be taken to speed up the delivery to the Caspian Sea of naval ships of all suitable types".[54] In August of that year after the arrival of four torpedo boats of the Baltic fleet in Rybinsk he sent a telegram: "I order the urgent completion of the loading of guns, shells and coal and their immediate despatch to Nizhny. This work must be finished in the shortest time. . . . Each moment's delay will entail

[53] S. S. Kamenev, *Notes on the Civil War and Military Construction*, Moscow, Voenizdat, 1963, p. 58 (in Russian).
[54] V. I. Lenin, *Complete Collected Works*, Vol. 50, p. 121 (in Russian).

a heavy responsibility and result in appropriate measures for those at fault. Telegraph the execution of this order".[55] By 24 August, torpedo boats had already arrived in Nizhny Novgorod and soon joined in the battles for Kazan. In October 1918 on the initiative of Lenin the Astrakhan-Caspian flotilla was formed.

In April 1919 Lenin, in a letter to the Petrograd organizations demanded that ". . . all measures and forces be deployed to get ready a flotilla on the Volga. *Repair* in particular".[56]

The strengthening, thanks to the vigorous intervention of Lenin, of the Volga and Astrakhan-Caspian flotillas helped to crush the White Guards and interventionists bent on capturing an area vitally important for the Soviet Republic.

The enthusiasm and martial mastery of the seamen made it possible in the most difficult conditions of disorder to form numerous flotillas and successfully fulfil a wide range of combat tasks. In the years of the Civil War over 30 naval flotillas were set up. As well as intact old ships the fleet at that time had over 2000 various river and lake vessels recast into fighting ships and manned in the main by naval seamen.

In the spring of 1919 the main battles unfolded on the eastern front, where Kolchak's troops went over to the offensive. In shattering this offensive and crushing the White Guards an important role was played by the Volga flotilla operating on the Kama, Vyatka, Byelaya and Ufa.

In an attempt of support Kolchak, Yudenich's troops and White Finns mounted an assault on Petrograd. To ensure the capture of revolutionary Petrograd the English concentrated in the Gulf of Finland large forces of the fleet, including over 100 warships. On the order of Lenin, the Baltic fleet developed active combat operations against the English ships. Losing 18 ships the fleet of the interventionists was forced to quit the waters of the Gulf of Finland, carrying off 16 damaged ships.

This was soon followed by the offensive of Denikin's armies in the south in connection with which Lenin's letter was published on 9 June 1919. "All in the fight against Denikin". It noted that the most critical moment of the socialist revolution was at hand.

On the flanks of our southern and south-eastern fronts, operating against the Denikinists, the seamen of the Dnieper and Volga-Caspian flotillas were in active combat.

In June 1920 Wrangel's army from the Crimea went over to the offensive to the north. To unite the counter-revolutionary forces of the Don and Kuban, the enemy tried to stage landings to the rear of our troops on the coast of the Azov Sea. These landings were smashed by concerted operations of the Red Army and of the Azov flotilla.

On all fronts of the Civil War the principal operations in the combat activity of the sea forces of the young Soviet Republic were the joint ones with the ground troops in which the seamen gave the troops fire backing, put ashore landing parties, fought against the sea and river forces of the enemy, ensured the crossing by troops of water barriers and transported military supplies.

[55] *Ibid.*, p. 167.
[56] *Ibid.*, p. 296.

The naval seamen defending the gains of the Great October Socialist Revolution performed wonders of heroism not only aboard ship but also on the land fronts where some 75,000 seamen fought. The names of A. G. Zhelaznyakov, B. F. Lyubimov, N. G. Markin. M. I. Martynov, A. V. Mokrousov, P. D. Khokhryakov and many others will never fade in the memory of their grateful descendants. The Soviet people still admire the devotion of these men to the cause of communism, their astonishing daring and courage—qualities which were characteristic of the intrepid band of sailors—heroes of great October.

The Navy in this hard struggle completely justified the trust of the Party, Government and people. The events of the Civil War once again confirmed the need to have as part of the armed forces of our country a powerful and comprehensively developed navy.

The main source of our victory in the Civil War was the leadership of the country and its armed forces by the Communist Party headed by Lenin. Naval seamen with a sense of special pride note that Vladimir Il'ich was the creator of our famous navy, all of whose fighting activity was stamped by his great genius. He created the foundations of Soviet military science, on the basis of which was also born Soviet naval art.

Leninist bases of Soviet military science

The scientific ideological and theoretical basis of the building of the armed forces of our State is the Marxist-Leninist theory of war and the army. Lenin said that in any field of Soviet construction it is necessary to take into account objective laws and regularities, the dependence of practical activity on political and economic conditions. This also applies to the armed forces. Therefore, the creation of armed forces of a new type also called for the creation of their own Soviet military science for, as Lenin pointed out, without science a modern army cannot be built.

For the successful waging of war against a strong enemy the armies and fleets must possess the necessary military knowledge. In this connection Lenin urged that one "learns the business of war in a real way."[57] That is why military questions received the closest attention at all the congresses of the Communist Party and Plenums of the Central Committee in the period of the Civil War. Lenin untiringly occupied himself with developing Soviet military science. His contribution to the treatment of the most important military problems and fundamental military-theoretical questions is inestimable. He made a scientific analysis of the laws of modern war and characterization of the ways of waging it. Unlike many authorities of the past who confine the content of military science simply to the sphere of military art, Vladimir Il'ich regarded the theory and practice of the business of war as an inseparable part of the social activity of people living in a class society. As far back as 1905 in an article *Fall of Port Arthur* he showed the effect of the objective patterns of modern war, the decisive role in it of the popular masses, the significance of moral and economic factors and concluded that the outcome of armed struggle depends not only on

[57] V. I. Lenin, *Complete Collected Works*, Vol. 36, p. 26 (in Russian).

the army but also on the whole people, i.e. on the rear (in the widest sense of the word).

Defining the scope of military knowledge necessary to the workers, Lenin noted that this knowledge includes both questions of tactics and questions of organization, the planned waging of the armed struggle, mastery of new complex military technique and modern ways of waging war. The workers need not only the A to Z of the business of war, he taught, but also knowledge of the laws, principles and rules of military art.

In analysing military forces Lenin pointed to the need of taking into account the number and preparedness of the members of the army and fleet and also the number and quality of weapons and military technology. He sharply criticized a dismissive attitude to the appraisal of the forces and potential of the enemy, and always insisted on studying the enemy together with his strong and weak points. "All will agree that unreasonable and even criminal is the behaviour of an army which is not ready to master all the types of weapons and all modes and techniques of struggle which the enemy has or may have".[58] At a theoretical level this thesis, of topical importance to us today, means that we make use of the individual elements and achievements of bourgeois military art.

Lenin oriented the Party to the principle that ". . . in any war, victory finally depends on the state of the spirit of those masses who spill their blood on the battlefield. Belief in the justness of the war, awareness of the need to sacrifice one's life for the benefit of ones brothers elevates the spirit of soldiers and makes them endure unheard-of hardships".[59] In the epoch of imperialism when wars are waged by peoples this tenet assumes special importance. Just wars generate patriotism, the high morale of the people and army and, conversely, unjust wars cannot produce in them a high morale since they are waged in the interests of the greed of the exploiters.

In the activity of all the organs of the Soviet state including military ". . . the primacy of the policy of the Communist Party must be frankly recognized".[60]

The leadership by the Communist Party of the armed forces and Party political work in the army and fleet were and remain one of the main sources of their might. Lenin considered that it was necessary to consolidate and ably support moral steadfastness with the whole force of ideological influence of the Party on the masses, the organizing role of the party organizations, political organs and the command staff. He repeatedly pointed out that where Party-political work is well defined, the better the discipline, the higher the spirit and morale of the troops and the greater the victories.

Leninist precepts played a tremendous role in working out the bases of Soviet military science. Their significance has even further grown in a century of technical progress, of the creation of fundamentally new armed forces and the building of a Soviet ocean-going fleet. They are the methodological base of Soviet military doctrine, the foundation of the military and naval sciences, and form the basis of the military policy of the Party, orienting the Soviet people to the need to keep the defence capacity of our state at the highest level.

[58] V. I. Lenin, *Complete Collected Works*, Vol. 41, p. 81 (in Russian).
[59] *Ibid.*, p. 402.
[60] *Ibid.*, p. 402.

Vladimir Il'ich Lenin paid much attention to military art and above all to strategy indissolubly linked with the policy of the state. The vitality of his military art resides primarily in its creative and scientific character, strict heed of the laws of armed struggle, its ability to determine unerringly the main direction of the war, to choose the time, place and method of delivering the decisive blow and also to use the tremendous revolutionary energy, initiative and enthusiasm of the people.

What marked Lenin as a strategist was flexibility in the choice of the forms of struggle, a surprising ability to determine the moment of transition to decisive operations. Under his guidance the most important principles of achieving victory were put into practice: to be stronger than the enemy at the decisive moment at the decisive point, to master all forms and means of armed struggle and rationally combine defence and offence, depending on the particular situation. The leader of the proletariat was an advocate of the most decisive offensive operations (to the point of completely smashing the enemy) and considered as one of the factors ensuring victory the suddenness of strikes, seizure and retention of the initiative. It is necessary to try to take the enemy unawares, he taught, and pick the moment when his troops are scattered. At the same time military vigilance taken to the highest limit is necessary. "To let go or lose one's head— is to lose all."[61]

Running like a red thread through all the Lenin directives, letters and instructions is the idea of the need for firmness and sense of purpose in fulfilling the plans set, the harmfulness of any kind of wavering and indecision at crucial moments of a battle.

One of the characteristic features of the military art of Lenin was the special care taken in preparing planned operations. "Any engagement", he pointed out, "involves the abstract possibility of defeat and there is no way of lessening this possibility other than the organized preparation of the engagement."[62]

The principles of strategy worked out in the years of the Civil War—study of the strong and weak points of the enemy, anticipating his thoughts, activity and boldness, strength of purpose and flexibility of plans, creation of superiority of forces and resources in the main directions, correct determination of the most dangerous grouping at a given moment and resoluteness of the operations—were further developed in the years of the Great Patriotic War and in the post-war period.

Many principles expounded by Lenin in his works, instructions and orders refer to operational art, for example, determining the goal of the operation, the deployment of forces and resources and the choice of the modes and forms of the operations on the scale of a front, fleet, army or flotilla. The requirement always to achieve unity of thinking and action of the forces in an operation, establishing strict control over the execution of orders, directives and dispositions, are still of tremendous importance for us.

He considered as the basis of correct and purposeful leadership the principle of leadership by one person, centralism and unity of will from top to bottom.

Lenin was not only a theoretician laying the foundations of Soviet military

[61] V. I. Lenin, *Complete Collected Works*, Vol. 39, p. 55 (in Russian).
[62] *Ibid.*, Vol. 6, p. 137.

science. His activity in the years of the Civil War was an unsurpassed model of the ability to anticipate the course of events, mobilize and concentrate the efforts of the whole country and its armed forces on gaining victory over the enemy. All the most important operations of the Red Army and Navy in that period were worked out under his guidance.

The very rich military legacy of Lenin gives a vivid idea of the leader as a fighting guide for defence of the Soviet state, a major military strategist, a commander of the revolutionary masses combining control of the armed forces with leadership of the country in a most complex internal and international situation.

The vitally creative ideas of Vladimir Il'ich and the unremitting organizational work of the Communist Party in putting them into practice found full support among naval seamen and served for them as a guiding star in the fight against the enemies of the Soviet state.

Restoration of the fleet (1921-28)

Crushing the interventionists and White Guards, our people set about peaceful socialist construction in extraordinarily difficult conditions of chaos and devastation of the country, and with a hostile policy of the imperialists aimed at destroying Soviet power, which still had to fight against the remnants of counter-revolution.

By that time the Soviet country had no fleet in the Far East and the North, nor did it really exist in the Black Sea since nearly all the remaining ships had been taken off by the White Guards to foreign ports. Only the Baltic fleet and a few river naval flotillas existed. Many ships were badly in need of repair. Over half the command staff were officers of the old Czarist fleet. Ratings and junior commanders were in need of replacement. Soviet command forces needed theoretical and practical training.

Assessing the state of the fleet of that time, M. V. Frunze wrote: "In the general course of the Revolution and the turmoil of the Civil War, particularly heavy blows fell on the navy. As a result we were deprived of the greater and better part of its material stock, deprived of the vast majority of experienced and knowledgeable commanders who played an even greater role in the life and work of the fleet than for other types of arms; we lost a whole number of sea bases and, finally, lost the main nucleus of Red Fleet rank and file. In sum, all this meant that we had no fleet."[63]

But unlike the pre-October period of the history of our motherland, when a characteristic feature of the ruling circles of Russia was failure to understand the role of the fleet, the Party and the Soviet Government attached great importance to its development, correctly assessing the need to have a fleet worthy of the Soviet state and its great ideas.

Fighting was still going on with the White Guards in the south of the country and in the Far East and Lenin was already concerned about the regeneration of the fleet. In October 1920 the Council of Labour and Defence adopted the

[63] M. V. Frunze, *On Youth*, Moscow, Molodaya gvardiya, 1937, p. 62 (in Russian).

decision proposed by Vladimir Il'ich to instruct the Petrograd Soviet of Deputies and especially the Committee for the defence of Petrograd to ". . . pay special attention to the stepping-up of work on the restoration of the Baltic fleet. . . ."[64] This was the first decision to strengthen the fleet and create the necessary material base for it.

A most important event in the early gigantic construction of socialism was the Tenth Congress of the Party in 1921 taking measures to buttress further the defence of our motherland. Its decisions served as the basis for developing large-scale and planned work in the country to restore the fleet. In the decisions of the Tenth Congress of the Party, on the initiative of Lenin, it was stated of the fleet: "Congress considers it necessary, in line with the general position and material resources of the Soviet Republic, to take measures to regenerate and strengthen the Red Navy."[65] The Congress also laid down specific measures for achieving this goal.

A major contribution to the creation of the Soviet fleet was made by the Lenin Komsomol deciding at the Fifth Congress (1922) to act as its patron. In the first two years in Komsomol recruitment drives some 8000 youngsters joined the navy and about a thousand Komsomol members were sent to naval training institutions. This improved the political health of fleet personnel.

A manifestation of the care of the people for the navy was the repeated holding of Red Navy Weeks, affording it considerable material aid.

In 1921, sustained work began to restore the ports and the shipbuilding industry. This already opened the way in 1922 to the repair of ships and vessels and to the formation of small units, capable of fighting.

By 1924 the Baltic fleet already had two battleships, one cruiser, eight destroyers, nine submarines and other ships. The Black Sea fleet by that time included one cruiser, two destroyers, two submarines and twelve ships of other classes. The flotillas on the Caspian and the Amur were all restored. An indication of the pace of restoration of the fleet was the growth in its total displacement which in thousand tons in 1923 was 82, in 1924—90, in 1925—116 and in 1926—139.

In December 1925 the Fourteenth Party Congress set a course for the socialist industrialization of the country. The impending development of industry opened up new prospects for strengthening the defence of the country and the technical renovation of the armed forces including the fleet.

Frunze at a conference of political workers in November 1924 said: "Some comrades because of the lack of resources in our country feel it better to concentrate all our attention on the land army. Such a view is quite false. . . . The Revolutionary Military Council firmly and unshakeably supports the view that the fleet is extremely necessary to us and that we must keep on developing it. . . . It is becoming increasingly necessary for us to embark without delay on the construction of new ships."[66]

What kind of a fleet does the country need? This question was on the agenda

[64] V. I. Lenin, *War Correspondence* (1917-1920), Moscow, Voenizdat, 1957, p. 256 (in Russian).
[65] *CPSU The Resolutions and Decisions of the Congresses, Conferences and the Plenums of the CC,* 8th ed. Revised and amended, Vol. 2, Moscow, Politizdat, 1970, p. 265 (in Russian).
[66] M. V. Frunze, *Selected Works,* Moscow, Voenizdat, 1951, pp. 286-287 (in Russian).

right from the start of the planned regeneration of the fleet. Its importance in that period was also dictated by the fact that limited material resources demanded strict economy in everything.

The answer to this question was given by the Central Committee of the Party which, on the basis of a thorough analysis of the main tasks of the fleet and the practical possibilities of building it, determined the role and place of the navy in the system of the armed forces of the Republic. In line with this in December 1926 the first six-year new shipbuilding programme was adopted. It provided for the building in the main of small ships (36 torpedo boats, 18 guard ships) and also twelve submarines.

In the period of restoration of the fleet perhaps the prime and most burning problem was the training of crews devoted to Soviet power, especially command staffs, since most of the officers of the Czarist fleet, because of their class allegiance, were in the camp of counter-revolution.

By decisions of the Central Committee of the Party thousands of communist seamen, who had gone to the Civil War fronts from their ships, now returned to the fleet. At the same time special mobilizations for the fleet of Communist and Komsomol members followed and in 1922-23 the first recruitment drives for volunteers were held amongst the latter.

All this made possible the successful solution of the problem of training not only among the ratings but also the command personnel of the fleet. Planned work was begun by training detachments, command and engineering colleges, and a naval academy where communist seamen who had emerged in the years of the revolution and the civil war came to train. Thus, in the first stage ships were restored and completed, new personnel trained and the organizational foundations of the fleet laid down. The fleet as a fighting force was regenerated.

Of course, these forces were small and the imperialists did not cease active preparations for armed assault on the young Soviet Republic. Therefore, work to strengthen the army and build the fleet steadily continued.

Because of the paucity of ship stock at that time, persistent searches were made for ways of solving the task of defending our sea borders with the forces of a small fleet in interaction with land forces. At the same time sustained creative military-theoretical work was done to look for effective ways of solving combat tasks by the limited forces of the fleet. In the course of the search was born the "theory of the small war" which starting from specific conditions defined rational means and forms of the struggle of the fleet against a stronger sea foe. This theory, as a whole, corresponded to the actual combat possibilities of our fleet at that time, the urgent tasks of the defence of the country, which had just seen the end of the Civil War and was forced to prepare to rebuff the next aggression, and to the economic possibilities of the Soviet state. Its essence was the delivery from different directions of short strikes on the main target of the adversary without separating from their bases the covertly concentrated, interacting diverse forces of the fleet. The basic form of interaction proposed was the concentrated (combined) strike of surface ships and craft, submarines, aircraft and shore artillery organized at a defended minefield headquarters. At that time this was the most effective, realistic and practical way of deploying the limited forces of the fleet for defending its coast in battle against a stronger sea foe. This was, as a whole, the defensive concept of a weak fleet.

In May 1928, the USSR Revolutionary Military Council revised and again clearly defined the role and place of the navy within the armed forces. The fleet was set the following main tasks: back-up of operations of the ground troops in the maritime directions, joint defence with land troops of the shores, bases of the fleet and the politico-economic centres on the coast, and operations on the sea communications of an enemy. The building of the fleet was oriented to the creation of light surface and underwater forces, strengthening the shore and mines-positional defence and also the creation of shore-based naval aviation.

Soviet naval seamen at that time, like many generations of their forebears—progressive figures of the Russian fleet—well understood the importance of the navy for strengthening the international prestige of the country, its military might, the defence of its immense sea borders and for protecting the state interests of the Soviet Union on the seas and oceans, and constantly looked for ways of strengthening its military power. In the search along these lines, in the conflict of ideas, views and trends, 1930 saw the introduction of the first Combat Regulations of the Sea Forces, which was the outcome of long research work of Soviet military specialists in which the experience of training formations, units and ships was generalized and the views of probable adversaries taken into account.

This regulated the combat activity of the ships of the fleet, naval aviation and shore defence units and laid special emphasis on their interaction and concentrated use in battle and operation. In the rules, oriented realistically to our limited and mainly coastal forces, preference was given to active forms of armed struggle and the endeavour to fulfil even defensive tasks by a decisive onslaught. Initiative and the wide use of new tactical procedures unknown to the enemy were encouraged in every way. Incidentally, these tactical aspects were further developed in later combat regulations and became in their own way a tradition on which even now the command personnel of our fleet are trained.

The first Combat Regulations of the Sea Forces were worked out from the basic principles of the Field Regulations of the Red Army, which are common both to land and sea forces. These basic documents reflected the unity of Soviet military doctrine which regarded the sea forces as an inseparable constituent part of the armed forces of the country. They were set the basic tasks of being ready for bold and resolute waging of battle with the enemy at sea, directed at the defence of the shores of the USSR, at support for operations of land troops of the Red Army and at keeping them supplied both from the sea and by river and lakes.

Building of the fleet (1929-41)

In the period of the pre-war Five-Year plans the Soviet people and the leadership of the Party in a short time carried through the industrialization of the country, the collectivization of agriculture, completed the cultural revolution, liquidated the exploiter classes and built the first socialist state in the world. Aircraft, automobile, electrical engineering and powerful defence industries were set up in our country and new shipbuilding yards reconstructed or built. All this led to a considerable growth of the economic and military power of the Soviet Union.

The material base was established, allowing the problem to be posed of building a large sea and ocean fleet meeting the interests of Soviet power.

Already in 1927 the first Soviet submarines of the *Dekabrist* type were laid down in the shipyards. In 1930-34 new submarines of the *Leninets* type, medium boats of the *Shchuka* and C types and small boats of the *Malyutka* type began to come into service. Soon oceanic submarines of the K type began to be built. In sum, the Soviet fleet received submarines of coastal, sea and oceanic types with tactical-technical features advanced for that time.

In the years of the second Five-Year Plan a new cruiser was commissioned, the number of destroyers and guard ships almost doubled, with three and a half times as many torpedo boats, almost three times as many minesweepers and over five times as many submarines. The air force situation substantially changed. The total fleet of naval aviation rose more than six and a half times with an almost treble increase in the stock of strike aircraft, over six times the stock of reconnaissance planes and more than eight times the number of fighters. The number of barrels of shore artillery of different calibres increased almost two and a half times. The decisions adopted in the pre-war years by the Party and Government on the construction in the country of an ocean-going fleet envisaged that we would have strong fleets in the Pacific and Baltic and greatly strengthen the Northern and Black Sea fleets. The need was also recognized for the fleet to have powerful shore-based aviation for combined operations with ship formations.

The shipbuilding programme adopted on the basis of these decisions was aimed at creating first and foremost large surface forces—battleships and heavy cruisers, surpassing in their qualities the corresponding foreign ships. In 1938-40 the first Soviet battleship of the *Sovetsky Soyuz* type and the cruiser *Chapaev* were laid down. The building of surface light forces was continued. At the same time it was planned to build powerful underwater forces including over 200 different submarines.

Carrying out the decisions of the Party and Government, the Soviet people, our shipbuilders and workers of kindred branches of industry made no small effort to fulfil the crucial and complex tasks of building up the fleet. As a result of the coming into service of new ships of modern type, the total displacement of ships of the Soviet Navy in the period from the beginning of 1939 to 1941 grew for the surface fleet by 107,718 tons and underwater by 50,385 tons. In only 11 months in 1940 the fleet received 100 different fighting ships, chiefly destroyers, submarines, minesweepers, and torpedo boats. At the end of 1940 a further 269 ships of all classes were under construction. Some of them were built in the first half of 1941 and took part in the Great Patriotic War. The ships were armed with new armament, fire control instruments, radio-navigational and other special equipment.

Progress was also made in building up the fleet air arm which in 1940 alone increased by 39 per cent. However, it was equipped with planes of the same type as other branches of the armed forces. While these planes could successfully operate with delivery of strikes on land targets, they were inadequately adapted to undertake combat tasks at sea. Because of low speed, limited flight range and low payload strike, naval aviation could not effectively use torpedo weaponry for ships at sea a long way from their aerodromes. We still did not have any special naval aircraft.

The fighter aviation of the fleet had limited possibilities of shielding ships at sea from air raids. Because of the restricted radius of the operations of planes, their weak arming and short time of stay in the air, they could not reliably cover ships at sea, even comparatively close to the coast. This seriously restricted the use of the main forces of the fleet in zones within reach of hostile aircraft.

A considerable growth in power was shown by the coastal shore defence of our fleet, which up to the 'thirties remained at the same level as in the First World War. Its material part was renovated and the areas of combat deployment extended. In 1940 alone the total number of shore defence batteries increased by 43 per cent.

In the years of the pre-war Five-Year plans, together with the building of ships, planes and the improvement of their equipment, major organizational measures were also put in hand.

In 1932 for the protection of the Far East sea lines of the motherland, by decision of the Party and Government, the Pacific fleet was created and in 1933 the Northern fleet. Then measures were taken to harness the Northern Sea route linking the Northern and Pacific theatres.

After Estonia, Latvia, Lithuania and Bessarabia became part of the Soviet Union, the areas of stationing of the Baltic and Black Sea fleets considerably widened. The Baltic fleet moved from the eastern part of the Gulf of Finland into the expanses of the Baltic Sea and the Black Sea fleet to the mouth of the Danube, where the Danube flotilla was formed.

The constant care shown by the Party and the Government for the fleet brought positive results. In a short time after the Civil War, steps were taken virtually creating anew a navy capable of conducting combat operations together with ground troops and independently in the seas lying next to our coasts, principally for the purpose of defending our coasts and disrupting enemy sea shipments.

As the economic power of our state grew stronger the fighting power of the navy increased. It was replenished with modern submarines, guard and other surface ships. Many of them in tactical-technical features were not inferior to the best models of foreign shipbuilding.

By the start of the Great Patriotic War our navy included four operational units: the Northern, Baltic, Black and Pacific fleets and also the Danube, Caspian, Pinsk and Amur flotillas. It comprised three battleships, seven light cruisers, 59 minelayers and leaders, 22 guard ships, 80 minesweepers, 269 torpedo boats, 218 submarines, 2581 planes of all types and 260 shore artillery batteries. As a whole, the fleet represented a considerable force, although it was segregated in separate theatres.

The subsequent period showed that the fleets were plainly short of mine-sweepers and auxiliary vessels. None of the fleets except the Baltic had marines. The forces and resources of anti-aircraft defence were feeble. The fleets did not have a sufficient number of non-contact mines or sweepers to combat them.

Together with the qualitative and quantitative growth of our armed forces and the perfection of their organizational structure, scientific elaboration of Soviet military theory rapidly moved ahead. The essence of this theory was most clearly given in the 1939 Field Regulations, which stated in particular: "Any attack by an enemy will be met by the Union of Soviet Socialist Republics by a crushing blow of the whole might of our armed forces. . . . We shall wage war offensively, carrying it to the enemy's territory. The combat operations of the Red Army will be aimed at destruction with the object of completely smashing the enemy . . ."

The idea was to solve combat tasks by the joint, concerted efforts of all branches of the armed forces and types of troops. The same notions also permeated the documents regulating the combat activity of the navy. The fleet was in the event of war to assist land forces in maritime directions and carry out independent operations at sea.

The navy at the start of the war had at its disposal a consistent theory of preparing and waging operations— a form of military operations still new at the time. It had clear recommendations on the main problems of operational art formulated in documents of that time. The command and staffs of the fleets and other operational units by the start of the war had been able to accumulate the necessary experience in organizing and planning sea operations. This gave considerable advantages in solving the main problems of operational deployment of forces in the armed struggle at sea.

Through all our instructions, manuals and regulations ran like a red thread the requirement to seek out persistently and attack resolutely the enemy, whatever the conditions of the situation.

The main method for solving the tasks by the fleet was considered to be the destruction of the enemy by delivering powerful strikes by superior diverse forces in the main direction with their coherent interaction, and utilization of tactical surprise and rapidity of the strikes delivered. A major role continued to be assigned to positional means of warfare—shore artillery, minefields and the formation of strongly-defended mine and artillery bases relying on which the ships and aircraft of the fleet were taught to inflict a defeat on the numerically superior forces of the fleet of the enemy. Thus, even at that time, based on the composition of the forces and their fighting possibilities the navy was set operational and strategic defensive tasks, in the main in the coastal zone, to protect the country from seaborne invasion.

With the development of the forces of the fleet the combat mastery of Soviet seamen grew. Combat preparation of the fleets was vigorously pursued, integration of the ships as part of tactical groups and formations perfected and the tactics of sea battle worked out. Attention was focused on organizing a joint strike by surface ships, torpedo boats, aircraft and submarines against any grouping of surface ships of the enemy at our defended mine and artillery bases set up in the narrows and approaches to naval bases.

At the same time analysis of the problems of naval art was dominated by the influence of the supporters of defensive views of the role and the use of the fleet in a future war. The result was the preservation of the traditions correct in their time of the "theory of the minor war" in new conditions, when our fleet had already become capable of waging combat operations beyond its coastal waters. This was an expression of the negative influence of this theory on the further development of Soviet naval thought. In essence, in naval art the view that the fleet should be used for defensive purposes predominated and the fleet itself was regarded as a defence factor, although its tasks on the operational and tactical planes were solved by offensive methods.

Such views, of course, affected the trend of the training of the leading personnel of the fleet. In none of our fleets was the question ever raised of conducting combat operations on the ocean, although they had submarines with quite a considerable range and the country was set on a course of building a large oceanic fleet. That is why the use of even such long-distance forces of the fleets as submarines, including cruiser submarines, was restricted to the narrow confines of primarily tactical use, chiefly in nearby regions. This is also confirmed by the distribution of the submarines between the theatres. In the Barents Sea, where the conditions for moving out into the ocean were most favourable, at the start of the war there were fewer submarines than in the Baltic or Black Seas.

A positive feature for Soviet naval art was the considerable headway made by moves to encourage the army and fleet to act together in conducting combat operations in maritime areas. During preparations for combat, the ships of the fleets were trained to give fire support to the marine flank of the army, stage landings (mostly tactical), and shield troops from action from the sea. For the first time in the history of naval art the 'thirties in our country saw the elaboration of the theory of the marine landing operation which was tested in the course of combat operations.

However, neither the building of landing ships nor the training of special landing troops were given due attention. All our fleets came into the war without having a single specially constructed landing ship. Nor did the fleets have a sufficient number of surface ships with the armament necessary for supporting the landing of troops.

All this limited the potential of the fleet in solving the tasks of assisting land forces and made it harder for it to stage landings from the sea, the need for which, as emerged in reality, arose from the first days of the Great Patriotic War.

Naval seamen nurtured by the Communist Party and the Young Communist League were distinguished by high morale and fighting qualities. Their comradeship in combat, loyalty to military duty and remarkable revolutionary and fighting traditions and devotion to the motherland served as an example for many formations of our armed forces. As a whole the combat readiness of the fleets on the eve of war was high. This was aided by the system organized and verified in peacetime conditions of bringing the forces into a state of raised combat readiness. The staffs of the fleets attentively followed the changes in the situation at sea in order to identify in time signs of the approaching war, which enabled the fleets promptly to fulfil a number of measures of a defensive character. Thanks to these measures, with the advent of a direct threat of attack by the enemy, all the fleets were rapidly brought into a state of immediate readiness and were able to forestall many harsh consequences of a sudden attack by the enemy.

The Soviet Fleet in the Second World War

The perfidious attack by Fascist Germany on 22 June 1941 interrupted the peaceful labour of the Soviet people. A bitter battle unprecedented in scale developed between the strike forces of imperialism and the first socialist power.

The start of the war did not take our fleets unawares. Although many naval bases were subjected to raids by hostile aircraft in the first hours of the war, our fleet did not lose a single fighting ship or plane from the first strike of the enemy. Nor did the Hitlerites succeed in reaching another goal—by laying magnetic mines in the areas of our bases, to stop ships from putting to sea.

All the fleets, right from the first day of the war, actively entered into battle against a strong foe who enjoyed the support of three air forces and, moreover, a number of important strategic advantages which allowed him to launch a sudden assault and take advantage of his starting positions. While each of our fleets could conduct combat operations only in its own theatre, the enemy was in a position to conduct an operational manoeuvre with his naval forces between theatres, intensify directions where the most important tasks were being solved and set up in them groupings surpassing the Soviet fleet in quantitative and qualitative composition.

For example, while at the start of the war the enemy in the Barents Sea had eight torpedo boats, six submarines and 35 guard ships and cutters, in 1943 here was concentrated a strong fleet including two battleships, three cruisers, two shore defence armour-plated ships, 20 destroyers, 21 submarines, about 100 guard ships and sweepers, 20 landing ships and some 300 planes. In 1944, the number of operating submarines in this theatre was up to 34 and in 1945 to 65 units.

In the tensest period of fighting at Leningrad, the German command concentrated in the Baltic Sea a large grouping of surface ships to destroy our fleet. A similar grouping including battleships was also formed in the North when the enemy tried his best to interrupt our external sea communications. In the period of the struggle for Odessa and Sevastopol, the Hitlerites switched powerful groupings of bombing and mine-torpedo aircraft from the Mediterranean to the Black Sea.

The possibilities for our navy of inter-theatre manoeuvre were very limited. Although the Northern sea route made it possible to move some of the fleet's forces from the Pacific to the North and back, this was feasible only for two to three months in the year. Inter-theatre manoeuvre with use of the inland waterways became completely impossible soon after the start of the war, since the main canals were in the zone of the land fronts. Nor could requirements be met by carrying cutters and small submarines by rail.

As the armed struggle unfolded, the conditions for the fleet bases steadily worsened. Soon the Baltic fleet could rely only on the bases of a confined area. Kronstadt-Leningrad was in a zone within reach of hostile artillery. The Black

Sea fleet could only be stationed in ports on the Caucasian coast not adapted for this.

The Soviet fleet from the first day of the war right up to the capitulation of Germany continuously waged active combat operations: submarines searched out and destroyed German warships and transports and laid down mines on their routes; aircraft and surface ships, especially torpedo boats, relentlessly sought out hostile ships and destroyed them at sea, in coastal waters and at the bases of the enemy.

The surface ships and aircraft of the Black Sea fleet delivered strikes on the naval bases of Constanza and the oil-producing regions of Rumania. The aircraft of the Red Banner Baltic fleet struck at hostile aerodromes where preparations were under way for mass raids on Leningrad, and aircraft, ships and the shore artillery of the Northern fleet hit enemy communication nodes in the Petsamo-Kirkenes region. The Danube naval flotilla already on the fourth day of the war put ashore several landing forces which took over the Rumanian shore of the Danube over a stretch of more than 75 kilometres. This obliged the enemy to bring strong units to fight the landing forces, thereby weakening the pressure on our troops in the main directions, which was of no little importance in that period of the war, so difficult for us. The enemy was badly damaged by ships of the Pinsk naval flotilla on the Western Bug River, a very effective unit.

The struggle for sea communications demanded enormous efforts. Throughout the war submarines, aircraft, torpedo boats, destroyers and often shore artillery too destroyed hostile transports carrying troops and cargoes. Such operations were conducted systematically and there was hardly a day without success in this task. Even when the submarines of the Baltic fleet to move out to sea had to negotiate the Gulf of Finland, literally strewn with mines, crisscrossed by anti-submarine lines, the enemy constantly had to bear the force of the strikes of our fleet. The Northern fleet kept under control the only sea route over which reinforcements were sent to German troops in Norway and Northern Finland and nickel carried from Petsamo.

The effectiveness of the strikes of the Northern seamen on German communications had even to be recognized by Hitler who, in directive No. 36 of 22 September 1941, stated that the "disruption by the enemy of our coastal communications inside the Arctic has still further limited the possibilities of executing the plans of the mountain rifle corps—to reach Murmansk this year."[67]

Black Sea seamen also inflicted heavy losses on the enemy's sea communications.

A convincing idea of enemy losses as a result of the operations of the Soviet navy in the course of the Great Patriotic War is given by Table 17, drawn up from confirmed data taken from two sources, including German.

As this table shows, in the course of the Great Patriotic War our fleet inflicted very telling losses on the enemy.

The destruction of naval transports seriously affected the fighting capacity of enemy troops. Thus, for example, one transport carried a cargo of air bombs,

[67] Top Secret! Only for the Command! p. 333, Moscow, Nauka, 1967 (in Russian).

the supplies for 2000 bomber flights; a medium tanker provided fuel for 1500 bombers or 5000 fighters. Destroying in the war years some 1300 enemy vessels in the shipping lanes, our fleet had no little influence on the course of the armed struggle on the Soviet-German land front where the fundamental question of the outcome of the war was decided.

An important place in the combat activity of the fleet during the whole war was taken by military shipments and their protection. They assumed special importance in the North after the enemy had severed the Murmansk railway. In the Black Sea they were vitally necessary in the period of defence of Odessa, Sevastopol, the North Caucasus, and for the Kerch-Feodosiya landing operation; and in the Baltic during the defence and evacuation of Tallinn, Hanko and the Moonsund Islands, for strengthening the troops on the Oranienbaum bridgehead and in the subsequent liberation of the Baltic Republics. An extremely crucial task was solved by the fleets and flotillas in ensuring military and civilian shipments along waterways close to the fronts, especially Lake Ladoga when a difficult situation was building up around Leningrad, and along the Volga.

TABLE 17

Losses of Ships and Vessels of Germany and its Allies resulting from the Action of the Soviet Fleet

Types of weapons of Soviet Navy	No. of sunk ships and auxiliary vessels	No. of sunk transports	Total tonnage of sunk transports, registered tons
Aircraft	407	371	800,296
	428	369	870,550
Submarines	33	157	462,313
	54	165	476,100
Surface ships	53	24	45,197
	106	60	138,400
Mines	103	110	250,101
	18	24	58,000
Shore artillery	18	14	28,646
	25	13	19,000
Total combat losses	614	676	1,586,553
	631	631	1,562,050
Losses due to unknown and other factors	94	115	251,666
	2	3	7,800
Total losses in the war	708	791	1,838,219
	633	634	1,569,850

Note. The numerator gives the number of ships and transports, the reliability of the sinking of which is confirmed from data from two sources; the denominator gives the number of ships and transports, the reliability of the sinking of which is still not confirmed by data other than our own.

All our theatres were supplied by sea routes in the war years with over 100 million tons of various cargoes of which a considerable part was made up of oil and oil products. The forces of the fleet ensured the transportation of 17 million tons of cargoes over external sea communications. Behind these figures were thousands of journeys of ships and flights of planes, many hundreds of combat clashes with surface ships and submarines of the enemy, the repulse of the strikes of hostile planes and, the negotiating of dense minefields.

In the years of the Great Patriotic War the Soviet navy completely fulfilled its duty to the motherland. Our naval seamen not only found the soundest tactical and operational solutions but also demonstrated their indisputable superiority over the enemy in the art of deploying new methods of armed struggle. Actions of officers and men were distinguished by mass heroism, iron firmness and endurance in defence, boldness and irresistibility of offensive strikes and great naval mastery enriching Soviet naval art. In the course of the war our fleets not only acquired rich combat experience but also developed essentially new tactics, theory and practice of preparing and waging sea operations. At the same time the continental character of the past war left its imprint on the content of our naval art.

The operations of our fleet against the sea foe formed an important part of the struggle as a whole. However, its principal efforts from the first few days of the war were aimed at solving the most important task—to assist ground troops, bearing the brunt of the defence of the country from the attacking enemy, and whose operations in the end determined the outcome of the war. In solving the tasks devolving on it, the fleet proved itself a powerful strike force capable of sharply changing the situation in the naval area of operations of land forces, making it much easier for them to fulfil operational and strategic tasks.

The Northern fleet under the command of Vice-Admiral A. G. Golovko, by the strikes of ships and aircraft on groupings of the German Fascist troops pushing towards Murmansk, repeated staging of sea landings, operations of the marines on shore and interrupting enemy sea shipments, played an important role in disrupting the onslaught of the German Fascist troops on the right flank of the Soviet-German front. Over 39,000 sailors and officers of the Northern fleet were sent to marines detachments.

The holding of the port of Murmansk, which does not freeze, and the Kola naval base was of exceptionally great operational and strategic importance since it made it possible to use throughout the war the shortest sea route of communication with the allies. This enabled the Northern fleet to solve successfully the tasks of protecting its communications, disrupting enemy shipments and assisting the ground troops in defence and then in offence.

The Red Banner Baltic fleet, commanded throughout the war by Vice-Admiral V. F. Tributs, together with the land forces protecting Liepaja, Tallinn, the Moonsund Islands and the Hanko naval base, pinned down a hundred thousand strong grouping of enemy troops driving towards Leningrad.

The robustness of the defence of Leningrad, especially at the start of the siege, was largely determined by the vigorous operations of the Baltic fleet ensuring the holding throughout the war of the Oranienbaum bridgehead drawing off large enemy forces. Over 110,000 sailors, petty officers and officers were sent by the Red Banner Baltic fleet to fight on land. At Leningrad there was not a single division in which Baltic seamen did not serve. The powerful long-range artillery of the fleet served as a strong fire-shield, the base of the defence of the near approaches to the heroic city. Its strike power was backed by matchless stubbornness and the irresistible attacks of the marines.

It is not possible to over-rate the role of the Black Sea fleet, led by Vice-Admiral F. S. Oktyabr'sky, in defence of the most important ports and in giving stability to the southern flank of the land front.[68] The successful and prolonged resistance deep in the enemy's rear in the Odessa defence region whose garrison mostly consisted of seamen and was led by the commander of the naval base Vice-Admiral G. V. Zhukov was possible only thanks to constant support from the sea of the fighting ships and continuous delivery to the besieged town of everything it needed. The heroic defence of Odessa, pinning down for over two months almost all the Rumanian army, which suffered heavy losses, held up the breakthrough of the southern flank by the *South* army group and badly upset the strategic plans of the Hitlerite command.

On 30 September 1941, with the threatened loss of the Crimean peninsula and hence the main base of the Black Sea fleet and the impossibility of defending simultaneously the Crimean peninsula and Odessa, the HQ of the Supreme Command decided to evacuate the Odessa area and to strengthen with its troops the defence of the Crimean peninsula.

Fulfilling the instructions of HQ, the Black Sea fleet evacuated the troops defending Odessa to the Crimea, where they helped hold up the enemy on the Perekop isthmus and then took part in the defence of Sevastopol.

The task of directing both the defence of Odessa and Sevastopol was entrusted to the fleet Command which, in the conditions pertaining, was the only correct thing to do. It was precisely the fleet which prepared, organized and ensured the defence of Sevastopol, which was directly led by the commander of the Black Sea fleet Vice-Admiral F. S. Oktyabr'sky. The fleet completely fulfilled the tasks set by HQ. The defence of Sevastopol, unmatched in history for heroism and for the duration of the siege, held down for eight months a three hundred thousand strong enemy grouping and did not allow it to join in the offensive in the south. In addition, keeping Sevastopol in our hands excluded the use of the sea route to the Azov Sea for supplying the southern group of armies, and impeded the breakthrough by Fascist troops to the ports of the North Caucasus.

The HQ of the Supreme Command, in a telegram to the defenders of Sevastopol on 12 June 1942, gave the following appraisal of the actions of the forces defending Sevastopol: "The selfless struggle of the Sevastopolians serves as an example of heroism for the whole Red Army and Soviet people."

The communication of the Soviet Information Bureau on 4 July 1942 in connection with the abandonment of Sevastopol said: "The military and political importance of the Sevastopol defence in the Patriotic War of the Soviet people is enormous. Pinning down a large number of German-Rumanian troops, the protectors of the town confounded and upset the plans of the German command. The iron firmness of the Sevastopolians was one of the main causes thwarting the notorious "spring offensive" of the Germans. The Hitlerites lost time and speed and suffered enormous losses.

"Sevastopol was abandoned by Soviet troops but its defence enters the history of the Patriotic War of the Soviet Union as one of the brightest of its

[68] Between April 1943 and March 1944 the fleet was commanded by Vice-Admiral L. A. Vladimirsky.

pages. . . . The incredible valour, fury in battle with the enemy and self-sacrifice of the protectors of Sevastopol inspire Soviet patriots to further heroic deeds in the fight against the hated occupiers."

With the abandonment by our troops of Sevastopol and the Crimean peninsula the way was open for the enemy to the North Caucasus, which meant a real threat of capture by the Fascists of this most important region and a change in the military-political situation in the Black Sea theatre in connection with the possible intervention of Turkey which still adopted a wait-and-see policy. The existence of the Black Sea fleet depended on the holding of the Caucasian coast by our army. But the resistance of the land troops defending the maritime regions of the Caucasus, in turn, could be ensured only by the operations of the fleet. And this task was successfully fulfilled by the Black Sea fleet, playing an important role in the outcome of the battle for the Caucasus.

In his book *The Battle for the Caucasus,* Marshal of the Soviet Union A. A. Grechko writes: "In the defensive period of the battle for the Caucasus, of nine defensive operations undertaken by Soviet troops between July and December 1942, the Black Sea fleet and Azov flotilla took a direct part in six. . . .

"The Black Sea fleet and the Azov flotilla closely working together with land troops gave them much aid in the defence and crushing of the Hitlerites in the Caucasus. . . .

"The Black Sea fleet and Azov naval flotilla gave substantial support to land troops also in the offensive period. By staging landings, the naval forces helped the troops to break through the strong long-term defence of the enemy. . . .

"The most important task set for the Black Sea fleet in the period of the battle for the Caucasus, the reliable safeguarding of our sea communications along the Caucasian shore—was successfully accomplished. . . .

"The Caspian naval flotilla . . . ensured the protection of sea routes extremely important for our country. . . .

"The Black Sea fleet and Azov and Caspian naval flotillas with honour discharged the tasks set before them in the battle for the Caucasus."[69]

In the war years the navy sent to the land fronts over 400,000 officers, petty officers and men who had completed naval training. From them were formed over 40 brigades of marines and naval rifle brigades, six separate regiments and a large number of single battalions and detachments. These formations and units were distinguished by high fighting qualities and were, therefore, used by the army command at key parts of the fronts. In the tensest period of the battle for Moscow, eight naval rifle brigades operated with the troops of the Western and North Western fronts.

In addition, naval units left as part of the fleets and flotillas, numbering in all some 100,000 men, engaged in the land defence of naval bases and islands and took part in many landings.

After the Soviet armed forces had seized the strategic initiative, aid to maritime groupings of troops continued to remain one of the main tasks of the fleet although its content considerably changed, the scale of the operations grew and the conditions for fulfilling them were made even more complicated by the

[69] A. A. Grechko, *The Battle for the Caucasus,* pp. 466, 467, 2nd ed., revised, Moscow, Voenizdat (in Russian).

fact that it was still not possible to use particular base areas. But despite this the fleets successfully solved all the tasks confronting them.

For the Red Banner Baltic fleet this was expressed in the participation of aircraft, long-range artillery and naval brigades in breaking through the Leningrad blockade, transporting large troop contingents to the Oranienbaum bridgehead, the staging of landings, backing up the troops on shore with artillery fire and air strikes. increasing the scope of the operations on the sea communications to destroy enemy troops evacuated by seas from Liepaja, Klaipeda, Swinemunde and other ports.

The Black Sea fleet, by mounting a large operational landing together with the 18th Army of the North Caucasus front, opened the way to the destruction of the Taman bridgehead of the enemy, ensured the forcing by our troops of the Kerch Strait and the capture of the bridgehead to the Crimea. The subsequent operations of the fleet cut the lines of evacuation of German troops from the Crimea, and the staging of a large number of sea landings hastened the liberation of the southern regions of our country, and of Bulgaria and Rumania.

An important role in destroying the enemy on the extreme right flank of the front and the liberation of the Pechenga region and Northern Norway was played by the Northern fleet.

In the course of defensive and offensive operations in maritime areas the Soviet fleet, using battleships and ships ill-suited for the landing of troops, put ashore in sea landings over 250,000 men with technical supplies and arms, or some 30 troop divisions. On average the fleet every fortnight of the war disembarked one landing force. At the same time active operations did not allow the Germans to stage a single landing on our coast although they possessed specially constructed landing craft and had the experience of the successful conduct of such operations in the Western European theatre.

Steeped in offensive operations, the combat activity of the Pacific fleet (commander Admiral I. S. Yunashev) and the North Pacific (commander Vice-Admiral V. A. Andreev) and Amur (commander Vice-Admiral N. V. Antonov) naval flotillas in August 1945 played a very important role in the rapid occupation by our troops of southern Sakhalin, the Kurile Islands and the ports of Korea and helped the rapid advance by Soviet troops deep into Manchuria. The fast landing operations of the men of the Pacific fleet upset the link between the Kwantung army of the Japanese and their homeland, and successfully completed its total encirclement.

Outstanding successes in the fight against the enemy were scored by the Azov, Ladoga, Onega, White Sea, Volga, Danube and other flotillas created on the inland seas, large rivers and lakes. They gave direct and important aid to land troops both in defensive engagements and in the period of the offensive.

The White Sea naval flotillas solved the tasks associated with the functioning of the sea routes in the Arctic regions and passages of ships and convoys via the Northern sea route. The Caspian naval flotilla reliably defended our chief oil link on the Caspian Sea. The Ladoga naval flotilla kept open the Life Road—the sole route linking besieged Leningrad with the rest of the country. The Danube naval flotilla fought its way over 2000 km up the Danube and took part in the liberation from the Fascists of six European states. In the course of combat operations ships of this flotilla carried along the Danube and ferried across it in all some 250 troop divisions. The operations of the Volga naval flotilla in the battle of Stalingrad are clearly appraised by Marshal of the Soviet Union V. I. Chuikov: "On the role of the seamen of this flotilla and their deeds I would briefly say: if it were not for them possibly the 62nd Army would have perished without munitions and without food and would not have fulfilled its task." [70] In the bleakest period of the Great Patriotic War, alongside the units of the Soviet Army, heroically fought the seamen of the Pinsk naval flotilla. In the bloody defensive battles at the river boundaries its craft supported the land troops and took part in the defence of Kiev. Regenerated in 1943, the Dnieper naval flotilla fought its way along the rivers and canals and ended its combat route on the River Spree in Berlin.

Thus, the navy throughout the war successfully fulfilled the task dictated by the requirements of armed struggle in the main theatre where its outcome was decided, that is, on the Soviet-German front. The operational and strategic deployment of the forces of the fleet was determined by the need for closely tying its operational plans to the plans of the fronts and armies, primarily in the interests of smashing the main enemy forces on land. The Soviet Navy made a worthy contribution to the achievement of victory over Fascist Germany and imperialist Japan. It demolished the sea power of the foe on the Barents, Baltic and Black Seas, ensuring the stability of the strategic flanks of the land front and all-round support for our troops in defence and offence. In this most difficult of wars the fleet justified the hopes pinned on it, the high trust of the Soviet people, and completely discharged its duty to the motherland.

The experience of the Great Patriotic War once again confirmed the validity of the basic tenet of our military doctrine that victory over a strong opponent can be gained only by the common efforts of all branches of the armed forces. The experience also showed that in a struggle even against a continental adversary an important role is played by the navy. Only the concerted efforts of all branches of the armed forces, full-blooded, harmoniously developed, well-trained, intelligently deployed and comprehensively supplied, can smash the military power of an aggressor and achieve complete victory.

From the very start of the war our fleet was faced with many major problems at technical and operational and tactical level. It was necessary in the shortest time in conditions of tense armed struggle not only to eliminate completely peacetime deficiencies coming to light in the course of the struggle, but also to solve many urgent tasks associated with waging combat operations. And it must be recognized that the personnel of our fleet were equal to the demands which the war placed on them. Improved ways were found of deploying the forces of the fleet in operations to assist land troops in defence and offence. In effect, the Soviet school of landing operations was created anew, the organization and ways of conducting them were defined using poorly-adapted shipping. Modern tactics for submarines and aircraft were devised, many problems of the defence of bases from the land side which appeared in the course of the struggle were solved, as were the organization of interaction of forces, their control and the supply of their operations.

[70] V. I. Chuikov, *Start of the Road,* p. 163, Moscow, Voenizdat, 1959 (in Russian).

For the needs of the fleet, Soviet industry made available a sufficient number of the necessary combat and technical resources. It was very hard to make good the losses of ships, owing to the loss by us of a number of shipbuilding yards and switching the considerable potentialities of the shipbuilding industry to the building of tanks and other arms for the army. During the war, therefore, mostly small fighting ships and cutters were built. Despite these difficulties, in the period of the Great Patriotic War the fleet received from industry two light cruisers, 19 destroyers, 38 minesweepers, 54 submarines and about 9500 various fighting ships. There was improvement in the quality of the armament and combat technical equipment—artillery, torpedoes, sonar communications and marine radar appeared. The mine-laying and mine-sweeping equipment, into the creation of which such outstanding Soviet scientists poured their talents as I. V. Kurchatov, A. P. Aleksandrov and many others, was greatly improved thanks to the introduction of non-contact technology. Naval aviation, particularly torpedo carrying, grew quantitatively and qualitatively.

Thanks to the heroic work of the Soviet people the fleets finished the war stronger than when they went into it, capable of fighting and in no way lost their leading place in their theatres. Also of no little importance was the experience gained in the bitter battles by the crews and their hardening in combat.

Thus, the Soviet Navy in the course of the war had to solve simultaneously two sets of tasks. First, to wage battle at sea against a strong foe bent on seizing the initiative and destroying the forces of our fleet. Secondly, our fleet had to ensure the stability of the strategic flanks of the front and assist land forces in defence and offence. Such deployment of the forces of the fleet in war was the only correct course to take and completely matched the situation. In simultaneously solving both sets of problems our fleet showed itself to be an active and powerful force capable of sharply changing the situation both at sea and in the maritime areas of the operations of land forces.

The bitter struggle unfolding in the sea theatres exceeded in scale and scope all the pre-war forecasts.

The figures given above on the losses of the enemy fleet, demanding many thousands of combat voyages of ships and flights of aircraft, numerous sea battles and operations, clearly show the continuity of the combat operations of the Soviet Navy against the enemy fleet. This struggle continuing day in and day out required exceptionally great stretching of the forces available. It must be stressed that our fleet operated as a rule in areas which were selected by the Soviet Command and were not imposed by the enemy. The forces of the fleet fought wherever they could inflict the heaviest damage on the enemy necessary for the general success of the struggle.

Our fleet by active and resolute operations not only contributed to the achievement of victory on the Soviet-German front, but lent support to the navies of our allies of the anti-Hitler coalition. Striking at bases and sea communications and hostile ship groupings, it made a weighty contribution to the fight against the enemy's fleet in the oceanic theatres. The German command under the influence of the activity of our fleet was forced not only constantly to hold considerable forces of the navy earmarked for battle against it, but also systematically to strengthen them with ships and aircraft from the

Atlantic Ocean and the Mediterranean and North Sea. Even in the tensest periods of the "Battle of the Atlantic", of 141 German submarines present in the areas of combat activity or in readiness at bases, on average about 30, that is, 20 per cent, waged combat operations in the Black, Baltic and Barents Seas in 1941-44. The number of enemy aircraft in these sea theatres was greatly strengthened in tense periods and reached as many as 1200 planes. Such massive deployment of German aircraft in other sea theatres was not noted after the attack by the Fascists on the Soviet Union.

By its combat operations the Soviet Navy helped the allies to solve the tasks of the "Battle of the Atlantic" to which they attached great importance, although this direction could not have a decisive influence on the outcome of the war. Even the German command did not consider it paramount, as is confirmed by the statement of Hitler in January 1943: "We must clearly realize that this submarine warfare will be useless unless we beat Russia in the East."[71]

Therefore, the USA and England, without special interference from the enemy,who was using all his resources on the Soviet-German front, were able in the course of the war to build a large new merchant fleet twice exceeding the losses on communication lines and also bring to bear enormous forces for fighting German submarines including 133 convoy aircraft carriers, 1,500 torpedo boats, frigates and corvettes, 1,900 submarine hunters, 1,000 minesweepers and several thousand planes. Consequently, no little credit goes to the Soviet Army and Navy for the fact that the allies were able to a certain extent to win the "Battle of the Atlantic".

This situation was correctly evaluated by many American and Australian soldiers who in a letter to Soviet troops stated: "While we were gathering forces for future battles you were fighting and spilling your blood."[72]

Thus, our navy throughout the war successfully solved in complex conditions the tasks set it.

Together with the navy in combat operations at sea, an active part was taken by the merchant and fishing fleets of our country. Merchant and other vessels made thousands of trips along internal and external communications, exposing themselves to attacks by enemy ships, aircraft and submarines, and participated in many landing operations. A considerable part of them after suitable re-equipment performed combat tasks in daily combat operations as part of the vessels at naval bases. Particularly important for the merchant fleet was the task of ensuring the transport of military and civilian cargoes.

In the war years the Soviet merchant fleet, with a comparatively small stock of ships, carried some 100 million tons of cargo necessary for the country and the front.[73]

Some of the ships of the merchant fleet were made over to the navy. From the start of combat operations 32 cargo vessels in hostile ports were seized by the enemy. The remaining ships, right from the first days of the war, independently

[71] S. Morrison, *The Battle of the Atlantic is Won* (in Russian), Moscow, Voenizdat, 1959, p. 80 (Ed. note).
[72] International solidarity of the workers in the fight for peace and national liberation against Fascist aggression for the complete destruction of Fascism in Europe and Asia (1938-45), p. 586, Moscow, Sovetskaya Rossiya, 1962 (in Russian).
[73] *Morskoi flot,* No. 8, p. 1, 1974.

fulfilled the tasks of carrying military and civilian cargo. Sailing and conducting loading-unloading operations in the zones of combat operations, our merchant fleet suffered considerable losses.

The losses in shipping were partly made good by supplies from the USA under Lend-Lease. But this could not radically improve the position. Success in carrying out transport was mainly due to the strenuous efforts of the forces, the heroism and fortitude of the seamen of the merchant fleet and perfection of organization to ensure shipments.

The heroic work of seamen was well described in 1942 by *Pravda*: "The Patriotic War of the Soviet people has demanded from the merchant marine and Soviet seamen sustained and warlike work. From the first few days of the war they have had to face the toughest working conditions. The enemy has carried out pirate attacks on Soviet vessels. . . . Merchant ships together with warships under the fire of the enemy are fearlessly delivering combat provisions, fuel and food to the valiant Soviet fighters. The enemy has tried and is trying to impede the sailing of our vessels undertaking foreign trips. . . . In the fire of war the seamen have passed the trial of combat. They have shown themselves to be courageous and worthy sons of the motherland."[74]

Truly heroic pages were entered into the history of war by the North Sea seamen not only by their crossings of the Atlantic but also by supplying remote garrisons and especially by journeys over the Northern sea route. The enemy persistently sought to interrupt the important northern communication, using for this aircraft, submarines and surface ships and even battleships. However, thanks to the valour and steadfastness of Soviet seamen the Northern sea route reliably served the cause of our victory.

From the first day of the war Baltic cargo vessels were also used for military and civilian shipments. Under the continuous strikes of the enemy they supplied everything necessary to the coastal and island garrisons in the Gulfs of Finland and Riga and briskly undertook the evacuation of the population and industrial equipment from the areas at risk.

Merchant vessels and warships protecting them sailed in this theatre against an extremely complex and dangerous mine background and were subjected to continuous air raids and torpedo attacks by the light sea forces of the enemy. But even in these conditions the seamen of the merchant fleet made their own contribution to the 900-day defence of Leningrad, undertaking important sea shipments between the dispersed garrisons in the eastern part of the Gulf of Finland and across Lake Ladoga—via the communication justly called the Life Road.

Merchant seamen of the Azov-Black Sea basin had to go through extremely tough trials. Together with naval seamen, they worthily maintained sea communications with the besieged towns and did much to make possible the 73-day defence of Odessa and the 250-day defence of Sevastopol, completely cut off on the land side.

Despite the violent counter-action of the enemy, in the Black Sea the communications successfully operated not only between Odessa and Sevastopol but also along the Caucasian coast playing an important role in the fight for

[74] *Pravda*, 9 June 1942.

Novorossiisk and the battle for the Caucasus. Solely in the period between the start of the war and the end of 1942, as a result of the close combat cooperation of naval seamen and the seamen of the merchant fleet, some one and a half million persons and a million tons of diverse cargoes were carried via the sea communications in the Black Sea.[75]

A truly outstanding role was played by seamen of the merchant and fishing fleets in staging audacious sea landings in the regions of Feodosiya, Kerch, Novorossiisk, expanding the forces of the landing troops and in providing them with all that was needed.

Seamen of the Caspian cargo vessels also fulfilled with honour their tasks in the war. They maintained an uninterrupted supply to the army and the country of oil coming from the main oil reservoir of Baku, and achieved the very difficult task of ensuring military and civilian shipments over the Caspian Sea including import cargoes coming through Iran from the Persian Gulf. The enemy stubbornly sought to interrupt our communications especially at the most vulnerable links–the Astrakhan roadstead, in the Volgo-Caspian canal and in the Makhach-kala region. But the defence ships and cargo vessels boldly joined battle with the enemy. In the second half of 1942, when the enemy succeeded in temporarily interrupting our land communications with the Caucasus, the main burden of supplying the troops operating there fell on the navy and the Caspian naval flotilla. The scale of the work done by seamen may be judged merely from the fact that in August to September 1942 alone they carried from Astrakhan and Krasnovodsk to Makhach-kala without loss two rifle and one cavalry corps with arms, playing an essential role in the battle for the Caucasus.[76]

A weighty contribution to the cause of victory was also made by seamen of the Far East fleet. Although at the start of the war their operating areas were not theatres of combat activity, already from December 1941 they became dangerous with the start of the war by Japan against the USA and England. It must be made clear that the naval forces of militarist Japan did not take much trouble to ascertain what came their way at sea—a ship of the enemy or a vessel of a neutral. Operating under the rules of pirates, Japanese submariners and airmen attacked Soviet cargo shipping. In the war years the Far East State Steamship Company lost from these hostile actions 25 cargo vessels,[77] or almost 30 per cent of their original stock.

No less heroic deeds were performed in this grim period by the seamen of the fishing fleet, a considerable part of whose vessels replenished the ranks of the navy. They selflessly waged battle against the mine danger and submarines and discharged other combat tasks. The crews of ships in normal service often came under attack from the enemy but courageously caught fish and other marine products to supply the fighters at the front and the workers behind the lines.

To ensure solution of the military-political tasks of the state, efforts have always been made to have armed forces, including a navy, and keep them up to date. As part of the country's armed forces, the fleet fulfils an important role as an instrument of policy of the state in peacetime and is a potent means of

[75] *History of Naval Art,* p. 285 (in Russian).
[76] *Combat Route of the Soviet Naval Fleet,* p. 416, Voenizdat, Moscow, 1974 (in Russian).
[77] *Morskoi flot,* No. 9, p. 9, 1974.

achieving the political ends of armed struggle in wartime.

A policy taking into account the need for the sea power of the country is an important factor determining the character of the building of the fleet. Even brief perusal of the question of the role of navies in wars and in the policy of states in peacetime inescapably leads to the conclusion that an important role has always been assigned to this component of the sea power of the state. With the aid of navies, maritime states have achieved important strategic goals in wars and also in peacetime by using them as a telling argument in disputes with rivals.

The real contribution of the fleets to attainment of the goals of this or that war has been determined by many conditions and factors, primarily the character of the war and the peculiarities of the armed forces of the opposing sides. In some cases the fleets have been given a leading role in war and in others they have acted as aids to the land armies. As a whole, fleets in the vast majority of cases have made a weighty contribution to the attainment of the goals of the wars waged with their active participation.

At the same time history gives us examples of how the fleets merely by their presence or even simply existence in one of the opposing sides have exerted a definite, sometimes very substantial, influence on the outcome of armed struggle in land theatres by acting only as a potential threat of further continuation of a war or change in its character in favour of the state with the stronger fleet.

This tendency, characteristic of many wars, found a new expression in the wars of the epoch of imperialism, especially in the Sino-Japanese, Spanish-American and Russo-Japanese wars in which the fleets played a decisive role in attaining the strategic goals of the armed struggle as a whole. But later, both in the First and Second World Wars, the character of the influence of the results of the operations of the fleets on the outcome of the war substantially changed.

With the aid of the fleets the armed forces of the opposing coalitions extended armed struggle practically to the whole World Ocean, giving it a global character. To create, develop and use the fleets in the sphere of their operations huge material and human resources were expended, the fight at sea was distinguished by its exceptional intensity, abounded in crisis situations and yet could not lead to the direct, rapid and decisive defeat of German Fascism. Only the heroic self-sacrificing uncompromising struggle of the Soviet Army smashing the strongest war machine of the capitalist world on land could lead the whole anti-Hitlerite coalition to a great victory.

In the Second World War the influence of the multi-facetted and intensive combat activity of the navies on the general course of armed struggle in its main theatre was only indirect, and was manifest here not through armed struggle as before. The results of the operations of the fleets, among which of the greatest importance was the struggle for sea communications, were able to influence the course of the armed struggle on the main Soviet-German front only as a partial weakening of the economy of Fascist Germany due to losses at sea. The share of these losses in the total balance of the economic resources of practically all of Europe utilized by the Hitler command in the war was very insignificant.

Only in the final stage of the war when the heroic efforts of the Soviet armed forces drastically undermined the strike power of the German Fascist army did the fleets of our Allies make a series of attempts to act on the course of the armed struggle on land by mounting large-scale landings in Sicily, Italy and then Normandy. As a whole, these operations were successful. They hastened to a definite extent the unconditional surrender of the already doomed German Fascist army and appeared only when the enemy had practically lost the ability to counter effectively the amphibious operations of the combined forces of the Allied fleets.

A different role was played by the fleets of those countries whose economy largely depended on sea communications which were, in effect, vitally important arteries feeding their military potential and ultimately determining their military power. For Great Britain, for example, in whose armed forces a leading place was occupied by the navy, the effectiveness of its operations was largely determined by its ability not only to continue fighting but also survive in war. But this proved real only when the bulk of the military potential of the Fascist bloc was being deployed on the Soviet-German front.

In other words, in the course of the First and, in particular, the Second World Wars the fleets of the maritime capitalist powers acted as a factor ensuring the sustained participation of these powers in the war waged to exhaust the enemy possessing large land armies. This function was performed by the fleets with heavy exertion of forces in the often critical situations, threatening the armed forces with heavy defeat.

The navies, especially in the course of two world wars, fully revealed such qualities of theirs as great strike power and high mobility, enabling them to concentrate large forces in different areas of the World Ocean for solving important tasks. They demonstrated their ability to achieve important results in a short time and significantly change the strategic situation in individual theatres of military operations. At the same time the fleets displayed great potential in solving multiple operational tasks of an offensive character both in opposing the enemy's fleet and in operations against the shore.

Another characteristic feature is the successive redistribution of the main efforts of the fleets from the sphere of countering the strike forces of the enemy fleet to the sphere of operations for communications and then against the shore, most widely adopted in the Second World War. This tendency became dominant in the post-war period when the general direction of development of the fleets became the formation of forces and resources capable of exerting a direct influence not only on the course but also on the outcome of armed struggle on the lands fronts, not merely in the context of hitting back at the enemy's fleets.

Analysis of the present distribution of forces in the international arena and the sharp increase in the ability of modern fleets to act decisively on all fronts of armed struggle give grounds for asserting that not only the absolute, but also the relative importance of armed struggle at sea has indisputably grown.

Our state—a great continental and maritime world power—at all stages of its history has needed a powerful fleet as an essential constituent of the armed forces.

The need to have a potent navy in keeping with the geographical position of our country and its political significance as a great world power has for long been clear. However, this problem became particularly acute in the post-war years when, as a result of the changes in the distribution of forces in the world arena, the USSR and other socialist countries came to be encircled by a hostile coalition of maritime states giving rise to a serious threat of a nuclear missile attack from the sea.

Therefore, the Central Committee of the Communist Party and the Soviet Government, continuing the policy of peaceful coexistence of states with different social structures and prevention of a new world war, are putting into practice the testaments of V. I. Lenin on the reinforcement of the defence of our country. They pay constant attention to the perfection of the defence power of the state, to the strengthening of its armed forces including a harmonious, balanced development of the forces of the ocean-going navy matching the demands of the time, capable of opposing any strategems of foes and of confronting a potential aggressor with the need to solve himself the very problems which he is creating for our country.

The care of the Communist Party and the Soviet People for the valiant armed forces of the country, including the navy, serves as a faithful pledge that the Soviet Union will continue to remain not only a very strong continental but also a mighty sea power, a faithful guardian of peace in the world.

CHAPTER 3

The Development of Navies after the Second World War

AFTER the end of the Second World War, as after all past wars, views on the further development and building of the naval forces were for some time determined on the basis of analysis of the combat experience gained—recognition was given to the increased role of aircraft-carriers, submarine and amphibious forces in the whole complex of armed struggle at sea. The use by the Americans in the last stage of the war of the atom bomb produced something like a shock state among naval theoreticians and government circles of the traditional maritime states. Because of this, for about ten years in the post-war period, the building of fleets practically ceased.

Military circles at that time engaged in ever wider discussion on the influence of nuclear weapons on the character of armed struggle in all its spheres—on land and sea. The minds of many military specialists were exercised by the problems of the status of the fleet in conditions of a nuclear war and the influence of nuclear weapons on the construction of ships, their arming, viability and other tactical qualities. Initially, in many countries, including ours, there was a tendency to regard this problem from a negative angle, which often served as a basis for expressing extreme views, going so far as to deny the possibilities of the operation of fleets in conditions when nuclear arms were used. The Americans rated in much the same way the potential of land armies, the desirability of which as part of the armed forces was never out of the US military press for a long time. All this occurred at a time of limited possibilities for the use of atomic weapons, which only the USA had available then. At that time the USA had very far from perfect atomic weapons. This applied to the atomic bomb which its sole carrier—the aeroplane— could use only from a comparatively short distance from the target by physically penetrating into a zone of the heaviest anti-aircraft defence.

It must be emphasized that the dissemination of views on the omnipotence of the atomic bomb was largely promoted by intentionally inflated propaganda emanating from imperialist circles of the USA in furtherance of many political goals. By all means at its disposal the propaganda sought to elevate the atomic bomb to the status of the sole "absolute" weapon. Using the monopoly in this means of combat, the American militarists wished to scare the peoples of the world and consolidate the military superiority of the USA, which was regarded as the most important pre-requisite for political leadership of the whole world.

This was promoted by the wide publicity given to atomic weapon tests, including those off the Bikini Atoll in 1946, carried out to establish the influence of damaging factors on ships of different combat classes.

But the possibilities of American propaganda for whipping up fear and stock-exchange gambling over the new weapon were far from boundless. The unrestrained boosting of this weapon and the deliberate exaggeration of its potentialities were transformed into its denial. The more strident became the propaganda of deterrence, the more vigorously grew the circle of people capable of grasping and uncovering the real possibilities of the new weapon. In many countries the voices were ever-increasingly to be heard of those who tried to find the real limitations and conditions in which the armed forces could act on land and at sea, to determine the principles of use not only of nuclear but also of conventional means of warfare in an actual combat situation. Among them we would note the French Admiral Barjot whose interesting book *The Fleet in the Atomic Century*[1] came out in 1956. It affirmed that the atomic weapons tests of Bikini Atoll did not take the fleets into a dead end, but on the contrary widely opened the door for them to the open sea.

The creation of nuclear weapons in the Soviet Union changed the whole approach to the problem of atomic warfare. It led to an end to the so-called American monopoly over the new means of struggle and to the collapse of hopes for world dominance. Many political and military figures of Western countries, tamely following in the wake of American propaganda, began a tormenting search for ways of properly evaluating the balance of forces created in the world. It may be considered that from that moment a new stage began in the development of the armed forces of the leading countries of the world, recovering from the stifling influence exerted by American publicity about absolute US superiority. The role and place of different branches of the armed forces in armed conflict were revised, new ways of delivering nuclear weapons to strike targets and means of protection from their damaging factors were sought. As a realistic appraisal of the potential of these weapons took shape, the more distinct became the general outlines of the armed forces capable of waging combat operations in all possible conditions.

This process marked the start of a military-technical revolution which in scope and depth transcended all the reforms and transformations which had previously occurred in the armies and fleets of the world. It made it necessary to revise not only tactics, which not infrequently brought about radical transformations of the armed forces, due to the appearance of the new weapons, but also many technical means of waging war. The influence of the technical transformation process on all aspects of military matters also increased in connection with the use of atomic-powered engines in naval shipbuilding and outstanding discoveries in the field of radio-electronics and rocket construction.

A radical transformation of the armed forces, of the structure of the weapons system, and of the command and organization of the rear became necessary. The need to take account of this circumstance considerably altered the concept of balance of the armed forces. Such forces had to become capable of executing their military tasks in the varied conditions which might arise in time of war.

[1] P. Barjot, *The Fleet in the Atomic Century* (Russian translation), Inost. lit., Moscow, 1956.

The Soviet Union could not be an exception in what had become a universal search, and, in the resolution of many questions, headed those who soberly estimated the enormous destructive potential of atomic weapons and their influence on the character of war, and at once began to fight for the banning of the use of means of mass strike.

But at the same time in our country, too, military research circles put forward extreme views, boiling down to a denial of the role of the separate branches of the armed forces and arms systems. The possibility of the fleet operating at sea was also denied and hence the country's need for it. And, with the appearance of rocket arms the same fate was also predicted for aircraft. Misunderstanding of the character of modern warfare and the influence on it of nuclear missile weapons and blind genuflexion to the "omnipotence" of the atomic and hydrogen bombs led to a tendency for the armed forces to develop in a one-sided way.

To the honour of our military research, rejecting subjectivism, firmly resting on Marxist-Leninist dialectics, historical materialism and Leninist teaching on war and the army, it not only refuted these basically unsound notions but opened the way to the rapid development of new views reflecting the real distribution of forces in the world arena and fully matching modern trends in the development of the armed forces.

Military Doctrines of the USA and NATO

The great victory of the Soviet Union over the most powerful war machine of the capitalist world—Fascist Germany and militarist Japan—greatly weakened the forces of world imperialism. In these conditions the USA headed the camp of imperialism with the aim of uniting all the anti-communist forces to wage battle day in day out against the strengthened forces of socialism. No sooner did the Second World War end than the imperialists began to prepare a new war against the countries of the socialist community.

In accordance with these plans the aggressive military bloc NATO was set up in 1949 including at first 12 and then 15 capitalist states, among them such maritime powers as the USA, Britain, France, Canada, Italy, Turkey, West Germany, Greece, Norway, Denmark. Soon a further two aggressive blocs were formed—CENTO and SEATO, the latter being joined by the USA, Britain, France, Australia, New Zealand, Pakistan, the Philippines and Thailand. All these military blocs are oriented to ensuring the pursuit of an expansionist policy of imperialism in the most important areas of the world.

In NATO the leading place was taken by the major maritime powers, notably the USA and Britain, the total displacement of whose naval fleets after the Second World War came to 10.5 million tons.[2] Denmark, Iceland, West Germany, Norway, Turkey and Greece, though not having strong fleets, occupy an exceptionally advantageous strategic position in the sea theatres, thanks to which NATO closed the western semi-circle around the Soviet Union and can exercise constant control over the outlets from the Baltic and Black Seas. Italy also does not have a strong fleet, but its advantageous position in the central

[2] The total displacement of the ships of the British Navy was 3.5 million tons.

part of the Mediterranean offers major facilities for stationing and maintaining the operations of the fleets of the USA and NATO in this most important theatre.

Thus, NATO is an alliance of maritime states, with powerful naval forces occupying advantageous strategic positions in the World Ocean.

The spheres of influence of the other aggressive blocs also extend to the Pacific Ocean. This allows the member countries of NATO and other blocs, notably the USA, to use numerous foreign military bases and coastal areas in the eastern hemisphere to threaten the USSR from the sea and to have prepared advantageously situated fortified positions and starting lines for deploying in the shortest time forces and resources in the oceanic zones they have selected.

The American military leadership made every effort to intensify the development of its own armed forces which, relying on nuclear weapons, were to occupy a dominant position in the world and have indisputable strategic superiority over the armed forces of the countries of the socialist community. Constant and unabated attention was paid to the development of the naval forces. For this was regularly set aside a considerable share of military appropriations, so enabling the strike power of the US fleet to be rapidly expanded. The oceans were gradually turned into areas of launching sites for strategic weapons. The endeavour in all cases to solve foreign policy issues by relying on the armed forces became the basic form of activity of the American imperialists, which together with the development of the general crisis of capitalism inevitably led to an escalation of the militarization of the country and to an arms race.

In line with this policy and in the interests of ensuring it, the military doctrine of the USA was evolved and modified.

The military doctrines of the other NATO countries stem from the doctrine of the USA—the leading state within this bloc. They were developed on the basis of the conception of so-called interdependence or military integration. The shaping of these doctrines was significantly influenced by the ever growing wish of most states of the bloc to pursue a policy more independent of the USA and to formulate national military-strategic conceptions. A definite role is also played by the fact that the strongest of the US partners are fighting for key positions in this bloc by seeking a solution, more advantageous to themselves, to the most important political problems of Europe.

In the development of their naval forces and in views on their combat deployment such traditional maritime powers as Britain and France follow the USA. However, their economic potential allowed them to set up only limited strategic submarine nuclear missile systems and aircraft-carrier forces.

Consistent with the concept of "interdependence", an auxiliary role is assigned to the fleets of other members of the NATO bloc—including West Germany and Italy. Their tasks are limited in the main to assistance to land troops and protection of sea communications. Therefore, it is quite logical to focus attention on analysis of the evolution of the military doctrine of the USA.

In the development of this doctrine, three main stages may be singled out, bringing forth three main strategic conceptions.

The first stage, covering the period from the end of the 'forties to the beginning of the 'sixties, is characterized by the birth, elaboration and official adoption by the American leadership in 1953 of the so-called new course in the national policy of the USA known as the policy from a "position of strength" and the strategy of "massive retaliation".

In this period wide currency was gained in the USA by the idea of a preventive atomic war against the Soviet Union, appearing even when the decision to destroy Hiroshima and Nagasaki was being taken. Such a barbarous demonstration of the "absolute" weapon manifestly pursued political ends and had no military basis. It was necessary to military-monopolistic circles bent on gaining world dominance, hoping that this action would "make Russia more accommodating in Europe". The atomic bombing of the two Japanese towns was aptly characterized by Professor P. Blackett, who called it not so much the last military action of the Second World War as the first in the "cold war" against the Soviet Union.

The intention to dictate his will to the world including the Soviet Union was most precisely demonstrated by the leader of the new claimants to world dominance—President Truman. "The USA today", he declared, "is the strongest power and there is no one stronger. . . . Possessing such strength, we must take upon ourselves the responsibility and leadership of the world."[3] Since the destruction of Hiroshima and Nagasaki had no influence on the policy of the Soviet Union, a wave of war hysteria was again whipped up. Now not only did the reactionary press call for a preventive war to be started against the USSR, but also voices were raised from the rostrum of Congress declaring that the USA "has strength" and must "use it now" while it still retains a monopoly over the atomic bomb and the biggest fleet and air force. The atomic bomb was "brandished" not only by the military but also by President Truman himself. Considering the atomic bomb very suitable for "pushing the Russians out of Europe", he took the decision to use it in Europe should "extreme circumstances" arise.

The idea of American omnipotence was widespread in higher military circles. The frightful destructive force of the atomic bomb gave rise to the view that it would enable the USA to police the globe and impose on the peoples a world in the American image.

To start with, the US air force consolidated its role as the main force in a nuclear war since one of its advantages was combat experience in the use of atomic bombs. Among the other advantages invoked were the "superior power" of American strategic aviation and "invulnerability" of the territory of the USA to a response strike of the enemy.

The Pentagon reckoned that, having a considerable number of long-range bombers and also a ring of military air bases situated in direct proximity to the Soviet borders, American nuclear forces would be in a position to break through the anti-aircraft defence of the enemy and destroy all or the vast majority of their targets.

Starting from these notions, the US leadership sharply intensified efforts to develop the air force and extend the network of its overseas bases.

[3] Quoted in Yu. N. Listvinov, *The First Strike*, p. 12 (in Russian), Mezhdunarodniye otnosheniye (International Relations), Moscow, 1971.

In June 1948 American Congress approved a bill to expand the size of the air force to 70 wings, and the USA also received the agreement of the British Labour Government to station in that country 60 B-29 bombers with nuclear bombs on board. After the signing of the North Atlantic Pact in April 1949, the whole of Western Europe was tied by American nuclear strategy. The number of US military bases by the end of the 'sixties had reached 3400. The gaps in this network on the sea and ocean routes were to be covered by naval forces. On the territories adjacent to the borders of our country, armies many millions strong were deployed, exceeding ten times the size of the armed forces of the allies in the main theatres in the years of the Second World War. All this was done on the assumption that the territory of the USA as in the past would be outside the range of retaliatory strikes and would thus not become a theatre of military operations. Assessing the significance of this treaty, the influential Congressman K. Cannon emphasized that the signing of the NATO pact gave the USA the necessary bases "for striking a blow at Moscow and all the other towns of Russia now . . . all we need are the planes for delivering nuclear weapons." (Retranslated from Russian.)

Under the influence of the advance of the Soviet Union in producing atomic weapons and the loss by the Americans of the "atomic monopoly", the gaze of the American military leadership began to turn more and more to the fleet which, as a potential carrier of nuclear weapons, depended less on the cramping influence of foreign policy factors expressed in different forms for aviation stationed on foreign territory. "Atomic power plus sea power will give such freedom of action to the country", wrote the journal *Military Review,* "that it can readily discharge our God-given right of leadership of the whole world." (Retranslated from Russian.)

Thus, in the circles of American militarists there was an ever clearer tendency towards partnership of the navy with the air force in the use of nuclear resources in a future war. This was the direct result of the atom-bomb tests off the Bikini Atoll, dispelling the doubts of the American military leadership on the possibility of using the navy in a nuclear war. Moreover, this was one of the manifestations of the intentions of the American imperialists to employ in the total nuclear war being prepared all the forces and resources at their disposal, to give a "universal character" to nuclear strikes on land targets in our territory and to make full use of the direction of armed struggle new to our country—the oceanic—where at that time the USA had a decisive lead in forces over our fleet.

It should be noted that this turn in the use of naval forces of the imperialist countries was plainly geared to the intention to direct the whole power of the American and British fleets primarily against the land. This direction of the operations of the navy was recognized as paramount. It later served as the basis for creating strategic nuclear forces as part of the fleet, giving rise to a continuing tendency towards strengthening the concentration of strategic nuclear means in the sphere of operations of a navy.

As doubts were increasingly dispelled on the possibilities of using fleets in an atomic war, momentum was gathered by the opposite conception, now defining the fleet as the most important branch of the armed forces, capable of solving, in a nuclear war, major strategic tasks and of exerting a direct influence on the course and outcome of a war.

In the second half of the 'fifties sharp and fundamental changes took place in views of the role and place of naval forces in a war and the importance of oceanic theatres of military operations. Starting from the alignment of forces in the international arena and considering the limited possibilities of the Soviet fleet, the Americans pushed into the background the traditional problem, bothering them for almost a century, of protecting oceanic communications. On the basis of the reports of the special Poseidon Commission, this problem in 1957 was relegated to second place and the oceans were declared no longer an arena of struggle for communications but extensive launching areas for releasing various carriers of strategic nuclear weapons intended to destroy important land targets located on the territory of the enemy.

However, in the strategy of "massive retaliation" officially recognized in the West, the emphasis was still on the superiority of strategic aviation which was then considered in the USA as the main means of delivering nuclear weapons to the target. This prompted the swaggering utterances of the Commander of the US Army Air Force that in a future war the new types of weapons would make it possible to finish off the war so quickly that the operations of artillery or the navy would no longer be needed. Nevertheless, this extreme point of view did not receive the support on which the air force leadership and military-industrial circles standing behind them counted. For over a century, American imperialism used the navy as the main instrument of its aggressive foreign policy in line with prevailing tradition and was impressed by the concept of sea power, which was presented as an irreplaceable means of achieving world dominance.

An attempt to remove this contradiction was behind the ideas of Admiral Nimitz who proposed that priority be kept for the fleet by uniting the fleet and aviation, producing an "air-sea hybrid" in the form of strike aircraft-carriers. This idea met with approval and was adopted as a doctrinal tenet of the "position of strength" policy of the US imperialists. "Nevertheless the core of the New Policy was its primary reliance on air-atomic power. The amphibious forces—i.e. ground troops—have but a secondary place in the New Policy. Massive retaliation by atomic blows from land-based and carrier planes is the essence of it."[4]

The use of these means in a war against the Soviet Union was based on the perfectly groundless assumption that the territory of the USA would be invulnerable to the means of strike when available in the Soviet Union. On this basis the strategy of "massive retaliation" assumed that only a global nuclear war would be waged against the Soviet Union and other socialist countries.

In line with this strategy the military-political leadership of the USA put the main emphasis on developing nuclear weapons and means of delivery, in the first place strategic aviation and strike aircraft-carriers to the detriment of the development of the conventional branches of the armed forces, especially of land forces. On this General Taylor wrote: "These percentages for Fiscal Year 1955 to Fiscal Year 1959 had been about 46 per cent for the Air Force, about 28 per cent for the Navy and Marine Corps, and some 23 per cent for the

[4]T. K. Finletter, *Power and Policy*, New York, 1954, p. 147.

Army. . . . In the vital area of funds for the purchase of new equipment . . . the Air Force in this period has consistently received some 60 per cent of the available resources, the Navy and Marine Corps about 30 per cent and the Army about 10 percent."[5]

In the 'fifties, the strategy of massive retaliation became the official military strategy of NATO. But in NATO it was transformed into the strategy of the "shield and sword". The role of the "sword" was to be fulfilled by strategic aviation and the strike aircraft-carriers of the USA and the role of the "shield" by the armed forces of the member countries spread out in Europe. Like the strategy of the USA, the military strategy of NATO assumed that the armed forces of this bloc would have to use nuclear weapons whether or not the enemy employed them. The possibility of a limited war being waged by NATO countries without use of nuclear weapons against the Soviet Union in Europe was practically excluded. The possibility of waging limited wars was admitted only in the "less developed areas of the globe outside Europe".

But soon the complete untenability of the strategy of "massive retaliation" became clear. The main reasons for its failure were the change in the balance of forces in the world arena, the growth of the military might of the Soviet Union and, above all, major advances in developing strategic nuclear missile weapons which not only made it impossible for the United States to reach its goals by means of the former strategy, but also deprived its territory of its past invulnerability. The American journal *Ordnance* wrote in an editorial article: "The principle of massive nuclear retaliation as the overriding basis for US military policy is thus made obsolete by loss of our nuclear monopoly and emergence of a mutual deterrence situation in which nuclear superiority as between the US and USSR is measured only in terms of overkill. Equally responsible for the significant change was the slow-in-coming realization that as the "big stick" of foreign policy it was too big for too many situations."[6]

In other words, the military leadership of the USA came to the conclusion that by pinning its hopes only on strategic nuclear means and on global nuclear war it could not achieve its main military-political ends. The military doctrine of the USA turned out to be inflexible. But they could not give up war as an instrument of policy and therefore the Kennedy administration at the beginning of the 'sixties undertook a partial revision of military strategy without, of course, changing the aims of US policy.

This paved the way for the second stage of the development of the American military doctrine. The French journal *Revue de Defense Nationale* in May 1964 defined the basic principles of the new US strategy thus:

"(1) The United States must have and maintain unquestionable superiority over the Soviet Union in the field of strategic and tactical nuclear weapons;

(2) The USA must possess sufficient means successfully to counteract the enemy in any situation without necessarily resorting to mass strike weapons;

(3) The USA must as it sees fit define (depending on the character and scale

[5] Maxwell D. Taylor, *The Uncertain Trumpet*, London, 1959, pp. 65-6.
[6] Quoted in *The Military Doctrines of the NATO Countries*, p. 71 (in Russian), and taken from *Ordnance*, September-October 1963, p. 156.

of the conflict) the scope and means of waging combat operations to remove any risk of the uncontrollable spread of the conflict."

Unlike the former strategy, the new military strategy of the "flexible response" envisaged the preparation and waging both of a global nuclear war and restricted wars with and without nuclear weapons against the socialist countries including those in Europe. A flexible response to the international situation obtaining and readiness to use military force in line with this situation was the keynote of the new US strategy. It proceeded from the need to prepare and wage wars of any kind—global nuclear wars or limited wars with use of nuclear or only of conventional weapons.

The USA considered that a universal nuclear war might begin in two ways: by a sudden nuclear attack or as a result of the build-up (escalation) of a limited war. A prominent place was taken by the execution of a sudden nuclear attack and the launching of a preventive war against the USSR and other socialist countries. Another approach was that the preparation for a sudden attack would be made under cover of propaganda depicting the USA as the defending side intent on delivering only a "response strike".

For a limited war the variant "waging two and a half wars" was put forward, according to which the USA started from the possibility of simultaneously waging two limited wars—in Asia and Europe, and one small local war—most probably in Latin America. For waging war in Europe the concepts of "suitable restraint" and "nuclear threshold" were advanced, stemming from the strategy of the "flexible response". According to the concept of "suitable restraint" a limited war in Europe might begin with use of conventional weapons only, having regard to the possible further development of the conflict. It was considered that the armed forces of NATO would initially use only conventional weapons but if the situation grew more complicated and threat of defeat appeared, the use of tactical nuclear weapons for achieving the goals set was envisaged.

The strategy of "flexible response" also set the scene for the development of the armed forces of the USA and other NATO countries. The Americans spread among the European member countries of the bloc a new variant of the principle of "interdependence", aimed at establishing in the framework of NATO balanced armed forces and on this basis specifying the responsibility of each country for developing such national armed forces as were necessary for achieving the political ends of the USA. The task of developing the strategic offensive forces was taken on by the USA and, in part, by England. The other NATO countries were to develop, in the main, land forces and comparatively minor air and naval forces. Such "interdependence" did not go down well with the European countries of NATO, in particular, with France and West Germany claiming a leading role in the bloc.

In addition, realizing that American strategic forces were in the first place a means of achieving the national goals of the USA and not in the interests of the European NATO countries and that the Americans might not even use them in a military conflict, if it did not touch the vital interests of the USA, the European member countries of NATO lost confidence in the efficacy of the US nuclear guarantee. Therefore, France in 1966 quit the military organization of NATO and independently went over to the building up of national strategic nuclear forces. Other countries (West Germany, Britain) put forward the suggestion of creating "European nuclear forces" of the bloc and urged the lowering of the "nuclear threshold" that is, the unrestricted use of nuclear weapons from the very start of the outbreak of a war in Europe. This produced serious disagreements within the NATO bloc because of the wish of the European member countries to free themselves even if only to a degree from American dictation. However, the dominant place of the USA in the Western bloc could not be eliminated since it possessed the basic nuclear power of the bloc. The European NATO countries depend on the USA in the field not only of strategic but also of tactical nuclear weapons. Operational tactical missiles, atomic artillery and a large part of tactical aviation are received by the European NATO countries from the USA; nuclear warheads are in the hands of the American command.

As in the strategy of the "massive response strike" in the strategy of the "flexible response" the strategic means of strike remain fundamental. However, while, firstly, the basis of these means was made up of strategic aviation and strike aircraft-carriers, secondly it became the so-called invulnerable missile forces to which were assigned *Minuteman* missiles and the *Polaris* submarine strategic system. No small part of the military leadership of the USA gives explicit preference to atomic submarine missile-carriers.

Taking as the basis of their strategic offensive forces, "invulnerable missile forces", the core of which became atomic submarine missile-carriers with whose aid a "nuclear missile ring" was to be set up round the Soviet Union, the US military command did not abandon the further development of the strike aircraft-carrier fleet which until that time had been the "backbone" of their navy. In the view of the American command, strike aircraft-carriers, together with tactical aviation, must form the basis of the strike power of general-purpose forces.

The recognition by the strategy of the "flexible response" of the possibility of waging limited wars against countries of the socialist community also gave the American command grounds for considering aircraft carriers with the aircraft on them as a force having greater importance in various armed conflicts than before. On this the Chief of Naval Operations of the US Navy Admiral McDonald declared: "Our fast attack carrier task forces, together with their mobile logistic support, enable us to project a United States base overseas and have it operable while moving."[7]

The third stage in the development of the US military doctrine began in 1971 with the proclamation of the "Nixon doctrine" and the military strategy of "realistic deterrence" worked out on the basis of it. The idea of the new strategy was to achieve the class aims of the general struggle of imperialism against peaceful socialism and the national liberation movement by conducting a policy of "deterrence" resting primarily on the military power of the USA and also on its allies in the military blocs. As a whole the new strategy is an updated strategy of the "flexible response" and the changes introduced into it do not affect the foundation of the military strategy of the USA, its anti-communist and anti-

[7] *Navy Air Force Journal and Register*, Washington, DC, 10 August 1963, Vol. 100, No. 50, part 1, p. 14.

Soviet orientation, the views on probable forms of warfare and their socio-political character.

The need to revise the strategy of the "flexible response" was due to its failure to match fully the military-political and strategic situation in the world built up by the start of the 'seventies and the principles of the national policy and strategy of the USA outline in the "Nixon doctrine". The basic principles proclaimed in the "Nixon doctrine" are: the principle of strength, the principle of partnership and the principle of negotiation. The principle of strength remains paramount, envisaging the military superiority of the USA and its allies over the USSR and the socialist community as a whole as the most important condition for the conduct of the policy of "deterrence" in mutual relations with them.

The principle of partnership consists in the maximum use of the military, economic and financial resources of the allied and dependent countries in the interests of maintaining the political influence and positions of the USA in the world. It is assumed that the implementation of this principle will help to reduce the direct participation of American troops in local wars. According to the estimates of the Pentagon, keeping a soldier of the allies is several times cheaper than keeping a US serviceman.

The principle of negotiation is given a subordinate role since it is considered that, merely relying on its military strength and the resources of the allies, the USA may conduct negotiations with the Soviet Union and other countries.

The essence of the strategy of "realistic deterrence" is to seek to solve international problems by relying on one's own strength, making the maximum use of the human and material resources of the US allies for which it is necessary to expand their military power and increase their role and responsibility for preparing and waging war.

The new strategy, like the preceding one, starts from the possibility of waging both local wars and a global nuclear war. However, the strategy of "realistic deterrence" lays much emphasis on "partnership"—the more active enlistment of the partners in aggressive blocs for executing the military-political plans of the USA, including the solving of the tasks of combating a national liberation movement by the method of "Vietnamization".

The new strategy and the strategic concepts springing from it determine the lines of development of the armed forces of the USA and its allies, the relationship between the different components of these forces and the criteria for fixing their levels. In line with this it looks forward to a sharp qualitative improvement in the armed forces, especially the strategic means and general-purpose forces; achieving technical superiority over the Soviet Union, especially in the field of developing and producing strategic nuclear missile weapons; increasing the strategic mobility of the American general-purpose armed forces; and increasing the fighting power of the armed forces of the allies of the US.

The main tasks in developing the US armed forces in the next decade remain the preservation and maintenance of "sufficient" strategic nuclear power as the basis of the "nuclear deterrent". The concept of sufficiency, in the view of American strategists, means the guaranteed destruction of the military potential, human resources and economic potential of an enemy even in conditions of a response nuclear strike unfavourable to the USA, and also the ability to maintain combat possibilities in any situation. This also conditions the most characteristic features of the current stage in the strategic arms race in the USA—the qualitative development of weapons and replacement of obsolete by new, more sophisticated systems.

As for the use of the general-purpose forces, the strategy of "realistic deterrence" envisages the dropping of the concept of "two and a half wars" in favour of that of "one and a half wars". Its essence is that the USA must maintain in peacetime general-purpose forces which, together with the forces of its allies, would be capable of simultaneously and successfully waging a major war in Europe or Asia and taking part in an insignificant conflict in any part of the globe.

An important role in the new strategy is given to the "strategic mobility" of the US armed forces which implies the ability to transfer and deploy them quickly in overseas theatres of military operations with the aim of strengthening the forces present there or creating new groupings. The need for "strategic mobility" springs from the global character of the military-political ambitions of the USA and is considered the most important condition for carrying out the strategy of "realistic deterrence". Special attention is paid to increasing the mobility of airborne and air-mobile troops and marines and in this connection to the development of transport aviation and the construction of universal landing craft.

In working out a military strategy and military policy for the 'seventies the American leadership placed special stress on so-called oceanic strategy as an important constituent of the strategy of "realistic deterrence". Its essence is the transfer of the main power of the strategic offensive forces to the expanses of the World Ocean. For this purpose the main efforts are concentrated on the development of general-purpose naval forces, raising the percentage of atomic missile submarines as part of the strategic offensive forces, and on the use of naval power as the principal means of military backing for the political course of American imperialism, which in the last analysis must secure the gaining of dominance at sea in the course of a war.

The following grounds for the desirability of moving over to an "oceanic strategy" are listed:

strategic nuclear offensive weapons located at sea would make it possible to create a dispersed arms system capable of ensuring the delivery of nuclear strikes on the territory of the countries of the socialist community from practically any direction.

the transfer of the launching sites of intercontinental missiles to the oceans would make it possible to remove from the territory of the USA the land installations for these missiles, which in the Pentagon's view will sharply reduce the number of objectives which might become targets for enemy missiles and hence considerably cut down the number of nuclear strikes which could be delivered directly on US territory;

submarine nuclear-missile weapon systems possess greater viability, ease of concealment and mobility than corresponding systems positioned on land;

the placement of the bulk of strategic forces at sea would lead to considerable dispersion of the nuclear missile strikes of the enemy in extensive areas of the ocean; bearing in mind the comparatively low vulnerability of missile boats and the complexity of detecting them at the start of first strike, it may be assumed that a considerable part of the nuclear missile power of the enemy would be dissipated fruitlessly and the bulk of the nuclear missile power of the US strategic forces maintained.

As missile carriers it is planned to use low-noise, atomic-powered submarines of improved design of the Trident type which will be discussed below. The strategic forces of the fleet would be left with the Polaris-Poseidon strategic submarine nuclear missile system.

As well as these strategic forces, "oceanic strategy" assumes that large general-purpose naval forces would be used for the control of strategically important areas. Among them a major place would be taken by the new multi-purpose ships described by the Americans as "ships for sea control".

The advocates of "oceanic strategy" consider that the naval forces, having effective strategic means represented by atomic-powered missile submarines, multi-purpose aircraft-carriers, a modern general-purpose surface and sub-marine fleet, considerable naval aviation and marines, and possessing such properties as manoeuvrability and comparative invulnerability, are the most promising and universal form of the armed forces for reaching the ends laid down by the "Nixon doctrine". It is also considered that "oceanic strategy" ensures the necessary flexibility in the use of military power, matches the current situation in the world, the potential of the United States and the principle of the strategy of "realistic deterrence".

Analysis of the basic pre-requisites of "oceanic strategy" and the practical measures of the American military command in the construction and use of the armed forces indicates that the chief goals of this strategy are consolidation of the military-strategic positions of the USA and securing its global presence by means of naval forces. These ideas are not new. They were borrowed from the ideologists of American expansion at the turn of the century, especially from A. Mahan, and updated in relation to the imperialist policy of the USA pursued in modern conditions.

Perusal of the content of the military doctrines of the imperialist states shows that whatever their name they are all aimed against the world socialist system and their principal task is to save capitalism which is doomed by history.

According to the theories of the ideologists of imperialism, the only means of saving capitalism is military force. At present, in their view, it can only be nuclear strike forces which in the post-war period have become the main argument used by the aggressive military doctrines of the chief imperialist countries. Among these forces a growing role is being played by the navy.

In the view of the American military and political leaders the advantage of naval forces is that the strike formations of the fleet may be rapidly and in time (before the adoption of political solutions) switched to so-called restive areas and may stay there for a long time in high combat readiness for solving tasks of any scale. In considering the advantages of naval forces in carrying out the strategic plans of the Pentagon, former US Defense Secretary Laird, in his testimony to a US Congress House Committee on Armed Services, meeting on 9 March 1971, and reporting on the military programme for 1972-76, stated that in some situations a timely response or presence would be of substantially greater importance than large forces which might be deployed in 60-90 days.

According to the assessment of the Chief of the Naval Staff Admiral Zumwalt, "... the naval forces, including the landing forces aboard ships, are the sole forces which can be rapidly and effectively brought into action irrespective of the presence of advanced bases, the presence of the right of flight of planes over certain territories or disembarking in this or that area, and also irrespective of other forms of support the use of which requires the permission of the authorities of the particular territories". (Retranslated from Russian.)

The plans, building programmes and practical measures carried out by the military-political leadership of the USA show that the USA as before is intent on stepping up the nuclear missile potential and strike power of its naval forces, raising the combat and mobilizational readiness of all branches of the navy. In the next few years the navy command plans to speed up the fulfilment of long-term plans of creating new strategic weapons systems and modernizing armaments, which was held up by the enormous expenditure of the USA on keeping going the war in South-East Asia.

It is no secret that these military preparations are directed against the peace-loving states, primarily the countries of the socialist community. This continuing nuclear arms race confirms anew the obvious truth that as long as imperialism exists, as long as it expands its military power, the real possibility of unleashing a war remains. Therefore the Communist Party of the Soviet Union "regards the protection of the socialist homeland, the strengthening of the defence of the USSR, the power of the Soviet armed forces ... as the most important function of the socialist state "[8]

The Development of the Fleets of the Imperialist States

In the post-war years the fleets of the imperialist states have steadily developed and become more sophisticated. Particularly great importance is attached by the USA to the development of the naval forces. Thus, according to the 1974 report of the US Defense Secretary Schlessinger to Congress, expenditure on the US Navy comes to about one-third of the total sum of US appropriations for all branches of the armed forces. In the 1971-72 financial year the US naval forces in appropriations came top, receiving 23,700 million dollars, that is 34 per cent of all the funds set aside for the three branches of the armed forces. It should be noted that the tendency for the appropriations set aside for the building of the US Navy to rise still persists. Thus, in 1972-73 the Navy received 25,400 million dollars (36 per cent), in 1973-74 27,600 million dollars (37 per cent), and in 1974-75 it was planned to spend 29,600 million dollars (37 per cent).

Speaking in February 1974 before the Armed Services Committee of American Congress, US Secretary of the Navy Warner specified the goals, as he put it,

[8] *Programme of the Communist Party of the Soviet Union,* pp. 110, 111, Moscow Politizdat, 1971 (in Russsian).

of the "maritime policy" of his country. In his words this is ". . . the maintenance of strong, strategic naval nuclear missile restraining forces and the ability
to ensure the freedom of sea communications in areas vitally important for the
national interests of the USA, including the all-round ability to influence events
in the terminal areas of sea communications to the point of waging offensive
operations and disembarking landing forces where this proves necessary."
(Retranslated from Russian.)

Developing and substantiating this idea, Warner declared that ". . . never
before in the history of the USA has the maintenance of strong naval forces and
marines capable of completely ensuring the attainment of the ends . . . of
maritime policy been so important as now. . . . During the life of our generation
dependence [USA-S.G.] on the sea has widened and extended to economic
security. For example, the USA now imports completely or in part 69 of the 72
materials extremely important for industry and over 99 per cent of the weight of
these materials is delivered by sea. . . . The ability to ensure the security of sea
communications has now become twice as important." (Retranslated from
Russian.)

In the post-war years major changes have occurred in the numerical and
qualitative composition of the fleets of the imperialist states.

As can be seen (Table 18), battleship and convoy aircraft-carriers, representing in the first post-war years a fairly large grouping, have been practically
excluded from the fleets.

TABLE 18
Changes in the Composition of the Forces of the Fleets of the USA, England,
France, Canada, Italy, West Germany, Japan and Australia

Class of ships	1945	1949	1960	1970	1974
Battleships	48	29	9	4	4
Strike (multi-purpose) aircraft-carriers	42	60	24	19	19
Anti-submarine aircraft-carriers	–	–	19	8	6
Convoy aircraft-carriers	117	68	22	–	–
Torpedo submarines	781	266	263	196	188*
Submarine missile-carriers	–	–	5	45	48
Cruisers	161	121	58	16	29
Destroyers, escort ships, frigates	2023	1053	1059	715	581
Landing-helicopter dock ships	–	–	–	12	19
Landing helicopter carriers	–	–	6	10	9
Tank-landing craft	1150	205	134	82	73

* Including 69 atomic-powered

The composition of strike aircraft-carriers has also changed qualitatively and
quantitatively. The almost two-fold fall in the number of carriers was compen-
sated by a considerable rise in their tactical properties as a result of the
realization of new achievements of science in shipbuilding, refitting for jet
aircraft and their conversion to floating bases as nuclear weapon carriers. The
reduction in the numbers of battleships and aircraft carriers brought in its wake
a corresponding sharp drop in the number of cruisers with armaments and also
of destroyers, frigates and escort ships.

But not only is this a measure of the degree of the transformation which has overtaken the fleets. The main point is that they have acquired a qualitatively new means of strategic importance—atomic-powered missile submarines, thanks to which they have increased many times the possibilities of undertaking operations against the land and of exercising a direct influence on the course of a present-day nuclear war.

The development of the American armed forces in the post-war period has been determined by a number of different strategies, although irrespective of the change in these strategies US and NATO naval forces have continued to remain the most important constituent part of their armed forces. Unceasing attention has been paid to their development, and the discussion on the desirability of building a fleet taking place in other countries after the advent of atomic weapons in the USA did not assume official form and did not go beyond the confines of the private views of individual authors.

The development of the fleets of the USA and other NATO countries in the first post-war years took the direction characteristic of the period of the Second World War. The main task was to ensure the safety of sea communications linking the overseas arsenal of war with the groupings of the armed forces deployed in the main, European, theatre and directed against the Soviet Union. Another task which was also decisive was connected with amphibious operations on a different scale, in a war primarily against the countries of socialism and the developing countries.

Later, after the American and then the British and French fleets had been equipped with strategic nuclear weapons, the decisive factor in the development of these fleets became their ability to solve the strategic task of destroying important land objectives situated deep in the territories of the countries of the socialist community.

The fleets of the USA, Britain and France were now already developed as a branch of the armed forces capable of decisively influencing the course of a world nuclear war. The new strategic qualities assumed by the naval forces determined their basic intention as a means for operations against land. These same qualities produced one of the basic tendencies in the development of the armed forces of the West: the continuous transfer of an ever greater part of the strategic nuclear missile potential to the naval forces. This tendency finally led at the end of the 'sixties and the beginning of the 'seventies to the proclamation of a military doctrine oriented for the first time towards the preferential development of the navy and finding its expression in "oceanic strategy".

As stated, before 1957 the main means of delivering nuclear weapons was aviation. That is why at that time special attention was paid to the universal development of strategic and aircraft-carrier aviation and strike aircraft-carriers which became the main strike force of the American fleet.

After 1957 when the Soviet Union demonstrated remarkable achievements in the field of rocketry, rockets began to be used with increasing confidence as nuclear-weapon carriers on land and at sea. At the same time this did not influence the role of aircraft-carriers in the system of Anglo-American naval forces. Today these ships form the basis of the sea power of the US fleet despite the ever-growing threat from sophisticated missile weapons.

The building of new aircraft-carriers in the USA was begun within only seven years of the end of the Second World War. Aircraft carriers of the *Forrestal* type were the ships of the first series. Their displacement was 78,000 tons and each of them carried on board over 80 planes. In addition, the finishing touches were put to the carriers already designed in wartime, the types *Midway* and *Oriskany* with a displacement of 43,000-62,000 tons and carrying up to 80 planes each.

The US fleet at the beginning of the 'sixties numbered 17 strike aircraft-carriers: one atomic of the *Enterprise* type,[9] six of the *Forrestal* type, three of the *Midway* type and seven of the *Oriskany* type. The position of the aircraft-carrier strike forces of the Americans was also roughly at this level by 1970. France has two multi-purpose aircraft-carriers and Britain one. A total of 1,500 planes are on these ships.

Strike aircraft-carriers are assembled into formations which operate in the Atlantic and Pacific Oceans and also in the Mediterranean. They have strong anti-submarine and anti-aircraft defences, the depth of which reaches several hundred kilometres.

The aircraft-carrier strike formations undertake intensive training to deliver nuclear weapons on land targets and assist their land forces.

At the beginning of the 'seventies the US naval command revised the projected programme of the development of general-purpose naval forces in order to bring it into line with the requirements of the new strategy. Significant changes were introduced into the programme aimed at the further expansion of the combat possibilities of these naval forces, in the first place the aircraft-carrier and anti-submarine forces.

The main element of the general-purpose naval forces continues to remain the aircraft-carrier strike forces which are the basic means of a strike by the fleet in local wars and a highly-trained reserve of strategic strike forces in a global nuclear war.

The US navy now numbers 14 strike aircraft-carriers including two atomic-powered ones. A further two atomic-powered aircraft-carriers of the *Nimitz* type are under construction.

To ensure the combat activity of atomic-powered aircraft-carriers the production-line building of atomic-powered frigates with guided missiles (guided-missile frigates) is under way, the idea being to have not less than four atomic-powered protection ships to each atomic-powered aircraft-carrier. Even now the USA possesses three atomic-powered protection ships and a further five atomic guided-missile frigates in different stages of construction.

Together with the building of new aircraft-carriers work is also being done to perfect the armaments and equipment of older ships. Exceptional attention is being paid to qualitative improvement in the plane complement of the aircraft-carriers, both by the continuous improvement of planes adopted for arming, and by producing planes with developed tactical and technical characteristics and more powerful armaments including missiles.

The development of the aircraft-carrier strike forces is along the lines of converting them into multi-purpose aircraft-carrier forces, the basic functions

[9] Its displacement was some 90,000 tons, main armaments up to 120 planes. The yard period for its construction was about four and a half years.

of which in the next few years may be shifted to the task of protecting extensive areas of the sea and ocean theatres. The Americans, in particular, have already embarked on refitting strike aircraft-carriers so that they can be used as a multi-purpose strike anti-submarine variant.

In the search for ways of extending the potential of the fleet for gaining dominance at sea in the USA and other NATO countries, together with the building of multi-purpose aircraft-carrying ships, the building of guided-missile atomic-powered submarines, missile ships and cutters is under way, including those on hydrofoil and an air cushion. The planes and helicopters of naval aviation are armed with missiles of the "air to ship" class.

Multi-purpose aircraft-carrying ships described in the USA as "ships for sea control" are intended to secure anti-aircraft and anti-submarine defence of formations of ships, landing detachments and convoys in transit at sea and also for backing from the air the disembarking of a landing force. These ships (displacement of some 14,000 tons, speed of travel about 30 knots) will house vertical take-off and landing planes and heavy multi-purpose helicopters.

In the 1974-75 financial year the US Navy asked for funds to be set aside to build a leading ship of such a class and by 1980 the Americans plan to build eight such ships. Great Britain has also begun to build multi-purpose aircraft-carrying ships similar to the Americans. In June 1973 the first such ship, the *Invincible,* was laid down. France and Japan also have similar plans.

An important line in the development of the American fleet was, and remains, the creation of forces for the defence of aircraft-carriers and convoys which include GMW cruisers, destroyers, anti-submarine protection ships and frigates. The US fleet by the beginning of the 'seventies had 253 such ships, the NATO countries 523 *in toto.*

In the American fleet in the post-war period great importance has been attached to the development of submarine forces, primarily nuclear weapon carriers. The first atomic-powered submarine *Nautilus* armed with torpedoes, a prototype of a multi-purpose vessel, was brought into commission in 1954. Within three years the USA embarked on the building of atomic-powered submarine missile-carriers intended for delivering strikes with ballistic missiles on land targets in the territories of the countries of the socialist community. At the end of 1960 the first atomic submarine missile-carrier *George Washington,* armed with 16 *Polaris* missiles, moved out for combat patrolling.

Developing strategic submarine nuclear forces the military-political leadership of the USA started from the premise that one of the main means of improving the combat resilience of offensive strategic forces was the creation of sea-base systems. Therefore, in 1961 Kennedy's government took measures to step up the *Polaris* programme.

In 1965, to increase further the combat effectiveness of the strategic missile forces the Johnson government adopted the *Poseidon* programme, to run from 1970 to 1976. This programme envisaged the development of a new *Poseidon*-C-3 missile with a multi-warhead of the MIRV type (each 10 nuclear warheads has a power of up to 50,000 tons) and the refitting of 31 atomic-powered missile submarines. The *Poseidon* programme was the main link in the chain of measures aimed at perfecting American strategic offensive forces.

In 1967 the USA completed the *Polaris* programme and immediately went ahead with modernizing it—re-equipping submarine missile carriers with *Polaris* A-3 instead of *Polaris* A-1 missiles. As a whole, the strategic submarine nuclear system of the USA includes 41 atomic-powered missile submarines armed with *Polaris* and *Poseidon* missiles, floating and stationary bases, the Loran radio navigational system and the space navigational system Transit.

The *Polaris-Poseidon* system is the most important part of the nuclear forces of the USA and the main strategic strike force of the fleet. However, aircraft carriers continue to remain an essential constituent of the forces intended for operations in nuclear and local wars.

By the beginning of 1975 20 submarines were already fitted with the *Poseidon* missile complex. After the fulfilment of the whole programme (by 1977) it is planned that strategic offensive forces of the American fleet will have 31 atomic-powered missile submarines fitted with *Poseidon* C-3 and ten with *Polaris* A-3 missiles.[10]

The number of nuclear warheads delivered in each salvo from missile submarines will more than treble as compared with 1970 and will exceed the number contained in each salvo of *Minuteman* missiles two and a half times.

TABLE 19
Planned Number of Missiles and Nuclear Warheads in the USA in 1977*

Type of missile	No. of missiles	No. of warheads	No. of warheads in Navy and Air Force (%)	Total TNT equivalent (megatons)
Air Force missiles				
Titan 2	54	54		540
Minuteman 2	500	500	27.4	750
Minuteman 3	500	1500		300
Naval missiles				
Polaris A-3	160	480		48
Poseidon C-3**	496	4960	72.6	248
Total	1710	7494	100	1886

 * According to data published in *United States Naval Institute Proceedings:* 1970, V, Vol. 96, No. 5 (807), pp. 204-223; 1972, V, Vol. 98, No. 5 (831), pp. 178-189; 1972, VI, Vol. 98, No. 6 (832), pp. 19-26; and also in 1970, Vol. 96, Nos. 4 (p. 22), 5 (p. 465) and 12 (p. 81); in 1971, Vol. 97, Nos. 4 (p. 107) and 11 (p. 87); in 1972, Vol. 98, Nos. 5 (p. 388) and 9 (p. 114).
 ** The head section of these missiles is divided into 10 warheads each of which is capable of hitting a separate target.

The development planned by the American command of strategic missiles and the growth of the missile share of the naval forces are indicated in Table 19.

Thus, the *Polaris-Poseidon* submarine nuclear missile system will become the main constituent of the strategic nuclear forces of the USA and NATO. Its importance in the general strategic arms system will increase in the future.

[10] Five submarines of the *George Washington* type initially armed with Polaris A-1 missiles were rearmed in 1964-67 with Polaris A-3 missiles. The rearming of five submarines of the *Ethan Allen* type with Polaris A-3 missiles, begun at the end of 1972, was due for completion in 1975.

In 1968, the Americans adopted the *Trident* programme which envisaged the development of a new type of atomic-powered missile submarines armed with 24 ballistic missiles with a firing range of up to 12,000 km. The missiles will be fitted with perfected warheads of the MIRV type. From analysis of the ten-year use of the submarine nuclear missile system the US military leadership concluded that this system has major advantages over ground-based missiles and aviation. It is not by chance that the coming to power in the USA of the Nixon administration was marked by the pursuit of a policy of further intensifying the nuclear missile potential of the US naval forces. The "oceanic strategy" is based on the notion of rehousing the main weapons of the country's strategic arsenal at sea and further developing the missile-carrying fleet.

The working-out and combat deployment of the *Trident* system has now received the status of a primary programme in the development of strategic offensive forces of the USA. At the end of 1971 it was decided to speed up the time for developing the *Trident* system and to bring into service the leading missile submarine not in 1980, as planned earlier, but in 1978. It was announced that the US Defense Department had decided to build the first series of atomic-powered missile submarines of the *Trident* system, ten in number, to replace the submarines of the *George Washington* and *Ethan Allen* types armed with *Polaris* A-3 missiles. The *Trident* system will later replace the *Poseidon* system.

The US military-political leadership, seeking to gain a substantial lead over the USSR in sea-based strategic missile forces, adopted a decision on the need to design a strategic guided missile with a range of about 3000 km intended for arming atomic-powered missile submarines.

On 20 June 1972, justifying before the Senate Armed Services Committee the programme to build strategic forces, the then US Defense Secretary Laird stated: "Work on the guided missile system for submarines is necessary to enable the USA in the future to decide on additional American forces if this proves necessary. The appropriations which we propose will make it possible to undertake accelerated study of the system of the "guided missile and the submarine" and begin to create tactical components such as the engine and guidance system . . .". (Retranslated from Russian.)

The US military-political leadership now regards the creation of a guided missile for submarines as the creation of the fourth element of the strategic offensive forces of the USA.[11] A budget message by US President Nixon to Congress published on 29 January 1973 says in particular: ". . . We shall maintain our present power in order to guarantee the viability of our forces of restraint. . . . We shall (1) continue to build the *Trident* sea-based ballistic missile system; (2) continue work on the latest piloted strategic B-1 bomber; (3) continue to change over the ballistic missile forces to the *Minuteman 3* and *Poseidon* systems; and (4) begin work on creating a strategic guided missile for submarines." (Retranslated from Russian.) Following the Americans, in the 'sixties France and Britain went over to the building of atomic-powered submarines. The building of the first British atomic submarine, the *Dreadnought,*

---

[11] The first three elements are: a submarine nuclear missile system, land-based strategic missiles and strategic aviation.

was finished in 1963. By the end of 1974 Britain had four atomic-powered submarine missile-carriers and France three with two under construction.[12] France intends to build a sixth missile submarine.

Thus, atomic missile submarines now form the basis of the strategic nuclear forces of Great Britain and are also the most important component of the national nuclear forces of France.

An independent line in the development of the submarine forces of the USA is the creation of strike, or, as they are called, multi-purpose atomic-powered submarines armed with torpedoes and torpedo missiles. These ships are chiefly intended for combating submarines.

In 1974, the fleets of the NATO countries had 69 atomic and over 100 diesel multi-purpose submarines. Their numbers are steadily rising.

The Americans have also started to design a tactical missile of the "submarine to surface ship" class. It is planned to arm some atomic-powered torpedo submarines of the Los Angeles type with this missile and also all future atomic-powered torpedo submarines. A similar missile is being developed for the French and British navies.

The American fleet has considerably developed amphibious forces intended for landing operations. The main demand placed on these forces is to ensure a rapid manoeuvre of troops and supplies across the seas and oceans and their speedy disembarkation on an unequipped coast in the presence of a strong counter-action from the shore and at sea.

In the post-war period the USA has designed fundamentally new landing craft. They include landing-helicopter carriers and landing-helicopter dock ships. The latter have a displacement of about 14,000 tons and carry on board six to twelve transport helicopters and landing-disembarking gear placed in the dock chamber. US landing craft are simultaneously capable of lifting, carrying by sea and landing on an unequipped coast about 50,000-strong marine formations with arms. The combat operations of these ships are secured by necessary protection and support forces. The US navy also has large contingents of marines numbering close to 200,000 men.

From all this it is clear that the main intention of the existing fleets of the Western powers is to engage in operations against the territory of the enemy. At the same time the US and NATO naval forces possess considerable potential in fighting against a fleet, notably submarines.

The submarine forces are being chiefly developed by expanding the number of atomic and diesel torpedo submarines,[13] renewing the ship stock of the anti-submarine forces, arming new anti-submarine planes and helicopters, equipping ships and planes with the latest anti-submarine weapons and creating long-distance sonar monitoring positional systems.

The USA has already embarked on the large-scale building of atomic multi-purpose submarines of the Los Angeles type (it is planned to build over 40 of this type) and large anti-submarine ships of the Spruance type (the building of 30 ships of this type has been approved), is finishing the building of 46 escort

---

[12] *Zarubezh. voennoye obozreniye, (Foreign Military Review)*, 1974, No. 11, pp. 68, 71 (in Russian).

[13] The US alone by the end of the 'seventies plans to have some 90 atomic-powered multi-purpose submarines.

ships of the Knox type and has begun to equip anti-submarine ships with new piloted anti-submarine helicopters, which will considerably improve the possibilities of monitoring and ASW beyond the range of ship radar and sonar devices.

All frigates, destroyers and escort ships being built in the USA and NATO will be armed with anti-submarine missile units and piloted helicopters.

Research and experimental design work to produce new types of anti-submarine ships, weapons and technology is gathering pace.

As a whole, the combat potential of the US and NATO naval forces in the second half of the 'seventies will substantially grow. The combat composition will qualitatively be largely renewed and be augmented with ships, planes and helicopters, combat technical supplies and weapons.

To strengthen the fire power of the surface forces of the fleet and extend their combat potential the US and NATO naval command have begun to take measures to produce ship guided-missile weapons systems of the "ship to ship" class and to fit them to built ships and ships under construction. In the USA a programme has been approved for building 50 missile escort ships with the Harpoon missile complex (firing range over 100 km). It has been decided to install this system on all built frigates and destroyers.

In the second half of the 'seventies the USA intends to build missile ships riding on a cushion of air with a displacement of 3000-5000 tons and a speed of travel of about 100 knots. Nearly all the leading maritime powers without exception have embarked on the production-line construction of missile boats including those on hydrofoil and a cushion of air.

Radical changes in the arming of the fleets and the new alignment of forces in the World Ocean have caused the Anglo-Americans to change their minds about the role of the fleets in a future war and on the sequence and importance of the tasks performed by them. Pride of place has been given to the destruction of land objectives and submarines, and such a traditional task as protection of one's own oceanic communications has been given secondary importance since about 1957.

An important factor determining such an approach was that the traditional adversaries of the Anglo-Americans, Germany, Italy and Japan, as a result of defeat in the Second World War, did not have any forces capable of operating in the oceans. In addition, West Germany and Italy became US allies in the aggressive NATO military bloc. The Soviet fleet, as they considered at that time, could not present a serious threat to the sea shipments of the USA and the countries of the aggressive blocs. Then the most rational move, in the view of the Anglo-Americans, was to develop the naval forces as a "deterrent". What the American military command meant by "deterrent" is amply conveyed by the report of one of the Committees of the House of Representatives on civil defence published on 1 July 1960, which may be found in the *Congressional Record,* for July, 1960 (Washington, DC). This report stated that if the American fleet did not have as its task the destruction of the strategic forces of the enemy before they were used against the USA, the building of naval strategic weapons systems "would inevitably lose much of its attraction for the people of the USA".

Expressing the hopes of the Pentagon kindled by this declaration, the journal *Air Force Magazine* (No. 9, 1960) frankly called it the long-awaited official recognition that now the enemy would reckon with only one form of "restraint"—the ability of the American fleet to strike first. This idea was expressed even more specifically by R. Strausz-Hupé, William R. Kintner and Stefan Possony in their book *A Forward Strategy for America,* published in the USA in 1961. They bluntly said that the US could not refuse to be the first to embark on the use of nuclear weapons.

As can be seen from these and a host of other statements, the concept of "deterrence" and its frequently-used synonyms such as "restraint" mean nothing else than maintenance of constant readiness for immediate sudden use of nuclear weapons on the most important strategic objectives in the territories of the countries of the socialist community. This task is considered paramount for the strategic forces, among which an important role is played by the naval forces. Guided by this, the military-political leadership of the USA and Britain regard the fleet as a resource possessing the greatest viability and universality in solving tasks in a world nuclear war. An important role is also assigned to it in local wars. Having as one of its components a strong marines force, the fleet commands a definite independence in operations on land, especially in wars against small nations and weakly-developed countries.

The brief characterization presented above of the process of the development of the naval forces of the USA and the other countries of NATO shows that they are now one of the most important strategic factors in modern war. They must be regarded as very mobile, highly viable forces capable of operating covertly and solving major tasks.

The Development of the Soviet Fleet

In the post-war years, the imperialists unleashed the "cold war" against the community of socialist countries and undertook frenzied preparations for a new world war. The threat to the security of our country from the oceans loomed ever larger. Could the Soviet Union, faced with such a threat, agree with the age-old dominance on the seas and oceans of the Western maritime powers, especially in conditions when extensive areas of the oceans have become the launching platforms of nuclear missile weapons? Of course not! In these conditions the only correct solution to the problem of the security of the country could be the creation of a situation capable of confronting the militarist circles of the West with the same problems which they had tried to thrust on us. The first task was to make the Pentagon realize that the ocean previously shielding the American continent from response strikes of the victims of aggression has completely lost its former role as a defence barrier, and that, should a war be unleashed by American imperialism, it would itself be faced daily with the terrible threat of response strikes as punishment for aggression. This indeed was the path chosen by the CPSU, and the development of our armed forces also proceeded along these lines. In terms of the Soviet fleet, this post-war development may be divided into two stages.

The first stage, which covers the period of the first post-war decade, saw the building of ships and planes armed with conventional armaments, torpedoes, and bombs. The building of the fleet was essentially based on the formation of squadrons of surface ships. The fleet continued to remain at an operational-strategic level, a defensive factor. It continued to be a coastal action fleet capable of conducting operations only within the framework of attaining the goals of major front operations. Views on the intention of the fleet and its tasks at that time were formed under the influence of Second World War experience and victory over a strong continental enemy.

It should be noted that in the first post-war decade, especially at the start of it, when decisions were taken to build the fleet, there were no real technical possibilities for creating fundamentally new forces. We still did not have nuclear weapons and the first missile models were only at the design stage.

In 1947 the Soviet Government declared that the atomic bomb was no longer a secret. And while at first the American leadership tried to ignore this claim, in September 1949 it was shaken merely by the undisputed recording of the first atomic explosion carried out in the Soviet Union. "At a stroke", wrote the prominent American military theoreticians Mills, Mansfield and Stein, "the whole military-political situation has been transformed. . . . The potential possibility of the total destruction of the enemy which we have more and more come to see as our main instrument of military strength has now lost the onesidedness which attracted us. The whole balance of world politics has undergone sharp and frightful changes. . . . This is a crisis—intellectual, moral and technical—far exceeding the usual crises of international relations."[14] (Retranslated from Russian.)

Roughly from the middle of the 'fifties, in line with the decision of the Central Committee of the CPSU, our country began large-scale work to build a powerful oceanic nuclear missile fleet. This paved the way for the second stage in the development of the Soviet navy.

The decision of the Central Committee of the Communist Party was based on deep knowledge of the special aspects of technical progress which by that time had assumed the form of a scientific-technical revolution, reversing many traditional lines of the development of technology. This, in turn, opened up possibilities for designing fundamentally new ships, arms systems and naval technology.

A most important factor which was taken into consideration was a firm recognition of the alignment of forces in the world arena, the strategic situation existing in the oceanic theatres in connection with the formation of aggressive blocs and the unrestrained expansion by the imperialists of naval nuclear arms, the prospects of developing naval technology and weapons and also the economic potential of our country. In the course of the construction of qualitatively new underwater and surface ships and weapons, all the latest achievements of science, technology and production were used.

As well as producing intercontinental missiles, a start was made on the intensive development of an ocean-going fleet, rapidly acquiring all the traits of a strategic factor in a modern war. The formation of an ocean fleet capable of

[14] Quoted in Yu. N. Listvinov, *The First Strike*, p. 19 (in Russian).

preventing the attack of an aggressor from the oceans was complicated in the Soviet Union by the fact that our country has no transoceanic and overseas territories and bases on which the fleet could rely in repelling strikes. The reports periodically appearing in the Western press on the presence of certain naval bases belonging to the USSR on the territories of countries friendly to us are patently defamatory, seeking to conceal and justify the efforts of the imperialist powers to extend their military bases in many areas of the world. It must be emphasized that the USSR, conducting a Leninist peace-loving foreign policy, is not after such acquisitions. A way of overcoming the difficulties associated with the long stay of our ships away from bases was found with the aid of engineering-technical and design solutions enabling them to be present for a long time in distant oceanic theatres and to meet all their requirements for material-technical supplies without replenishing them from stationary bases.

Our country has built a modern fleet and has sent it out into the ocean to ensure its state interests in order to defend itself reliably from attack from extensive oceanic directions. And if now in the pages of the foreign press and the utterances of political and military figures the rhetorical question is often raised "Why does the Soviet Union need an ocean fleet?", this is done essentially for propaganda reasons in order to justify constantly inflated expenditure on armaments and intensification of the preparations for a new world war. Politicians, sowing doubts on the true purposes of the development of our fleet and ascribing to it aggressive intentions, seek with their demagogy to hide the improper activities of their own fleets, performing gendarme functions in suppressing national liberation movements and acting as the main strike force of imperialism in the World Ocean.

The Communist Party of the Soviet Union at all stages of the existence of our state has firmly kept to a course of building the material base of communism, is consistently practising the policy of strengthening peace and friendship between peoples and states. It pays the necessary attention to strengthening the defence capacity of our country. At the will of the Party, the Soviet armed forces were to become a strong shield, an insurmountable obstacle in the way of new claimants to world dominance, capable of holding back and cutting short aggression at its very start, confronting the imperialists with the inevitability of inescapable retaliatory strikes. The latest achievements in science, technology and production have been marshalled to ensure the safety of the country and form the basis for producing modern weapons and military technology for all the branches of the armed forces.

A most important event in this stage was the ending of the US nuclear monopoly. It is now no secret that already at the beginning of 1954 the Soviet army and navy possessed nuclear weapons of varying power including hydrogen bombs, and embarked on the practical study of these weapons and means of combat operations with their use.

With this was connected the start of a new stage in the development of the nation's fleet—the stage of forming and developing a Soviet ocean-going atomic fleet armed with nuclear missile weapons, strengthening the position of our country as a great maritime power. The practical implementation of the preliminary plans of the Party to build an ocean fleet completely matching the task of defending our country in the atomic century, its conversion into a real force capable of ensuring the state interests of the Soviet Union in the World Ocean, successfully countering the strong fleet of the enemy and warding off his strikes from the ocean, played an enormous role in strengthening the defence capacity of our country and the entire socialist community.

The leadership of the Communist Party of the Soviet Union through tremendous work in creating a powerful ocean fleet, the self-sacrificing years of toil by shipbuilders, scientists and naval seamen, all ensured the building in a short time of a qualitatively new ocean fleet of our country completely answering to Soviet military doctrine.

As is known, ". . . military doctrine means the system of views adopted in a given state and its armed forces on the character of war and the ways of waging it, preparing the country and army for it. . . .

"Military doctrine is the result of a complex process of developing state ideas on the solution of military tasks. All its basic tenets stem from actual conditions and above all from home and foreign policy, the socio-political and economic structure, the level of production, the means of waging war and the geographical position both of one's own state and of a probable enemy."[15]

Soviet military doctrine springs from the policy of our Party, meets the most important requirements of the Marxist-Leninist theory of war, the army and the armed defence of the socialist motherland. It embodies all the wealth of progressive military technical thinking and also the military experience of the Soviet state and the experience of many past wars. Soviet military doctrine—the doctrine of a peace-loving socialist state—is diametrically opposed to the current aggressive, reactionary military doctrines of the imperialist states including the "bloc" military doctrine.

In the post-war period our military doctrine has continuously developed, which is due in the first place to the steady growth of the power of the Soviet Union and the whole camp of socialism, the growth of the national liberation movement in the world and changes in the physical means of waging war. However, the essence of this doctrine and its fundamental direction have remained unchanged.

At all stages of development Soviet military doctrine, solving the problems of the structure of the armed forces, has paid and is paying the necessary attention to the navy which is unfailingly regarded as an important branch of the armed forces capable of solving major tasks in a war. And in connection with the equipping of ships with nuclear missile weapons it recognizes the ability of the fleet to solve important strategic tasks. The principles of Soviet military doctrine concerning the fleet were an important factor determining the general direction of its development, the main tasks, balance of its forces by different criteria and the direction of operational and combat training. They were a guide in the development of all aspects of operational strategic use of the fleet and the tactics of its forces.

The development of the navy in the post-war period and the ending of the lag in the general sea power of our state were particularly favourably influenced by

[15] A. A. Grechko, *The Armed Forces of the Soviet State,* pp. 314, 315, Moscow, Voenizdat, 1974 (in Russian).

the scientific and technical achievements and discoveries of the post-war period.

One of the most important achievements of modern scientific-technical progress was the discovery and working out of ways of using a practically inexhaustible new source of energy—the nucleus of the atom. This made it possible to create fundamentally new nuclear missile weapons of unprecedented power and also of atomic power for fighting ships, which sharply raised their fighting possibilities. A tremendous role in the production of the latest weapons and combat technical means was played by the application of chemistry to modern production, opening the way to the use of fundamentally new artificially-produced substances and materials with properties known in advance.

Of outstanding importance were the achievements in the fields of radio-electronics, on the basis of which striking results were achieved in the automation of the most complex process of controlling the forces, computer technique was widely introduced, mathematical methods of calculation were applied to solve the problems of building the armed forces and developing military art.

The Communist Party by its practical activity created all the conditions for the achievements of scientific-technical progress to be used for strengthening the defence power of our motherland, including the building of the navy, one of the branches of the armed forces most saturated with complex combat techniques. The navy has always been a focal point in the latest technological achievements and always stays highly sensitive to their development and changes. This dependence of the fleet on the achievement of scientific-technical progress is to be explained by the fact that, together with the particularly complex constructions that ships are, it comprises virtually all kinds of troops and weapons at the command of the armed forces. Naturally, even minor changes in the armament of any of the branches of the forces significantly affect the state of the fleet as a whole. Profound qualitative changes in the main resources for armed conflict bring about truly revolutionary transformations not only in the whole material-technical base of the fleet, but in all the constituent parts of naval art that ensure its combat use.

The main lines in the qualitative transformation of the fleet under the influence of the scientific-technical revolution have been: going over to the building of an atomic-powered submarine fleet; the introduction of missile and nuclear weapons and the creation of strategic submarine nuclear-missile systems; the arming of the fleet with long-range aviation—oceanic aviation; the introduction into the navy of ship aviation; qualitative change in the resources for clarifying an underwater situation, the forces and resources for combating submarines; and the introduction of various kinds of radio-electronics, automation of weapon control and of combat techniques, and also mathematical methods of investigation, using computers.

Fast scientific and technical progress is revealing even more possibilities where its achievements can be used to develop the navy and further improve the sea power of our motherland.

Among the factors governing the post-war development of our fleet the economy of our country and its military-economic potential are decisive.

Engels already scientifically demonstrated the dependence of the ways of waging war on the economic bases of society, the development of production: "Nothing so depends on economic conditions as the army and the fleet. Armaments, complement, organization, tactics and strategy depend first and foremost on the level of production reached at a given moment and on the means of communications."[16]

The military-economic potential of the state is determined by such factors as natural resources and above all strategic raw materials satisfying the needs of production; industry—factories, mills, power stations; agriculture; the transport and communication network; labour productivity; human resources satisfying the high requirements of modern production both on the quantitative and qualitative side; the level of development of science and technology; and state material reserves.

The state of these main indices enabled our country to create the ocean fleet it needed for its defence. It permitted the wide use of the achievements of science and technology and the building of precisely those ships the need for which was determined by Soviet military doctrine, of course within the limits of the resources which our country could set aside for the fleet's requirements.

Military-geographical conditions have always acted as one of the most important factors in the development of any branch of the armed forces, but they have special importance for the navy since it is necessary with its diverse forces to operate on and under the water, in the air space over the water, on the shore, in the most varied climatic conditions and zones, at different times of the year and day. The importance of this factor in the development of the navy is also due to the character of the distribution of forces in the World Ocean, the development of the system of stationing the forces of opposing sides, mutual disposition of strategic positions ensuring the deployment and use of the available forces and means for solving a complex of operational and strategic tasks.

From this point of view the fleets of the imperialist states possess advantageous positions in the World Ocean. Having naval bases in the direct proximity of the territory of our country and acquiring ever new areas for stationing their forces, they are concentrating efforts in the strategically important zones of the World Ocean. Even in peacetime, in establishing control over straits and narrows, they are seeking to create all the pre-requisites for achieving dominance in these areas immediately after the start of a war.

The imperialist states are also using their positions to advantage in building ships, systems of accommodating them and various supplies. Even in determining the operating range, independent operating potential or repair capacity of ships they have no need to attach to these tactical elements the importance they have for our fleet, since the wide system of bases encompassing nearly all the World Ocean means that ships can be supplied with all that is necessary in the shortest possible time.

Historically, things have so worked out that our navy, not having overseas bases, to move out into the ocean is forced to cover enormous distances and force narrows and straits either controlled by the fleets of the imperialist states or permanently under surveillance by their allies in aggressive military blocs.

[16] K. Marx and F. Engels, *Works,* 2nd ed., Vol. 20, p. 171 (in Russian).

In addition, most of our naval bases are located in areas with a severe climate where for a long period of time a complex ice situation obtains, making it hard for ships to manoeuvre and take measures to ensure high combat readiness of the forces of the fleet.

All this naturally leaves its mark on the building of fighting ships and auxiliary vessels of our fleet and working out ways of using it in war and peacetime.

In this connection, special importance for us is assumed not only by the seaworthiness of ships but also operating range, independent operational potential, ability to counter numerous strikes by the enemy using various means of warfare, that is, high combat resilience, extremely high reliability of the systems of machinery and high horse-power. Under the influence of military-geographical conditions our fleet has to create special forces and means for backing up operations in distant areas of the oceans and take special measures for the specialist training of ship crews, including repair training.

The basic historical condition influencing the post-war development of our fleet was the experience of past wars. Armed struggle has always acted as an arbiter determining the degree of correspondence of pre-war views on the use of the forces and resources, in the course of a war during which its weapons, military technique, the basic principles of the operational-tactical and strategic use of forces are verified. It allows important conclusions to be drawn concerning the development of weapons and military art in each post-war period. Therefore, the skilful generalization of the experience of military operations is an important task not only for military historians but also for leaders determining the direction of construction of the fleet.

At the same time it should be remembered that after the end of the Second World War the armed forces of all countries were developed on a fundamentally new technical basis. Missile and nuclear weapons became dominant. The armed forces were created and trained essentially for solving tasks in a nuclear war. Therefore, the experience of the Second World War had less influence on the post-war development of the forces than did the experience of the First World War. This, however, does not exclude the need to study with care those lessons and results of armed struggle which were taken into account in the post-war building of the fleets and in the working out of methods of using them in a nuclear war.

The Second World War showed the increased significance of armed struggle at sea and the strengthened link between military actions and operations on land with actions at sea. This reconfirmed views on the need for the comprehensive development of the fleet as an essential part of the armed forces of the country.

The experience of combat operations in the sea and oceanic theatres showed that the main, most universal and effective kinds of forces of the fleet have become submarines and aircraft. Therefore, there was a sharp decline in the importance of large ships with armaments and such a use of the forces of the fleet as sea engagements of the surface forces in the course of which major operational results were achieved.

The post-war development of many fleets was greatly influenced by the experience of using aircraft-carriers for destroying land targets and forces of the fleet of the enemy. This influence was expressed in the further development of aircraft-carriers and the forces maintaining their operations. Attention was directed to the creation of forces and means capable of fighting aircraft-carrier formations.

An important role in the course of post-war development of the fleets was also played by experience of conducting numerous minor or major sea-landing operations. This found reflection in the creation of a large number of special landing craft capable of ensuring the landing of troops with heavy combat supplies on an unequipped coast using fast disembarking aids and helicopters.

In the production of new ships and weapons of the post-war period, note was also taken of wartime lessons for oceanic and sea communications.

Much attention was paid by many countries to the experience of using mine weaponry by the various branches of the fleet for attaining diverse ends. This found expression in the creation of new mine models and their mass use, for example, by the American fleet for blockading the approaches to the ports of the Democratic Republic of Vietnam from the sea and its internal water communications.

A most important means of controlling forces and weapons is the communications systems, which play a particularly important role in navies since their forces are constantly present in different areas of the oceans, often far from their shores. Therefore, a modern fleet needs global communications capable of ensuring the control of forces many thousands of kilometres away. Moreover, it is necessary to ensure the control of the forces of the fleet operating on water and under water, in the air and on land. It is not hard to see that the creation of such a communications system represented a problem of enormous scientific and technical complexity. Many countries have worked on this. This task is being solved successfully in our fleet.

Particularly valuable was the experience of the use of radar, promoting the wide development of this technique in the post-war period and its use on all ships and planes, in the shore surveillance system and on auxiliary vessels.

In looking at premises influencing the post-war development of our fleet, it is necessary to note the following.

Each of them exerted on the development of the fleet its own specific varying influence. For example, the policy of the CPSU and the military-economic potential of the country were paramount and decisive.

The character of the influence of these premises also varied. Thus, the influence of the military-economic potential was "all-embracing" in the depth of its impact on the whole complex process of development of the fleet, whereas the development of the fleets of the imperialist states chiefly influenced the building of forces necessary for solving our defensive tasks. These premises as they developed altered the degree of their influence on the building of the fleet, with a steady growth of the importance of achieving scientific and technical progress.

As well as by these premises, the building of the fleet was specifically influenced by the development of naval art which sought, under the influence of the material means of armed struggle, to match them to their internal operational tactical properties, and hence depending on them, itself helped to stimulate the development of ships and naval arms systems. Herein is expressed the dialectical unity and mutual influence of the material means and the art of waging armed struggle at sea.

Strict attention to all these premises allowed the Central Committee of the CPSU to carry out scientific management of the building of our fleet in the post-war period, make this process a reality, put it on independent lines without copying but only rationally using the experience of world naval shipbuilding.

The development of the navy is a most complex process which is by no means limited to the replacement of outdated arms systems by new ones more in keeping with the current level of development of technology and the requirements of armed struggle at sea. Such replacement is merely the final outcome of a tremendous amount of work to define the optimal variants of solving the many operational-strategic and operational-tactical problems and also a colossal number of technical matters. The point is to concentrate in each ship the maximum combat possibilities with the most economic "expenditure" of size and displacement, and ensure the effective solution of the tasks with minimum economic outlay.

The modern fighting ship is an elaborate combination of technical devices, systems and complexes which are the latest achievements of science, engineering thought and industry. These are nuclear power, gas and steam turbines with a high specific output, strategic and operational-tactical missiles, homing submarine weapons, automatic armament, technical supplies ensuring the comprehensive automation of the process of control, precision storm equipment, very elaborate sonar and radar complexes, etc. The creation of a modern ship involves many hundreds of factories of different branches of industry. Its building is preceded by thoroughgoing scientific studies.

The idea underlying the creation of each ship is so to build it that it is best fitted to discharge the tasks particular to it. Account is also taken of the traditions of shipbuilding in our country and our national production potential.

To solve the problems associated with the building of a fleet work is done aimed at determining the optimal combination of strike and defensive possibilities of a fighting ship and such factors as arming, automation, speed of travel, operating range, independent operation and living conditions for the crew, etc. For submarines, in addition, the depth of submergence, noise, advantageous precavitation speeds, etc. are determined. The ship's displacement, with a general wish to reduce it within reasonable limits, is regarded only as a function of such a basic argument as the ability of the ship to solve and fulfil all those tasks for which she was built.

To ensure the ability of the fleet to fulfil its operational-strategic tasks, research work is carried out to determine the character of the balance of the navy, the general quantitative and qualitative composition of ships and planes and the distribution of these forces over theatres and stationing areas.

Thus, the development of the fleet calls for serious and thorough scientific investigation. Here any manifestation of free choice or subjective principles is out of the question. The closer the attention paid by the leaders taking crucial decisions on the development of the navy to the recommendations of the research institutions and the views of naval officers on active service and their appreciation of the possibilities of industry, the sounder will be their decisions and the more painless the process of building the fleet, and in the end the less it will cost to build and the more powerful it will be. Such an approach to the problems of building the fleet pre-supposes the all-round development of scientific methods of management which requires wide comprehensive research work in the field of engineering-technical and operational problems. It implies a strict system of optimization ensuring the selection of the most rational variants of solutions based on a quantitative analysis and military-economic validation bases on consistent criteria and tolerance limits.

An important constituent of the process of building the fleet is the shaping of technical policy, the bases of which are determined by the political leadership of the country with reference to the conditions of use of the fleet and the special aspects of its interaction with other branches of the armed forces.

Until recently the scientific method of managing the building of the fleet was based only on the analysis of the current possibilities of science and technology and their development in the near future. Now, into this sphere has come scientific forecasting based on estimated lines of weapon development, electronic technology, power, shipbuilding theory and a number of non-military sciences, the state of which influences the development of a fleet.

Characterization of the most important lines of the scientific-technical revolution shows that they are based on the development of science, that they are essentially the result of coalescence of branches of science with industry. The mutual relationship between science and engineering has become much closer. Science, augmenting the volume of knowledge, ensures favourable conditions for the revolutionary development of technology. All the latest achievements of technology are now directly linked with discoveries in the natural sciences. The development of technology and production in turn creates a corresponding technical base which determines the rapid pace of scientific discovery and introduction into practice by military enterprise.

With the current fast pace of the development of science and technology, it is very important to anticipate new qualitative changes in the development of the fleet, determine in good time the appearance of new means of warfare, their role and place among existing resources and the principles of their use.

Naturally, a particular scientific discovery cannot be reliably planned. In solving major military-scientific problems there always exists a certain degree of indeterminacy due to incomplete data at our disposal on the enemy, and insufficient information on a number of other questions. The presence of indeterminacy makes it necessary to calculate several variants of solutions with analysis of their positive and negative sides. This is greatly facilitated by achievements in the field of mathematics and the wide use of computer techniques.

The present arming of the navy is characterized by extreme complexity, diversity and has specific features. In the light of this, the fleet constitutes a complex dynamic system, the development and functioning of which demand considerable expenditure of various material resources.

No one country can invest unlimited resources in armaments. In each country a permissible level of expenditure on military needs is fixed. A consequence of economic limitations is, that of the large number of tasks brought forward by new scientific-technical achievements, it is necessary to choose the most important, the solution of which is necessary for maintaining the fighting capacity of the armed forces at the requisite level.

Important strategic tasks devolve on our navy in present-day conditions. Its specific contribution to the armed forces is continuously growing. This, in turn, makes necessary increased scientific management of the development of the fleet to ensure in good time the creation of the most effective forces and means, having regard to the real possibilities at the command of the country's economy.

A major role in the development of scientific methods of managing the building of the fleet is played by a well-organized and reliably-functioning system of scientific information helping to shape views on the development and use of the forces of the fleet in a modern war and in peacetime.

The most important of the demands made on it is to get efficiency in analyzing scientific information and deciding who among the users should receive it.

The development and use in practice of scientific methods of management in building a fleet has already brought important results, finding their reflection in the practical solution of many major problems making up this complex process. Above all, this means a solution to the problem of balancing different features and characteristics of the forces of the fleet, the determination of rational ways of building the fleet, with priority given to the most effective means, and the preferential development of missile weapons as the most promising means of combat at sea among other means constituting the armaments system of the fleet. On the basis of thorough scientific investigation, many optimal combinations of tactical elements of submarines and surface ships and the rational limits of automation of control of forces, ships and their arms systems have been determined, criteria found for evaluating the combat robustness of weapon-carriers and the combat effectiveness both of single carriers and tactical groups formed in different combinations and permutations.

This, of course, does not exhaust the range of those problems which have already been solved and which are at the stage of solution by scientific organizations. They merely show the scope of this work, the main tendency in the development of this process consisting in the further spread of scientific methods of validating all the crucial decisions adopted by various bodies in ensuring the development of the navy.

As a result of extensive and many-sided research work, views were evolved on the place and role of the fleet as part of our armed forces and the line of development of all its branches of forces and weapons.

In connection with the advent of the atomic and then the hydrogen bomb, and other technical discoveries, a search began for new lines of development of the armed forces of the great powers.

Abroad, this was expressed in the creation of different strategic nuclear weapons systems. At first these were aircraft-carrier strike formations and land-based strategic aviation. Then an increasingly important place in the plans of the Pentagon began to be assigned to the *Polaris* submarine nuclear missile system. In the development of general-purpose forces of the fleets, emphasis was laid on the building of new, more powerful and sophisticated forces and means of anti-submarine warfare. In the armed forces, various means of automation and radio-electronic warfare began to be widely introduced everywhere.

However, this happened only after the practical value of all the scientific discoveries available at that time to the opposing camps of imperialism and socialism was realised.

For the American and British fleets, mostly able to renew the fighting stock of their ships in the war years, the question of their further development in connection with the appearance of atomic weapons was very complex. Therefore, at first they tried to speak only in a whisper of the possibility of using nuclear weapons in an armed struggle at sea, so as not to cast doubts on the reality of the strike power of the strongest fleets of the world of that time.

In the first post-war years, when the US still had a monopoly over atomic weapons, in the leading circles of the war ministries of the Western countries the only question was that of updating the ships, replacing weapons and equipping them with various types of radar, since it was felt that the fleet, even as it was, would be able to discharge its tasks in the war against the USSR for which they were preparing.

The decisions of the Central Committee of the Communist Party, aimed at the further development of the fleet, were based on a profound recognition of the peculiarities of the scientific-technical revolution upsetting many traditional lines in the development of technology. This, in turn, opened up possibilities for creating fundamentally new ships, arms systems and naval supply systems, based on the use of the latest achievements of science, technology and production. Some twenty years have since elapsed and in this short historical period the Soviet fleet has been transformed into an important strategic factor potentially capable of countering aggression from the sea and of resolving in the World Ocean major tasks connected with our country's defence. Today submarines and naval aviation, equipped with the most up-to-date weaponry, in which missiles play a major part, constitute the main type of forces of our fleet. To give combat resilience to submarines and ensure their comprehensive supply, to combat the submarine and anti-submarine forces of the enemy and solve other specific tasks our fleet comprises diverse fighting surface ships and planes. They are armed with torpedoes, multi-purpose missiles, guns and other types of naval weapons. The navy widely uses radio-engineering devices and means of control based on computers, analogue and modelling systems.

It should be noted that by virtue of a number of conditions the Soviet fleet developed in a distinctive way in the post-war period. This distinctiveness was based on strict scientific allowance for the specifics of building and use of its forces in armed struggle at sea. It was manifest in the design features of the ships and planes, the character of the balance of forces of the Soviet navy and the organization particular to it alone.

The Improvement of the Forces and Resources of the Fleets

Submarines

In the Second World War, submarines proved themselves as a branch of the forces of the navy, capable of actively operating in the oceans and seas and of solving important tasks. In some areas the operations of submarines formed the core of the armed struggle at sea. As stated, submarines in the Second World War sank more merchant and fighting ships than did surface ships and aircraft taken together. We would recall that Britain, the USA and their allies (without the USSR) and neutral countries lost from the weapons of the German and Italian submarines 2,770 merchant vessels with a total tonnage of 14.5 million registered tons, that is 69 per cent of the total tonnage of ships destroyed. Japan, as a result of the operations of American and British submarines, lost about 62 per cent of all the tonnage sunk. Under the influence of the heavy losses from hostile submarines the allies were compelled to develop effective forces for anti-submarine warfare. These forces, in the conditions of quite unsatisfactory combat and operational backing by the German command of its own submarines, frustrated German plans for unrestricted submarine warfare. The losses of German submarines in the course of the war grew and the goal set before the submarine forces by the German supreme command—strangling England by a blockade—was not achieved.

Because of such contradictory results in the use of submarines the world press for the first time in the post-war years widely discussed the problems of the effectiveness of submarine forces. Can submarines, despite constant improvement in the means of anti-submarine defence, achieve strategic goals in war at sea?

The answer to this question demanded much research. All of it invariably confirmed the high effectiveness of submarines when rightly used and given proper combat backing. This conclusion proved particularly convincing in relation to atomic-powered submarines.

After the end of the Second World War our submarines were converted into a branch of the forces capable of solving important tasks in the oceans. They became the main combat power of the fleet. Of no little importance were military-economic considerations which also encouraged our fleet to concentrate on the switch-over to building primarily submarine forces.

In determining the lines of development of the navy in the nuclear age, one could not fail to take into account, for example, the fact that the imperialist states opposing us possess an enormous surface fleet and a powerful shipbuilding industry. Even for us to match in numbers the main classes of surface ships would have taken many years of estimating the relative potentials, involving the expenditure of enormous material and monetary resources. The achievement of superiority in such conditions was very problematical since a fleet, by virtue of the specifics of development, possesses superiority over another fleet, which can keep it at comparatively low cost.

The priority given to the development of the submarine forces made it possible in a very short time to increase sharply the strike possibilities of our fleet, to form a considerable counter-balance to the main forces of the fleet of the enemy in the oceanic theatres, and, at the cost of fewer resources and less time, to multiply the growth of sea power of our country, thereby depriving an enemy of the advantages which could accrue to him in the event of war against the Soviet Union and the countries of the socialist community.

However, this far from exhausted the importance of the new nuclear missile fleet based on atomic-powered submarines. The qualitatively new technical base helped to put paid to the centuries-long tying of our fleet to coastal areas and closed theatres, to widen out the sphere of its operations in the oceans and, in the event of the imperialists unleashing a war, to fulfil its operational and strategic tasks, hitting back at the fleet of an aggressor in the areas of the ocean chosen by us. But a particularly important point was that, having new means of armed conflict, the navy acquired the ability to open up new directions of warfare for the armed forces, including those which from ancient times have been considered inaccessible to us. This refers to the oceanic areas in which our fleet has become capable of solving our strategic tasks of defence.

All this radically altered the situation built up over the centuries in the oceanic expanses where the fleets of the imperialist powers had hitherto enjoyed unshared dominance. This was an invasion into the holy of holies of imperialism, where it strove not to admit even its companions in aggressive military alliances.

Two stages may be noted in the post-war development of the submarine forces. In the first stage, lasting about ten years, improved submarines of new designs were created with diesel-powered engines. In the second stage which is still continuing, mostly submarines with atomic-powered systems are being built.

In the first stage it was possible to focus attention only on a certain improvement in the tactical-technical features of submarines, including increase in speed and operating range, using diesels and ensuring the possibility of prolonged sailing and charging the accumulator battery during movement of the submarine at periscope depth. In building diesel submarines, note was taken of the experience of the Second World War, the character and conditions of solving the tasks in a future war and also the possible perspectives of the development of anti-submarine forces and resources of foreign fleets.

In this period, diesel torpedo submarines of two modifications were built—sea and oceanic. This made it possible to use submarines not only in seas lying next to our territory but also in fairly extensive oceanic areas. The new diesel submarines had a speed of travel under water and depth of submergence appreciably greater than those built before the war. They were equipped with the latest means of surveillance, radar and sonar units, modern means of communication, control instruments and highly effective torpedo weapons.

In the second half of the 'fifties some of the post-war-built diesel submarines were further improved and were armed with winged and ballistic missiles. However, the increase in the speed and operating range of submarines under water before the introduction of nuclear-powered systems was limited by the size of the power equipment determined by the potential of the diesel-electrical installations. The depth of submergence of submarines was increased thanks to the use of new high-quality materials and improved hull designs.

Diesel submarines are improved and powerful ships and they undoubtedly will find wide application also in modern conditions. Even now, when we regard the state of submarine shipbuilding in the light of the tremendous achievements of scientific-technical progress, we cannot fail to be struck by the important role which has been played by the experience of building diesel submarines of post-war construction, which has helped to solve a host of problems of a scientific and technical character on going over to the building of fundamentally new atomic underwater ships.

In the course of building diesel submarines in the post-war years our industry acquired the necessary experience in creating many new combat and technical means, thanks to which the new ships fundamentally differ from the best models of submarines built before and during the war. The building of new oceanic and sea diesel submarines, the mastery of them by the fleets during combat training, long sailings and voyages created all the pre-requisites for passing to the second stage of the post-war development of submarines. This second stage is characterized by the building of submarines with atomic power, radically changing the combat possibilities of the submarine, making it in the full sense an underwater ship. The high-power equipment of atomic submarines enables them to stay for a long time in the oceans, complete distant transits at high speeds of travel, remaining in immediate readiness for delivery of strikes at the enemy. They can draw close to fast surface ships of the enemy, pursue them for a long time, attack repeatedly, rapidly re-deploy from one direction to another and successfully dodge hostile anti-submarine forces.

The powerful sonar complexes with which atomic submarines are equipped provide a high search potential and hence considerable possibilities in struggle against hostile submarines.

The ability to stay under water practically throughout the period of independent action, the great depth of submergence and sailing on low-noise courses give atomic submarines high concealment of operation. Thus, in atomic-powered submarines are concentrated all the main factors characterizing the power of a navy: high strike power, high mobility and concealment, ability to conduct combat actions on a global scale to destroy important land objectives, submarines and surface ships of the enemy. Therefore, in modern conditions atomic-powered submarines are a strategic resource for the armed forces of maritime powers.

In world submarine shipbuilding two basic trends can be discerned: creation of submarine missile-carriers and creation of multi-purpose submarines.

Submarine missile-carriers are carriers of powerful, long-range strategic missiles intended to destroy important land objectives of the enemy. They are the main component of the fighting power of the leading fleets of the world including the Soviet fleet. These are the largest of all existing underwater ships. Thus, for example, the American submarine missile-carrier *George Washington,* built at the beginning of the 'sixties, has a displacement of about 8,000 tons and a length of 116 m.

It should be noted that the displacement of submarine missile-carriers continues to grow. The Americans consider as inevitable their growth to 10,000 tons and more. Thus, the displacement of the new atomic-powered missile submarine *Trident,* designed in the USA, is estimated to be around 18,000 tons.

Atomic-powered submarine missile-carriers are the "youngest" ships. They were created when numerous models of ballistic and guided missiles and the latest surface ships and submarines of other types had already been worked out and brought into use. Therefore, on submarine missile-carriers are concentrated all the very latest achievements in the field of shipbuilding, missile weaponry, means of ascertaining the underwater situation, automation of control and navigational-storm equipment.

The need for the rigid limitation of the mass-dimensional characteristics of missiles for submarines demanded the creation of special sea ballistic missiles. The Americans tried to use army missiles for arming submarines but because of their large mass and considerable size they had to abandon this idea. Each country with submarine missile-carriers is now using for their arming relatively small-sized ballistic missiles. They are being constantly perfected in terms of increase in the range of flight, in the accuracy of hit, and creation of more powerful warheads (in the latest American models they are separable). At present the only countries producing their own sea ballistic missiles are the USA, France and the USSR. Britain uses ballistic missiles produced by the Americans.

Increase in the flight range of missiles and the use of separable warheads are the main trends in the development of this weapon (Table 20), which widens the areas of strike and also of combat patrolling by missile submarines.

The drive to increase the flight range of missiles is leading to growth in their mass. Thus, while the mass of the *Polaris* A-1 missile was equal to 12.7 tons, the mass of *Polaris* A-2 increased to 13.6 tons and in the following modification *Polaris* A-3 reached 15.0 tons. The mass of the new *Poseidon* missile is 30 tons. This missile already has a flight range of 5600 km and a separable warhead. It is assumed that the effectiveness of this missile, despite the fact that the power of each warhead is only 50 kilotons, will be several times greater than that of the *Polaris* A-1 missile.

TABLE 20
Change in the Flight Range of American Ballistic Missiles of Atomic-Powered Submarines

Missile	Year of adoption as armament	No. of warheads	Flight range with monobloc warhead, km	Flight range with separable warheads, km
Polaris A-1	1960	1	2200	–
Polaris A-2	1961	1	2800	–
Polaris A-3	1964	3	–	4600
Poseidon	1970	3–14	–	5600–2800
Trident	1978	10	–	Up to 12,000

Submarine missile-carriers are also armed with torpedoes which are necessary to them primarily for self-defence.

Modern atomic-powered submarine missile-carriers, forming part of the fleets of the Soviet Union, the USA, Britain and France, are weapons of the strategic nuclear forces of the country.

American military specialists consider that the missiles of submarine carriers have indisputable advantages over *Minuteman* ground missiles. Among these advantages they see higher concealment and mobility, deployment and dispersion beyond the territory of the country and lower vulnerability. This explains the well-defined tendency in the USA in the distribution of nuclear missile resources, directed at a continuous extension of the role of the sea-based forces, as Table 21 shows.

TABLE 21
Distribution of Strategic Nuclear Missile Resources between the Branches of the US Armed Forces

	1960	1970	1975
Number of missiles	48/29	656/1054	656/1000
Percentage of total number of missiles	62/38	38/62	25/75
Number of nuclear missile warheads	48/29	2384/1314	5440/2000
Percentage of total number of nuclear missile warheads	62/38	65/35	73/27
Total TNT equivalent in megatons	24/290	183/1923	290/1050

Note. In the numerator the data refer to the Navy's missiles and in the denominator to the Air Force missiles.

In the USA great attention is paid to the refinement of the qualitative characteristics of strategic nuclear missile resources. Keeping the number of missiles practically unchanged since 1970, the Americans achieved a sharp increase in the number of nuclear warheads directed to targets. This is particularly noticeable on submarine missile-carriers where the very same 656 missiles can release almost 2.3 times as many nuclear warheads. Because of this, the percentage of nuclear strategic missile warheads placed on submarines rose in five years from 65 to 73 while the percentage of land-based warheads fell from 35 to 27. Such in practice is one of the expressions of the reorientation of the American leadership to an "oceanic strategy".

Multi-purpose atomic-powered submarines are intended for destroying surface ships and merchant vessels of the enemy and also for combating submarines.

The displacement and main dimensions of multi-purpose submarines, as noted, are considerably less than for submarine missile-carriers. For example, the first such American ship, *Nautilus,* had a displacement (submerged) of 4,040 tons. Twelve years after the coming into service of *Nautilus* the American fleet was augmented by the multi-purpose vessel, *Jack,* with a displacement of 4,300 tons. In the future, the displacement of such craft will apparently be at the level of 5,000 tons or somewhat higher. Some of the multi-purpose submarines of the American navy will be built especially as an anti-submarine variant. They are distinguished by less noise, higher speeds of travel and equipped with powerful sonar complexes.

Just how important is the place of sonar on multi-purpose submarines is indicated by the following fact. On American submarines of the *Thresher* and *Sturgeon* types, for the sonar antenna, the diameter of which is about four metres, is set aside the whole volume of the bow which is usually taken up with torpedo equipment. In connection with this the torpedo equipment is placed along the sides of the ship at an angle of about 10° to the centre line. Thus, the weapons of submarines have been ousted from their traditional place by the technical resources intended to ensure the use of these weapons.

In our fleet the appearance of atomic-powered submarines laid the foundation for the creation of powerful submarine forces capable of solving strategic tasks in the ocean.

The first submarines with atomic power units have already proved themselves as fully modern, powerful and reliable weapons and were rapidly mastered by the crews. On the basis of the experience of their design, building and service, industry started to build more powerful and sophisticated atomic-powered submarines. The latest technical achievements of world shipbuilding found application in the designs of these ships. These submarines, possessing higher fighting qualities than the first, considerably increased the navy's potential to solve strategic tasks.

Soviet atomic-powered submarines are first-class modern universal all-purpose fighting ships possessing operational combat properties enabling them to solve a wide range of tasks in the World Ocean. They are not only the carriers of tactical weapons, but form an inseparable part of the strategic nuclear shield of our motherland. Aggressors know this too. And they cannot but reckon with the direst consequences of retaliation which may befall them from the ocean if they dare start a nuclear war. The remarkable qualities of our atomic-powered submarines have been confirmed in many exercises and distant voyages. Soviet submariners have more than once reached the North Pole. A group of atomic-powered submarines performed without surfacing a round-the-world journey unmatched in history.

The technical improvement of modern submarines has enabled a quite different approach to be taken to the questions of organizing their combat operations. In the conditions of the Second World War submarines operated mostly on their own and only in operational liaison with surface ships and aircraft, but the complexities of mutual identification and communications made surface ships avoid encounters with their submarines. The position has now radically changed—the possibility has appeared of achieving close interaction in combat and operation of submarines and surface ships, which greatly enhances their combat effectiveness.

It should also be noted that our submarine forces are today equipped with completely up-to-date weaponry, constantly being improved, and which include, in addition to strategic submarine missile-carriers, submarines equipped with guided missiles and torpedoes. This line of development of the submarine forces was the result of major scientific research aimed at seeking the most rational ways of combating the forces of an enemy fleet.

Surface ships

These ships, already conceding in the period of the Second World War the role of the main branch of the sea forces to submarines and naval aviation, continue, however, to remain an important constituent of modern navies.

In the second stage of the post-war development of the navy, when our country stressed the creation of powerful submarine forces, the building of surface ships, in particular oceanic, began to lag. This was also due to the appearance of fundamentally new means of armed struggle represented by nuclear weapons. At first it was not clear what tasks surface ships would have to solve in the ocean and what properties they would need to have to take an effective part in armed struggle with use of nuclear weapons. As noted above, foreign military specialists, mesmerized by the omnipotence of atomic weapons, were convinced that in the new conditions all surface ships would lose combat value. The only exception allowed was aircraft carriers because they possess inherent sufficiently strong aviation cover from air attack. Only a few of these specialists saw the high mobility of the fleet as a means not only of surviving under the blows of the enemy but of conserving the ability to solve combat tasks. Among them we would note the already-mentioned Admiral Barjot, who was able to grasp the essence of the events and correctly appraise the influence of nuclear weapons on the development of the fleet and ways of using it in a nuclear war when he wrote: "A decisive factor is that the ship is guaranteed a future in the atomic century since the sea itself gives it in unlimited quantity material (non-contaminated sea water) thanks to which it can be in zones of radioactive contamination. This possibility, allowing the ship to remain unscathed, has profound implications. . . . Modern naval doctrine must start from the assumption that the fleet needs ships of different types which provide a large radius of action and high mobility."[17]

It must be recognized that at first our fleet did not show due confidence in many theoretical postulates of the role and place of surface ships in armed struggle at sea in connection with the growth of the destructive factors of modern weapons, since all theoretical formulations related to surface ships built in the first post-war years and not fundamentally differing from their predecessors, especially in means of defence and protection. The most vulnerable link in the defence of these ships was anti-aircraft defence the development of which lagged behind the development of the strike power of aviation. Surface ships deprived of reliable shelter from air attacks as soon as they emerged from the "umbrella" of continental anti-aircraft defence became a tempting target for bombing and torpedo-carrying aviation.

Modern surface ships materially differ from those which were built in the years of the Second World War and soon after its end. Their flak equipment has been considerably strengthened, enabling them to counter more successfully hostile aircraft and repel the combined attacks of other branches of the fleet of the enemy, thus solving their chief task.

The modern means of struggle have given quite new combat qualities to formations of surface ships, extended their possibilities in the combined use of long-range multi-purpose missiles, guns and torpedoes, thanks to which they are capable of successfully fighting back against the mixed groupings of a hostile fleet and using in concert surface and submarine forces and aircraft.

Surface ships remain the basic and often sole combat means of ensuring deployment of the main strike forces of the fleet—submarines. The First and Second World Wars showed the fallacy of the view that the submarine by virtue

[17] P. Barjot, *The Fleet in the Atomic Century* (Russian translation), pp. 261-262.

of its concealment after emerging from its base can itself ensure its own invulnerability.

An important positive attribute of surface ships is the possibility of maintaining continuous two-way links with them by shore command points. This makes control much easier and ensures the timely transmission to ships of all the necessary information and dispositions, which is extremely important in conditions of an eve-of-war situation when the time factor assumes special importance.

Surface ships form the basis of the land disembarking aids and forces of support for a landing. They have the chief role in the fight against the mine danger and in protecting communications.

In closed theatres and in coastal areas surface ships may be employed for operations on sea communications. An example of this is afforded by the operations of missile boats of the Egyptian fleet, which sank the Israeli destroyer *Eliat,* and also the operations of the Indian fleet in striking a blow at the forces of the Pakistani fleet, concentrated in Karachi.

As shown by the conflicts of the post-war period surface ships are capable of solving a large range of tasks in local wars. They were widely used for giving armaments backing to land forces operating in the coastal areas of Korea and Vietnam, for staging seaborne landings and for blockade operations. With the aid of surface ships, American marines penetrated along rivers and canals into the hinterland areas of South Vietnam.

The development and building of surface ships are in keeping with their potential in the creation of a modern balanced nuclear missile fleet. Numerically the largest group is made up of anti-submarine surface ships. They are divided into ships capable of operating in the ocean for a long time and coastal ships.

The former include large anti-submarine ships and also anti-submarine cruisers. Coastal anti-submarine ships include specially-built small fast ships which can successfully seek out and destroy multi-purpose atomic and diesel submarines of the enemy operating in the closed sea and coastal areas of the oceanic theatres.

It must be stated that our anti-submarine surface ships, in their design, arming and power, differ a good deal from the corresponding ships of the fleets of Western countries.

The surface ships of the forces of our fleet have modern fast missile ships and cutters.

Missile boats can operate not only in closed sea theatres but also in the coastal areas of the oceans, fulfilling the tasks of destroying the surface and merchant ships of the enemy.

The powerful armaments-missile flak weapons set up on missile cruisers and other missile ships, and radar stations for detection of air targets and weapons control, make it possible to rebuff successfully air attacks from the enemy.

As stated above, our fleet during the Great Patriotic War constantly felt the need for specially-constructed landing craft. The specific conditions in which our fleet was forced to operate made this problem, generated by an imbalance of its forces, particularly acute. While well grasping the need of the fleet for these ships, we could not build them even in the first post-war decade, as the shipbuilding industry was engaged in building mostly large fighting surface ships (cruisers, destroyers, escort ships) and also vessels for the merchant marine. Only in the second post-war decade did the fleet receive specially-built landing craft.

The surface forces of our fleet, represented by diverse oceanic and coastal ships, are now capable, independently and in interaction with submarines and aircraft, of solving a large range of tasks in the oceans and closed sea theatres.

The development of the surface forces of the fleet is moving along the lines not only of building new displacement ships with higher tactical-technical characteristics and more effective armament than in their predecessors. Scientific and technical progress has provided a real opportunity to produce fundamentally new surface ships with a number of tactical features which cannot be achieved in displacement ships.

On the basis of research and experimental design work intensively pursued since the beginning of the 'fifties in the USSR, USA, Japan, Britain, France and other highly-developed countries, a considerable number of types of fundamentally new ships have now been built, known in world shipbuilding by the general name of surface skimmers. They include ships with hydrofoil, air cushion, and others.

Ships with dynamic principles of support are largely free of the many defects peculiar to displacement ships, such as high vulnerability to torpedoes and mines, too low speeds of travel, limitation of the areas of combat use over the depths of the sea and in an ice setting, etc.

Abroad, fighting ships on an air cushion and on hydrofoil are used as patrol, landing-disembarking, ammunition and look-out ships and also for coastal protection and seaboard service.

The first ships with dynamic principles of support were ships on hydrofoil, best developed abroad in the USA, Italy and Japan.

The building of ships on hydrofoil was a notable achievement during development of a surface fleet. However, the basic defects peculiar to displacement ships could not be avoided since ships on hydrofoil are not capable of being completely severed from the water medium. Moreover, they are ill-suited for solving certain combat tasks, for example, the speedy disembarking of seaborne invasion forces, especially in shallow areas because of the high risk of damage from the ground to the hydrofoil.

Thus, ships on hydrofoil may be regarded as a transitional step to the creation of modern surface ships differing in principle from displacement ships. Such are ships on an air cushion and ram-wing vehicles, to the design of which much attention is being paid abroad. The principle of an air cushion is applicable to vessels of different displacements, up to ocean-going. Possessing a speed of travel of over 100 knots such an ocean vessel is capable of crossing the Atlantic Ocean in 30-40 hours, while an ordinary cargo vessel takes eight days and even longer.

Ships on an air cushion have a low specific use of power units, diminishing with rise in size, and high coefficients of utilization, growing with increase in carrying capacity. Their relative useful carrying capacity is higher than in displacement ships.

The main tactical property of ships on an air cushion is that they are capable of moving over the water surface and land, including an ice cover, negotiating shallow areas, freely passing from water to land and ice cover, and back. All this, combined with high speed of travel and high carrying capacity, give the new ships a number of very substantial tactical advantages.

It is perfectly obvious that with such qualities, ships on an air cushion will be able to find the widest combat applications. Foreign experts consider that in the future they will be used as landing craft, aircraft carriers of strike ships armed with missiles and flak-missile installations, and also for seeking out and destroying fast submarines and for mine-laying. Ships and vessels of this type may play an important role as supply ships at sea, in carrying out military shipments, solving the tasks of anti-mine defence, protecting the forces of the fleet en route at sea, etc.

Abroad, over 140 ships and vessels on an air cushion have now been built, although most of them (about 70 per cent) have relatively low size (up to 10 tons) and limited speed of travel (up to 80 per cent of the ships have a speed of about 60 knots).

Attaching much importance to ships on an air cushion, the USA, Britain and France have developed work aimed at building in the next few years new ships and vessels of this type with a displacement of 4000 tons and over, with a speed of travel of about 100 knots including vessels with atomic-power units.

In the field of ram-wing vehicle construction, research and technical problems have been defined abroad, mostly concerning the building of ocean-going ram-wing cargo vessels. A little over ten flying models of ram-wing vessels and a number of ram-wing vessel designs with a mass from 100 to 2000 tons have been built. Although the experience of the building and operating of these ships is still insufficient, even now their potential can be seen. As compared with ships on an air cushion, ram-wing vessels will possess greater speed of travel or, to be more precise, of flight, with less energy expenditure and hence, other things being equal, greater range of operations. In addition, they are capable of overcoming obstacles of great height.

Thus, in many countries work is well under way to realize the latest achievements in science and technique in the field of surface ship-building. The building of ships with dynamic principles of support has already become a reality. There is no doubt that the appearance in large numbers of such ships as part of the fleets will increase their combat possibilities and that the surface forces will be able to solve more successfully combat tasks and acquire quite new qualities.

The further development of surface ships of different classes will be an important stage in the creation of a modern balanced fleet.

The process of merging aviation and surface ships, the material expression of which was the creation of aircraft carriers dating back some time, is continuing even now but on a wider technical basis. Together with the development of aircraft-carriers, fleets of different countries are paying increasing attention to the construction of qualitatively new helicopter-carrier ships. Our navy also has them and such ships are being built in the USA, France and other countries.

Many fleets are seeking to have as many ships as possible of all classes capable of carrying helicopters. The main reason for this is that the helicopter is increasingly becoming a "constituent" part of modern surface ships of different classes, giving them quite new combat qualities. The participation of helicopters in submarine search, for example, not only widens the range of "vision" of the ship carrying them but substantially increases its possibility of keeping track of the detected opponent, increasing the reliability of striking him with anti-submarine weapons. Taking advantage of their considerable superiority in speed over the submarine and also the advantages in the possibilities of mutual detection, helicopters create for the submarine conditions in which it becomes harder for it to evade encounters with an anti-submarine surface ship.

Ship helicopters are introducing many and fundamental changes into the tactics of landing operations. For example, US naval forces employ a tactical procedure of fighting for a landing with the aid of helicopters known as vertical enveloping of the opponent. It relieves one of the need to traverse minefields in the water and on the shore and, above all, considerably increases the speed of disembarkation and the swiftness and irresistibility of seaborne landings.

Ship helicopters also perform many other functions which make them indispensable in a modern sea battle. Primarily these are good reconnoitering and target designation for weapons, transport and transfer of various items to other ships under way, crew rescue, complex operations in servicing a variety of technical needs and many others.

Naval aviation

Before the appearance of missiles, aviation was the main and sole carrier of nuclear weapons and therefore on it fell the tasks of wrecking and destroying important objectives on land, and also of demolishing the strike grouping of the forces of the fleets at sea and in their bases, on which other branches of the armed forces could not effectively act.

The advent of land- and sea-based missiles opened up the new possibility of delivering nuclear warheads over long distances. A tremendous qualitative leap in development of ship nuclear weapons led to sharp change in the character of armed struggle at sea. The new possibility of effectively acting against fixed objectives helped to free naval aviation from strikes on them. This, of course, does not mean that naval aviation will not be invoked for delivering strikes on stationary shore objectives. Modern aviation has all that is necessary for such strikes and can consequently discharge these tasks. However, in modern conditions such operations by it must be regarded as the exception rather than the rule since the tasks which in the not-too-distant past it was supposed to solve have now changed. Now it can direct its main efforts against strike formations of surface ships, submarines and merchant vessels, including those carrying troops, and cargoes en route or in port, and also destroy the most varied mobile, highly manoeuvrable, small-sized objectives at sea.

The change of task is leading to a redefinition of the place, role and importance of each branch of aviation and the direction of its development. For example, comparatively recently, before the appearance of atomic missile-carrier submarines, the main task of aviation in combat operations at sea was the wrecking of the strike grouping of the ships of the enemy fleet. This undoubtedly had a serious influence on the development of aviation systems which were envisaged as being used to strike against surface ships. But as an ever larger number of atomic submarines came into the fleets of different states, primarily missile carriers, and began to be widely constructed, the main task of aviation became the fight against them. Therefore, the role and importance of anti-submarine aviation, capable of effectively seeking out and destroying submarines in distant areas of the oceanic and sea theatres, is sharply rising.

In view of the complexity of the tasks solved by aviation, and bearing in mind the possible character of armed struggle at sea, it is quite logical to consider that the importance in it of aviation is considerably greater than in the last war.

As for the factors influencing the use of aviation at sea, it is necessary to take a closer look at the probable conditions under which it can overcome the counter-action of anti-aircraft defences. In this connection we would note that in the past the possibilities of anti-aircraft defence were comparatively limited since groupings of ships at sea chiefly possessed flak artillery and the range of detection of air targets was low. With the appearance of flak missiles and radio-electronic means of monitoring in the air, the feasibility of anti-aircraft defence sharply grew (there has been increase in depth and degree of sensitivity of the field of radar monitoring air targets at medium and high altitudes, the combat possibilities of ships and fighter-planes of the screening forces have grown), but the designers of aviation missiles were able to provide their carriers with a sufficiently long distance for launching the missiles away from the target, freeing them of the need to enter, on delivering the strike, the actual flak-fire zone. This, of course, does not mean that final superiority of aviation over anti-aircraft defence has been reached. The age-old rivalry between means of attack and means of defence will continue with unabated intensity.

The possibilities of aviation in the struggle at sea were greatly influenced by the development of aviation techniques and weapons. It is significant that in nearly all countries the tendency to specialization stood out most clearly, i.e. the construction of aircraft for solving quite definite tasks. Therefore, most of the countries use for arming aviation specially constructed search-strike systems for combating submarines, strike systems for attacking surface ships and reconnaissance systems for monitoring the sea situation. The material published in the foreign press shows that the possibilities of aviation increase if so-called aviation systems (plane carrier, means of search and strike) are deployed in concert for solving quite definite problems, akin in content and conditions of fulfilment. It is assumed that these systems will enable aviation to conduct operations by the principle of "independent search—detection—attack" and with reference to the high effectiveness of aviation, nuclear missile weapons will allow it to fight successfully the forces of the navy at sea and enhance its self-sufficiency, mobility and combat readiness.

Particularly fast headway is being made by modern radio-electronic means of search for surface ships (round- and side-view radar stations, radio-engineering and radio-reconnoitering equipment, infra-red instruments, television and other devices) which allow aviation to detect the targets at sea several hundred kilometres away, often much earlier than the ships notice the reconnaissance plane. Using these means of search it is possible not only to identify targets but also to specify the composition of the ship groupings and the parameters of their movement.

A much more complicated matter is that of the search for submarines, especially atomic-powered ones with high speeds of travel and depth of submergence. Search for them and their detection, despite constant improvement of equipment, presents no small difficulties.

The expanded combat possibilities of aviation units, increase in the launching range of missiles by them and the ability to overcome the counter-action of active forces and resources of ship anti-aircraft defence by these missiles, have made aviation nuclear missile strikes on sea targets practically irresistible. Such an enormous qualitative leap in the combat possibilities of aviation units and formations in delivering strikes on sea targets, together with other factors, pre-determined profound changes in application including the principle of their use, ways of solving tasks, organization of interaction, control and all forms of supply.

The combat possibilities of naval aviation are one of the salient indicators of the strike power of our modern navy. Naval aviation has, in fact, become oceanic, it has been converted into a most important means of armed struggle at sea.

Weapons and technical combat resources

Immediately after the end of the Second World War all countries widely engaged in work to produce qualitatively new means of armed warfare, including marine armaments.

As is known, Soviet rocket weapons in the Second World War were used for the first time. These were uncontrolled army-type missiles, the use of which on torpedo boats had to be made by guidance equipment like that designed for the famed *Katyushas*.

The Americans in the years of the war were very sceptical about these weapons. Only after the first intelligence reports on work done in Fascist Germany on the production of V-2s did this attitude begin to undergo radical change. Then the USA took no little trouble, on the one hand, to get hold of specific information on the German rockets and, on the other, to conceal such data from the USSR. This was also promoted by the situation existing at that time.

At the beginning of 1944 when, after the massive raid of Allied aircraft on Peenemunde, the V-2 trials were switched by the Nazis to occupied Poland, the Anglo-American war command used their communication with Polish partisans to obtain test models of the main types of German rockets, sometimes falling well away from areas where German search parties sought them.

The interest of the Pentagon in the new weapon is also confirmed by the fact that, before the landing of the allies in Normandy, the American military command carefully worked out a plan for the secret *Paperclip* operation to take captive Nazi rocket scientists. The designer of the V-2, Von Braun, and his team made this task much easier. With the approach of Soviet troops they fled to the West to meet the leading American units.

With the aid of Von Braun the Americans acquired the first batch of 102 highly-qualified Nazi scientists. In addition, the American command took care to remove all the rockets found, both assembled and ready for assembly.

For the quickest mastery of pilotless systems of delivering nuclear warheads to the target, the USA, immediately after the war, embarked on a programme of building aerial craft with air-feed jet engines or missile planes. Some of the projects forming part of this programme—*Regal, Regulus-I, Regulus-II* and *Matador*—represented medium-range missile planes, the idea being to launch the missiles of the first three types from surface ships or submarines above water and the missiles of the last type from American military bases in Europe or Japan.

Two other projects also developed as part of this programme—the *Snark* and the *Navaho*—concerned weapons of the intercontinental classes and their flight range was to vary up to "more than one quarter of the distance around the globe".

The programme to build purely rocket means of delivering warheads began to expand at almost the same time. In this field the USA had already chalked up some, albeit modest, advances. By the end of 1944, American rocket men successfully carried out the first experimental launch of a prototype of a ballistic rocket and in 1945 one of the trial rockets of this type reached a height of 64 km.

With the arrival of German experts in the USA, work was begun to assemble and test the V-2 and then perfect it. No less vigorous efforts were made by the American leadership to develop submarine nuclear-missile systems.

In 1946, the design team led by the naval engineer Rickover began to design an atomic-powered submarine missile-carrier. Much later, in November 1955, after work had stopped on missile planes, to arm submarines a joint working party of the Navy and Air Force was set up with the brief of examining the possibility of adapting the *Atlas* missile so as to launch it from surface ships and submarines. However, this team quite soon broke up and it was replaced by another, led by Admiral Raeburn, which began to develop the *Polaris* naval missile.

In September 1955 the *Polaris* programme was officially given the rank of a top programme of national importance. Gradually, the missile programme was speeded up to achieve the swiftest acquisition of the "absolute" weapon. A statement of the then Secretary for Defense Wilson that the missile programme was executed on the basis of unlimited financing cannot be considered exaggerated: by the spring of 1957 no less than 100,000 persons were engaged in carrying out the American missile-programme; 20,000 plants and 22 branches of industry worked on it; already in 1952 the appropriations set aside for carrying out the missile programme topped 1,000 million dollars and the total expenditure on these goals in the first post-war decade exceeded 17,000 million dollars. "Congress", later wrote the *New York Times* "has always passed all the budget bills of the government for the development of missile weapons". (Retranslated from Russian.)

Naturally, in the face of such a formidable danger we were compelled to take all necessary steps to defend our country. Therefore, simultaneously with the creation of new missile weapons systems for land forces and aviation and the improvement of existing models, which had brilliantly withstood the test in the Great Patriotic War, our country began to explore the possibilities of arming ships with qualitatively-new missile weapons.

Scientific research already then made it possible to determine the tremendous advantages of missile weapons over such traditional means of conflict at sea as armament of different calibre, including the largest. These advantages consisted primarily in the incomparably greater firing range and ability with a high probability of hitting the target. However, the accuracy of travel of the combat part of the missile to the target depends not so much on the technical qualities of the missile itself as on the accuracy and reliability of target designation, since the flight range of a missile is considerably greater than the "reach" of the means of ascertaining the above-water situation on a rocket-carrying ship, and also on the system of flight control of the missile.

It was also necessary to bear in mind that the replacement of guns by rockets inevitably had to overcome major difficulties connected with placing large-sized rockets on the then existing ships. But the problem facing us was: either explore the possibilities of replacing armaments by rocketry or, if this fails, build qualitatively new ships.

Another important job done at that time was the creation of a winged rocket for sea aviation. The intention at first to use this missile for arming sea aviation was dictated by the imperfection of the motor then installed on the missile, limiting the possibility of launching from the side of a ship. Its release from an aeroplane did not have these limitations.

In the course of the work to perfect this missile a new, even more promising line in the development of missile weapons took shape. Therefore, the development of shore and aviation complexes temporarily ceased and attention was focused on a universal missile complex which it was planned to use for arming planes, surface ships and shore launching installations. This work was basically successful and in the middle of the 'fifties the winged rocket was used to arm sea aviation and shore missile units.

The next step in the development of guided missiles was the production of missiles specially intended for arming low-displacement ships. This was a big advance in the development of arming the ships of our fleet, thanks to which the ships assumed quite new qualities; their potential fundamentally changed as did the modes of the operational-tactical use of surface forces of the fleet in armed warfare at sea. Missile weapons make practically equal the strike power of ships of the most varied classes. Even gun-boats (the use of which in a battle with surface ships had earlier been out of the question thanks to their arming with missiles) were capable of attacking ships of practically any class.

However, it should be noted that for many years the ships of our navy alone were armed with guided missiles. The fleets of other countries took a very cautious approach to the evaluation of the potential of such weapons, and even if they recognized them as effective were in no hurry to use them for arming. Only after the sinking by an Egyptian missile boat of the Israeli destroyer

Eilat did guided missiles gain recognition even in the fleets of the traditional maritime powers, which then began to step up work on the production of guided missiles for surface ships of different classes.

Thanks to guided missiles, fast missile boats were recognized as a strike force in a modern fleet. In Norway, for example, missile boats were adapted for arming with four launching installations, and 20 gun-boats were refitted for guided missiles. The building of missile boats was pursued in West Germany, Denmark, Italy, Israel, Greece and other countries. The building of missile boats was also taken up by such maritime powers as the USA, Britain and France. Many foreign naval experts now agree that missile boats give to small fleets offensive possibilities out of proportion to the size of these fleets.

Qualitative changes also took place in the anti-aircraft armament of ships which also became, in the main, missile. The solution of the problem of flak missile armaments opened the way to a new approach to the appraisal of the real combat potential of modern surface ships. Considerably raising the defensive qualities of formations of surface ships, flak missiles created conditions in which surface ships could successfully fulfil combat tasks far beyond the range of their continental anti-aircraft defence, since they are sure of the reliability of their anti-aircraft defence.

Unlike missile weapons for surface ships, which replaced guns, in the first place main guns, missile weapons for submarines were a qualitatively new arms system which radically altered the submarines themselves, their function and combat potential with all the inherent implications.

Missile weapons for submarines were developed along two lines. The first envisaged the creation of guided missiles for hitting large surface ships and for destroying land objectives. The fitting of submarines with such missiles extended their possibilities in combating the surface forces of an enemy fleet. They acquired the ability to use the various means in the most advantageous combination for combating strongly-protected ships of the enemy and delivering strikes on them without entering into the zone of effective anti-submarine defence.

Another independent line in the development of missiles for submarines was the creation of the ballistic missile with a long firing range. The first model of such a missile appeared in our fleet at the beginning of the 'fifties. Then, on the basis of it more sophisticated models of ballistic missiles were devised for arming submarines. At the end of the 'fifties submarines received for arming their first effective combat ballistic missile. However, it was not free of such a serious defect as above-water launching, to undertake which the submarine had to surface. Therefore, a continuous search was made for ways of ensuring underwater launching of missiles and at the same time increasing their flight range. As a result of a strenuous search and numerous experiments, our submarine fleet received a missile launched from under the water which paved the way for the creation of a strategic submarine nuclear system for our armed forces. Thanks to ballistic missiles launched from under water carrying a nuclear warhead of tremendous power and having long flight ranges running into thousands of kilometres, submarines became able to fulfil strategic tasks.

The process of perfecting the missile weapons of submarines, surface ships, aviation and shore units is also continuing today. The range and accuracy of fire is increasing, the combat effectiveness of missiles and their carriers is growing. Missile weapons have firmly taken a leading place in the arms system of the fleet and the fleet has acquired a solid arsenal of strategic resources for ensuring the solution of complex tasks in war. Today the fleet is capable of successfully fulfilling strategic tasks not only by destroying important objectives on hostile territory but also destroying submarine carriers of nuclear weapons at sea.

After the end of the Second World War in the fleets of different countries the view was widely held that the then existing means of combating submarines, even if still not ideal, were at least coming close to it. The basis for such a view was the very special rivalry between the means of attack and defence in the sphere of submarine operations in the years of the Second World War. It consisted in the fact that the development of submarines in that period was chiefly along the lines of their partial improvement on the basis of the pre-war material-technical base. These improvements, even very substantial, influenced only the individual tactical properties of submarines without at the same time changing their main qualities and without freeing them from those deficiencies which were organically peculiar to this class of ship. This process was most clearly in evidence in submarines of the Fascist German fleet.

The anti-submarine forces of the fleets of the Allied countries were created on a new technical basis with reference to the latest achievements of science in this field. Therefore, in the period of the Second World War, the gap existing in the pre-war years between the potential of the means of attack and defence against submarines substantially narrowed. But the claims that submarines did not stand up to this competition and were defeated, as we have already noted, were very wide of the mark.

As soon as the first diesel submarines built post-war appeared, making concerted use of all those improvements which had occurred in the various fleets in the years of the Second World War, and as soon as the depth of their submergence was doubled and the speed of their underwater travel raised, the gap between the potential of the means of attack and defence again proved to be even more perceptible. None of the fleets was then able to create the means of underwater observation which would extend the sphere of "vision" of the anti-submarine units to values comparable with the ranges of reach of anti-submarine weaponry used by surface ships, planes and anti-submarine ships. The partial increase in the ranges of "underwater vision" which was achieved in our and foreign fleets did not solve this problem since the ability of submarines to move from the field of their operation became much greater than before.

At the same time, submarines gained growing recognition in all fleets as the basis of armed struggle at sea and were considered the main threat to surface fighting ships and merchant vessels. Another important factor was that in the first post-war years in a number of countries a search was begun for ways of building atomic-powered submarines, which even according to the ideas of that time was bound to introduce very substantial changes in the conditions of armed struggle at sea as a whole, and in solving the tasks of fighting submarines in particular. Therefore the question of the development of anti-submarine resources remained as topical as ever, and had become increasingly acute.

The intensive development of submarines, in particular the appearance of missile submarines with atomic power, the fight against which assumed the character of a state task, raised the question of a further and sharp rise in the effectiveness of anti-submarine weapons. Even then it was clear that the solution of this problem was essentially to be sought not by perfecting the available means of combat, the technical possibilities of the development of which were coming close to the limit. The question was one of developing entirely new principles of combating submarines, which also determined the new demands for combating them.

The main requirement was that to ensure a hit on atomic-powered missile submarines it was necessary to increase sharply the range of action of the means of detecting submarines and to design weapons capable in the shortest time and with a high probability of hitting submarines over the entire range of depths of submergence. The development of anti-submarine weapons proceeded in relation to these requirements which stemmed from the new combat properties of submarines.

In the course of the post-war development of the fleet the need to use on fighting ships power units with a high specific output became particularly clear. This need is met in several ways, the most important of which is the design, improvement and introduction of nuclear-powered plants and also the development and introduction of improved steam-turbine, gas-turbine and diesel plants with increased output.

Nuclear power, greatly raising the duration and range of operation of ships, has also considerably increased their combat possibilities. However, it imparts fundamentally new qualities chiefly to submarines which are being converted into truly underwater ships combining to the highest degree such basic indicators of fighting power as speed, force of strike and concealment of operations. Submarines are also becoming complete anti-submarine ships capable of detecting submarine missile-carriers of the enemy, keeping track of them and if necessary striking at them.

The use of nuclear power in submarines made it possible to increase sharply their power equipment, operating range under water and speed of travel. The introduction of nuclear power in surface ships is also substantially raising their combat qualities: their operating range at high speeds of travel is increasing and at the same time the dependence on shore bases and supply vessels diminishing.

The improvement of steam and gas turbines and diesels helped in the design of new surface ships with increased operating ranges, independence and speed of travel and also opened the way to the design of fundamentally new surface ships with dynamic principles of support discussed earlier.

In the course of development of the forces and resources of combat at sea a special place has been taken by radio-electronics, not only forming the technical basis of the systems of control of the forces, but also entering into the most important complexes as their inseparable elements.

All the forms of activity of the navy are to a greater or lesser degree necessarily connected with the use of radio electronics. Tendencies towards the automation of the process of control of ship gear, weapon complexes, ships and formations testify to the growing role of radio electronics in the functioning of all control and arms systems. Therefore, superiority in the field of development of military radio electronics is becoming one of the essential conditions for military superiority over an enemy.

However, while raising the combat potential of forces and weapons, radio electronics at the same time is making the systems of means of control more vulnerable to the action of the enemy. Control can now be upset not only by wrecking the systems of control themselves but by electronic counter-measures, as was convincingly demonstrated in the course of the Arab-Israeli wars of 1967 and 1973 and combat operations in Vietnam.

Overall, radio electronics, extensively used in all the spheres of operation of the armed forces, occupies an important place in systems of control for the forces and weapons in all links. At all levels it is assuming the role of one of the decisive factors determining the real balance in the forces and resources of opposing sides.

This is of special importance for the navy in the sphere of whose operations radio-engineering devices are being put to much wider and more diverse use than in any other branch of the armed forces. The arming of the navy now includes the latest radio-engineering complexes which are divided into ship (including aircraft) and stationary. They are distinguished by a large range of operations, accuracy of measurement of the co-ordinates of the targets, high reliability and extensive automation. All this ensures rapid analysis of the data of observations, putting out of target designation, flow co-ordinates and the choice of optimal solutions for using forces and weapons.

The waging of combat operations is now impossible without the use of radio-engineering aids. Naval weapons themselves (missile and even armament shells) have various radar devices.

The need to have a multiplicity of radar units and systems on a ship requires ship spaces of large volume for accommodating equipment and service personnel and also strongly-developed superstructures and masts for a large number of antennae. The further extension of the tasks and potential of radar will saturate ships even further with radar equipment. This wide use of radar has made it an important factor in modern armed struggle at sea.

Radar as a system of arming the navy has introduced major changes into the organization and waging of combat operations of its forces, making it necessary to work out the principles of the combat use of radar devices as an inseparable part of the tactics of the fleet.

Of the greatest importance in modern conditions are the devices for ascertaining the underwater situation, among which a special place has come to be taken by sonar stations and complexes intended to detect submarines and surface ships, search for mines and ensure ship navigation and rescue operations. Sonar means are being intensively developed in all fleets and have already become an inseperable part of the equipment of submarines, surface ships, helicopters, planes and stationary systems. The wide use of sonar devices had a considerable influence on the development of the fleet and naval art. The possibilities of sonar are still far from exhausted and work to make it more effective, especially in combating submarines, will continue and therefore more effective ways of combating the forces of the enemy fleet will also be developed.

Well known to all are the measures which in the last few years have been adopted by the Central Committee of our Party and the Soviet Government to bring about a radical improvement in scientific management in all spheres of the life of our country. The Party teaches that on the scientific organization of control largely depends the creation of the material-technical base of communism and the formation of a new man—the man of communist society.

The importance of control has now grown so much that it determines not only the degree of effectiveness and the outcome of the activity of society but the very possibility of this activity. In armed struggle at sea this is particularly clearly manifested. The character of armed struggle at sea will be distinguished by its global scale, the highly transitory nature of combat clashes and considerable increase in the impact of combat operations as compared with operations of the past. These circumstances greatly increase the responsibility of each commander in decision-making and putting such decisions into effect without delay and confront him with the need to display exceptional operational understanding corresponding to the course of events in progress.

Until quite recently, in the years of the Great Patriotic War, even a commander of a fleet could observe the field of engagement in the main decisive direction in an operation, issue the necessary orders and thus directly influence its course. Combat means and their rapid action were to a certain degree commensurate with the possibilities of man. Control of the forces was achieved by means of previously evolved methods familiar to all, without use of complex machines and equipment. Only three decades have since elapsed and the former approach is largely outdated. The immense power of the means of strike, increase in their length of range, the scope of combat operations and the growth of rapid operation of the means of combat to such a degree that it is already incommensurate with the physical possibilities of man, are forcing one to take a fresh look at the most important aspects of waging struggle at sea—the resources, ways and organization of the control of the forces of the fleet.

In the case in question we are considering only those means without which the control of the forces of the fleet is now inconceivable, not only in extensive oceanic expanses but also in comparatively small areas of the seas, even in solving by the forces of the fleet of tasks of a tactical character limited in scale. Among them a special place is assigned to the means of communication which, from ancient times, have been most important in control of forces and weapons of any branch of the armed forces. But for none of them is the range of operation of the means of communication as important as it is for the navy, the forces of which may be virtually in every area of the World Ocean including the most distant. A modern fleet needs global communication capable of ensuring the control of forces tens of thousands of kilometres away from the areas of their stationing.

Each of the branches of the armed forces has a specific area of operations within which the control of its forces is brought about by the different means of communication used in a given medium. The fleet in this respect, too, significantly differs from all other branches of the armed forces. It needs such means of communication as will ensure the simultaneous control of its forces in different media: under water, above water, in the air and on land.

A further specific feature of the forces of the fleet as an object of control is that its forces operate not as a compact structure, as, say, aviation or land troops, but in split-up combat order and even as single ships a very long way apart.

Because of these objective causes, the navy needs such organization of communications as allow it to control confidently its highly-mobile forces at enormous distances from their bases, operating in different areas, in split-up formations extending over many thousands of kilometres along the front and the same distances in depth. Bearing in mind the special features of modern warfare this link must be fast-acting, constant, resistant to interference by the enemy and necessarily two-way.

These features and requirements were taken into account in the construction of the system of communications of our navy, gradually spreading far beyond the seas touching our territory as the forces of our fleet harnessed ever newer and more distant areas of the World Ocean. Ships, planes and the command points of the navy are now fitted with powerful means of communication which ensure reliable control of the forces of the fleet over large distances.

The process of control including the sphere of the activity of the fleet is based on the work of the persons carrying out or ensuring this process. This most complex work can be reduced in all cases to two forms of mental activity of man—analysis and synthesis of the information or, as is commonly said in the armed forces, to appraisal of a situation and the preparation and adoption of a decision.

The effectiveness of the process of control essentially depends on the fullness, subtleness and accuracy of the analysis, on the one hand, and on the maximum soundness (faultlessness) of the synthesis of information on the other. The completeness and optimal correlation of these two special processes are expected to ensure the maximum effectiveness of the work of the command and staff bodies in the sphere of control of the forces of the fleet.

In preparing decisions on the basis of which all the combat and daily activity of the forces and organs of control of the fleet will take place in modern conditions, the commander must without fail identify the possible alternatives, i.e. different paths of reaching the goals, different methods of solving each task, with analysis of the merits and drawbacks of each of them in order to pick the optimal variant.

It is perfectly obvious that the realization of these requirements in the course of organizing and planning the combat and daily activity of the fleets and even more so in waging operations on a different scale, extending over extensive spaces of the oceans, is unthinkable without wide use of modern technical aids based on the use of computer techniques.

In parallel with the work developed in industry in the post-war years to set up a new computer technology, in the navy scientific investigations were undertaken in the course of which a method was worked out for the practical use of computers for raising the effectiveness of the combat use of the forces of the fleet.

The post-war period in the development of our armed forces is a special stage in their history. In this period the foundations of the ocean-going nuclear missile fleet of the Soviet Union were laid.

The special aspects of the forces of the fleet—their high manoeuvrability, ability to concentrate covertly and to form, unexpectedly for the enemy, powerful groupings and better resistance than the land forces to the action of nuclear weapons—have brought the navies into the first rank of modern means of armed warfare. Their use in conditions of a nuclear missile war is connected with the introduction of much that is new into tactics and operational art, the design of ships and their technical supplies and equipment.

An important factor determining the direction of the building of our fleet was that in the World Ocean the post-war period for the first time saw a strategic situation characterized by the unified planning of the development and use of the naval forces of the imperialist states. At the same time, when the main weapon of the fleet became missiles of different combat classes, this enabled it to dispense with traditional criteria in determining the strength of the groupings of the forces at sea.

And although military-technical progress is continuously introducing something new in all fields of the business of war, the final goals of armed struggle at sea remain the same: crushing the enemy, destroying his life force and material resources, i.e. his ships and crews and stores of weapons or shore objectives, within reach of modern means of attack from the oceans.

The qualitative transformations occurring in the naval forces have also changed the approach to appraisal of the comparative power of the fleets and their combat groupings, and to the possibilities of achieving these goals—comparison of the number of the ships or a particular class, their total displacement (or the number of guns in a salvo, or the mass of this salvo) have had to be dropped in favour of a more complex but sounder evaluation of the attack and defence power of ships on the basis of mathematical analysis of their potential and qualitative characteristics.

The tremendous amount of work done on the building of the oceanic fleet and its development in the post-war period brought in its train the elaboration of a corresponding theory of naval art which is now characterized by new categories and a kind of distillation of former concepts and principles. The area of use of the fleet and the range of tasks to be solved by it have widened. In other words, cardinal changes have taken place in the sphere of operations of navies in the post-war years, both in connection with the new alignment of forces in the world arena, and with changes in the forces and resources. And this naturally has affected the modes of armed struggle at sea, the tasks of the fleets and the role which the navy is called upon to play in defence of the country from attack by an aggressor. The fleet undoubtedly will continue to develop until the threat of attack by an aggressor on our country has disappeared. And if it is true that a fighting ship embodies the latest achievements of technical progress, then the ships of the future will reflect the level of development of science and industry of their country.

It is now hard to say what peaks can be reached by human thought in twenty or twenty-five fast-moving years, but one thing is certain—ships will be quite dissimilar from present craft.

This "dissimilarity" in the first place, as we see it, will be manifest in the ever wider replacement of the now customary and traditional systems of armaments and torpedo equipment by missiles and new electronic systems. Even now the Americans are working on laser techniques in general and high-energy lasers in particular, which, in their view, will lead to the development of a quite new military technique and hence to the appearance of new tactics.

We have no doubt that for ships of the future, electric power units of colossal output will be needed, guaranteeing not only the fast movement of ships in different mediums but also the requirement of an ever-growing number of the most varied electronic devices, instruments of observation, control and communication. Aircraft-carrying and other fighting ships will be more and more equipped with vertical take-off planes and other aerial craft of the modern helicopter type but, of course, more sophisticated. Combat operations will to an even greater degree pass into the underwater and aerial spheres.

In concluding this chapter it may be said that the disposition of forces in the international arena and the increased ability of modern fleets to act on all fronts of armed warfare give grounds for considering that the absolute and relative importance of conflict at sea in the general course of a war has grown unquestionably.

Now our armed forces comprise a fully modern ocean-going fleet, equipped with all it needs for successfully solving the tasks given it, in the expanses of the World Ocean, to ensure the security of our country and protection of its interests at sea.

It is necessary to emphasize again the radical difference in goals, to which ends they have been created and maintained, between the navies of the imperialist states on the one hand, and the navy of the Soviet Union on the other. While the naval forces of the imperialist states are an instrument of aggression and neo-colonialism, the Soviet fleet is a powerful factor in creating favourable conditions for the building of socialism and communism, a factor in the active defence of peace and strengthening of international security.

The Central Committee of the Communist Party and the Soviet Government, putting into practice the testaments of Lenin on the strengthening of the defence of the country, are paying unflagging attention to the strengthening of the armed forces of the state and the harmonious, balanced development of the ocean-going fleet, meeting the requirements of the times and capable of discharging the tasks facing them. By the efforts of the Soviet people, such a fleet will continue to grow and develop and improve on the basis of swift scientific and technical progress.

CHAPTER 4

Problems of Naval Art

NAVAL art is a historical category, since each period of history has its own theory and practice of armed conflict at sea suitably reflecting the point reached in the development of material means for such conflict.

In the course of the centuries-old history of navies, naval art has developed unevenly. It has known smooth, gradual movements ahead and tempestuous surges, raising it to a height previously appearing unattainable. Periods of decline mostly coincided with a strengthening of reaction and the stagnation of economic and political life. Flourishing periods usually corresponded to revolutionary events in the life of nations. Such was, for example, the radical change in military affairs associated with the victory of the Great October Socialist Revolution which opened a broad path to creativity of the popular masses, cleared the way for great revolutionary transformations in military matters necessary to the young socialist state for the struggle against the imperialists, seeking to take from the people the power they had gained.

Naval art, like any other scientific theory, is intimately connected with practice, and rests on the lessons from past wars and the many-sided experience of operational and combat training conducted in peacetime. Practice is a criterion of the truth. Without study of the experience of past wars and its critical application, the development of naval art cannot be ensured. Study of historical experience on the basis of dialectical materialism is a method of grasping the patterns of armed struggle at sea, the laws, lines and directions of the development of naval art.

The development of naval art is closely tied to the development of military art, despite the fact that for all the identity of the goals of land forces and navies, the tasks and modes of their operation, determined by the medium and means of struggle, substantially differ.

Fleet against Fleet and Fleet against Shore

The main tasks of land forces, as is known, has always been the destruction of the opposing foe in order to take over his territories and possessions. In a given case the tasks of the operations of land forces in the purely military sense might be figuratively expressed by the phrase "soldier against soldier". This is not so in the sphere of the navy. As well as the tasks of fighting an enemy fleet, it is also faced with tasks associated with the operations against territories and groupings of troops therein. Thus, the formula "soldier against soldier", translated into terms of the fleet, takes on the form "fleet against fleet and fleet against shore".

The correlation of these two tasks throughout history has naturally not always been constant. Among the operations of fleet against fleet one may include battles and operations to destroy the ships of the enemy at sea and in the bases, and the struggle on oceanic and sea communications (disruption, defence). A vivid example of this is provided by the campaigns, sea operations and battles of the First World War, in the course of which the fleets acted little against the shore. But history also provides many examples of active operations of the fleet against the shore.

Traditional were the staging of sea landings of varying size and the delivery of strikes of ship armament on targets located on shore. The new modes of operations of a fleet against the shore consist in delivering a strike of carrier aviation on ground targets and groupings of troops, and in the destruction by nuclear missile strikes from submarines of land targets of great strategic and economic importance.

Since the goals of a war were achieved mostly by taking over the territory of the enemy, successful operations of a fleet against the shore brought a better result than the operations of fleet against fleet. In the first case the fleet solved a direct "territorial" task, whereas in the second, victory over the enemy's fleet merely created the pre-requisites for the later solution of territorial tasks.

True, such pre-requisites in individual cases were of paramount importance as compared with the actions of land forces connected with them. For example, the defeat by the English navy of the so-called invincible Spanish Armada in the Atlantic Ocean completely excluded the possibility of invasion of the territory of England by Spanish land troops. The defeat of the French squadron at Aboukir Bay already mentioned, pre-determined the failure of the Napoleonic plan to conquer Egypt. The crushing by the American navy of the Spanish squadrons in the Greater Antilles Islands and of the Philippines in fact decided the fate of the territorial claims of the Americans and the outcome of the Spanish-American war.

The decisive and active operations of the Soviet navy in the sea theatres in the period of the Great Patriotic War forced the German command to abandon completely attempts to use their fleet against Soviet land forces and the capture of territory from the sea directions, even when they had the strategic initiative.

Let us take a closer look at the relationship of these two main directions in the combat activity of navies.

The final results of the operations of a fleet against an enemy fleet have been achieved by different methods, determined by the material-technical base at the disposal of the fleets in a particular period of history.

Characteristic of the fleets of antiquity was the clash of a mass of vessels passing into a disordered tussle, as the victor of which emerged the fleet with the larger complement and possessing ships of greater strength than the enemy. In the age of sailing fleets, this struggle had the character of rivalry between comparatively small squadrons of battleships in mutual display on extensive sea expanses and occupation of a more advantageous position for manoeuvre and use of one's own weapons. Ever greater importance was assumed by the combination of manoeuvre and fire-power of the battle forces, representing the highest concentration of strike power of the fleet against similar forces of the enemy. This aspect of the operations of essentially homogeneous forces also persisted in the initial stage of development of steam fleets, the principles of the use of which differed little from those adopted in sailing fleets.

As fleets developed, with formation of diverse forces (submarine and aircraft) and also the widening of the arsenal of naval weapons (guns, torpedoes and mines), the opposition of fleets at sea assumed ever new features. The gun duels of different ships were augmented by attacks of light, rapid, non-armoured torpedo forces, submarines and aircraft. The operations of fleet against fleet therefore required great diversity in planning. Sea tactics began to look at battles of diverse forces with their wide interaction in combination with major defence measures and other forms of maintenance. The appearance of rocket weapons accentuated this tendency. Its latest expression is the fight against weapons which has assumed almost the same importance as the destruction of ships—carriers of these weapons. In individual cases it may become the sole means of ship defence.

The evolution of forms of combat operations of the fleet helps to define the tendency towards a further complication of this process considered.

The use of missiles with nuclear warheads, for example, generates major and complex problems associated with the appraisal of the balance of forces in the operation of fleet against fleet at sea and in protection of its forces.

Now the criterion of comparability of the potential of fleets is the ratio of their overall combat power in different combinations of diverse forces and resources for different variants of a situation. An objective approach to the determination of fighting power of the forces of the fleet helps to determine a necessary and sufficient composition of forces in the most rational combination, which we called balanced.

Analysis of sea engagements, battles and operations suggests that despite very decisive operations in counterposing the forces of the fleets, their results, as a rule, were no more than operational. Some exceptions are, for example, the results of the sea engagements in the 1898 Spanish-American War, the 1904-05 Russo-Japanese War and also the attack of the Japanese fleet on Pearl Harbor in December 1941. At the same time the totality of the operations of a fleet against an enemy fleet in war was often of strategic importance. Thus, for example, of undoubted strategic importance were the sea campaigns of the Russian fleet in the Mediterranean in the eighteenth to nineteenth centuries, the struggle for Atlantic communications in the First and Second World Wars and also the operation of the Soviet fleet in the years of the Great Patriotic War in the sea theatres adjoining our territory. Should world imperialism launch a new world war the prevention of nuclear strikes from the sea would undoubtedly be of a strategic character.

An important feature of the forces of a fleet in operations against an enemy fleet is their relatively greater independence than in operations against the shore. This is largely determined by the fact that the operations of fleet against fleet occur predominantly in areas of the seas and oceans distant from the coast, where the forces of the navy can in the main fulfil their combat tasks. In this sphere the fleet makes fullest use of such qualities as high readiness for immediate action, mobility, ability to be at sea for a long time and wage a battle with the enemy fleet a long way from the areas of its permanent home. The realization of such qualities, as indicated by numerous examples from wars of the past, has always given advantages to that side which has been able to combine and use them for achieving the goals of war.

The tendency now taking shape towards a mutual interlinking of the spheres of combat operations by branches of the armed forces, due to the development of military technology, introduces certain corrections into this thesis. However, at the present time too the fleet has a leading role in the fight against an enemy fleet.

The operations of fleet against fleet encompass the extensive field of the operational and strategic use of this branch of the armed forces in sea and oceanic theatres. Such use of the fleet may be regarded as a bitter struggle waged in two main directions.

The first is based on operations of the forces of fleet against fleet in pure form, i.e. not directly connected with the simultaneous solution of other tasks, either in sea or continental theatres.

The hub of these operations in the past was the fight of the main forces of the fleets of the adversaries against one another with the aim of gaining dominance at sea and seizing and keeping the strategic initiatives in the theatre to ensure the solution of the next tasks stemming from the aims of the war or campaign.

In the epoch of sailing fleets these were general engagements of the battle forces. Later, steam fleets tended to conduct such engagements according to established tradition, right up to the end of the First World War. The last such engagement was at Jutland. The final result of this engagement was totally unlike what each of the opposing sides wanted to see. This expressed the objective pattern of the development of the fleets and naval art, consisting in the fact that general engagements which before could materially change the situation at sea in favour of one of the belligerents not only lost their importance but became practically unrealistic. At the same time the sphere of use of the main strike forces of the fleets for taking on equals, in the hope of gaining dominance at sea, narrowed. There was an ever stronger tendency, becoming paramount in the course of the Second World War, for the general scope of the operations of the forces of fleet against fleet through successive and simultaneous operations and battles in different directions or theatres to increase, both independently and in interaction with other branches of the armed forces.

Examples of this may be afforded by the operations of part of the forces of the English fleet in destroying the grouping of ships of the Italian fleet at Taranto. As a result of this operation, the British in fact gained dominance in the Mediterranean, but could not retain it in the course of the war. They ended up in a difficult position after a strong grouping of German aviation, specially switched there, developed active operations in the Mediterranean.

One year after the operation in Taranto, the Japanese, using the aircraft-carrying forces of their fleet, struck at the main grouping of the US Navy in Pearl Harbor with the aim of gaining dominance in the Pacific.[1]

[1] The Americans lost 18 large fighting ships, of which four battleships were destroyed and four put out of action for a long time.

Thus, the Second World War, with little exception, did not in fact provide classical examples of the independent operations of fleet against fleet to gain and hold dominance at sea.

The second direction of this form of combat operations of fleet against fleet is provided by actions associated with operations against the shore and also to ensure trans-oceanic or sea communications. Without exaggeration it may be stated that most of the combat clashes of the major forces of the opposing fleets in this war took this direction. Thus, the battles off Midway Island and in the Philippines Sea and in the area of Wake Island, Rabaul and Port Moresby and others were a constituent part of sea-landing operations in the Pacific. At the same time clearly falling within the category of operations associated with maintaining communications are the battles off Cape Matapan, the operations to destroy the German battleship *Bismarck,* and others.

The equipping of the fleets with nuclear missile weapons has now accentuated the manifestation of the tendency for the importance of the operations of fleet against shore to grow.

Analysis of the views of specialists in different countries on the direction of development of the forces and resources of the fleets in the last ten to fifteen years suggests that in modern conditions the role of opposition of the fleets, undertaken to achieve the objectives of other operations, continues to grow. An exception may be operations in theatres limited in size where the possible attempts of one of the opposing sides to attain dominance in a given theatre cannot be discounted. Such a course of events may be characteristic of a situation when one of the sides has indisputable superiority in a given specific theatre. Here, we have in mind events similar to those which came about in the Gulf of Tonkin during the war against the Vietnamese people, where the American Seventh Fleet, possessing overwhelming superiority in force, sought throughout the war to transform this superiority into dominance at sea in the zone of operations of its main forces.

However, the course and outcome of a major war will be determined by events on a global scale and by decisive objectives, to attain which each of the opposing sides will strive. This will be precisely the idea behind the use of strike forces of the fleets. In other words, all spheres of opposition of the forces of the fleets in modern conditions will be increasingly influenced by the use of ways and means of deploying the forces directly connected with the operations against the shore. The transition of the operations of the fleet from operational-tactical to a higher strategic level brings these operations into the category of determinant, overriding all others, including those directed at gaining dominance at sea. And while earlier the crux of the efforts of a fleet was directed against the enemy fleet, now the chief goal of a fleet is becoming that of ensuring the fulfilment of all tasks associated with action against enemy ground objectives and the protection of one's territory from the strikes of his fleet.

In speaking of the operations of the fleet against the shore it must be emphasized that they are just as old a form of using the fleet as the operations of fleet against fleet. The most vivid examples are those connected with the "marche-manoeuvre" of troops across the sea and their landing on hostile territory (invasion force), which have been undertaken by fleets throughout their history.

As far back as the fifth century B.C., in the course of the Greek-Persian Wars, the Persians used the fleet for landing troops in the rear of the Greek army. In the third century B.C., during the so-called Punic Wars, the Romans undertook large landing operations which played a major role in the battle against Carthage.

In a later period, one may mention the numerous landings of the Russian fleet staged on the Swedish coast in 1720-21 in the course of the Northern War, and on the island of Corfu, the landing of the Japanese on the Liaotung peninsula in 1904, the landing of German Fascist troops in Norway in 1940, the landing operations conducted by the Soviet Navy in the years of the Great Patriotic War and also landings during the Second World War.

The role and significance of landings and the intensity of this form of operations of the fleet have changed in different periods of history. In many cases the emphasis has been on landings in war. For example, Napoleon in his plans to crush England (at a time when the French still had hopes of gaining dominance in the English Channel) envisaged disembarking on the British Isles a strategic invasion force for which was trained the so-called Boulogne expedition which, however, was not undertaken because of the setbacks of the French fleet in the struggle against the Royal Navy. It should be noted that this event is seen by the English and, by following them, other historians to be the outcome of the indisputable superiority of the English fleet and its naval art over the French fleet and the art of its deployment. But the actual causes of the success of the English consisted primarily in that onesidedness of the strategy of Napoleon which stemmed from his fondness for operations in land theatres and a misreading of the role of the fleet, the neglect of its possibilities in a war and hence inability to use it in a struggle against a maritime opponent, as was England at that time.

This onesidedness of the strategic thinking of Napoleon was undoubtedly grasped by Napoleon himself, as witness his intention to shift the blame for blunders in the use of the fleet on to his admirals. Therefore, he was evidently not altogether frank when, in connection with the failures of the fleet he wrote to his naval minister: "All the sea expeditions undertaken since I became head of government have always been unsuccessful because the admirals do not see things as they are and have learnt—I do not know how—that one can wage war without risk."[2] (Translated from Russian.)

The trouble here was, of course, not only the admirals and their passivity, although they were distinguished neither by resoluteness nor high fleet command art. When Napoleon needed talented marshals to realize his plans of campaigns on land, he was able to find them in the army. And the fact that the French fleet in the course of these campaigns repeatedly sustained defeats serves as further confirmation of the inability of Napoleon to evaluate in good time the possibilities available to the French fleet and to use it in the struggle against the enemy.

Later, in the course of the Second World War, the Japanese and Americans

[2] Quoted in B. B. Zherve, *The Naval Strategy of Napoleon*, p. 34, Petrograd, 1922 (in Russian).

set much store by landing operations in the Pacific Ocean. It should be noted that the decisive sea engagements of this theatre occurred precisely during landing operations. These engagements naturally assumed the form of the operations of fleet against fleet, although their general purpose was the purpose characteristic of operations of fleet against shore.

It must be added that the opening of a second front, that is, the staging of a strategic landing in Europe in the period of the Second World War, due to the successes of Soviet troops in the fight against the Hitlerites, depended on the ability of the Allied fleet operating successfully against the shore.

At the same time one cannot help noting that in the course of the First World War only five landings were staged and the biggest landing operation undertaken by the English, in an attempt to disembark off the Dardanelles, failed completely.

The operations of the fleet against the shore in the form of landings in the Second World War assumed such wide proportions and were of such great importance that they gave rise to a special direction in the development and building of fleets—the creation of numerous transport-landing and disembarking devices. In the period of the war over 600 landings were mounted. These number about nine landings a month or, on average, one landing every three days. In ten major landing operations alone some 1,700,000 men were put ashore. Over 18,000 ships took part in the landing operations. It is significant that nearly all the landings were successful. The Soviet navy also widely employed seaborne landings.

It should be noted that landing operations of the fleets in the Second World War were mostly of a tactical and operational character and only individual landings were of strategic importance.[3]

The fleets throughout their history have also made wide use of such a form of operations against the shore as armament strikes on objectives located in the coastal belt. Here we have in mind not the armament preparations conducted in the course of a battle for disembarking an invasion force by specially planned ordnance strikes, the delivery of which exhausted a given combat operation. Such a form was best developed in the period of the Second World War and also in local wars unleashed by the imperialists in the post-war period.

As an example Table 22 gives some data characterizing the operations of the British Navy in naval bombardment of objectives in the coastal belt in the Second World War.

Large forces of the fleet were mustered for gun strikes on shore objectives. The formations set aside for solving this task included battleships, cruisers and destroyers. In the war against Vietnam the Americans for this purpose took out of mothballs and brought into service the battleship *New Jersey*. The groupings of forces operating against the Vietnamese shore in composition were essentially operational and the result achieved by them did not go beyond the limit of tactical. Such operations of the fleet against the shore, as a rule, did not produce the results expected despite the enlistment of considerable forces.

[3] Among the strategic landings of the Second World War we may include: the landing of German Fascist troops in Norway in 1940, the Japanese on the Philippine islands in 1941-42, the Anglo-Americans in North Africa in 1942, in Italy in 1943 and in Normandy in 1944, and the Americans in the Philippines in 1944.

The swift development of aviation and shipbuilding brought into being in the course of the Second World War such a new form of use of the forces of the fleet against the shore as the delivery of strikes by carrier-based aircraft on the territory and troops of the enemy.

TABLE 22

Results of Armament Strikes of the British Fleet on Coastal Belt Objectives in the Second World War

Target of strike	Composition of strike grouping of forces	Losses from gun fire
Mers-el-Kebir 3 July 1940	Force H: 2 battleships, 1 battle cruiser, 1 aircraft-carrier, 2 light cruisers, 11 destroyers	Battleship *Bretagne* sunk; the battleships *Dunkerque* and *Provence* and one destroyer damaged.
Genoa 9 February 1941	Force H: 2 battleships, 1 aircraft-carrier, 1 light cruiser, 10 destroyers	Electrical plant and arms factories badly damaged. Fires and explosions at the base and in the town. No ships in the base.
Tripoli 21 April 1941	The combined Mediterranean Fleet: 3 battleships, 1 aircraft-carrier, 4 light cruisers, 13 destroyers, 1 submarine	Three cargo vessels sunk, some cargo vessels and other ships damaged. Fires, destruction of several buildings.

Note. the attacking forces suffered no losses.

Admittedly, the experience of such operations was limited to the use of aircraft-carriers of only three countries—Britain, Japan and the USA. However, it became convincing proof of the desirability of using this form of operation, which led to a considerable expansion of the building of aircraft-carriers. While at the start of the Second World War the three countries had respectively seven, six and five carriers, in December 1941, by the start of the war in the Pacific, Britain already had in service twelve carriers, Japan ten and the USA seven. In the war years 221 aircraft-carrying ships were built. By the end of the Second World War the USA had 118 carriers, including twenty strike carriers, that is, capable of attacking not only warships but also enemy ground objectives.

At first, aircraft-carriers were regarded only as ships providing fighter cover from air attack for surface forces and cargo vessels. Then on them fell the task of destroying the fighting surface ships of the enemy at sea and at the bases. Later, carrier aviation operated widely against ground objectives also in the course of landing and anti-landing operations, likewise in operations and combat actions aimed at weakening enemy aviation groupings.

Examples of this are provided by the strikes on the Gilbert, Marshall, Wake and Marcus Islands and on Tokyo in 1942. These raids were carried out under the motto "hit and run". Important ground objectives, including naval ones, came under attack in the operations to destroy the forces of the enemy fleet at the bases. The most characteristic examples were British carrier aircraft at

Taranto in November 1940 and Japanese carrier aircraft at Pearl Harbor in December 1941.

The operations of aircraft-carriers against the shore came into the widest use in landing operations when aircraft were used for "softening up", subduing the anti-landing defences of the enemy and giving aid to their troops in solving the tasks on shore after landing. The experience of the Second World War in the use of carrier aviation against ground objectives was widely used by American militarists in local wars, especially for striking at troops, towns, bases, aerodromes and ground communications in the wars against the Korean People's Democratic Republic and the Democratic Republic of Vietnam.

The introduction of nuclear weapons into the fleets of the great powers considerably widened the sphere of the use of the forces of the fleets against the shore. At first carrier aviation, and then ballistic missiles launched from submarines, determined the enormous possibilities the fleet had to strike at the territory of the enemy. The operations of fleet against shore assumed fundamentally new significance in war as a whole. They constituted an important part of its strategy.

Today, a fleet operating against the shore is able not only to solve the tasks connected with territorial changes but to directly influence the course and even outcome of a war. In this connection the operations of a fleet against the shore have assumed paramount importance in armed conflict at sea, governing the technical policy of building a fleet and the development of naval art. Confirmation of this is that in the USA atomic-powered missile submarines are assigned to the strategic forces and all other ships to the general-purpose forces.

The new possibilities of a fleet in operations against the shore and the resulting serious threat from oceanic directions have determined the character of the main efforts of a fleet in the struggle against an enemy fleet. The most important of them has become the use of the forces of the fleet against the naval strategic nuclear systems of the enemy with the aim of disrupting or weakening to the maximum their strikes on ground objectives. Thus, the fight of a fleet against the fleet of an enemy in the new conditions since nuclear weapons have appeared has become a secondary task as compared with the operations of a fleet against the shore.

This also changes the significance of the operations of the fleet fulfilling such traditional tasks as disruption of the sea communications of the enemy and protection of one's own. These operations are now the most important constituent part of the efforts of a fleet, aimed at undermining the military-economic potential of the enemy, that is, at solving one of the special tasks arising from the main tasks of a modern fleet in war.

Operations to disrupt and cut off the sea shipments of the enemy, which used to come directly into the sphere of use of a fleet against an enemy fleet, are now assuming a new direction. Forming part of the general system of operations of a fleet against the shore, they are accentuating the special function of a fleet which it has acquired thanks to modern means of combat—the ability to fulfil strategic tasks of an offensive character by directly acting on the sources of the enemy's military power.

Thus, the traditional operations of fleet against fleet which, since ancient times, have been characteristic of the struggle against sea communications of the opposing sides, are now being used in a new, decisive sphere—operations of a fleet against the shore. This trend in the operational and strategic use of the fleet is becoming increasingly prominent and assuming the features of the main field of operations of a fleet, governing all others at all operational levels.

Some Theoretical Problems of Naval Art

Naval art and the ways of using the navy in modern conditions of possible combat operations will greatly differ from those which have dominated in past wars, including the Second World War. Therefore, in considering the navy as the most important of the components of the sea power of the state, we shall deal, though briefly, with certain principles of the use of a modern fleet which the theory of naval art is now evolving.

A most important feature of the current stage in the development of naval art is the intensive extension of its size and composition and the increasingly many-sided elaboration of new forms and ways of using the forces of the fleet at different operational levels. This is due primarily to the influence of scientific and technical progress, resulting in sharp qualitative changes in modes of combat, which ultimately means profound qualitative transformations in the material-technical base of armed struggle at sea. The formation and verification in the course of combat training and the constant improvement of new forms of using the forces of the fleet, new modes of operations in a different situation are naturally connected with change in the many categories, forming in their entirety the content of naval art. These categories are most sensitive to the transformation of all factors influencing the development of naval art. Therefore, changes in these categories may be regarded as the first manifestations of an objective multi-facetted process of the development of naval art as a whole.

Change in many categories of naval art and the impact of objective factors is manifest at all its levels. For example, one may speak of the interaction of the forces and control of them in their strategic, operational and tactical aspects. This applies in equal measure to such concepts as manoeuvre, strike, concentration, and many others. At the same time such concepts as battle, attack and others are characteristic only of tactics.

Without considering the whole variety of categories relating to the field of naval art we shall dwell only on those which may be used as an example, as it seems to us, to trace the general tendencies of the development of this branch of naval science.

Scope of Conflict

Increase in the potential of the fleet for solving strategic tasks determines the growth of its role and importance in war.

A modern navy possesses universality and mobility and is capable of concentrating strike power which may be used not only for fighting a sea foe but also in the sphere of operations of other branches of the armed forces. Thanks to this, the scope of the armed struggle at sea is increasing to global proportions.

In looking at this category from the strategic angle it is also necessary to note the constantly growing ability of nuclear fleets to achieve ever more decisive objectives in a modern war. This particularly applies to the operations of the forces of the fleet aimed at wrecking the military-economic potential of the enemy, which may have a direct impact on the course, and even on the outcome, of a war.

The individual operations conducted by a fleet are greater and greater in scope. The expansion of the potential of a fleet in solving the tasks of destroying ground objectives results in an extension of the front and an increase in depth of the influence exercised by naval strategic weapons systems. For example, the potential of this influence by the American submarine strategic nuclear *Polaris-Poseidon* system in the past ten years has more than doubled. Hoping to go over to the new *Trident* submarine nuclear missile system, on which the Western press writes so much, the Americans expect to double its influence as compared with the *Polaris-Poseidon* system. It is also planned to widen its front of influence. With the completion of the change-over of the American armed forces to an oceanic strategy, apparently operations against ground objectives will also assume global proportions. The further extension of the spatial sweep of operations against ground objectives is not only a present but also a future tendency of the development of the naval art of nuclear fleets. Probably it is also manifest in operations in the sphere of combating naval strategic nuclear weapons systems which may encompass almost the whole extent of the World Ocean and assume a global character.

In looking at such an element of the scope of operations as the composition of usable forces, it must be noted that the sharp expansion of the potential of the forces in offence and defence is more and more often being achieved not only and not so much in the traditional way—simple increase in the number of ships and other weapon carriers. Increasing prominence is being assumed by such a factor as the increased ability of each ship to solve diverse tasks, using more sophisticated weapons. In other words, the prevailing criterion in evaluating the actual potential of the groupings of forces is now becoming not the number of carriers but their quality, expressed in the aggregate strike power of the weapons concentrated on them and combat tactical resources. For example, after the end of the Second World War in 1945 the submarine forces of the US fleet were represented by 263 submarines. Now, according to the data of Jane's reference work for 1973-74, this fleet totals only 127 submarines, 41 of which are atomic-powered missile carriers, 61 multi-purpose atomic ships and 25 diesels, although their total power bears no comparison with the power of earlier submarines. Thanks to their power they are a most important part of the strategic resources of the fleet of that country.

Groupings of other branches of the armed forces may, on an ever-increasing scale, form part of the forces enlisted to take part in operations in the oceanic theatres. This determines the new possibilities for total realization of a further category of naval art, stemming from the strategy of armed conflict in the oceanic theatres of military operations—interactions. Its advent in the framework of a unified military strategy, in turn, is nothing other than an expression of the continuing process of shaping the categories of naval art corresponding to the modern material means of waging armed conflict.

Strike

The growth of the power of naval weapons at a particular stage of its development brought a quite new understanding of such a category as strike. Earlier, the concept of strike was accompanied by the modifying adjectival definitions "gun", "torpedo", "bomb" and at one time "ram"; that is, this category was considered only a tactical concept and only in individual cases, for example in the expression "strike from the sea", did it assume the importance of a concept of operational status. Now the concept of strike has been extended to the attaining of strategic goals. It is considered that strike is becoming the dominant form of use of forces since it allows modern combat operations to realize to the full their potential from enormous distances and different directions, and thereby even attain such a strategic objective as devastation of the military-economic potential of an enemy.

In operational art, the strike is increasingly asserting itself as one of the basic methods of solving combat tasks. The strike in each operation is not only the totality of the specific combat actions welded together by unity of purpose or tasks. It may also be independent and even a single-act operation of a single weapons carrier or a group of them. For example, a strike on a grouping of surface forces may be delivered by a group of ships armed with guided missiles. Naval aviation is equally able to discharge such a task.

In the tactical link the strike, unlike in the past, when it was only one among elements of a battle and was regarded as a set of attacks, held together by the unity of a tactical task, is increasingly becoming tantamount to a battle. For example, by delivering a strike on a submarine of the enemy or the missiles launched by it, the combat task may be solved. A large surface ship may be destroyed by a strike by one submarine using long-range missiles. The further development of this tendency is promoted by the constant increase in the range and power of naval weapons, which makes it impossible in certain conditions to solve tactical tasks not by sustained and stubborn opposition but by a unilateral, single-act action against the enemy.

Thus, strategic, operational and tactical objectives can be reached by strikes. In individual cases the strike delivered "under the norms and rules of tactics", for example, by missiles from a submarine on land targets, can immediately bring strategic results. This is an already new quality in a category as customary for us as the strike, which is undergoing changes in the process of development of the material base of armed struggle at sea and its necessary naval art.

Battle

The battle always was and remains the main means of solving tactical tasks. For a long time it remained the sole form of combat use of the navy. Like any phenomenon, battle undergoes continuous evolution. One of the features of this process is increase in the distances of combat clashes and their spatial sweep, determined by the growth of the range of action of naval weapons, manoeuvrability in different planes and media, independent operational potential and range of sailing (flight) of its carriers and also by participation in battle of other branches of the forces of the fleet, primarily aviation. At the dawn of the development of the fleets it was practically impossible to say anything about the distances over which battles were fought, since the solution of the task was determined by the possibilities of capturing an enemy by boarding or by ramming him. Gradually, the range of action of weapons increased and ships on opposing sides became capable of striking the enemy at ever greater distances. Already in the years of the Second World War they began to exceed not only the range of optical visibility but also the range of the technical means of observation existing at that time.

The first battle at sea which paved the way for "non-contact" combat operation of ships was the engagement off Midway Island on 4 June 1942. In modern conditions these ranges already run into several hundreds of kilometres. And it may be confidently stated that in the future the sea battle will, as a rule, proceed over enormous spaces, and ascertaining the situation will be possible only with the aid of special essentially aerial or cosmic devices.

Development of the sea battle as a form of utilization of fleet forces has always been attended by change in its three-dimensional character. At first the battle represented a clash of the surface forces only on the surface of the water, then it embraced the underwater and aerial media. Ever-growing importance in a modern sea battle is being assumed by its specific attributes, expressed in the fact that the opposing sides are directing an ever greater part of their efforts at combating the torpedo or missile already released by the enemy, gradually cutting down the share of the efforts aimed at destroying the carriers of these weapons. Thus, the sea battle is already assuming a new quality.

In many cases the battle may not include such an obligatory element of the past as tactical deployment. Deployment may be carried out in good time. In this case, to construct the most rational combat orders with change in the tactical situation as a result of a manoeuvre by a probable enemy or with change in the composition of his forces, the forces may be pre-deployed. It is assumed that the elements of tactics forming the content of the classical scheme of the sea battle—seek out the enemy, tactical deployment and delivery of strikes after the weapon carrier has moved into the release position—will also persist in the future.

The strike and defensive potential of the forces of the fleet is constantly increasing and this gives grounds for asserting that in the future, to overcome the organized and deeply-staggered defence of the enemy in a battle, tactical interaction of diverse forces will be necessary. However, in individual cases, because of the sharp growth of the strike potential of the forces of the fleet, outstripping their defensive capacities, the waging of a battle with homogeneous forces will apparently also remain realistic.

The further growth of the destructive power of weapons and timely deployment will shorten the time for solving combat tasks. The quickening of the pace of development of events will introduce changes in a category such as the battle. It will become more fleeting, dynamic and productive.

A special feature of the sea battle is that it has nearly always been waged to destroy the enemy. The equipping of the forces of the fleets with nuclear weapons is further accentuating this feature.

Interaction

Interaction is, as is known, one of the most important categories of naval art. The rational combination of offensive and defensive potential of diverse groupings, compensating the weak points of some forces by the strong points of others, helps to solve tasks considerably exceeding those which are solved by the usual co-ordination of homogeneous forces.

The organization of interaction, as the range of action of weapons, their diversity, power and speed of their carriers increased, has steadily become more complicated. At present its importance and potential are growing, thanks to the development of the means of communication and control.

Under the influence of scientific and technical progress, technical means of combat are becoming more sophisticated and therefore new possibilities for mutual penetration into the spheres of combat actions of other branches of the armed forces are appearing. The importance of tactical and operational interaction in solving any task by the fleets is growing. Tactical interaction of non-homogeneous forces in combating nuclear missile weapon-carriers will be organized where there is an acute need to solve the task in the shortest time possible.

The potential for other branches of the armed forces operating jointly with the fleet in the sphere of tasks of the latter, like the possibilities for the fleet solving tasks on land and in the air, will steadily increase.

The extension of the spheres of combat operations of branches of the armed forces will undoubtedly complicate the organization of their interaction at operational and strategic levels.

Thus, in the near future the organization of interaction will become even more complicated, the degree of its importance will grow and its forms and methods will become more varied.

Manoeuvre

The manoeuvre is the oldest category of naval art. Fire and manoeuvre for long practically formed the core of naval tactics. Thanks to the manoeuvre, the forces of the fleet were able to bring weapons to such a level where the possibilities of these weapons could be fully realized in a strike, and, in addition, in certain cases the necessary concentration of forces be achieved. It should be noted that as the range of weapons lengthened, manoeuvre in battle carried out at tactical deployment stage constantly contracted linearly. With the appearance of naval guns, it was no longer necessary to draw up to the enemy and the manoeuvre became shorter. When naval ordnance became rifled, it contracted still further and after the advent of rockets, with a flight range beyond the horizon and high accuracy of hit of the target, assumed new qualities. The replacement in considerable measure of the manoeuvre of the weapon carrier by the manoeuvre with trajectories of weapons proved quite realistic. For example, the area within which it is possible to strike at the enemy with naval armaments with a firing range of 20 km is 1256 sq. km. With use of missiles with a firing range of 200 km, this area will be equal to 125,600 sq. km. If it is remembered that with increase in the firing range of weapons by one order of magnitude the area which can be hit by them increases by two orders of magnitude, then it is not difficult to imagine the scale of the potential of the manoeuvre with trajectories of rockets with a flight range of several thousands of kilometres. However, from this it does not follow that the importance of the manoeuvre of forces in a battle will decline, but it will be simpler to undertake.

On the other hand, the manoeuvre of forces beyond the limits of observation of the enemy who, in turn, takes measures to occupy an advantageous position, also beyond the limits of observation, requires it to be backed by reconnaissance and target indication data. The manoeuvre will be carried out on the basis of data received from different radio-electronic sources and in the conditions of the most intensive electronic counter-measures which, given correct organization, may completely paralyse the system of monitoring the situation and the receipt of information. Therefore the carrying-out of the manoeuvre and use of different technical means for monitoring the situation and target designation demand true art. The acute need arises for coherent interaction of strike groups, not only with the reconnaissance forces but also with the units of external target designation. Undoubtedly, it will still be necessary to secure a manoeuvre and concentrate forces, equipped with such short-range weapons as the torpedo and guns, which unquestionably will continue to remain for arming the fleets of the future.

Manoeuvre with ship forces in the future will become swifter with the wide introduction of ships with dynamic support principles into many fleets of the world.

In considering the manoeuvre from the operational angle, we would note that its importance as a form of operation aimed at ensuring the operational deployment of forces and concentrating them in particular areas of the oceanic theatres will greatly grow in the future.

Speed

This is a characteristic category of modern naval art particular to all forms and variants of combat operations at sea. Its expression is connected with the development of the means of armed struggle, thanks to which the former ways of waging a sea battle, made up of a sustained manoeuvre of the forces and their repeated and prolonged action on the enemy, have gradually lost their importance and have been replaced by dynamic, swift, decisive and increasingly productive combat clashes.

Scientific and technical progress is leading to the creation of ever more mobile weapon-carriers and long-range high-speed means of attack. In the future, therefore, speed will be an integral feature of any operation, battle or strike.

Its manifestation in the operational link will be expressed in further contraction of the duration of action on an enemy, with a simultaneous rise in the power and impact of strikes and combat operations, making up the content of sea operations.

It is precisely the speed of the different groupings of forces aimed at the most important enemy objectives which will become a decisive factor in choosing how they are used. Speed ensures the fullest use of all the combat potential of the forces for the quickest attainment of their objectives in operations and makes their strikes inescapable and irresistible.

The saturation of armed struggle at sea with swiftly-moving operations, strikes and other combat actions makes this struggle particularly dynamic and highly effective. Therefore the combat activity of fleets in the future will be a complex combination of simultaneous and successive swift, rapid combat actions culminating in the attainment of decisive goals and exerting in particular cases a direct influence on the course and outcome of the armed conflict as a whole.

The importance of speed—this most important factor in armed conflict at sea—will grow and the ability to carry out swift actions will become the most important of the indicators of the mastery of naval art.

Time

With the development of naval technology, increase in the speeds of weapon carriers and the range and power of weapons, naval art was faced with the need to solve growing tasks more and more rapidly.

Already in the years of the Second World War the destruction of a particular grouping of the enemy was not always limited to a strictly defined time interval. If, for example, the task was to destroy an enemy convoy en route at sea, it could be solved at any moment during its passage, lasting days and even weeks. And whether the task set was accomplished at the start or end of this period was not of fundamental importance. The only important thing was to accomplish it while the grouping of enemy ships was at sea.

Now such an approach will often be inapplicable. In a number of cases the groupings of the forces of an enemy fleet will have to be destroyed in a definite very short time interval, before they can make full use of their weapons.

An important feature of the change in the significance of the category considered is that the time necessary for solving strategic tasks by the fleet after the start of military operations will be of the same order as the time necessary for solving tactical tasks.

As the means of armed conflict at sea continue to develop, this will become increasingly obvious. The growing demands for shortening the times of solving tasks decisive for the development of all forms of armed conflict at sea have made it necessary to keep the forces of the fleet in readiness for immediate delivery of strikes on the enemy and all-round automation of the control of these forces.

In considering the categories of naval art it is also desirable to take a look at the creation of certain conditions which ensure the attainment by the forces of the fleet of the goals set. Without going into the whole diversity of such conditions, we feel it necessary to dwell on those ensuring the freedom of action of their forces in a battle and operation, and, at the same time, creating serious interference for the enemy. In other words we have in mind what is often called dominance in the area of operations of one's forces or simply dominance at sea.

Dominance at sea

This is a special category particular solely to the armed conflict in marine theatres. The naval forces do not form a line of a front, they are mobile, their operations are not connected with moving through, capture or retention of certain spaces. They operate on "no man's water" in stretches where there is no "sovereign" ruler since international conventions recognize the principle of the sea open (free) to all. Victory in a sea battle or an operation does not always mean the achievement of territorial changes. Moreover, the victor is often in a hurry to quit the battlefield as is done, for example, by submarines after an attack, although it may have resulted in heavy enemy losses. However, any fleet always seeks to create in a particular area of the sea the regime necessary for it, for example, to gain control of shipping and ensuring its safety, freedom to deploy one's forces, etc.

Naval losses are hard to make good. Therefore, each defeat inflicted on an enemy means not only the achievement of the goal of the given combat clash but the creation of favourable conditions for quite a long time for solving the next task. It largely deprives the enemy of the possibility, sometimes for a long time, of undertaking organized action of an offensive nature and creates a very specific situation. This situation is characterized by the fact that the victor is free to choose the time, directions and character of the offensive operations, sometimes using for this even weak groupings of his forces.

Depriving the enemy of the possibility of staging a determined counter-action, the victor can exploit this victory by severing the sea shipments of the enemy by blockading his ports, bases and coastal areas, seizing islands and some distant territories or can deliver without hindrance strikes against the shore.

For the defeated side, if its economy was closely dependent on sea communications or if its fleet was the main part of its armed forces, loss of dominance at sea in the distant past could have meant even defeat in a war.

In speaking of the "age" of this category of naval art, then without fear of error it may be boldly asserted that history does not know of a more ancient and hardier concept. The idea of dominance at sea appeared when the use of the sea spaces began to be used in wars by specially-created organized naval forces.

Close attention to dominance at sea was paid in the period of colonial seizures, carried out with the aid of the fleets of the powers of western Europe, primarily England, which, to justify her striving for world dominance by colonial robbery and piracy, used the flighty expression of the well-known English adventurer and pirate Walter Raleigh: "He who is master of the sea is master of world trade. And he who is master of world trade is master of the riches of the earth and of the earth itself". This ominous assertion was more than once repeated by Winston Churchill and now serves as the banner of bellicose circles of English and American imperialism.

The regular Russian navy, the creation of which is associated with the name of Peter the Great, by its resolute actions convincingly demonstrated an understanding of the essence of the idea of dominance at sea and the ability to put this idea into practice. Shattering the sea power of Sweden in the Baltic, it gained for itself freedom of action in the most important areas of the theatre and skilfully used it to force the enemy to sign a peace treaty. The idea of dominance at sea was maintained and developed by the great Russian military chiefs—Suvorov, Potemkin, Ushakov, Spiridov, and others.

On dominance at sea and its importance in the course of a war, Engels wrote in 1865: ". . . If one dominates at sea . . . this is an *advantage*."[4]

In the textbook on naval tactics written for the Russian naval corps in 1873, twenty years earlier than work on this question appeared in England and the USA, Lieutenant-Captain Berezin clearly outlined the theory of dominance at sea and ways of achieving and keeping it. There it was stated: "When a war begins, involving the fleets, attaining dominance at sea is usually the first and principal task. If the forces are greatly incommensurate this task is solved by direct blockade of the roads or the harbours where the hostile squadrons are, and then, of the whole shore; in absence of such incommensurability it is necessary to gain this dominance by inflicting defeats (squadron engagements) on the hostile fleet and only then establish a blockade seeking to destroy the sea trade of the enemy and all his transport by sea." Further Berezin asserted that dominance cannot be absolute, that as well as blockade it is necessary to send cruisers in pursuit of separate vessels of the enemy, that inshore landing operations are possible even without dominance at sea, etc.

Unlike the interpretation of the idea of dominance at sea adopted in Russia, in England, the biggest colonial power in the world, where the "exploitation of the colonies was the principal source of enrichment of the British bourgeoise and maintenance of colonial dominance constituted its principal military task,"[5] political meaning was vested in this concept. In this connection the maintenance of dominance at sea became for the English capital a matter of survival. This idea became the basic guiding principle of English military doctrine.

The idea of dominance at sea was taken as the basis of English military doctrine by Admiral Colomb and his followers. The USA, hurrying by the beginning of the epoch of imperialism, to occupy a leading place among the claimants to world dominance, developed its own theories of dominance at sea, the progenitor of which is recognized to be Admiral Mahan.

Both these authors in their expositions fulfilled the social mission of nascent imperialism and therefore transformed the category of naval art into a political concept of the bourgeoisie bent on world dominance, into an ideological banner

[4] F. Engels, *Selected Military Works* (in Russian), pp. 666-667, Moscow, Voenizdat, 1956.
[5] M. V. Frunze, *Selected Works* (in Russian), Vol. II, p. 12, Moscow, Voenizdat, 1957.

of imperialism. The gaining of dominance at sea was proclaimed as the sole aim of armed struggle at sea, the attainment of which ensures, in their view, the establishment of world dominance.

It is known that serious attention was paid to dominance at sea as a category of naval art by Lenin, making a profound scientific analysis of the causes of the defeat of Russia in the 1904-05 Russo-Japanese war. He wrote: "The Japanese have so far more rapidly and heavily reinforced their military forces after each major engagement than the Russians. And now having won complete dominance at sea and the total destruction of one of the Russian armies they will be able to send twice as many reinforcements as the Russians."[6]

Subsequently, the category of dominance at sea was studied and elaborated in the Soviet navy. Thus, in the 1930 Combat Regulations for the naval forces it was emphasized that it is necessary to create such conditions as will guarantee the secure movement of forces at sea from their bases and the solution by them of the combat task. These conditions include: countering a blockade of the enemy, both by correct choice of the support points, making it difficult for him to continue a blockade, and by combat operations proper to make a blockade impossible or lessen its effectiveness, countering enemy reconnaissance and patrol service.

It must be noted that from its very inception Soviet naval science has completely rejected attempts to equate the concept "dominance at sea" with the concept of "dominance over the world". It always saw the gaining of dominance at sea not as an end in itself but merely a way of creating certain conditions enabling the forces and resources of the fleet to solve successfully particular tasks in specific areas of the theatre in a defined period of time. Therefore, in the Soviet fleet in pre-war years, the term "favourable operational regime" was more widely adopted. In our Regulations it was stressed that this term means the conditions promoting successful solution of the tasks set before the fleet. By these conditions were meant those elements of the situation which make it possible to form the necessary groupings of the forces of the fleet, deliver strikes and perform the combat tasks set without seriously departing from the scheduled plan. To create these conditions it was necessary to wage a stubborn and sometimes quite long struggle with the use of different forces and resources at sea, in the air and in a number of cases in the coastal areas.

In the course of the Great Patriotic War in the basic documents regulating the combat activity of the fleet, the actions of its forces to create the necessary situation for its operations were classified as actions creating the most favourable and stable operational regime in the stationing areas and on the most important communications. Analysis of the combat experience of our fleets helps to define more clearly a number of definitions relating to this category of naval art. At the end of the 'forties, dominance at sea was regarded as the creation of conditions promoting the successful conduct by the fleets of operations at sea and by the sea fronts on land. Strategic dominance at sea (in a theatre) was recognized as the best of these conditions. It was characterized by a favourable position (ratio of forces, their stationing, equipment of theatre, etc.) when the enemy in the whole theatre was not in a position to disrupt operations

[6] V. I. Lenin, *Complete Collected Works* (in Russian), Vol. 9, p. 154.

undertaken by us. In passing we would note that the concept of the sea theatre of combat operations then only referred to the seas directly adjoining the territory of the Soviet Union.

If strategic dominance in a sea theatre was absent, and this was very typical of that time, then the necessary condition for the successful conduct of sea operations was recognized to be the gaining of tactical dominance. By such dominance was understood superiority in forces and resources in the direction of the main strike, achieved by wide and bold manoeuvre with the forces, both in the preparatory stage of the operation and in the course of it, and skilful utilization of the geographical features of the sea theatre and of its equipment.

The difference between strategic and tactical dominance, in the views at that time, consisted only in the size of the space controlled and the duration of the time interval in the course of which this dominance could be held. If strategic dominance served the ends of waging war or a campaign, then tactical dominance served the ends of conducting an operation, a series of battles or even one battle.

The inner content of these two concepts—favourable tactical situation gained for conducting an operation or battle in a particular area of a sea theatre in a period necessary for the reliable warranty of success and a guarantee against the disruption by the enemy of preparation and waging of an operation or battle—remained the same.

With the advent of nuclear weapons, and then missiles, many theoreticians claimed that the question of gaining dominance at sea had receded into the background because new combat and technical means of armed conflict at sea had radically altered the conditions of conducting operations and combat activities, and hence the means of maintaining them.

One of the arguments for denying the need to gain dominance at sea was the claim that since combat activities had become swift and productive, the forces waging a struggle at sea did not need the creation of favourable conditions. Often the question was even posed thus: "What will a fleet do in a nuclear war—destroy the enemy or gain dominance, running the risk of being destroyed by the enemy before he can reach his goals?"

As shown by history, with the development of the material-technical base of the fleets and increase in their combat potential new features of the struggle for dominance at sea came into being, although this struggle itself remained a reflection of the objective reality, determined by the specifics of combat actions at sea.

The growth of the speed of ships and other forces of the fleet and the improvement of the means of communication and reconnaissance have considerably shortened the time span during which dominance at sea can be held. Thus, the English sailing fleet after the battle at Aboukir (1798) established its dominance in the Mediterranean for some years, which accounted for the failure of the Napoleonic expedition to Egypt, despite the fact that French troops had already been landed and had won a series of major victories in land engagements. Dominance of the Japanese fleet gained at the end of 1941 as a result of the smashing of the battle forces of the US Navy in Pearl Harbor and sinking of English battleships in the Gulf of Siam lasted no more than four months.

From these examples it will be seen that the period of keeping the dominance gained at sea tends to shorten and the struggle for gaining it becomes even tougher. This tendency still persists, since the forces and resources of the fleets are being vigorously developed, nuclear missile weapons perfected and naval aviation is coming into ever wider use. It is particularly important to note that submarines have become the main branch of the forces of modern fleets. A major role is also played by the new strategic orientation of the fleets for struggle against the shore. All this is making more necessary the all-round backing of the actions of the forces solving strategic tasks. Therefore, the struggle to create, in a particular area of a theatre and in a particular time, favourable conditions for successfully solving by a large grouping of forces of the fleet, the main tasks facing it, and at the same time creating conditions such as would make it more difficult for the enemy to fulfil his tasks and prevent him from frustrating the actions of the opposing side, will apparently be widely adopted.

The creation of the conditions for gaining dominance at sea has always taken a long time and demanded a number of measures even in peacetime. Among these measures are the creation and preparation of the necessary forces and resources for keeping them in readiness to solve combat tasks, form groupings of forces and such deployment of them in a theatre as to ensure positional superiority over the enemy, and also the equipping of the sea and oceanic theatres of military operations, the corresponding organization of the forces and system of emplacement, the system of control of them, etc, and which serve their purpose.

The interrelationship and interdependence of combat actions of the fleet in solving the main tasks in gaining dominance at sea consist and will evidently continue to consist in the fact that the areas and directions in which dominance at sea is achieved and the time it is held, completely depends on the conditions of fulfilment of the main tasks. Combat actions, the aim of which is to secure dominance at sea in selected areas or in particular directions, may either precede the solution by the fleet of the main tasks or be conducted simultaneously. Consequently, the attainment of dominance at sea is a factor ensuring the success of the actions of the forces solving the main tasks. The successful solution by the fleet of these main tasks ensures the further securing of it of dominance at sea and widening of the sphere of its implementation.

The experience of the Great Patriotic War showed that the success of the actions of land forces and the capture by them of new coastal areas also help to gain dominance at sea. An example of this is the gaining and securing of dominance of our fleets in the Black, Baltic and Barents Seas as a result of the operations conducted by land forces together with the fleets. The German command strove for dominance in the Black and Baltic Seas by capturing the bases of the Soviet fleet from the land. However, the Hitlerites failed to reach this goal. Their plans were foiled by the joint actions of the Soviet army and navy. From this it may be concluded that the gaining of dominance at sea depends both on the solution of the main tasks set before the fleet and on the general course of the armed struggle as a whole.

One cannot help noticing that in undertaking military preparations the imperialists are seeking to create the conditions for gaining dominance at sea at the very start of a war. The idea is to widen the sphere of dominance at sea to the depths of the oceans and the air space above them.

From all this it follows that such a category of naval arts as the gaining of dominance at sea retains its topicality and therefore the elaboration of it in all its aspects relevant to the present, forms one of the important tasks of naval science.

Consequently, the general perspectives of the development of naval art are connected with the continuous growth of demands for the most effective use of the means of combat, the stiffening of the norms of training and use of weapons, rise in the intensity of combat actions, shortening of the times of decision-making and increase in the responsibility of the flag officer. The appearance of long-range and homing weapons, highly-effective cybernetic and automated systems is increasing still further the role of humans in armed conflict at sea.

Important tendencies in the development of naval art are the progressive widening of the object of its investigation, the fields of optimization, and an increase in the role of engineering-technical and physico-mathematical sciences definitely required for solving the theoretical questions of naval art.

Awaiting elucidation are the perspectives of development of such elements of naval art as reconnaissance, camouflage, operational and tactical deployment, combat orders, defence, rear back-up and others.

The Fleets in the Local Wars of Imperialism

The ending of the Second World War did not bring the nations the long-awaited peace. This was impeded by the aggressive, rapacious policy of the imperialist powers seeking to achieve their political ends by the means of an unrestrained nuclear missile arms race and preparations for unleashing at a "suitable time" a nuclear world war. However, bearing in mind the balance of forces in the world arena, continuously changing and not in their favour, the imperialists are trying to achieve their goals in individual areas of the globe by using an extensive arsenal of different methods and forms of activity, an important place among which is taken by local wars, that is, wars limited to the participation of two or a few states. Consequently, they are also limited in their tasks, the territory of operation and the scale and means employed in the armed conflict. The aim of all these wars remains unchanged. It consists in strangling the national liberation movements, keeping former colonies in social and economic dependence, weakening the world socialist system and the capture and holding of strategically important areas of the globe. To wage local wars the imperialists are expending enormous funds and human and material resources. Thus, for example, the war against the Korean People's Democratic Republic cost the USA 20,000 million dollars. Taking part in it on the side of the aggressors were over a million men, over 200 warships, up to 1000 tanks and

1600 planes. Against the national liberation forces of Algeria, France threw in over 500,000 officers and men, some 1500 planes and 1000 tanks.[7]

On the war against the people of Vietnam between 1961 and the beginning of 1973, the USA, according to the official, plainly understated, figures of the Pentagon, spent 140,000 million dollars (according to the figure of Senator Mansfield, almost 400,000 million). At one time and another in this period in Vietnam there were 2,500,000 American servicemen, the number of whom in action in the tensest periods of the war reached 549,000 men. The carrier, strategic and tactical aviation of the USA dropped on towns and villages of Vietnam some 7,500,000 tons of bombs, more than three times the tonnage of the whole Second World War. Despite this, the aggressors were unable to taste the sweetness of victory: with a casualty list (according to Pentagon figures) of about a million officers and men killed and wounded and a loss of 8612 planes and helicopters, the American-Saigon side was forced to recognize the impossibility of achieving the goals set by military means and their own *de facto* defeat in the war.

As shown by experience in local wars, the imperialist powers assign an important role to the naval forces. Thus, for example, the fleets of the USA and Britain have always been unfailing participants in all local wars and conflicts provoked by imperialism in the post-war period. However, the experience of the combat use of the fleets in these wars is very specific since the aggressors, in practice, had no sea adversaries and their fleets operated, in fact, in proving-ground conditions. Yet this experience permits certain conclusions on the development of the fleets and their combat use.

First of all it must be stressed that the fleets of the biggest imperialist powers, the main purpose of which is to solve strategic tasks in a nuclear missile war, are at the same time busily preparing for local wars where they are given a leading role in the suppression of the national liberation and other progressive movements of the peoples. The present-day imperialist powers—the USA, Britain and France—are, in conformity with this, building up their navies which consist both of strategic strike forces equipped with nuclear missile weapons and general-purpose forces, i.e. forces intended to take part both in a nuclear missile war and local wars.

The role of the fleet in local wars is determined by the fact that among the other branches of the armed forces it is best fitted to carry out, on a wide scale, military actions against countries well away from the territories of the aggressor. In the last two decades in all military conflicts where the geographical conditions have allowed, an active part has been taken by large forces of the fleet of one and sometimes several imperialist powers which, it is true, have far from always succeeded in reaching the goals set before them.

In most cases the forces of the fleet have been sent in good time to the areas where it was planned to provoke a sharpening of the situation. Information on the displacements of the groupings of the naval forces of the imperialist states in the World Ocean has often served as a sure sign that a military conflict was coming to a head in a particular area of the globe.

Naval forces are also regarded by the imperialists as the most suitable

[7] See V. Matsulenko, *Local Wars of Imperialism* (1946-68), *Voennoistorichesky zhurnal,* 1968, No. 9, p. 39.

instrument for local wars because they possess high mobility and are capable of remaining for a long time in constant combat readiness in areas of probable military operations without violating the sovereignty of other states too soon and without producing premature international complications.

Another factor considered important in the west is that in local wars the attacking fleet is vulnerable to the response actions of the side subjected to attack since the latter usually does not have sufficient naval and aviation forces.

The high operational combat potential of the forces of a modern fleet give the imperialists the possibility of widening the field of their use in local wars. Thus, the ability of strike aircraft-carriers to deliver strikes on objects as far as 2,000 km away has brought them into the rank of the most important forces in a local war. This circumstance has to no small degree been promoted by the fact that aircraft-carriers were often the only means for bringing the bases of strike aviation closer to the areas of combat operations.

In local wars, as experience shows, a considerable role may also be played by other surface ships—missile carriers, gun-boats, anti-mine and landing ships. They are capable of transporting and landing troops, backing with fire the sea flanks of the groupings of their land forces, delivering missile-gun strikes on the coastal objectives of the country subjected to aggression and performing other tasks. In local wars and conflicts, as one of the main strike forces, wide use has been made of the marines since their formations and units are most suitable groupings and are in high combat readiness for moving by sea or air to the area of aggression.

The idea of the extensive use of naval forces in local wars and conflicts finds expression in the creation by the imperialists of the system of stationing the fleet and also the choice of the areas of its permanent presence in the ocean. Together with deployment of large nuclear missile strategic groupings of the fleet, aimed first and foremost at the Soviet Union and the countries of the socialist community, aggressive circles of the leading imperialist powers are at the same time seeking to keep permanently in strategically important areas of the globe powerful groupings of the fleet intended for waging local wars and for provoking conflicts. These forces of the fleet are always at the ready to fulfil gendarme functions in suppressing national liberation movements in the maritime colonial countries or the developing countries that have recently freed themselves from colonial dependence.

A vivid illustration of this may be afforded by the situation existing in the Mediterranean where are concentrated a large grouping of the atomic-powered missile submarines of the USA pointing their missiles against the socialist countries, the American Sixth Fleet and the maritime forces of other NATO countries, the core of which is formed by strike aircraft-carriers. Under the flag of the Commander of the Sixth Fleet alone are usually two strike aircraft-carriers (150-180 deck planes), several cruisers, up to fifteen escort ships and also a landing force with means of supply.

To safeguard the interests of British imperialism England also permanently keeps forces of her fleet in the eastern part of the Mediterranean. The true intention of these forces is exemplified by the aggression in 1956 when the strikes on Port Said were delivered by the British and French fleets totalling 185 ships (six aircraft-carriers, one battleship, three cruisers, tens of destroyers and escort ships) and also marines and strategic aircraft. The British fleet had also earlier often played the role of an organizer of military conflicts in the Persian Gulf and other areas of the Middle East.

Similar tasks are performed by the American Pacific Fleet numbering hundreds of fighting ships, including a squadron of atomic-powered missile submarines and a considerable grouping of strike aircraft-carriers. These forces are constantly present in different areas of the Pacific Ocean, in particular in the seas washing the countries of South East Asia. In the last few years the Indian Ocean has come into the sphere of the operations of this fleet. A squadron of US ships is permanently present and new naval bases are being built.

A favourite technique of the imperialists is also to conduct military-political shows of strength by the fleet to put pressure on democratic governments not to their liking or on national liberation forces acting against unpopular regimes enjoying the patronage of the imperialists. Such displays, as experience shows, are usually run for a short time and often pass either into direct independent combat use of the forces of the fleet or into operations to support land forces.

The imperialists have mustered for local wars considerable forces of the fleet, the specific composition of which has been determined by the prevailing situation, the course of events and the character of the conflict. For example, against the small countries of Latin America (Panama, Dominican Republic, Guatemala, etc.) the US Navy has employed forces necessary only for disembarking units and divisions of the marines and supporting their operations on shore.

The Americans took a different line in the period of the Caribbean crisis directed against the "Island of Freedom". The USA used strike aircraft-carriers, large formations of other surface ships and large contingents of marines. At the same time vigorous preparations were made to use nuclear weapons and stage a large seaborne landing on the Island of Freedom. Military-political moves were made on a global scale to put pressure on other countries to make them refrain from supporting revolutionary Cuba.

In all military conflicts, whatever their scale, the imperialists seek to create and maintain overwhelming superiority in forces over their enemies. This also happened in the 1950-53 war in Korea, during the events in the Lebanon in 1958 and, in particular, in the 1961-73 war in Vietnam. Off the Vietnamese shores were permanently present the main forces of the US Seventh Fleet. In the final stages of the war, from the spring of 1972, combat operations were conducted here by four to six strike aircraft-carriers, 60-65 large ships of other classes and up to 180 patrol ships and vessels. Over 30 ships and as many as 390 patrol and landing ships of the US allies engaged in combat operations.

During the war in Vietnam, of the 17 strike aircraft-carriers belonging to the US Navy, 15 took part in combat operations, of nine helicopter carriers six, and also three-quarters of the combat complement of guided missile ships—cruisers, frigates and destroyers (48 of 58)—and the vast majority of destroyers (163 of 179).

Among the forces of the fleet taking part in local wars the main role has been played by aircraft-carriers with their aviation and other surface ships. These forces carried out the task of knocking out the troops and objectives of the enemy on shore, supporting the operations of their own units by air raids on distant targets and attacks on coastal objectives by ships' guns and, in part, uncontrolled missiles. Blockade of the sea coasts was also widely employed. Submarines in these wars were used on a limited scale. Their task was no more than backing up the operations of surface ships, shielding them from possible counter strikes and conducting reconnaissance.

With the appearance of new means of armed conflict at sea, the sphere of use of the forces of the fleet in local wars will apparently widen as indicated. For example, ships on an air cushion were used for the penetration by divisions of the US fleet into the hinterland areas of South Vietnam along small rivers until then not considered navigable. There they conducted military operations far from the sea coast, in very swampy areas and jungles.

Naval art in local wars has been characterized by two features: firstly, the endeavour to make wide use of the forms and modes of operations already tried out in previous wars, and secondly, by the verification of new modes of armed struggle corresponding to modern weaponry. This has turned such battle fields into a kind of proving-ground for testing newly-created models of arms and combat logistics.

In the local wars conducted by the imperialist states after the Second World War, various forms of deploying the fleet have been used: landing of troops (chiefly marines) from ships on the coast, the use of carrier aviation for supporting their troops, the delivery of strikes of ships' guns on objectives on shore and sea blockade with use of mines. The practice of shipping sea and air supplies has also been widely adopted.

Staging of seaborne landings

The disembarking of seaborne landing parties is one of the most common means employed by aggressors for directly backing reactionary regimes and suppressing national liberation movements. Landing operations were used most widely in Korea and were conducted to a lesser degree in Vietnam.

The composition and tasks of the invasion forces and the forces maintaining them and the organization and numerical size of the landing of troops in local wars have varied with the balance of forces of the sides and the course of the armed struggle on land. When the troops of the aggressors suffered a defeat, for example, in Korea, landing operations assumed a large scale. The troops landed in the rear or on the flank of the advancing patriotic forces and tried to halt or hold up their advance to enable the interventionists to gain the time necessary for regrouping and strengthening their forces. Such a character was assumed by the generally-known Inchon landing operation in Korea, one of the most important events of that war. In other cases large operational invasion forces were disembarked to ensure the fast pace of the advance of the land forces.

Tactical invasion forces have been widely used in local wars, consisting, as a rule, of units and divisions of marines landed on shore backed by aviation and the gunfire of ships. How landing forces disembark has recently been considerably developed. While in Korea the landing of a party was carried out directly from landing ships, in Vietnam a combined method was used: personnel and light combat equipment were landed on shore by helicopters and heavy combat equipment by landing ships.

US marines have begun to practise new tactical techniques of landing, so-called vertical enveloping and eagle flight. After quelling the defences of the area to be taken by assault bombers and ship armament, direct-fire support helicopters were sent to the landing area to isolate it, to ensure the landing of forces from transport helicopters and with fire back-up from commandos. After fulfilling their combat task the landing divisions were picked up by helicopters and sent to take over the next lines or objectives.

Let us look a little more closely, from the purely military stand-point, at the Inchon landing operation we mentioned. The idea of this operation was to land a force from the sea, deep in the rear of the Korean People's Army, seize Seoul, push to the east, cut land communications, disorganize the control of the troops of the Korean People's Democratic Republic and their supplies, and, advancing simultaneously from the north and the south, to surround and destroy the main forces of the Korean People's Army by joint strikes of the land forces, fleet and aviation. Then it was planned to move up to the frontiers of China and thereby end military operations in Korea.

Large ships were enlisted for direct participation in the landing: the US Seventh Fleet, strengthened by American, British, Canadian, New Zealand, Australian, French and Dutch ships, numbering up to 300 units, including six aircraft-carriers, one battleship, seven cruisers, over 40 destroyers and escort ships, 18 mine-sweepers, 76 landing ships and 66 transports; air units, including over 500 planes of different classes; the American Tenth Corps (the First Reinforced Marines Division and the Seventh Infantry Division) totalling over 40,000 men.

In preparing the operation the interventionists built up a more than twenty-fold superiority in forces and, in addition, guaranteed for themselves absolute dominance in the air and at sea.

Units of the People's Army defending Inchon and the reinforcements sent stoutly waged battle with the advancing enemy, inflicting on him heavy losses in lives and equipment. The forward units of the interventionists in heavy fighting for each line had therefore managed by 16 September to advance only 10 km and to occupy positions 15 km from the Kimpo airfield and 20 km from Seoul. The planned swift offensive from Inchon to Seoul was blocked.

To ensure the development of the offensive in the Seoul direction, on the evening of 16 September an airborne party, forming part of an airborne regiment, was disembarked in the area of the Kimpo airfield. Capturing the airfield and using it as an air base, the Americans were able to use aircraft to back the forward units advancing on Seoul.

An active role was played by carrier aircraft, taking off more than 500 times a day.

Despite the concentration of large forces, the interventionists were able to take Seoul only 14 days from the day the operation began. In the course of the operation they achieved tactical success but the strategic task—the wiping out of the main forces of the People's Army and early ending of the war in

Korea—was not fulfilled. In the Inchon landing operation, tactical procedures applied in the Second World War were repeated.

The success of the disembarkation and operations on shore was achieved only thanks to the creation of a many times greater superiority in forces on land with complete dominance at sea.

A distinguishing feature of the operation was the staging of a sea landing directly in the port, situated in the operational defensive depth of the defenders.

Without wide, active use of the fleet, the interventionists could hardly have escaped military defeat in Korea. The fleet was the force which materially influenced the course of the war as a whole. Thanks to the use of the fleet, the Americans were able to create in a narrow portion of the front a powerful strike grouping of forces enabling them to avoid total defeat in Korea.

The operations of aviation in local wars have right from the start of a conflict pursued the aim—by concentrated massive strikes on aerodromes, a iti-aircraft defence forces and the control system—to deprive the defenders of the possibility of hitting back in an organized manner at the aggressor. At the same time air strikes were carried out on densely populated areas of the country to spread panic among the population, demoralize and sap the will of the people to resist and disorganize the running of the country. Usually the first strikes were delivered by large forces of carrier aviation operating in small groups over a wide front. To hit the best-defended objectives, massive strikes of carrier aviation, operating from different directions at different heights, were undertaken. Characterizing the operations of aircraft in the war against Egypt in 1956, one of the French journals wrote that its main purpose before staging the landing was to destroy or neutralize Egyptian aircraft for two or three days and then go over to air psychological warfare with dropping of leaflets and nightly bombing of populated areas. It was assumed that the depression of morale which ensues after bombings "might . . . possibly lead to the unconditional surrender of the enemy . . . without having to put a single soldier on land . . ."[8] (Translated from the French.)

The same tasks also fell on carrier aviation in the war against heroic Vietnam. Provoking the "Tonkin incident" as an excuse for so-called countermeasures, on 2 August 1964 the American Seventh Fleet with strikes of its carrier aircraft on populated areas sought to demoralize the population of the Republic and demonstrate their determination to hold positions captured in South East Asia at any price and to force the Vietnamese patriots to give up the liberation struggle. Not achieving its ends by these barbarous raids, the United States in February 1965 went over to systematic, ever-mounting air strikes on populated areas including the country's capital Hanoi and the most important nodes of sea and ground communications. The USA—forced under the pressure of world public opinion to call a halt to the air bombing of the Democratic Republic of Vietnam—from 1 December 1968 nevertheless continued individual military actions of its aircraft against the country and in April 1972 made a last desperate attempt to smash the heroic resistance of socialist Vietnam. This time it concentrated off the shores of Vietnam the biggest grouping of the fleet in the whole war, consisting of six strike aircraft-carriers and a large number of other

[8] Admiral P. Barjot, *La Revue Maritime*, 1959, No. 1(151), p. 46.

ships, renewed with a special ferocity the bombing of the Vietnam Republic with carrier, strategic and tactical aircraft, but still failed to achieve its aims.

Carrier aviation in this, the biggest of the local wars, was very intensively used. With, on average, 1.4 crews per plane each pilot performed monthly 20-28 combat sorties and in 1965-72 carrier aviation monthly undertook up to 8,000 sorties.

The raids of carrier aviation on the Democratic Republic of Vietnam were carried out in conditions of heavy opposition from the anti-aircraft defence system, as a result of which each carrier lost 10-15 planes a month. The operations of the air force against South Vietnamese patriots encountered far less resistance from flak fire. But the air force operated with an intensity 1.2-1.5 times greater than against targets in the Democratic Republic of Vietnam. Here, the planes, from carriers in the main, solved the tasks of air backing of the American and Saigon land forces and marines. A general idea of the intensity of the operations of carrier aviation is given by some results of the fighting for the town of Khesan, besieged by the patriots in 1968 where in 77 days fighting the aviation of the American aggressors made more than 25,000 sorties (on individual days as many as 1600), dropped 100,000 air bombs and fired 700,000 shells.

The intensity of the use of US carrier aviation in the Vietnam war is eloquently demonstrated by the following figures. It accounted for over 50 per cent of the total number of sorties for all branches of US aviation taking part in the bombing of targets in South Vietnam. During 1969, Task Force 77 of the US Seventh Fleet, operating in Vietnam, included eight strike aircraft-carriers and one anti-submarine aircraft-carrier. The daily schedule of carrier aviation was: for one carrier 178, for two up to 311 and for three up to 350 sorties. In the course of a year carrier aviation undertook 74,965 sorties, including 53,481 (71 per cent) for strikes and 21,484 (29 per cent) for back-up.

From the beginning of systematic raids on the Democratic Republic of Vietnam, from April 1965 up to the temporary halt on 1 December 1968, carrier aviation undertook 200,000 sorties, solely for delivery of strikes.

Although the combat manoeuvring of US carriers was undertaken in simple conditions, in the absence of any real threat to them, the US Naval Command nevertheless envisaged a whole complex of measures to defend and protect the carrier strike groups: the ships manoeuvred in dispersed combat order, were constantly shielded in the air by fighters and took anti-submarine, anti-mine and anti-ship defence measures.

As stated, carrier aviation was also employed to give direct support to the attacking or defending troops of the aggressor. An example is the defence by the Americans of the Pusan bridgehead in 1950 and also their operations in the area of Khesan in South Vietnam.

Carrier aviation supported the attack by US troops on Seoul after the staging in Inchon of the seaborne landing.

American troops, pushed to the sea in the area of Hungnam, largely owe to carrier aviation the fact that they avoided total defeat and destruction in Korea in 1950.

In the course of the combat use of American aviation against the Democratic

Republic of Vietnam, radio-electronic countering of the anti-aircraft defence system was greatly developed. The wide use of passive interference by radar devices was combined with strikes on them by anti-radar missiles of the *Shrike* and *Standard* ART type. Electronic bombs (SMART) were also used, controlled by television or guided by a laser beam.. The operations of aircraft were safeguarded by tactical target reconnaissance and pre-reconnaissance and the anti-aircraft defence system carefully carried out by operational-tactical masking.

It is worth looking at the aid given by ships' guns to ground troops in local wars, illustrated by the examples of the intervention in Korea and Vietnam.

In the war in Korea, ship armament was widely used by the interventionists against the shore. On it fell the tasks of backing up the troops, destroying military objectives and personnel, securing the sea flanks of the front and interrupting the ground coastal communications of the Korean People's Democratic Republic. Single ships and whole formations were mustered to solve these tasks. The use of ship armament, according to the claims of American specialists, in individual sections of the front sometimes took on decisive importance.

Ship armament was used most intensively and massively by the Americans in 1950 in preparing for the landing at Inchon, when, for almost three months, ships 89 times shelled military and other targets of the People's Army on the east coast.

In 1952 the battleship *Wisconsin,* the heavy cruisers *Saint Paul* and *Rochester* and the light cruiser *Manchester* for ten weeks kept under fire the forward positions of the People's Army, thereby backing up units of the marines. In this period they fired 977 shells of 406 mm calibre (with an average firing range of 16 miles), 1661 of 203 mm (with an average firing range of about 11 miles), and 470 of 152 mm shells (with an average firing range of 11 miles). The troops of the People's Army lost as a result about 470 dead with 450 wounded; six artillery installations were destroyed and 18 damaged, 225 bunkers and shelters destroyed and 252 damaged. The American Command considers that the armament support given in this period to the troops on the shore was effective and justified itself.[9]

In looking at the experience of use by the Americans of ship armament against shore targets in Korea, one cannot help noting that its intensive use was possible only because American ships did not meet due counter-action from the aviation and naval forces of the Korean Republic at that time, which long-range means of combat.

Where events unfolded in areas defended without numerically small artillery of the People's Army, without it often became a serious obstacle to the ships of the interventionists.

Use of ship armament against the shore was possible only because of specific, almost perfect ground conditions.

The interventionists also widely employed ship armament in Vietnam. Here, to shell the coast groups of ships were formed usually consisting of one to three

[9] See M. Kagle and F. Manson, *The Sea War in Korea,* Moscow, Voenizdat, 1962 (in Russian).

cruisers and one to five destroyers. Target reconnaissance and direction of gunfire were carried out by planes and helicopters and also by ground directing posts separated from the ground troops and marines.

Analyzing the experience of combat operations in Vietnam, the US Naval Command concluded that although the use for constant action on coastal objectives of 203 mm and 152 mm guns of cruisers and 127 mm guns of destroyers was not sufficiently effective, it was more effective and economical than use of aircraft, as the former depend less on weather conditions.

Therefore, to expand the power of gun strikes on coastal objectives the Americans sent to the shores of Vietnam the battleship *New Jersey,* armed with 406 mm guns with a firing range of up to 38 km. The idea was to ease the position of other ships of the US fleet which had been badly mauled by counter-action of the shore artillery of the Democratic Republic of Vietnam.

Thus, American intervention in Vietnam also showed that ship armament continues to hold an important place in the arms system of a modern fleet.

Sea blockade in one form or another has been employed by the imperialist powers practically in every conflict and local war. Its aims were to isolate the victims of aggression, deprive it of support from friendly states and ultimately suppress its ability to resist the interventionists. To carry out a blockade the fleet of the aggressive side usually set up several blockade zones at the approaches to the sea coast, constantly controlled by ships and planes. On the approaches to the Vietnamese coast, for example, two blockade zones were set up: distant and near. In the distant zone large surface ships and aircraft kept under observation the approach to the shores of Vietnam of cargo vessels from countries friendly to it. In the near zone patrolling American ships, cutters and planes hunted for Vietnamese cargo vessels and junks engaged in inshore navigation. However, the hunt for Vietnamese junks did not produce the expected result. Vietnamese patriots delivered a considerable quantity of military cargoes by sea and along inland waterways. Moreover, most of the cargoes from friendly countries got to the ports of Vietnam. Therefore, grossly flouting all the norms of international law, widening the criminal, undeclared war in Vietnam, the United States, to increase the effectiveness of the sea blockade, on 9 May 1972 went over to the wide use of mines.

On one night, according to a plan carefully worked out in advance, planes from aircraft-carriers sowed mines in the approaches to all the ports of the Republic. At the same time the inland waters were also mined. The minefield activity of the American fleet went on right up to the end of the war in Vietnam. As a result extensive stretches became dangerous for international shipping and the legitimate rights of other states to enjoy the freedom of the open sea were impaired. A blockade organized to suppress popular liberation movements and interfere in the internal affairs of other countries is under all circumstances an act in breach of the norms of international law proclaimed in the UN Charter and in a number of international agreements.

From the purely military point of view the blockade operations of the USA in the war in Vietnam, as in other local wars, are not very instructive since they were conducted in conditions of an absence on the defending side of real naval forces capable of putting up proper resistance to the aggressor.

Seaborne military shipments in local wars have played a very important, sometimes decisive, role. Their use has grown particularly in periods of the heaviest fighting on land. Thus, for example, the defeat of the American troops pushed to the sea at the Pusan bridgehead in 1950 was largely prevented by the fact that the Americans were able to send in time by sea from Japan to Pusan five divisions with reinforcements. *In toto* in the years of the Korean war some 5,000,000 men were transported by sea from the USA and Japan, and between the ports of Korea. For each soldier landed in Korea there were four tons of diverse cargo. In the 37 months of the war the American fleet brought to Korea 44 million tons of dry cargoes and 22 million tons of oil products. For comparison we would note that in the period of the Second World War for England—a country for which the problem of sea shipments is a question of survival— the minimum necessary annual imports of strategic raw materials were 16 million tons, for which it was necessary to keep permanently at sea 2,000 vessels and pass through the ports daily 350 cargo vessels.

Oceanic and sea shipments were also of very great importance in the Vietnam war. The Americans monthly imported into South Vietnam 85,000 tons of munitions, 320,000 cub.m. of fuel and 15 million daily food rations that is, on average, 35 kg stores per man a day.

According to foreign information, the total monthly volume of oceanic shipments in South Vietnam was at the level of 1.5-2 million tons. Over 300 vessels were permanently engaged in shipments, ocean transport accounting for up to 98 per cent of the volume of cargo shipments and up to 35 per cent of the volume of transport of personnel.

The practice of oceanic shipments confirmed the great advantages of container ships which we discussed in the first chapter. It took only 18 hours to unload such a vessel in port instead of five to seven days. Container transport enabled helicopters to be widely used for unloading operations and delivery of cargo over considerable distances from the off-loading points.

Also of great importance were transoceanic military air shipments, the total volume of which in the period of the Vietnam war was: in 1965—110,000 tons, in 1966—225,000 tons, 1967—540,000 tons and in 1968—910,000 tons.

Thus, from study of the experience of the use of the US naval forces in local wars it may be concluded that large groupings were mustered to fulfil a wide range of the tasks examined. In some cases more ships and planes took part in the combat actions than in individual major operations of the Second World War. The forces of these groupings usually included carrier aviation, surface ships and marines. Carrier aviation, as a rule, was the main strike force.

The operations of the forces of the fleet of the aggressor were marked by diversity and concentrated use. A characteristic feature was the close interaction between carrier aviation and ground troops. It took the form of direct-fire back-up and was also expressed in the timely formation and movement into certain areas of operational groupings of naval forces in support of the actions of ground troops. Military shipments across the ocean were of great importance. Despite the growing role of transoceanic air communications, a large part of the personnel and the bulk of the combat equipment and other cargoes continued to be carried by oceanic and sea transport.

Experience of these local wars confirmed that the aggressive actions of the imperialists led to success only in the absence of due counteraction. In the presence of well-organized resistance by the freedom-loving peoples, supported by the powerful socialist community and other progressive forces at the time, the imperialists were unable to achieve their military-political goals in a local war.

The Fleets in Peacetime

The armed forces throughout the history of their existence have been a most effective means in the policy of states not only in war but also in peacetime. Now—in the period of the most acute ideological contradictions of two social systems, capitalist and socialist, the growth of the national liberation struggle in all continents, unprecedented scientific and technical progress placing at the service of states their discoveries, sharply changing the concept of the power of weapons—this statement is all the more true, and proof of it can be seen everywhere. It is known that immediately after the end of the Second World War, relying on monopoly possession of nuclear weapons, the USA took upon itself the mission of "representing" the interests of all mankind. In connection with its temporary monopoly of atomic weapons, the American leaders reduced their policy and diplomacy to atomic policy and diplomacy, and military strategy to nuclear strategy. The main aim of American monopoly capital became the achievement of power over the whole world. As a result of the strenuous efforts of Soviet scientists, the American nuclear monopoly was soon wiped out and the imperialists were deprived of a material base for conducting in relation to the socialist countries a policy of nuclear blackmail. However, the pretensions of US aggressive circles to world dominance did not cease even after the loss by them of a monopoly over nuclear weapons.

Both in the 'forties and the 'fifties the striving for world dominance was quite openly proclaimed by the ideologists of American imperialism, with the emphasis on nuclear weapons and the fleet. As the American journal *Military Review* wrote, ". . . Atomic power plus sea power will give such freedom of action to our country that it can easily carry out its God-given right to lead the whole world."[10] (Retranslated from Russian.) An active supporter of the policy of establishing world dominance by the USA, a Colonel Reinhardt, hoping that atomic weapons would provide the key to establishing world dominance, wrote; "Technology, by making the world smaller, for the first time in history is creating conditions which allow effective dominance over the world by a single power."[11] (Retranslated from Russian.) In the way of American imperialists striving for world dominance stood as an insurmountable force the USSR and the whole socialist camp. And the fact that despite threats to destroy communism, imperialism hesitated to unleash a new world war finds its explanation above all in the enormous growth of the military might of the USSR, changing the military balance of forces. This serves as a graphic confirmation of

[10] Quoted in Z. M. Solontsov, *The Diplomatic Struggle of the USA for Dominance at Sea,* p. 385, Moscow, IMO, 1962 (in Russian).
[11] *Year Book of World Affairs,* p. 5, Washington, 1958.

the obvious truth that the real military power of the armed forces of the Soviet state is having a sobering effect on the aggressive forces of the imperialist camp unable to give up their demented ideas of destroying the countries of the socialist community and, notably, the Soviet Union. This is recognized by the ideologists themselves of numerous military and other doctrines of "overthrowing" and "destroying" communism. Already in 1959 the Senate Foreign Affairs Committee in a report noted that ". . . The ending of the American nuclear monopoly and growth of the strategic potential of the Soviet Union have increased the difficulties connected with maintaining the military position necessary for achieving established American goals."[12] (Retranslated from Russian.) The Committee was forced to conclude that ". . . the military position of the United States has worsened: our country which used to be indisputably safe is now open and vulnerable to a direct and destructive attack."[13] (Retranslated from Russian.)

Such statements by bourgeois leaders cannot but be taken into consideration in assessing the balance of forces. They are very telling, especially if it is borne in mind that the imperialists are compelled to recognize one or other achievements of the socialist countries only when life itself makes them do so.

The invincible military power of the Soviet Union forms an integral part of the military potential of the whole socialist community, it ensures the safety of fraternal countries and radically alters the balance of forces in the world arena in favour of a peaceful revolutionary process and world peace. At the 1969 International Conference of Communist and Worker Parties, the representatives of the fraternal countries and parties emphasized the tremendous international significance of the defence power of the USSR. "Now, in conditions of a revolution in military- technology and military science", said the First Secretary of the Central Committee of the German Socialist Unity Party, W. Ulbricht, "the defence power of the Soviet Union is more than ever a decisive guarantee for the protection of all socialist states and also of progressive states which have achieved national liberation, a guarantee for the protection of peace in the whole world."[14]

Among the many components making up the power of the Soviet armed forces, a most sobering effect on the advocates of preparing a new world war and the new-styled claimants to world dominance is exerted, along with nuclear weapons, by the rich arsenal of the means of their delivery at the disposal of our country; and primarily those, thanks to which the American continent has become just as vulnerable to punitive strikes of retaliation as other areas of the globe which the American strategists consider as springboards for an attack on the USSR. This essentially refers to the means of delivering nuclear weapons of intercontinental range at the disposal of strategic missile troops and the navy. Largely a means of restraint and, if need be, of cutting short the aggressive actions of the imperialists are the air force, ground troops and other branches of our valiant armed forces.

---

[12] Quoted in *Military Strategy,* Moscow, 1963, p. 79 (in Russian), using material from "Developments in Military Technology and their Impact on United States Strategy and Foreign Policy"—a study prepared at the request of the US Senate Foreign Affairs Committee, 6 December 1959, p. 1.

[13] *Ibid.,* p. 3.

[14] *Pravda,* 11 June 1969.

Policy, as Lenin taught, is a concentrated expression of the economy, the state of which primarily determines the power of such an important instrument of policy as are the armed forces of the nation. It is precisely in the state of the armed forces of a given country that its economic power is reflected.

Graphic confirmation of this and a conventional indicator of the level of development of the economy of a country may be the navy.

"The modern fighting ship", wrote Engels "is not only the product of heavy industry but also at the same time its model. . . . A country with the best-developed heavy industry will enjoy almost a monopoly of building such ships. . . . Political strength at sea, based on modern warships is not at all "direct" but on the contrary mediated by economic strength."[15] These words were written at the very dawn of the development of the steam fleet. Now their significance is much greater.

To build a modern warship, a high level of development of all branches of industry and science of the country is needed. The building of an individual ship meeting modern requirements is possible only with the widest co-operation, only if each of the branches of industry connected with shipbuilding supplies products of the highest quality. As a rule, several hundred establishments take part in the building of a fighting ship. The creation of a fleet as a whole, sufficient in complement to solve the tasks facing it with all the means of supply for its normal service, is possible only for states with a powerful economy.

The long time taken to develop the material-technical resources of a fleet, the relatively short service life for ships and the attendant danger of morale decay of the forces of the fleet make special demands on science, which must lay down the guidelines for building a fleet for years and even decades ahead.

The navy, as a constituent part of the armed forces of the state, has a further distinctive feature, namely the ability to demonstrate graphically the real fighting power of one's state in the international arena. This feature is usually utilized by the political leadership of the imperialist countries to frighten off potential adversaries. It should be noted that the arsenal of the means for such displays, used by the diplomacy of these countries, is constantly expanding.

As is known, in the last few years it has become common to hold displays of missile weapons, combat aviation and various military equipment on an international scale, pursuing as well as a commercial, another aim: to surprise potential enemies with the perfection of this equipment, exert on them a demoralizing influence by the power of one's weapons even in peacetime, instil in them in advance the idea that efforts to combat aggression are futile. This technique has often been employed throughout the history of military rivalry. True, such a propaganda technique far from always reaches the goals set, primarily because the means of war displayed impress the viewer merely as a potential force. The navy is another matter. Ships appearing directly offshore represent a real threat of actions, the time and ways of realizing which are determined by their command. And if such a threat was quite great in the past, it has now considerably grown since modern ships are carriers of nuclear missile weapons and aircraft, the zone of reach of which may extend to the whole territory of a state.

Demonstrative actions by the fleet in many cases have made it possible to

[15] F. Engels, *Selected Military Works* (in Russian), pp. 17, 18.

achieve political ends without resorting to armed struggle, merely by putting on pressure with one's own potential might and threatening to start military operations.

Thus, the fleet has always been an instrument of the policy of states, an important aid to diplomacy in peacetime. To this corresponded the very nature of a navy, the properties peculiar to it, namely, constant high combat readiness, mobility and ability in a short time to concentrate its forces in selected areas of the ocean. In addition, the neutrality of the waters of the World Ocean means that the forces of fleets can be moved forward and concentrated without violating the principles of international law and without providing the other side with formal grounds for protests or other forms of counteraction.

The ability to threaten potential enemies with the very fact of their existence has transformed the navies of the capitalist countries into a force of intimidation and has raised their construction to the rank of one of the most important problems in political struggle in the international arena.

Thus, England took economic, military, diplomatic and propagandist measures to create the strongest fleet which, in fact, played an important role in the attainment of the goals of English policy not only in war but also in peacetime, and helped to turn England into the biggest colonial power. Her fleet was widely used in so-called gunboat diplomacy—suppression of the liberation movement of oppressed peoples and extension of colonial dominance.

The importance of navies in peacetime is confirmed by many examples from the history of Russia. The power of the Russian fleet under Peter the Great was the main factor which restrained the bellicose intentions of the English seeking to come to the aid of Sweden, which sustained a defeat in the war against Russia.

In 1780 Russia, using the increased power of her fleet, acted as the initiator of the declaration of freedom of neutral sea trade, which promoted the development of world sea trade and was a blow to the baseless pretensions of England to their private right to undertake sea trade only on English vessels.

In 1783 the Czarist government, using the superiority of its fleet in the Black Sea, without a war annexed the Crimea and made it part of the Russian state, and in 1830, without waging military operations, concluded an advantageous defensive alliance with Turkey. Thanks to this alliance, the presence of large forces of the Russian fleet and land forces in the area of the Bosphorus and the Turkish capital was established. It seemed that in the conditions of peacetime the solemn goals of Russian Czarism had been reached—freedom of navigation from the Black Sea into the Mediterranean, although the military-political blackmail of the Western states, primarily England, resting on stronger forces than the Russian, did not allow the success won by Russian diplomacy to be secured and Russian Czarism was forced without a war to submit to the dictation of the Western powers.

The special importance of navies for states is confirmed by a series of acts regulating international relations. Thus, under the 1856 Paris Peace Treaty the Russians were forbidden to have a navy in the Black Sea.

The 1902 Anglo-Japanese alliance specially stipulated that an allied fleet outnumbering the fleet of Russia be kept in the Pacific.

In discussion of the draft of the Portsmouth Peace Treaty after the end of the

Russo-Japanese war, Japan tried to include in it a demand that the complement of the Russian fleet be limited in the Pacific, but this was not endorsed, since England, France, the USA and the other interested states feared the excessive strengthening of Japan.

In the peace treaties concluded after the First and Second World Wars, special attention was paid to restrictions concerning the navies of the defeated states. The characteristic features of these treaties were the demand for the total destruction of submarines and an unconditional ban on the defeated countries building or acquiring them.

As well as restrictions and bans placed on the navies of the defeated states, the victors divided them up with special care. Thus, the Berlin Conference of the three great powers (July-August 1945) fixed the order of dividing up the fleet of Hitlerite Germany. All surface ships, including those under construction and repair, were equally divided between the USSR, the USA and England. German submarines were scheduled to be destroyed, apart from thirty which were also divided up between the victorious countries. Together with ships all the stores of the German fleet were handed over. The ships of Japan, after its capitulation, were also divided up on the basis of these principles. It is significant that similar measures were not taken in respect of other branches of the armed forces.

The special importance of a navy in the policy of the major states is also indicated by the repeated attempts to limit the building of fighting ships made at international conferences in 1922-35. True, the decisions of these conferences held back the building of the fleets of the biggest states only up to about the middle 'thirties, after which the naval arms race proceeded unhindered.

The role of navies in the policy of states may also be traced by looking at the events which led to the weakening of England, so long occupying the place of leader of the capitalist world. It is interesting that England was cast from the throne of "ruler of the waves" by the USA, not only not at war with her at the time, but her unchanging ally. The United States managed without a war to achieve what Germany could not do in two world wars.

The weakening of England began in the First World War and was distinctly in evidence immediately after its end, when England was forced to abandon the "two-power standard" and agree to equality between its own and the American fleets. But the process of weakening developed at the fastest pace in the course of the Second World War and a most important role in it was again played by the navies. Of course, this process had deeper roots and was determined by the influence of the law of unevenness of development of capitalist countries and also by the influence of the revolutionary and national liberation movements, encompassing the whole world. However, even allowing for these underlying causes, the role of the navies in the weakening of England cannot be underestimated. The point is that the USA directed the efforts of its fleet not only against the fleets of the Hitler coalition but also, at the same time it pursued the aim of eliminating its old imperialist competitor—the British Empire—and of taking its place in the world. The USA conducted such a policy over a long period and especially in the course of the Second World War, using naval forces as the main means.

The Americans "ousted" England from the seas adjoining the American continent and wiped out its former power in the Western hemisphere, in the area of the Mediterranean, the Indian Ocean, the Far East and the Pacific basin. In the toughest period of the war they placed before England the question of her fleet moving, in the event of defeat, to the bases of the American continent. In the course of the war, the entire gold stocks of England were shipped across the ocean.

Moreover, the conditions created, and a powerful economy, enabled the Americans to concentrate considerable efforts on building up their fleet and creating in the period of the Second World War tens of thousands of diverse fighting ships and boats. The number of ships of the main classes of the US naval forces by the end of the war had become equal to the number of ships of the fleets of all other capitalist states taken together, and were twice the number of ships of the English fleet.

In its qualitative features, the American fleet also surpassed the fleets of the other imperialist powers. In 1945 this was the most modern fleet, 75 per cent of whose ships were not more than five years old, that is, in essence it had been completely renewed in the period of the war and, in addition, had been transformed into an aircraft-carrier and submarine fleet, the most up-to-date of its day.

In the post-war period, the USA moved into the ranks of the leaders of imperialism and their navy began to be widely used as an instrument of imperialist policy. At present the US Sixth Fleet (and not the English) is permanently present in the Mediterranean—in the past the traditional arena of dominance of Great Britain, being the main means of threat and political pressure on a number of countries of the Mediterranean basin. It is used as the main means of combating the national liberation movement of the Arab peoples and also supports in every way the aggressive tendencies of Israel and the economic expansion of the American monopolies in the Middle East, Africa and southern Europe.

The US Seventh Fleet is widely used in the fight against the national liberation movements, democracy and progress in South East Asia. It constitutes a forward grouping of the imperialist armed forces and has more than once unleashed in this area of the globe open wars against the progressive forces of the young states of the Indian-Chinese continent.

The growth of naval forces has enabled the Americans to develop expansion on a considerable scale into various countries of the world, including the countries of the British Empire. The United States and not England has become the centre of a system of post-war aggressive alliances, uniting a large number of states, the binding element of these alliances being the American navy.

It is hard to find in the world an area where American politicians have not used their navy against progressive forces. With the aid of the navy they conducted the blockade of revolutionary Cuba and landed on its territory detachments of counter-revolutionaries, suppressed the democratic movement in the Dominican Republic, helped to overthrow the progressive regime in Chile and assisted anti-democratic forces in other countries of Latin America.

In addition, the USA is also using its fleet to put pressure on the member allies of pacts possessing relatively weak forces at sea designated to help solve auxiliary tasks.

It is interesting to note that whenever within these alliances, under the influence of imperialist contradictions or in other cases, tension mounts, US politicians put forward plans to create different groupings of so-called joint naval forces, seeking to strengthen in this way the alliances and creating the impression of parity of their members. This was the case in 1962 when the US Secretary of State Dean Rusk proposed that multi-national naval nuclear forces be created. Subsequently a plan was suggested for creating a surface nuclear fleet of 25 ships with multi-national commands and a plan for a combined squadron of several destroyers in the Atlantic Ocean, etc. However, the United States does not go beyond the symbolic creation of international sea forces, leaving the undivided use of the navy for itself.

Times are changing, as are also the ways in which different states use the fleets as an important instrument of policy in peacetime.

In the post-war years, when present-day capitalism is striving in every way to adjust to the new situation in the world, the forms of use of the fleets have changed. In conditions of opposition to socialism, the ruling circles of the countries of capitalism are resorting to ever more ingenious ways of showing force and using intimidation, going as far as nuclear blackmail in an attempt to preserve or restore their dominance over the peoples of former colonies or other countries tearing themselves from the clutches of capitalist exploitation.

The show of force of the fleets of the leading maritime powers of the capitalist world against our country and her navy has become the daily practice of the military command of the member countries of different aggressive military blocs. This also includes patrolling by atomic submarines in different areas of the World Ocean and demonstrative actions of aircraft-carriers in the seas lying close to the territory of our country, also the numerous shadowing flights by planes of our ships and vessels and demonstrative visits by ships to the Black, Baltic, Japanese and other Seas. All these plainly provocative acts have been realistically appraised by us and have not reached the goals pursued by their instigators.

The growth of the might of the Soviet state and its prestige in the world arena has made the leaders of many countries realize the futility of such practices, as a result of which in 1972, as noted above, for the first time in the practice of maritime legal mutual relations a Soviet-American agreement was concluded on the prevention of incidents at sea, which greatly cleared the air in areas where Soviet and American ships operate.

The Soviet navy is also used in foreign policy measures by our state. But the aims of this use radically differ from those of the imperialist powers. The Soviet navy is an instrument for a peace-loving policy and friendship of the peoples, for a policy of cutting short the aggressive endeavours of imperialism, restraining military adventurism and decisively countering threats to the safety of the peoples from the imperialist powers.

With the emergence of her navy on the oceanic expanses, the Soviet Union has gained new and wider possibilities for its use in peacetime to ensure her state interests. And this potential is being successfully realised. Finding themselves in foreign ports, Soviet naval seamen—representatives of the various Soviet nations and specialities—feel themselves ambassadors for our country.

Friendly visits by Soviet seamen offer the opportunity to the peoples of the countries visited to see for themselves the creativity of socialist principles in our country, the genuine parity of the peoples of the Soviet Union and their high cultural level. In our ships they see the achievements of Soviet science, technology and industry. Soviet mariners, from rating to admiral, bring to the peoples of other countries the truth about our socialist country, our Soviet ideology and culture and our Soviet way of life.

They demonstrate high awareness, organizational capacity and culture, with deep respect for the peoples, for national idiosyncracies and the customs of those countries where they happen to be. On the evidence of Soviet diplomatic representatives and a number of officials in such states, our mariners worthily represent their people abroad and contribute much to the growth of sympathies and friendly feelings to the Soviet Union and her high human ideals. Thus, on 10 January 1969 the newspaper *Afro-American* wrote: "Kenyans are struck by the fact that Soviet seamen, unlike the seamen of the American and English navies, did not leave the slightest trace of disorder behind them in port. . . . Soviet seamen are so serious and behave so well that they appear to be persons from another planet." (Retranslated from Russian.)

Soviet seamen also see the achievements of the peoples of countries friendly to us who have won the right to manage their own affairs, see too the consequences of the centuries-old rule of the colonizers and the social contrasts of the capitalist countries which are so carefully glossed over by bourgeois propaganda.

Official visits and the working calls of our ships to foreign ports make a substantial contribution to the improvement of mutual understanding between states and peoples and to the enhancement of the international authority of the Soviet Union. This is convincingly confirmed by the numerous examples of the expression of warm feelings for the land of the Soviets on the part of the population in each foreign port, and the enormous interest in the life of the Soviet people, our seamen and ships. This is also testified by the remarks of many official representatives. Suffice it simply to refer to a statement of the Minister of Foreign Affairs of the South Yemen on the occasion of a first visit to the port of Aden by Soviet ships when he said: "For the first time in history our country has been visited by ships of a friendly country. In the past to Aden came many warships, but bearing the banner not of friendship but of threat, violence and enslavement."

The large "Okean" manoeuvres conducted in April-May 1970 by the Soviet navy were also completed by visits of ships to more than ten foreign ports situated on the four continents of the globe. Usually, after large-scale exercises, inspections of the forces involved in them are held. However, because of the global, spatial scope of the sea manoeuvres, such an inspection could not be made. Therefore the calls of Soviet warships at foreign ports were a kind of inspection of the forces of the fleet of the great Soviet power, guarding the peace and safety of the peoples. They helped to strengthen friendship with the peoples of these countries and towards the development of the international ties of the Soviet Union with a number of developing sovereign states.

Problems of Balancing Fleets

While our fleet was being built, close attention was and is being paid to efforts to ensure that all the elements making up its fighting power are constantly in the most advantageous combination, or, as is now commonly said, are balanced.

The correct definition of the character of balance of the forces of the fleet is possible on the basis of thorough scientific analysis of all the earlier-discussed premises, objectively influencing the trend of its construction. The problem of balance of a fleet is the subject of modern naval science, embracing such important areas as naval art, history and naval technology.

This problem is also unquestionably of considerable interest from a purely cognitive standpoint. All this gives us grounds for a more detailed examination of this question in its theoretical and historical aspects.

The balanced development of a fleet must be based on a military doctrine which defines its role and place in the system of the armed forces of the state, its tasks in armed struggle and also the purpose of the branches of the forces forming it.

The balanced development of a fleet pre-supposes in a particular historical period the preferential development of those branches of the forces which are most capable of solving effectively the main tasks facing the fleet.

Today a leading place is given in navies to those forces capable of solving important strategic tasks, pursuing the goal of undermining the military-economic potential of an enemy and shattering his nuclear sea power. Scientific analysis of the experience of past wars, the presumed character of a future war and the trend in the development of the fleets of the imperialist states suggest that such forces are atomic-powered submarines armed with ballistic and guided missiles and naval missile-carrying and anti-submarine aviation. They have enormous strike power, possess high mobility, can conceal operations and have the ability to deliver strikes on important military-industrial and administrative centres of the enemy located on the coast and deep inland and on nuclear missile groupings of the enemy in the ocean.

The preference given to the development of submarines and sea aviation not only does not exclude but, on the contrary, implies harmonised development of other branches of the forces of the fleet, without which the successful use of the main forces and fulfilment of all the tasks facing the navy in a modern war is inconceivable, as is also the operation of all forms of combat and material and technical back-up in which a most important role will be played by surface ships.

From this it may be concluded that the balance of a fleet consists in the fact that all the elements making up its fighting power and their protection are constantly in the most advantageous combination, in which the fleet can completely realize the quality of universality it has, that is, the ability to fulfil different tasks, in conditions both of a nuclear and any possible war.

Another aspect of the problem is determination of the quantitative composition of a fleet, starting from the basic demand made of it—to be a composition of forces present in peacetime, capable of fulfilling the tasks assigned, having regard to geographical location and the possibility of undertaking a manoeuvre between theatres.

It should not be forgotten that making good the forces of the fleet in conditions of a nuclear war, unlike other wars, would be very complex or virtually impossible. Consequently, the problem of creating a modern balanced fleet must be resolved essentially during its construction in peacetime.

The character of the balance of the fleet is not constant. In certain historical conditions it may change. The main factors determining such changes are the general political situation (new alignment of forces, presence of military blocs, change of regimes in individual countries, etc.), the potential of the economy and growth of the military-economic potential of the country, the development of science and technology at home and abroad and change in the tasks devolving on the fleet.

Of all these factors the main ones are the tasks set before the fleet by the political leadership and the level of the economy of the country, in the first instance the potential of the shipbuilding, tool-making, aircraft and other branches of industry mustered to build ships, planes, weapons and combat equipment.

It is false to try to build a fleet to the model and likeness of even the strongest sea power and to determine the requirements for the building of ships for one's fleet merely by going on quantitative criteria and ratios of ship composition Each country has specific requirements for sea forces which influence their development. For a socialist state this requirement is determined by the tasks of defence.

At the heart of the management of the building of our fleet and determination of the character of the balance of its forces lie the problems of the defence of our country and the decisions of the Central Committee of the CPSU stemming from them. An important place is held by scientific methods of management, based on careful consideration of the above-indicated factors and mathematical and logical analysis of the possible perspectives of their changes. The crux of these methods is a systems approach to scientific research and investigations conducted with the aid of modern computer techniques for defining the optimal quantities of the types of ships, planes, arms complexes and other means of combat and also their ratio, helping to solve successfully the tasks set before the fleet in varying conditions of a modern war.

The wide scope of scientific research and specific scientifically-based conclusions obtained as a result of them help to the utmost in avoiding mistaken subjective decisions concerning the development of the fleet and make it possible to concentrate the efforts of design and engineering thought and also material-technical expenditure on the creation of optimal forces and means of combat capable of achieving with the least losses the best ways of resolving their particular tasks.

History provides many instructive examples of what happens when underestimation of the problem of fleet balance or sheer neglect of the fleet, when limited economic potential, erroneous military doctrines or a short-sighted policy by states, leads either to the defeat of fleets in war or to the extreme overtaxing of such countries' economies, faced, during a war, with setting right earlier blunders.

On the eve of the 1904-05 Russo-Japanese war, the Czarist government and the supreme military command of Russia were unable to determine the main political and military goals and tasks deriving from them, to fulfil which the fleet had been created. As the fleet was being built, attempts were made to achieve numerical superiority in ships of the main classes over the fleet of the probable enemy, although it was already clear that one could not be guided simply by this criterion. The acquisition by Japan of several foreign-built armoured ships and cruisers nullified the efforts of Russia to achieve superiority at sea. Russia's economy did not allow the ratio of forces built up by the start of the war to be rapidly changed and therefore her fleet, neither in quantitative composition nor in quality of ships, was able to meet the goals for which it had been built.

At the moment when the fleet by its actions ought to have decisively influenced the outcome of the war, it was plainly unprepared to discharge this task and was in effect bottled up in its bases.

The short-sightedness of the foreign policy of Czarist autocracy and the helplessness of the Russian naval command only accelerated the destruction of the Pacific fleet. An attempt to put right the position in the course of the war by sending a squadron to the Far East, as is known, ended in its tragic defeat in the Tsushima Strait.

On the eve of the First World War the fleet of Great Britain retained numerical superiority in powerful battleships over the fleets of other European powers. Kaiser Germany was striving to make the strike power of its fleet equal to that of the English fleet, primarily in number of battleships.

The development of the English and German fleets was determined by a single purpose—in a general sea engagement gain a victory which would lead to the attainment of dominance at sea. Therefore from the experience of the Russo-Japanese war were extracted solely those lessons which only partly confirmed the postulates of Colomb and Mahan, based on the combat experience of the use of sailing fleets. It was planned to improve the tactical characteristics of battleships, cruisers, destroyers and above all their weapons and armour. None of the naval theoreticians of the west drew fundamental conclusions concerning the lines of development of the fleets, their role, the composition of their forces and use, although the Russo-Japanese war had already made the need for this clear.

Even then, from analysis of the changes in armed struggle at sea, brought about by the development of the material-technical base of the fleet, it was possible to conclude that it was necessary to differentiate the forces of the fleet starting from its basic task in war. Although the need was a consequence of an objective law, it went unheeded in all the fleets of the maritime powers, which continued to be guided by outmoded ideas, on the basis of which the necessary ratio of the forces and resources was maintained only to the degree to which the main battle forces of the fleet needed to be used in a battle. The ratio of the different classes of ships was determined by the principle: ensure the entry into action of battleships, and the waging by them of the battle in advantageous conditions.

Each of the potential adversaries on the eve of the First World War started from the premise that their navy would be able to achieve the goals fixed only with the aid of decisive offensive actions against the main forces of the fleet of the enemy, represented by squadrons of battleships and heavy cruisers.

Therefore, the building of the fleets was based on the tasks of creating strike forces—battleships and cruisers capable of conducting offensive operations against an enemy fleet. The solution of defensive tasks was considered a forced measure and the building of new ships for this was not contemplated. Such tasks if they appeared in the course of the war were to be solved chiefly by obsolete ships which could not take part in a general engagement.

Thus, the forces of the fleets of the Western powers were virtually not allocated to specific tasks and the problem of their balance on the eve of the war was unresolved.

The consideration that the main purpose of use of the fleet in war was that of gaining dominance at sea narrowed in advance the sphere of its deployment, artificially limited the content of combat operations at sea, precluded the determination of its main task and differentiation of existing and new forces and means of the fleet for armed conflict.

Nor was the requirement for a balanced development of the fleet fully realized in Russia, even when the Russo-Japanese war had graphically confirmed the need to create a more universal fleet than envisaged by the shipbuilding programmes of the Western powers.

The segregation of the sea theatres adjoining the coasts of Russia, differences in their military-geographical conditions, the characteristics of the fleets and the intentions of probable adversaries in these theatres and, hence, the main tasks falling on the Baltic and Black Sea fleets required a different solution to the question of what forces should be created and how big each of them should be.

In addition, the creation of a balanced fleet was to help to restore the sea power of Russia after the Russo-Japanese war. But this demanded time, people and money. There remained little time, there were few knowledgeable, capable and energetic persons in the leadership of the country and fleet and there was even less money. Therefore, the Russian fleet on the eve of the First World War developed in very complex conditions.

After the Russo-Japanese war Russia built ships intended chiefly for fulfilling defensive tasks. Although battleships of the *Sevastopol* type built in 1915 in the country's yards and the two heavy cruisers of the *Izmail* type, laid down but not completed, were first-class ships at that time, they were few in number and so could not form the fighting core of the fleet and did not take part in combat operations.

The light forces of the fleet made the greatest headway: destroyers of the *Novik* type with universal fighting qualities, thanks to high speed of travel and quite strong gun-torpedo armaments and also minelaying and anti-mine ships—minesweepers.

It must be emphasized that individual surface ships, especially destroyers built to the designs of Russian engineers in our own yards, were distinguished by high tactical properties and in a number of respects surpassed the best foreign ships. However, as a whole, because of technical and economic backwardness at the start of the First World War, Russia could not create a fleet capable of competing with the fleets of the traditional maritime powers.

Possessing small, though quite modern forces and resources, the Russian fleet was prepared to fulfil an extensive range of defensive tasks in the coastal areas of the sea theatres and continued to remain a coastal action fleet which could exert only a local influence on the course of armed conflict in the maritime directions of the land fronts.

The choice of the direction of the development of the fleets, the determination of their tasks and hence the quantitative and qualitative composition of the forces was crucially affected by the absence of unity of views of the supreme military and naval command of many states on the character of a future war and the role in it of each of the branches of the armed forces. Before the start of the First World War, military theoreticians assumed that although the strategic use of the fleet and land forces pursues the same final end—defeat of the enemy—these branches of the armed forces must exist and develop independently. The army and navy were looked upon as two independent forces. It was recognized that combat operations of the fleet and land forces could be conducted jointly, although the constant co-ordination of their efforts on a large scale was considered nonsensical.

This view, characteristic of the traditional maritime powers, was also held by the military leadership of Germany although its army and navy were under the single command of the Kaiser. There were serious disagreements in matters of strategy between the senior officers of the German navy and army. Army officers, like civilians and the government, believed that the First World War would go through two stages: at first the land forces of France and Russia would be destroyed and then it would be England's turn. The naval forces would need to be used only in the second stage. At the start of the war the German army command did not demand from the navy that it prevent by its operations the despatch to the continent of the "Contemptibles".

But the war did not go the way many military specialists, including naval ones, had imagined. Since Italy at the start of the war remained neutral and then joined the side of the Entente, the heavy engagement in the Mediterranean on which many hopes had been pinned did not work out this way. The weak Austrian fleet stood in the Adriatic ports and its role was merely confined to pinning down certain forces of the enemy, not allowing them to be used in other areas.

Only 22 months after the start of the war did a heavy (in composition of the forces involved) engagement take place between the German and English navies in the North Sea known in history as the Battle of Jutland. In this engagement, not having any strategic or operational link with the combat actions on the land fronts both sides avoided a decisive encounter and its results did not change the position at sea.

The imbalance of the fleets of the opposing coalitions was ever more strongly felt in combat operations at sea. After a long search to find a way out of the strategic impasse and ways of overcoming the crisis in the use of the powerful but inactive British Grand Fleet and the German High Sea Fleet, both warring sides concluded that it was necessary to widen the range of tasks of their fleets in armed conflict at sea. Each of them solved this problem in their own way.

The English Admiralty, in August 1915, not reckoning with the fact that the Royal Navy did not have any special landing ships (that it was not balanced in respect of the given task), decided to deliver, by the forces of the fleet of the allies, a combined strike on the southern flank of the Austro-German front, to stage a large landing on the Gallipoli peninsula and under its cover have the fleet break through the Dardanelles to capture Constantinople.

The twelve battleships, four cruisers, sixteen destroyers, seven submarines, air transport and a large number of transports lined up for this operation were unable to ensure the successful staging of the landing, involving 157,000 men. The English had no landing ships or special ships for giving the troops fire back-up. The main forces of the fleet, represented by battleships and cruisers, were not trained to operate against a fortified coast. Moreover, the organizational capacities of the leaders of the Admiralty and the Command of the Mediterranean Fleet left much to be desired.

The attempt to use ships not adapted to the staging of a landing and therefore eliminate pre-war miscalculations in determining the necessary composition of the forces of the fleet, like the planning of armed struggle at sea, could not have a happy end and resulted in the failure of the operation. This had such a serious influence on the military theoreticians of England and some other countries that right up to the start of the Second World War they considered as unrealistic the use of naval forces in a struggle against a shore defended by a strong enemy and the fleet was not trained for it.

In passing we would note that the Russian fleet as a whole successfully fulfilled the tasks of backing the land forces in the Baltic and Black Seas. It frustrated an attempt by the Germans to mount a landing on the Moonsund Islands in 1916, landed its parties on the coast of Lasistan, a district of the Turkish Black Sea coast between Trebizond and the USSR frontier, supported from the sea army units by gunfire from ships, ensured military shipments and the manoeuvre of land forces in the maritime areas of the theatres near the coast. This in no small measure was promoted by somewhat better balance, than among the English, of the Russian fleet for the tasks appearing in the course of the war.

The miscalculations of the English Admiralty in respect of the balance of the fleet were even more distinctly manifest in the course of the fulfilment of tasks to protect oceanic and sea communications of vital importance to Great Britain. The protection of communications was not a new problem from the very start of the war but assumed special urgency after the Germans, in the search for a way out of the strategic impasse on the land front, turned their gaze to the sea.

Convinced after the Battle of Jutland of the futility of attempts to gain dominance at sea, the German Command came to the conclusion that the German fleet, inferior to the fleet of the allies in number of battleships, could with the aid of submarines achieve major successes on the sea and oceanic communications of the enemy. The switching of the operations of German submarines in the course of war against allied merchant vessels occurred comparatively quickly. The British fleet could not actively counteract this. Enormous in number of ships and total displacement but not in balance, it proved helpless in face of the obvious danger and was forced to react by limited defensive measures to changed enemy combat techniques, going over to a determined offensive. The English in the course of the war itself had to create the necessary forces and means to combat submarines, mobilize their own and Allied resources and work out ways of using ships unprepared for this in order to reduce the losses in merchant ships and cargoes. In the USA it was estimated that the cost of the means of combat necessary for successfully fighting submarines exceeded 19 times the expenditure needed to build submarines. Objectively, the situation was such that Germany, which had paid attention not only to the building of a surface fleet but also to the development of submarines, was in a favourable position in two ways. Firstly, it confronted the enemy with the need to open up in a hurry a new front of armed struggle at sea. Secondly, it was able, thanks to this, to add considerably to the strain on the English economy which was in any case in a perilous state, forcing England to expend enormous resources to speed up the building of anti-submarine forces.

The miscalculations in the determination of the direction of development of the British fleet and their grave consequences were eliminated only thanks to the assistance of the American fleet supporting its partner in a dangerous situation. A complex of measures of an operational-strategic character and huge material expenditure enabled the Allies at the cost of heavy losses to reduce sharply the success of the activities of German submarines.

Without exaggeration it may be said that the main burden of the armed struggle at sea was taken on by the forces and resources of the fleet created in the course of the war, that is, those with the aid of which the fleets of the warring states were balanced only in the course of the armed struggle and not as a result of scientific foresight in building the fleet.

The experience of the First World War made it crystal clear that the range of tasks discharged by the fleets had considerably widened and combat activity had become much more diverse in form and content. The scale of military activities at sea and the scope of operations had immeasurably grown. Military activities took in the oceanic expanses. The fleets needed to have forces intended to upset the sea and oceanic communications of the enemy, protect their own communications, support from the sea land forces operating in maritime directions, fight against enemy fleets at sea, etc. In addition, it became necessary to distribute the forces of the fleet capable of fulfilling these tasks in near (coastal) and distant (oceanic) areas.

Despite the obvious need to use the experience of the First World War in the subsequent balancing of the fleets, the traditional maritime states continued to cling to conservative, pre-war ideas of gaining dominance at sea by smashing the power of the battle forces of the enemy fleet. The question of the balanced development of fleets, the coherent distribution of their forces according to the main tasks and area of operations was not posed even at theoretical level and was ignored in analyzing the combat experience of the First World War. The fleets of these states went on preparing battleships for battles in the open sea. The yards of the USA, England, Germany, Japan and Italy continued to build new battleships armed with large-calibre guns.

After the failure of the Dardanelles operation, the English and French naval commands, as noted earlier, considered the operations of the fleet against the shore if not impossible, then at any rate extremely complex. Therefore, before the start of the Second World War the allied staffs planned no operations of the fleet against land and did not create any special forces for this.

Not a few other miscalculations and mistakes were made in solving the problem of balancing the forces of the English fleet on the eve of the Second World War. The real reason for this lay not so much in the conservatism and limitation of the military thinking of naval theoreticians as in the shortsightedness of the foreign policy of Great Britain and the erroneous forecasting of events on the eve of the war. Helping Germany to restore its military potential after the First World War, the ruling circles of England were convinced that they would succeed in directing aggression against the Soviet Union and in the course of the war consolidate their position as a leading maritime power.

However, subsequent events made nonsense of these calculations. England had to go through several heavy defeats in the struggle at sea, that is, precisely in that sphere where she was considered the strongest among the big maritime powers. Moreover, England was forced to concede primacy irrevocably to her ally—the USA—which rushed to take advantage of this, and without special difficulty came to head the imperialist camp.

During the Second World War the English fleet was again faced with the need to reduce the disproportions in its forces. At the start of the war the operations of the fleet were sharply limited by German mine-laying, to combat which it lacked the necessary forces and resources. The inability of the English fleet to protect its sea communications was strikingly manifest even in the period when the number of German submarines suitable for operations in the Atlantic did not exceed twenty and conditions for their deployment were extremely limited. The British fleet was unable not only to stop the U-boats from moving out into the Atlantic but even to organize reliable counter-action to them on the approaches to the English coast. As a result, the merchant fleets of England and the Allied countries began to suffer systematic losses, which in 1940 and in the first half of 1941 exceeded 300,000 tons a month.

Only the redeployment of the armed forces (including the navy) of Fascist Germany to the east for the war against the Soviet Union and in this connection the limitation of the intensity of the operations of the German navy in the west gave England and her allies an appreciable respite. The losses of their merchant fleet from the strikes of U-boats sharply dropped: while in the first half of 1941, 787 ships with a total tonnage of 2,822,000 registered tons were sunk, in the second half this was down to 276 ships with a total tonnage of 1,375,000 registered tons.[16]

The English fleet felt a particularly acute need for coastal action anti-submarine and anti-mine ships, capable of combating submarines and the mine danger at the approaches to the ports and bases of the homeland. No less important was the question of anti-submarine forces and resources intended for protecting convoys in the open sea and ocean a long way from sea and oceanic communications posts.

[16] *History of Naval Art,* edited by Admiral S. E. Zakharov, Moscow, Voenizdat, 1969, p. 333 (in Russian).

From the first days of the war the English shipbuilding industry had to be reconstructed, to pay even more attention to the building of anti-submarine and anti-mine ships. It was necessary to master the building of escort aircraft-carriers, patrol-escort ships, frigates and corvettes. By the end of the war the English fleet numbered 138 frigates and 141 corvettes, and over a thousand submarine hunters, each with a displacement of 65-70 tons, were built for shore protection. In addition, the fleet comprised 32 American escort-carriers, 88 frigates and 15 corvettes handed over under Lend-Lease.

Since the 42 minesweepers operating at the beginning of the war could not ensure even to a minimum degree protection from the mine danger, the English had to take emergency measures to bolster anti-mine defence. They were forced to appeal for aid to the Americans and to use a considerable number of their sweepers. A multiplicity of fishing trawlers and drifters was mobilized and the building of new sweepers accelerated. By the end of the war the English fleet already had 126 specially-constructed squadron sweepers and 453 small sweepers.

The English fleet before the war did not have the necessary number of means of transport. Even in May 1943 senior officials in Great Britain continued to complain that the main obstacle to the execution of their plans of attack was lack of sea tonnage. Then Churchill pointed out that this limited the scope of all the actions of Great Britain. As stated by the head of the Imperial General Staff, the lack of sea tonnage "strangles our operations ' and the First Lord of the Admiralty emphasized that "it will make difficult and already in effect is making difficult the execution of the whole of our offensive strategy". (Retranslated from Russian.)

True, one must look critically at these statements, especially in those cases in which they were made to justify the non-fulfilment by England of her commitments to the Soviet Union.

The naval aviation of England was also unprepared to solve tasks at sea and as in the First World War was given an auxiliary role. The English air force was prepared in the main to defend the British Isles from air attack and to deliver strikes on military-economic targets of the enemy. These tasks also determined the direction of the development of fighter and heavy bomber aircraft. One consequence of the under-estimation of the role of naval aviation was that the debate on its role and place in the arms systems of the fleet ended only shortly before the start of the Second World War, with the result that its formations were included in the fleet only in 1939. The naval aviation of England proved insufficiently prepared to solve tasks at sea and was very small in number.

The British Government more than once tried to use the imbalance of the fleet and the difficulties in eliminating pre-war miscalculations in an attempt to justify its questionable actions to delay in every way the opening of a second front. This was done precisely at a time when the Soviet armed forces were under the heaviest strain in the struggle against the foe.

Only by the end of the war, thanks to US aid and the full use of its own resources, was Great Britain able to balance the fleet more or less in relation to the tasks set before it. There was an appreciable rise in the ratio of the number of aircraft-carriers, destroyers, anti-submarine and anti-mine ships and submarines in relation to the fleet as a whole. Major changes in the balance of forces were brought about by the accelerated construction of landing craft; their numbers by the end of the war had increased by many hundreds. At the same time the number of battleships and cruisers considerably fell, although by the end of the war they still represented about half the tonnage of the English fleet. Analysis of the change in the ratio of the forces of the English fleet suggests that the Admiralty could balance the fleet by the end of the war in respect of the goals, tasks and areas of operations only with the aid of their ally, the USA, and only thanks to the fact that the main tasks of the Second World War were resolved on the Soviet-German front.

The navy of Fascist Germany, in balance of forces in respect of these criteria, fundamentally differed from the naval forces of England. Getting ready to attack the Soviet Union, the German Command paid prime attention to the development of the land army and the air force. The efforts which Germany expended on preparing for the combat operations at sea against the Western powers were extremely small. The preparation for the war against England and hence the expanded building of the fleet was scheduled for a later time, after the ending of the war in the east. The general plan evolved with reference to this operation of building the fleet (Z plan), adopted in February 1939, envisaged the building, by the time of the possible start of the war against England, of six battleships (including three "pocket" ones), five heavy cruisers, two aircraft carriers and 190 submarines. After the execution of the Z plan it was planned to bring into service 13 battleships, 33 cruisers, 4 aircraft-carriers and 267 submarines.

Under the Z plan, the main aim of the operations of the fleet was the disruption of the sea and oceanic communications of England. For this it was planned to use all the forces of the fleet, the emphasis being on surface ships. To fulfil this task long-range forces were created, notably fast battleships and cruisers with a long operating range and independent operational potential, capable of attacking the fighting ships and merchant vessels of the enemy at distant points of the open sea. Submarines were also allocated to the long-range forces. The German fleet on the eve of the Second World War had 57 of them. The total displacement of submarines was only 9 per cent of the total displacement of the fleet, whereas battleships accounted for 46 per cent, cruisers 31.5 per cent and destroyers 13.5 per cent.[17]

The German Command under-estimated the role of aviation in the operations at sea. This to no small degree was promoted by the resistance of Goering to the creation of naval aviation. He considered that all the aviation of the armed forces must be concentrated in the Luftwaffe and, depending on the situation, must be used either in the interests of the navy or for fulfilling independent tasks, that is, for strategic bombings. The German Command also paid close attention to the development of short-range forces intended for defending the stationing areas, combating the mine danger, ensuring the development of the main forces of the fleet at sea and maintaining an advantageous operational regime in their coastal waters. Thus, the fleet of Fascist Germany on the eve of

[17] L. M. Yeremeyev and A. P. Shergin, *Submarines of Foreign Fleets in the Second World War*, p. 11 (in Russian).

the war was oriented to the disruption of enemy oceanic communications. Its buildings and training moved along corresponding lines.

The improvidence and adventurism of the German Sea Command, reflected in the choice of the direction of the building of the fleet and also the views on its use, were the main reason why German raiders were destroyed by the forces of the fleet of the allies in the very first year of the war. The switching of the operations of strike aviation to the Soviet-German front in the summer of 1941 resulted in only German submarines waging battle on the communications of the allies. The German Command regarded the encouraging results of their combat activity at the start of the war as a stimulus to go ahead with the intensive building of boats and the accelerated training of their crews. The successes of U-boats were largely promoted by the passivity of the English and American armed forces on land and in the air, and also the irresoluteness of the operations of the English fleet at sea.

On 30 December 1939 Germany approved a new shipbuilding programme in line with which, by the end of 1941, they were supposed to build 392 submarines. In the summer of 1943 a further programme was adopted for the accelerated construction and the coming into service by February 1943 of 288 *series XXI* submarines and by October 1944 of 140 *series XXIII* submarines.

The use of large contingents of the work force (hired foreign workers, workers of occupied countries, prisoners of war, women) and other extreme measures enabled German industry to increase considerably the construction of submarines. While in 1939 six of them were built, in 1940 this figure was up to forty, in 1941, 219 and in 1942, 222. The largest number of submarines was built in 1943 and 1944 (292 and 283 respectively). In all the war the Germans were able to bring into service 1131 submarines.[18] However, the intensified building of submarines did not improve the position of Fascist Germany at sea since no forces were created capable of ensuring the operations of these submarines, opposing the fleets of England and her allies, and assisting its land forces from the sea.

The development of essentially one branch of the forces—submarines—was in the end to lead to the sharp restriction of the range of tasks of the German fleet in the fight against the fleets of its enemies and pre-determined its passivity in all other spheres of the struggle at sea. Thus, the German Fascist Command put itself at a disadvantage at sea by facilitating to a certain extent the operations of the fleets of its enemies and promoting the specific development of their anti-submarine forces.

Another reason why Germany could not enjoy the fruits of such a tempestuous and, in equal measure, distorted development of its fleet was that it lost much time, allowing its enemies to take suitable counter measures. In addition, by creating armadas of submarines, the German Command did not bother about the fight against the anti-submarine defence of the Allies. And, finally, the most important thing, the tremendous strain of the struggle on the Eastern front deprived Germany of the possibility of setting aside more material resources for her fleet. The scale of the struggle and a number of very heavy defeats on the

[18] L. M. Yeremeyev and A. P. Shergin, *Submarines of Foreign Fleets in the Second World War* (in Russian), p. 27.

decisive Eastern front did not allow the German Fascist Command to set aside aircraft for use against English and, later, American shipping, for reconnaissance backing of the activity of submarines the laying of mines and combating anti-submarine forces at sea. In addition, the very powerful shipbuilding industry of England and the USA remained unaffected, so that the replenishment of the cargo fleet from 1944 began to exceed its losses in the war and the stepping-up of the pace of building the anti-submarine forces finally led to the collapse of German plans of unrestricted submarine warfare.

All these factors deepened even more the pre-war miscalculations of the German Command, which was soon to affect the combat operations of the German fleet as a whole.

The balance of the fleet of Fascist Germany in the course of the war was also constantly influenced by the operations of the Northern, Baltic and Black Sea fleets, to combat which the German Command was force to muster, along with the near-range forces, a considerable part of the forces from the sea and oceanic communications. This increased the disproportions in the German Fascist fleet and limited its possibilities in the fight against the fleets of our allies.

One of the merits of the Soviet armed forces was that, by displaying unshakeable steadfastness in defence and delivering strikes when on the offensive, they did not allow the German Command to remove the disproportions in the development of the fleet and to create in the course of the war balanced forces for fulfilling the main tasks at sea.

Taking advantage of the fact that the Soviet Union waged a bloody war against Fascist Germany face to face, drawing on to herself nearly all its forces, the Anglo-American Command, evading for almost three years the direct waging of active combat operations in a decisive land theatre, expanded unhindered and, finally, mustered enormous forces of the fleet and aircraft to combat German submarines.

According to the most conservative estimates, this task was fulfilled by over 1,500 shore-based planes, over thirty aircraft-carriers and some 3,500 escort ships of different types. English and Canadian aviation alone took off from ground aerodromes 44,000 times for escorting convoys and 75,500 times for patrolling sea areas to seek out hostile submarines. To this it should be added that the German shipbuilding establishments, especially the factories and yards building submarines and producing equipment for them, starting from 1943, were subjected to frequent mass raids by Anglo-American aircraft.

Already in that period German diesel submarines, remaining in effect at the 1939 technical level as a result of the sharply-diminished level of training of the crews and decline in their morale, were incapable of successfully overcoming the counter-action of the carefully trained and technically more sophisticated forces of the anti-submarine defence of the opponent. The losses of German submarines in trying to break through the anti-submarine lines and in the course of attacks on English and American convoys began to grow substantially, while the losses of the merchant fleet of Britain and her allies appreciably diminished. This is made clear by Table 23.

Foreign historians often use these statistical data to demonstrate the fanciful idea that submarines, like battleships, were vanquished in the last war. But the

TABLE 23
Merchant Shipping Losses for Britain and Her Allies and German Submarine
Losses in the Course of the Second World War

| Years | Losses of merchant ships | | No. of German submarines sunk | No. of vessels sunk per submarine destroyed | Gross tonnage of vessels sunk per submarine destroyed reg. tons |
	No. of vessels	Gross tonnage reg. tons			
1939	114	421,156	9	12.6	46,795
1940	471	2,186,158	22	21.4	99,375
1941	432	2,171,754	35	12.3	62,050
1942	1160	6,266,215	85	13.6	73,720
1943	463	2,586,905	237	1.5	10,915
1944	132	773,327	248	0.5	3118
1945	56	281,716	145	0.4	1949
Total	2828	14,687,231	781	3.6	18,806

See L. M. Yeremeyev and A. P. Shergin, *Submarines of Foreign Fleets in the Second World War* (in Russian).

decline in the effectiveness of the combat activities of submarines on sea communications in the course of the war was nothing other than the expression of the process of struggle between the means of attack and means of defence, the development of which proceeded in unequal conditions: the former were slowly improved without changing their technical level and the latter were created on a new technical basis. And, if thanks to the massive use of anti-submarine forces and resources, the English and Americans achieved certain successes in the fight against submarines, there is no doubt that the appearance of essentially new types of submarines with more sophisticated arming would have altered the position in Germany's favour. In other words, if the German Command was not in a position to use on a wide scale the new submarines and new means of combat before Germany had been crushed on land by Soviet troops, this in no way means that submarines as a means of combat on sea communications were somehow discredited.

The success of the Allies in the armed struggle at sea is largely explained by the imbalance of the German fleet, used only for the fulfilment of one task. The adventurism of German sea strategy, turning the fleet from a universal branch of the armed forces into a narrowly-specialized force and limiting the sphere of its use merely to operations on the enemy's communications, was one of the basic causes of the defeat of the German fleet in the "Battle of the Atlantic". The imbalance of the fleet did not allow the Hitler command to use it effectively either against the strike forces or against the shore or to combat the landings of the allies which virtually encountered no determined resistance at sea.

At the same time the use of the various forces and resources of the German fleet in the sea theatres lying next to the territory of the Soviet Union, their periodic bolstering with submarines, anti-submarine forces drawn off from the oceanic directions and first-line aviation, greatly complicated the struggle of our fleets. However, the operations of the Soviet fleet were helped to a certain extent by the absence in the German fleet of large amphibious and special means for supporting from the sea land forces in maritime directions.

The active combat activity of our fleet did not allow the Germans to compensate the imbalance of their forces at sea by various improvisations. Therefore, the German fleet throughout the war was unable to provide decisive support for its troops in the maritime directions even when they were sustaining heavy defeats.

It cannot be said that the US navy came into the war balanced in relation to its goals and tasks. On the eve of the Second World War this oceanic fleet, the biggest in complement, was also oriented to the waging of combat against battle forces in the open sea. All the large ships, including aircraft-carriers and cruisers forming part of the squadrons, were supposed to ensure the entry into battle of the battle forces.

A fairly large number of US submarines were chiefly intended for combating the surface fighting ships of the enemy, although the possibility of using them for destroying cargo vessels on the sea and oceanic communications was not denied.

The distribution of the forces of the fleet for specific tasks did not go beyond this, if one disregards the fact that for the struggle on communications it was planned to use some of the surface ships forming part of the squadrons. Therefore the American command was compelled to solve the problem of balance directly in the course of armed struggle.

After the attack by the Japanese on Pearl Harbor the Americans "like Adam and Eve, found themselves naked."[19] A large part of the "basis" of their fleet lay at the bottom in the form of a mass of useless scrap. The loss of eight battleships, three cruisers, three destroyers and other ships shook the hierarchy of the American fleet. It took six months to reorient the fleet to the fulfilment of the main tasks in the fight at sea with the forces of aircraft-carriers. It took a battle in the Coral Sea to show convincingly that battleships had finally lost their leading role, irrevocably surrendering it to the carriers of strike naval aviation—aircraft-carriers.

The urgent need for carriers made the US naval command step up their building in every way. At the same time the building of battleships, cruisers and destroyers was accelerated. In the years of the war 9 battleships, 45 cruisers and 379 destroyers were built.

The Second World War introduced fundamental changes into the ratio of forces of the American fleet. While at the start of it the ratio of battleships to that of the entire fleet was 45.6 per cent, cruisers 22 per cent, destroyers 19.1 per cent, aircraft carriers 9.3 per cent and submarines 4 per cent, by the end of the war it was 24 per cent for battleships, carriers 23, cruisers 23, destroyers 19 and submarines nine per cent.

These figures confirm the conclusion that already in the course of the Second World War battleships had lost their former importance and had ceded the main role in armed conflict at sea to aircraft-carriers and submarines which are today the basis of the fighting power of the US navy.

The American navy came into the war totally unprepared to protect merchant vessels from submarine strikes. The enormous losses of the merchant fleet and the continued activation of the operations of German submarines in the

[19] J. Fuller, *The Second World War 1939-45,* p. 56, Inost. Lit., Moscow, 1956 (in Russian).

Atlantic placed before the US naval forces the priority problem of producing patrol-escort ships. With the aid of emergency measures and heavy financial expenditure, the Americans were able to develop comparatively quickly the large-scale building of these ships. While at the end of July 1941 280 patrol-escort ships were taking part in the fight against submarines, a year later it was 527 and after a further two years 1260.

Thus, in the years of the Second World War the US practically built a new powerful anti-submarine ship force. Taking into account the insignificant losses suffered in the course of combat actions, by the end of the war they numbered 73 escort carriers, 358 escort ships, 77 frigates, eight corvettes and 659 submarine hunters.

At the start of the war with Japan the USA was also faced with the need to fill the gap in landing ships. At that time the American fleet had only a few experimental ships of this class. The USA embarked on accelerated production-line construction of landing-disembarking devices of various types and large vessels for moving troops across the ocean and taking an invasion force to the areas of disembarkation in the course of the war itself. By the end of the war, the US naval forces had 17 landing ships (headquarters), 1090 large landing ships (tanks), 554 landing ships (tanks), 454 landing transports (infantry), and 23 landing transports (docks). In addition, thousands of various landing-disembarking small vessels were built.

The mass construction of anti-mine defence ships was undertaken. And while at the start of the war the American fleet had almost none, by the end of it it already had 223 squadron and 74 base sweepers and 450 minesweeper boats.

Thus, only in the course of the war was the American fleet balanced in its tasks, qualitative and quantitative properties and areas of operations. The operational-strategic goals of the use of its forces in war were re-defined, which demanded the creation of new classes of ships, including purpose-built anti-submarine and landing ships.

The US naval forces, earlier geared to waging battle with an enemy surface fleet, were transformed into a universal-purpose branch of the armed forces on which also fell major tasks in conducting large-scale amphibious operations, the defence of the oceanic communications of the Allies and upsetting the enemy's communications.

The successful solution of the problem of balancing the forces of the American fleet in the course of the war was promoted by the fact, advantageous to the USA, that the strategic tasks of the war were being resolved by the Soviet armed forces on the main Soviet-German land front and therefore the fleet of Fascist Germany, especially starting from 1943, was not in a position to wage struggle against the communications and fleet of the USA in the Atlantic, thanks to which US industry was not exposed to the action of the enemy and worked in the war in the most favourable conditions.

However, even in these conditions, American industry took years to create anew the forces of the fleet capable of waging battle with German submarines in the Atlantic and the large amphibious forces for the invasion of Europe by Allied troops.

The imbalance of the forces of the Japanese fleet in goals and tasks came to light from the very start of military operations in the Pacific and was one of the main causes of its defeat in the Second World War. The direction of the development of the Japanese fleet in the pre-war period was determined on the same premises which underlay the military doctrines of the Western powers. The only difference was that the Japanese envisaged the building of ships and vessels for staging sea landings. But no modern forces for anti-submarine defence of oceanic communications were created, although the island position of Japan and dependence on imports by sea of strategic raw materials were always its vulnerable point.

The rapid thrust of the Japanese in a southerly direction and the seizure of extensive island areas in the south-west part of the Pacific at the start of the war led to the dispersion of the forces of its fleet enlisted to protect merchant shipping, and placed a very great strain on the coastal anti-submarine forces, the composition and fighting qualities of which ruled out combat operations over large stretches of the Pacific.

The Japanese military leadership, getting ready for a war against the USSR, started from the premise that if even limited anti-submarine forces could block the exit of Soviet submarines from the Sea of Japan, all the tasks of protecting the Japanese communications in the Pacific would be solved. For this, the massive use of minefields and anti-submarine nets, covered by ships and coastal artillery in the straits, was considered sufficient.

The losses sustained by the Japanese merchant fleet already in the first year of the war greatly exceeded all the calculations of the Japanese command. However, the obstacle to any decisive measures to ensure and protect sea shipments was the limited potential of the productive and raw material base of the country, not geared to build in a short time the necessary number of anti-submarine ships. The general complement of escort forces of the fleet continued to remain insufficient. In 1943 the Japanese fleet numbered only fifty anti-submarine protection ships (including fourteen specially constructed), including several destroyers built in 1920-25, but they were chiefly used for protecting large surface ships.

The convoying of cargo ships at sea was in the main by coastal escorts with weak anti-submarine armament. The four escort aircraft-carriers forming part of the anti-submarine forces were able to take part in convoys only in 1944.

In an effort to remove the consequences of the miscalculations in balancing the forces of the fleet, the Japanese Sea Command brought into the struggle against American submarines an enormous number of motor and sail fishing craft not adapted for this. Such vessels were not fitted with sonar and radar equipment and could have no effect in the fight against submarines.

Seeing the failure of its strategic plans, the Japanese military leadership, in addition to fourteen special anti-submarine ships in service, planned to build in 1942-45, 233 escort ships. However, this intention, beyond the potential of industry, was not realized.

The weakness of the material-technical base and unpreparedness of the Japanese fleet for anti-submarine defence created highly favourable conditions for the operations of American submarines on the sea and oceanic communications of Japan. Not meeting any serious opposition, they sank 1150 Japanese vessels with a total tonnage around 4,860,000 registered tons or about 62 per cent of the total losses of the Japanese merchant fleet.[20]

From the weapons of submarines the Japanese lost over 80 fighting ships including 1 battleship, 8 aircraft-carriers, 12 cruisers, 37 destroyers and 24 submarines.[21]

The Japanese fleet also proved to be insufficiently prepared to repel air strikes. In the period of the war the American air force destroyed 750 merchant ships with a total tonnage of 2,467,000 registered tons or 31.5 per cent of the losses of merchant tonnage and also 112 large fighting ships including 6 battle-ships, 13 aircraft-carriers, 20 cruisers, 51 destroyers and 22 submarines.[22]

Thus, analysis of the condition of the navies of the capitalist states in the period of the Second World War, the dynamics of their development, changes in the structure and ratio of forces in the course of combat actions brought about by unforeseen circumstances, suggests that the problem of the balance of the forces of fleets was not solved in any of the warring imperialist maritime powers on the eve of the Second World War.

Wherein lie the main causes of the under-estimation of this important problem in the pre-war period?

Of course, the point is not at all that the economies of such imperialist states as the USA, England, Germany and Japan were unable in the conditions of peacetime to create the naval forces necessary in fighting qualities and quantitative composition. One hardly agrees, either, that the military thinking of these countries was incapable of determining the goals and tasks of the navies in a future war stemming from the foreign policy of the states and formulating a scientifically-based programme of fleet building.

The true causes of such a situation are:

– major irredeemable miscalculations in the foreign policy of the ruling circles and military leadership of the USA and England, who were unable to recognize in time a potential foe in Hitler's Germany, to determine the character of the Second World War and the role and place in it of their fleets:

– the adventurism of the policy and strategy of Fascist Germany and militarist Japan; the endeavour, doomed to failure, of achieving, by war, world dominance in a short time;

– the neglect by the military leaders of both coalitions of the rich experience of the First World War; over-estimation of the combat possibilities of big-gun ships; underestimation of the strike power and perspectives of development of submarines and aircraft which, in fact, became the main forces of the fleets in the armed struggle at sea;

– the imbalance of the forces of the fleets in relation to the tasks was already obvious in the course of the developing armed struggle at sea, which confronted all the warring powers with the need, in a hurry and at the cost of enormous efforts and extreme strain on the economy, to put right the miscalculations made. And only at the moment of the ending of the war did the American and

[20] V. A. Belli *et al.*, *Blockade and Counter-Blockade* (in Russian), p. 706.
[21] *Sea Atlas* (in Russian), Vol. III, Part 2.
[22] *Sea Atlas* (in Russian), Vol. III, Part 2.

British fleets become balanced to the highest degree in relation to the tasks arising;

– the limited economic possibilities of Fascist Germany and militarist Japan, as compared with the possibilities of the USA and England, were used only for developing those forces of the fleets on which fell the main burden of the armed struggle at sea at different periods. This substantially narrowed the range of the tasks of the fleet, deprived it of such an important quality as universality. Objectively favourable conditions were created for the enemy, allowing him to concentrate the forces of his fleet only in limited directions, ensure their operations precisely in this narrow sphere and achieve success at the price of comparatively little effort and material cost.

Using mostly submarines for the struggle at sea, the Germans made the enemy experience no few bitter disappointments in his anxiety to protect his oceanic communications. However, as a result of the one-sideness in its development the German fleet proved no match for the Anglo-American fleet.

The navy belongs to the branch of the armed forces most difficult to restore and the replenishment of the losses of ships and weapons involves heavy expenditure of time and material. Economically-strong states coped with this task in the course of the war in curtailed times only because of exceptionally favourable military-political conditions. In the absence of these conditions, replenishment of the forces of the fleet and, even more so, the balancing of them in the course of the war were practically insoluble problems. Particularly instructive in this respect is Japan, which did not have the necessary raw-material base and its industrial objectives were constantly subjected to strikes by the Americans.

The industrial establishments of Fascist Germany also came under attack from Allied aircraft, although, as a rule, not sufficiently to rob her completely of the possibility of making good the losses sustained by the fleet.

British industry at the start of the Second World War had much trouble in making good the losses in ships since her shipyards were subjected to fierce German air raids. Only after Hitlerite aviation ceased mass raids on England, concentrating all efforts on the Soviet-German front, and only after enormous aid from the USA, was there a sharp increase in the pace of building anti-submarine ships, landing ships and sweepers and also cargo vessels of the merchant fleet.

The Second World War showed that none of the warring capitalist countries whose industry had experienced strikes of the enemy could, without the assistance of the Allies, get rid of disproportions in the balance of the fleet and organize and carry out replenishment of the forces and resources of the fleet in the course of the war.

Only US industry was in a position to solve this task independently. This was helped by the fact that the American continent was out of reach of the then existing means of armed conflict and also by the considerable capacity and high level of the economy and war industry of the USA.

The absence of unity in operational-strategic thinking resulted in failure to determine correctly the directions of the creation of the various types of weapons and branches of the armed forces, which was expressed in particular in the under-estimation of the operations of the fleet against the shore. Only the practice of war somewhat changed this position and made the Anglo-American command in a number of cases set up a combined land-sea leadership for conducting operations against the shore, developed in the main in the Pacific theatre.

A nuclear missile war, if it were to be unleashed by the imperialists, would create new conditions for the economy of all countries making it impossible to eliminate miscalculations in the pre-war building of the fleet.

Today, all the apologists of imperialism are faced with the immutable truth that no ocean will protect an aggressor country from the strike of strategic nuclear missile forces launched from any area of the oceans or from another continent.

Problems of the balancing of the Soviet navy in pre-war and war periods (1921-45).

The initial stage of the emergence of the Soviet navy as a branch of the armed forces coincided with the period of the breakdown of the national economy, when the country could set aside very limited resources for the development of the armed forces. There was plainly not enough such resources to build new ships. Therefore, the Tenth Congress of the RCP (B) decided to bring into service ships left over from the old Russian fleet. Attention was focused on those ships which could be restored and used to protect the coast from attack by a foe from the sea. But there could be no question of balancing the fleet at that time.

At the same time work began on the elaboration of the theoretical bases of Soviet naval art. The trouble was that it was not possible to take advantage of the theoretical legacy of the old Russian fleet and bourgeois naval theories, as they rested on altogether different ideological and political principles, not to mention the quite different economic potential.

Soviet naval theory took an independent course. Theoretical postulates of a so-called minor war oriented towards defensive actions of the fleet in its coastal waters were taken as the basis.

In numerous disputes and discussions, different points of view were advanced. However, practical meaning naturally attached only to proposals, the realization of which did not go beyond the economic potential of the country. The development of the fleet was directed to creating, at the cost of the least material expenditure, forces capable of successfully rebutting an attack by an enemy on the coast from the sea. This concept for many years determined the main function of the fleet—to assist land forces in solving the tasks in the land theatres of military operations which, as the armed forces developed, assumed different forms: from direct support by the fleet of the army from the sea, to the conduct by it of independent operations but with the same operational objective.

The basis of the fleet was then provided by the short-range forces—torpedo boats, shore-based aviation, shore artillery and mine weapons. Their combined use, especially on positions prepared in good time with the support of sub-marines, big-gun ships and coastal artillery batteries present in very small numbers as part of the fleet, provided a more or less effective counter to a hostile fleet intent on delivering strikes on our coast or staging seaborne landings.

Thus, in the development of the fleet the starting point at that time was the need to solve with its aid the main tasks: to ensure the defence of our coast essentially in the form of support of the flank of the army by fire power. However, in solving this task we were not able to avoid errors. Like the fleets of the capitalist countries, our fleet did not have and did not build special landing craft. In rare cases during combat training so-called handy means and unadapted transports were used. These erroneous views on the development of our fleet persisted right up to the Great Patriotic War. And it was during the war, when there emerged the problem of staging landings as a very widespread form of combat activity, carried out on the sea flanks of the Soviet-German land front jointly with the army, that we had to pay a heavy price for the neglect of this form of combat preparation of the fleet and army.

As industry was restored and the economic potential of the country grew, new perspectives for the development of the fleet opened up. In 1926, the Council for Labour and Defence approved a new six-year programme of naval construc-tion which envisaged the creation of surface ships and submarines, intended in the main for operations in their own coastal waters.

As noted above, in 1928 the Revolutionary Military Council of the Republic confirmed that the main purpose of the fleet is to assist land forces: which thus continued to remain the basic starting point determining the demands on the building of the fleet in the new stage. In the years of the first two Five-Year Plans the fleet began to be augmented by new cruisers, destroyers and sub-marines, guard ships and torpedo boats.

The programme of building a large ocean-going fleet, adopted in 1938, called for the building of big-gun ships capable of standing up alone against a strong enemy in the open sea. The problem of the balance of the forces of the fleet in relation to the new conditions was not resolved either in the theory or in the practice of building the fleet.

In the last pre-war years, Soviet military thought was oriented to the creation and use of squadrons of large surface ships headed by powerful battleships and cruisers, and insufficient regard was paid to the high combat possibilities of aviation as a strike force in the armed struggle at sea. At the same time Soviet military theory, oriented to surface ships, was not able to validate the need to have as part of the ocean-going fleet aircraft-carriers capable of ensuring the cover of ships with weak flak arming beyond the zones of reach of shore-based fighter aircraft. As a result, it was not possible to reckon on the success of the operations of the ships in relatively distant areas of the sea and even more so in zones controlled by hostile aircraft.

Thus, the ocean-going fleet created could operate in fact only in its coastal areas and its tasks continued to remain aid to the troops in the land theatres and support of the army. It was considered that the fleet might also perform such a task as disrupting the sea communications of the enemy, but the creation of special forces for this was not contemplated.

Nor were the tactical-technical demands on the new submarines built scientifically based. The starting point here were retrospective requirements which had come to light already in the years of the First World War and no allowance was made for possible changes in the conditions of armed conflict in the near future. The bulk of the submarines built had a low operating range and independence of action. Submarines capable of operating in the ocean were planned to be built in small numbers.

As is known, the programme of naval construction adopted in 1938 could not be realized by the start of the Great Patriotic War. Therefore our fleet, though considerably augmented by surface ships, submarines and planes, in fact was not in balance with those tasks which lay ahead of it. And in the course of the war the fleet had indeed to solve quite new tasks not envisaged in the rationale of its construction. Instead of assisting in-depth offensive operations of land forces, the fleet was forced to secure defence from sea and land of naval bases besieged by the enemy, the evacuation of these bases and the coastal towns and hastily undertake the formation of numerous flotillas for waging defensive operations in the Azov Sea, on the rivers and lakes and deep in our territory. For the Baltic and Black Sea fleets it was necessary to set up in haste a new system of bases in the areas under enemy attack.

In this situation a particularly sharp impact was made by the absence of special landing craft, the necessary number of sweepers, anti-submarine ships and other means of transport. In addition, there were not enough sweeps for combating non-contact mines and mines with non-contact explosives.

The absence in the fleet of the necessary number of anti-mine ships resulted in the period of the Great Patriotic War in losses of our fighting ships on mines, amounting in the Black Sea to 24 per cent, the Baltic 49 per cent and in the North Sea 22 per cent of total losses. Mines were responsible for the destruction of 52 per cent of all destroyers lost by us in the war. One cannot help noticing that losses on mines of fighting ships of the capitalist states in the Second World War were only 7.7 per cent of total losses and the loss of destroyers 10.7 per cent, i.e. five times less than the losses in our fleet.

The woefully inadequate number of auxiliary and military-transport vessels caused serious difficulties in ensuring military shipments, for which it was necessary to use fighting ships and cutters, taking them from other duties. In the Red Banner Baltic Fleet, for example, in the first months of the war over 70 per cent of the runs of torpedo boats were made to carry various military cargoes.

The air force of our fleet before the Great Patriotic War included a large number of planes. However, special naval aviation was represented only by coastal water reconnaissance flying boats. We had no anti-submarine aviation. At first the flying boat MBR–2 was adapted for anti-submarine defence purposes and then the wheel-planes the *D–3, Pe–2, Il–4* and the *Douglas*. These planes had no special means of search for submarines and in effect were armed reconnaissance planes. To cover ships and vessels from air attack at sea, one had to confine oneself to conventional front-line aircraft with a low radius of action which made it more difficult to use surface ships and in a number of cases led to heavy losses.

Our ships and vessels in the course of the Great Patriotic War operated with an acute and constant lack of air cover. For this reason their losses from enemy aircraft were: in the Black Sea fleet 47 per cent, in the Red Banner Baltic fleet 26 per cent, and in the North Sea 48 per cent of the total number of ships and vessels lost.

The change in the character of the balance of our fleet in the course of the Great Patriotic War was, in part, brought about by the entry into the navy of ships mobilized from the People's Commissariat of Internal Affairs, the merchant fleet and the river fleet, the construction of new ships and planes in the country's factories and the receipt of some ships from the Allies.

Over 1,600 different vessels and boats were mobilized from civilian organizations. Armament was set up on many of them and some were refitted. However, they all had low tactical-technical quality and could solve only secondary combat tasks or fulfil the function of auxiliary vessels. Therefore, the receipt of such ships, boats and vessels did not introduce any fundamental corrections into the character of the balance of the forces of the fleet.

The shipbuilding industry of the USSR before the start of the Great Patriotic War built ships of all classes. The main direction of its work was the building of first- and second-rank surface ships and also submarines. The organization of production technology and character of cooperation were all subordinate to this.

With the start of the war, the direction of naval construction sharply changed. By the decision of the State Defence Committee adopted in July 1941, the building of large ships, demanding heavy labour expenditure, long time schedules, materials in short supply, equipment and arming, was stopped. Emphasis was placed on the completion of light surface ships and the building of various combat craft.

With the evacuation of the southern factories (about 30 per cent of gross production) and the development of the building of tanks in some of the biggest shipbuilding yards, naval construction was in effect wound up. The production capacity of the shipbuilding industry and the workers engaged in it fell by 50 per cent. Therefore, the Soviet shipbuilding industry, in the uncommonly difficult conditions created for it, could not fully meet the need of the navy for ships.

To a certain extent this need was satisfied by ships received under Lend-Lease (22 sweepers, 108 submarine hunters, 86 torpedo boats and some frigates). However, these measures had no practical influence on the balance of our fleet and by the end of the war it was only partly in balance.

Problems of balancing the Soviet Navy in the post-war period

In the first post-war decade, the main tasks determining the building and development of the navy continued to remain assistance for land forces in conducting operations in maritime directions and disrupting the near-lying sea communications of the enemy. To fulfil these tasks, the fleet had to possess a considerable number of surface ships of different classes, submarines, strong naval aviation, marines and shore artillery. However, the severe wounds inflicted on our country by the war did not allow an immediate start to be made after the capitulation of Fascist Germany on building such a fleet. For a long time it continued to remain imbalanced in relation to its tasks.

The navy did not have the necessary number of oceanic submarines, anti-submarines and anti-mine ships. The fleet did not have landing ships. Naval aviation had a low radius of action and anti-submarine aviation was absent. Fighters could cover ships at sea only in a narrow belt lying next to the coast and flak armament of ships remained weak. The auxiliary fleet was represented chiefly by base craft of doubtful seaworthiness.

Thus, the navy continued to remain coastal and hence, at an operational-strategic level, in war with a strong sea foe, was a defensive factor.

The main requirements for balancing the fleet could be clearly defined only in the second post-war decade, that is, after the restoration of industry and with the start of the technical revolution in military matters.

The technical revolution in the military sphere, expanded economic potential and the outstanding achievements of Soviet science and technology, the introduction into the fleet of nuclear missile weapons, atomic power and radio-electronic devices, enabled the Central Committee of the CPSU and the Soviet Government to set the course for the building of a modern ocean-going fleet completely matching the defence requirements of our state in conditions of a growing threat to it from the oceans. In the briefest time a qualitatively new fleet was built, capable of fulfilling tasks of a strategic character and waging a successful struggle with a powerful sea adversary.

On the basis of thorough scientific research into the combat possibilities of the new forces and resources of the fleet, analysis of the post-war development of the naval forces of the leading imperialist states, and experience in operational preparation of our and foreign fleets, all the directions of naval science were determined, the operational-tactical requirements on the new forces of the fleet worked out and a consistent theory of naval art created, opening the way to the planned development of these forces and their use in war. Operational-tactical requirements were based on the thesis that a modern fleet, by virtue of the universality of the tasks facing it, must have diverse specialized forces. The optimal quantitative ratio of submarines, surface ships, aircraft units, marines, shore artillery missile forces, and also auxiliary vessels and other means of supply must allow the formations and tactical groups created independently or in liaison with the formations of other branches of the armed forces to overcome the counter-action of the enemy and successfully execute the tasks falling on the fleet.

Scientific investigation confirmed that such requirements may be met only by a balanced fleet, and we already have its basis.

A modern fleet, as noted above, is a very complex and multi-faceted organization. A modern fleet comprises diverse combat forces including, as well as submarines as the main strike force, surface multi-role fighting ships, naval aviation, shore artillery missile forces with marines and varied means of supply. The quantitative composition of these forces and their combat possiblities are determined by the need to create groupings for solving all the tasks which might arise in the most unfavourable variants, that is, in those cases in which these tasks have to be fulfilled not successively but simultaneously.

At present the conditions of activity of the fleet have changed, and the forces of rear back-up—supply of ships and ship repair—have begun to act in a new capacity. To solve these tasks, a balanced fleet must have a floating rear, the basis of which is made up of seaworthy oceanic supply vessels, floating shops and floating bases.

The quantitative composition of these facilities and their equipment must secure for the use of the oceanic forces high operational resilience to meet the situation prevailing in oceanic and sea theatres.

Briefly looking at the main problems of the use of the sea power of states, principally their navies, in wars and in peacetime, one may draw the following conclusions.

(1) One of the main qualities of modern naval forces is their universality. It is expressed in the ability of these forces to solve multiple tasks.

The development of the means of armed struggle at sea has not merely raised the effectiveness of the operations of the fleet and has not only widened the sphere of its possible use, but has also continuously influenced those tasks which have fallen to it.

Thus, in a particular stage of the development of fleets there were operations connected with warfare against a fleet of the enemy, in the course of which tasks were solved to gain dominance at sea, especially necessary in the age of sailing fleets.

Today the dominant role has been assumed by operations of the fleet against the shore. The operations of the fleets against the shore were earlier qualified by tasks in the fight against an enemy fleet; in present-day conditions, the function of the factor determining the development of fleets and their naval art is performed by operations directly against the shore.

In considering historically changes in tasks solved by the fleets, one cannot but notice that the most "ancient" of them, but retaining its importance even in present-day conditions, are the conflict on the sea communications and sea landings.

(2) A specific variant of military operations in modern conditions is provided by local wars which have been waged by the imperialist states practically continuously since the end of the Second World War. The experience of these wars shows that the navy plays an enormous role in them and may be used (within the framework of use of conventional weapons) for solving all possible tasks known to modern naval art and military doctrines.

The operations of the fleets in local wars bring the solution of tasks into the sphere of "fleet against the shore". The available experience of the use of fleets in local wars is characterized by a certain onesideness due to the character of these wars, waged as a rule by the big imperialist powers against small countries which have just freed or are freeing themselves from the yoke of colonialism. Nevertheless, study of the experience allows one to see the changes in the resources and ways of using "large" fleets and the evolutionary development of individual categories of naval art. In general, the experience of the use of sea forces in local wars has a definite influence on the development of the fleets and naval art. However, it is not fully applicable to the waging of armed combat at sea with use of nuclear weapons or to encounters between equivalent naval forces.

(3) The navy, as a branch of the armed forces and a most essential component of sea power, and with specific properties, has often had to act as one of the most important instruments of the policy of states in different historical conditions. This peculiarity of the fleet is actively used by imperialist states in relations with weak states. Attempts have been made to employ this form of using sea power also against the Soviet Union, although without result.

The Soviet navy, in the policy of our Party and state, acts as a factor for stabilizing the situation in different areas of the world, promoting the strengthening of peace and friendship between the peoples and restraining the aggressive strivings of the imperialist states.

(4) The multi-faceted activity of the navy in wars and peacetime, the wide range of the tasks solved by it, each of which requires the participation of diverse forces and means, have governed the need for balancing the forces of the fleet by different criteria and forms. Analysis of the combat experience of the fleets in past wars shows that the imbalance in their forces was manifest not only in the limitation of the possiblities of solving that task for which the given forces were created, but also in fulfilling a number of contiguous, attendant tasks. For example, the absence of sweepers affected not only the location of the actions of the mine weapons of the enemy but also the waging of struggle in the open sea by surface ships and submarines and the solution of all tasks of the fleet in coastal areas. In this connection the balancing of the forces of the fleet may be regarded as a definite specific form of actual material possibilities.

In the light of this position as a whole, a stronger (in overall displacement and number of ships) but imbalanced fleet may be inferior in its integral operational potential to a numerically weaker but properly balanced fleet, since the use of this latter will be affected by the favourable influence of the interaction of its diverse forces, which is determined not simply by summing up the potential of the groupings of forces, but by the advent of a new quality, representing a higher stage in the unity of offensive and defensive potential. The problem of the complete balance of a fleet crucially depends on such a complex process as the scientific management of its building. The solution of the problem of the balance of a fleet calls for much material expenditure, since, in fact, it can be regarded as the creation of the fleet necessary to a given state.

All in all, it may be taken as indisputable that the victories of the fleet and the art of using its forces in any war for which it is created significantly depend on the correct solution of the problem of its balance.

Conclusion

AMONG the many factors characterizing the economic and military might of our country, an ever-growing role is being played by its sea power, expressing the real ability of the state to make effective use of the World Ocean in the interests of communist construction. The higher the level of development of the economy of our country, the greater will be the significance assumed for us by the World Ocean as an inexhaustible source of energy, raw materials and food and as a sphere for the further development of political, economic, scientific and technical links with the countries and peoples of all continents of the globe.

Scientific and technical progress conditions the need to develop all the components of sea power in their integral meshing and uncovers new possibilities of realising them in different branches of the national economy. From the point of view of economics and international relations a leading place is taken by the merchant and fishing fleets, ensuring the exploitation of the wealth of the World Ocean and the further extension of economic, scientific and cultural ties with the people of many countries of the world.

Ever-increasing significance is being assumed by study of the World Ocean as an important factor influencing the status of the sea power of the state and opening up of new possibilities in the earth's hydrosphere, for satisfying the rapidly-growing requirements of our country for energy and fuel, useful minerals and foodstuffs.

But a special role belongs to the military side of the sea power of the country, characterizing the real possibilities of the Soviet navy to protect the inviolability of the sea lines of the homeland and ensure its state interests at sea.

The important place which the navy occupies among the other components of sea power of the state in modern conditions is determined by the striving of the imperialist powers with the aid of the armed forces in general and the fleets in particular to turn the course of world development in their favour. Rapacious wars are alien to the Soviet Union. But the Soviet people-will resolutely protect socialist gains, using all the power of our country, including sea power represented by such a component as the navy.

The creation in our country of an ocean-going nuclear missile navy has wrought profound changes in the views of its role in the system of the armed forces of the country and ways of using it. This gives rise to an acute need to generalize the historical experience of armed conflict at sea where it links up with current problems of building and using the fleet.

This was the goal the author set himself, while realizing that the present work is far from an exhaustive attempt to make such a generalization.

In the course of the exploration of the lines of development of the fleets, forms and ways of using them in wars and in peacetime, a point constantly borne in mind was that they have always been a constituent part of a single whole—the armed forces of the state, and also that the interrelationship of all the branches of the armed forces and the mutual interaction of their operations have constantly grown. The share of each branch of the armed forces has changed with the composition of the coalitions of adversaries, the political goals of war and arming and its combat properties.

In many wars, especially those in which the main adversaries have been separated by expanses of sea, the fleets have played a decisive role in winning victory. In essence this was characteristic of the wars of the pre-imperialist stage of the development of capitalism and of the first wars of the age of imperialism, including the Russo-Japanese war.

In the course of the First World War, despite the growth of the scale of military operations at sea, the fleet became relatively less important. A similar position, despite the further rise in the scale of armed conflict at sea, may also be noted in the Second World War. As is known, in the course of it a decisive role was played by the struggle on the Soviet-German land front.

Scientific and technical progress in the military realm has brought forward new criteria for determining the real fighting power of each of the branches of the armed forces, the principal one being the ability to use most rationally such a decisive resource of armed struggle as nuclear missile weapons. Therefore, forces possessing nuclear missile strategic weapons of intercontinental range have come to the fore.

Scientific and technical progress has produced submarines as the most perfect carrier of modern weapons, the launching site of which is in effect the whole World Ocean. The fleet concentrates in itself numerous mobile carriers of strategic weapons, each of which may carry a very large number of long-range missiles and is capable of manoeuvring with launching sites over an area exceeding many times the area which land-based missile troops can use. Sea carriers of strategic means also possess the ability to manoeuvre in depth, sheltering themselves by width of water and using it not only for protection but also for masking, which greatly adds to the viability of naval strategic weapons systems. Thus, objective conditions of armed conflict in a nuclear war produce as a strike nuclear missile force the missile-carrying fleet, rationally combining the latest achievements of science and technology, enormous strike power and mobility, viability of strategic means and high readiness for their immediate use.

In the course of the scientific-technical revolution, naval forces have assumed the significance of one of the most important strategic factors, capable by direct action on enemy groupings of troops and vitally-important objectives on his territory, of exerting a very considerable and sometimes decisive influence on the course of a war.

The influence of the struggle at sea on the course of a war, as a whole, is essentially expressed in how far the fleet can realise its ability to strike at ground objectives on land and undermine the strategic nuclear potential of the enemy at sea.

The growing importance of the navies in armed conflict is reflected in the military doctrines of the imperialist states, the principal ones of which are oriented to an oceanic strategy. This strategy reflects not only military but also fundamental economic and political interests of the leading powers of the capitalist world at sea. Thus, analysis of the present-day alignment of forces in the international arena and the swift development of navies in the post-war period give grounds for asserting that the importance of the struggle at sea has grown and will continue to increase.

The most important period in the history of the development of navies and the art of using them is the post-war period. It is precisely at this time when the most significant and profoundest qualitative changes have taken place in the material base of armed conflict at sea and also in operational art and tactics of the navy.

A characteristic feature of the post-war period is the universal recognition of the growing role of armed conflict at sea and hence the importance of oceanic directions and theatres of military operations in a modern war. This is confirmed by the fact that, unlike the Great Patriotic War, against us now stands a coalition of maritime powers possessing powerful modern fleets capable of solving strategic tasks in a war. The imperialists are turning the World Ocean into an extensive launching-pad, less dangerous in their view to their countries as compared with land, of ballistic missiles, of submarines and carrier aviation trained on the Soviet Union and the countries of the socialist community. And our navy must be capable of standing up to this real threat.

But the military aspects examined by us have not only exerted an influence on the role of the navies. Remaining a very effective and an essential means of armed struggle, they are constantly used as an instrument of the policy of states in peacetime. The sea is no-man's-land and, therefore, the fleets do not encounter in their activity the many limitations which stand in the way of the use for political purposes of other branches of the armed forces in peacetime.

The fleets in this regard have assumed special importance in modern conditions in connection with the growth of their strike power. The mobility of the fleet and its flexibility where limited military conflicts come to a head enable it to exert an influence on coastal countries, employ and extend a military threat at any level, starting from a show of military force and ending with the mounting of landings.

Confirmation of this may be provided by the activity of the Sixth American Fleet in the Mediterranean, where it put pressure on the holding of elections in Italy and Greece, openly acted as an avant-garde grouping of the aggressors in 1956 by landing marines in the Lebanon, and has been repeatedly used for various military shows of strength.

However, this does not exhaust the causes leading to further extension of the role of the navies. A new stage in the struggle to divide up and take over the oceans for economic and military purposes may now be observed. The World Ocean is becoming the object of a kind of expansion by the imperialist states. It is obvious that in this struggle navies, as an instrument of policy, will occupy an important place.

The interest in harnessing the World Ocean is explained by its truly inexhaustible riches. They can all be most fully utilized in the interests of mankind only if the seas, oceans and their floor remain a sphere of peaceful cooperation, if they are not seized and turned by the imperialists into bridgeheads for housing new forms of weapons. And many facts indicate the far-reaching plans of extremists of different kinds to seize and appropriate whole areas of the World Ocean.

It is clear that the new expansionist ambitions of imperialists on the oceans, directed against the countries of socialism, can be countered by our sea power which is capable of exerting a sobering influence on them.

Our fleet is an integral part of the armed forces of the country, standing guard over the security of our motherland. Its development is the subject of close attention by the Party, the Government and the whole Soviet people. The direction of development our fleet adopted was determined by the Central Committee of the CPSU. Already in the mid-fifties it was planned to build in the first place powerful submarine forces and sea aviation, fit the fleet with nuclear missile weapons and use atomic power in submarine shipbuilding. A definite role was assigned to the building of surface ships, without which the solution of a number of tasks facing the fleet is impossible. The need to balance the forces of the fleet was taken into account.

The creation of a modern navy became possible thanks to the powerful military-economic potential of our country, the major achievements of Soviet science and technology and thanks to the introduction of scientific methods into the process of management of the building of the fleet. The creation of our ocean-going nuclear missile fleet, capable of solving strategic tasks in the oceans, was an outstanding event, dashing the illusory hopes of imperialist aggressors that in the sphere of armed conflict at sea they would have no strong opponent. The creation of the Soviet oceanic fleet may be put on a par with the most important events of the recent past, having a decisive influence on world politics, such as the creation of atomic weapons, signifying the end of the monopoly of the American imperialists of the most important means of armed struggle and the creation of intercontinental ballistic missiles, marking the end of the unreachability of the American continent.

The Soviet fleet is a reliable means of protecting our motherland and one of the factors restraining aggression. It serves as an important instrument of policy in peacetime, undertaking the protection of the interests of our country and support for friendly countries. It should be noted that the methods of solving many technical problems in the production of ships and naval weapons of our fleet are of a clearly marked specific character. The ships of the Soviet fleet and their weapons constitute a new, original line in the development of world fleets.

In the search for the lines of development of our fleet we started not by simply copying the fleet of the most powerful maritime power of the world. The composition of the fleet, its weapons, ship design and the organization of its forces were primarily determined by the tasks which are set before the armed forces and hence before the fleet by the political leadership of the country, its economic potential and by the conditions in which the fleet will have to solve these tasks.

The revolution in military affairs has led to substantial shifts in all fields of military theory and practice. It has also brought changes in the organization of the navy, invaded the field of naval theory and touched on the content of naval art from tactics to the strategic use of a navy. This has brought in its train the elaboration of modern naval art, characterized by new categories and a kind of distillation of former concepts and principles.

However, at a particular stage this art coexisted with the elements of the "old" art.

Examples of this may be afforded by the operational art and tactics of the navy taking place at the start of the process of introduction into the fleet of nuclear weapons and missiles. Then, the traditional tactics of strike surface forces based on the combat use of ships' armament and conventional torpedoes had to adjust to the use of carriers of fundamentally new weapons with much greater combat possiblities. Operational art had to devise rational methods of planning and conducting operations in conditions of use of nuclear missile weapons together with conventional ones.

This determined the special aspects of combat orders and operational construction of forces, and ensured maximum effectiveness with use of "mixed" strike groupings or echelons of forces.

The general building of the fleet is now oriented towards creation of a comprehensively developed, that is, balanced, fleet. Our fleet has at its disposal a theory of the employment of forces in modern conditions and a system of training personnel. Relying on this sound base and already acquired experience, our country will continue to realize the conditions and pre-requisites created for the further consolidation of its sea power.

The development of the means of armed struggle is placing ever higher demands on the morale and fighting qualities of personnel. Victory in a present-day war can be won only by the armed forces, consisting of fighting men boundlessly devoted to the Party and the Soviet people, disciplined, possessing high general and special training, physically hardened and resilient. Ever more stringent demands are placed on crews of the fleet, especially the commanders of ships. Therefore, with the growth of the material base of the fleet and the development of naval art there is an objective need to work out new ways and forms of training and education, helping to form true masters of their craft, skilful sea-farers and specialists in military matters.

In the course of the struggle for building a communist society, our motherland has had to go through many tough trials. The imperialists, since the day of the birth of the Soviet state, have not ceased to hatch plans for its military conquest. They have already tried more than once to destroy it by military force.

In the years of the Civil War the main power on which imperialism relied was the land forces of the interventionists and internal counter-revolution. The fleets of the imperialist powers in this struggle played only an auxiliary role. They could not strangle our revolution. The Red Army created in the fire of war, with the support of the fleet, crushed the forces of the foe, driving them out of our state and defended the gains of October. But imperialism has not changed its aggressive nature. It fostered Fascism, its most hideous creation, and in 1941 drove this force against our motherland. A battle unrivalled in scale and ferocity unfolded between the strike forces of imperialism and the first socialist power. And again the imperialists brought forward as the main force in this struggle the land armies of Hitler Germany. The navies once again played an important, albeit secondary, role. The valiant land forces of the Soviet Army with the full support of other branches of the armed forces smashed the armed forces of reaction, the mightiest in the whole history of mankind. The Soviet Army showed itself in this struggle as an uncrushable force.

And after the victory in the Second World War of the forces of socialism and progress, imperialism did not put away its weapons. It continued to hatch plans for military conquest of the countries of the socialist community. The imperialists not only did not give up hopes of revising the outcome of the historical battles of the twentieth century and establishing world dominance, but sharpened even further aggression in all fields: economic, political, ideological and military. The face of modern imperialism is manifest above all in militarization of the economy, creation of a military-industrial complex and a frenzied arms race. The main intention of its armed forces is to prepare for war against the Soviet Union and the other socialist countries and suppress national liberation movements.

Unlike the past, when the main armed force of imperialism was made up of land armies, in present-day conditions one of the principal roles in armed struggle against the countries of socialism is assigned to naval forces. However, bearing in mind the experience of history, demonstrating the total untenability of military doctrines oriented to the use of one branch of the armed forces or one kind of weapon, the imperialists contemplate the development of ground, air and also missile forces while at the same time laying the main stress on naval forces.

One of the reasons for the switch of the centre of gravity to naval forces is that the aggressive forces of imperialism are now represented by a bloc of maritime powers possessing powerful naval forces relying on numerous bases and occupying advantageous strategic positions. In addition, the introduction of achievements in the scientific and technical revolution has radically altered the tasks of the fleets. Their main tasks have become strikes from the sea on objectives in enemy territory. They have become capable of rapidly and decisively acting directly on the course of armed conflict in practically all theatres of military operations. The naval forces are gradually becoming the main carrier of nuclear weapons capable of striking at the enemy in all continents and seas. In this connection the imperialists are giving increasing preference to oceanic strategy, to war from the sea against the shore. A considerable role in the shift of the centre of gravity to the naval forces was also played by the historical experience of the failures of the campaigns against the USSR of the most powerful land armies of imperialism.

As a result of the consistent implementation of the peace programme adopted at the 24th and developed at the 25th Congresses of the CPSU, the process is continuing of easing international tension, important stages of which were the successful completion of the Helsinki Conference on security and co-operation in Europe, and also the series of recent fruitful encounters of the leaders of the Soviet Union and a number of leading capitalist states.

The current advances on the road to peace were preceded by radical changes in the ratio of the economic forces in favour of socialism. This became possible thanks to the wise leadership of the Communist Party, decades of selfless labour by the Soviet people, the mass heroism of Soviet fighters in the years of severe military trials, and the enormous labour and political upswing with which the whole country is continuing to fulfil the wise plans mapped out by the Party.

However, on our planet still exist and actively operate the forces of imperialist reaction and aggression, not abandoning attempts to undermine the process of strengthening peace and clarifying the international situation. These forces have not been rendered harmless and the danger of war has still not been removed. The Party teaches that as long as there persists imperialism, the aggressive nature of which has not changed, a real danger of the outbreak of a new world war remains. In the leading capitalist states there is no slackening of preparations for the material-technical base for war, military budgets are growing, and new arms systems, above all, the latest submarine nuclear missile systems are being actively created.

All this has determined the need and rationale of the efforts which are being made in our country to develop the navy—the basic component of the sea power of the state capable of withstanding the oceanic strategy of imperialism. The sea power of our country is directed at ensuring favourable conditions for building communism, the intensive expansion of the economic power of the country and the steady consolidation of its defence capability. Therefore unflagging attention is being paid to the development of the components of sea power, increasingly resting on the achievements of scientific and technical progress.

Index